He Heard

A Different

Drummer

The Cold war Memoirs of
a Scientist, Explorer, Naval Officer and Spy

Volume I

JANUARY 2016

To CAPTAIN MARTY SHELTON,
My old Navy INSRL Colleague of
MANY YEARS —— Enjoy !

Leonard A. LeSchack
CAPT USNR (RET)

Synopsis: He Heard a Different Drummer

If a man does not keep pace with his companions, perhaps it is because he hears a different drummer. Let him step to the music he hears, however measured or far away—Henry David Thoreau

HE HEARD A DIFFERENT DRUMMER is a memoir of the Cold War, a seemingly endless conflict beginning at the end of World War II in 1945, but eventually concluding in 1990. The story is the saga of Leonard (Len) LeSchack: scientist, explorer, naval officer, spy, and ardent lover of women. Born a first-generation American of Ukrainian descent at the height of the Great Depression, his life experiences were strongly influenced, not only by his own makeup—he was a classic maverick—but by many of the historic events that occurred during that Cold War period. It was a time when the United States was pitted in a life or death struggle against the Soviet Union. Len LeSchack took part in that struggle.

In The Cold War, journalist Robert T. Mann wrote:

"The Cold War continues to profoundly impact the lives of everyday Americans in all sorts of ways. Its legacy still impacts our politics, military strategy, and national diplomacy. Our culture bears its scars and influences. And the fields of medicine and technology continue to benefit from its scientific advances. As much as World War II—perhaps even more so—the Cold War shapes what we are as a people and as a nation. The war may be over, but we still live in its enormous shadow."

The Cold War had a seminal impact on Len LeSchack, and it continues to do so.

But LeSchack brought his own persona to this Cold War and dealt with it on his own terms—as he attempted to do with everything else. He never saw active combat—due to a quirk in American history—resulting from a peculiar political decision by President Lyndon Johnson *not* to call up the Reserves for the war in Viet Nam. While never intending as a child to be a soldier, there in 1959, however, he was a commissioned officer in the U.S. Naval Reserve and on Active Duty at the Office of Naval

Research (ONR}. While on active duty he was highly decorated, receiving distinction just days after the 1962 Cuban Missile Crisis ended; the decoration was for designing and execution of a successful dangerous James Bond-like intelligence mission against a Soviet listening station in the Arctic earlier that year—just as Ian Fleming's character, "James Bond," with his glorious assortment of lovely nubile women as well as the unusual espionage tools produced by "Q" were then beginning to become popular. It was not surprising, therefore, from the inception of LeSchack's Project Coldfeet, he was accused by Navy officialdom of trying to be "the American James Bond!"

From the moment when this young, ebullient junior officer , Lt (jg) LeSchack first proposed the clandestine investigation of a just abandoned Soviet Arctic drifting station by parachuting a two man intelligence team onto the abandoned Soviet drift station in the high Arctic, then conducting a comprehensive study to determine whether specific clandestine Soviet military tasks had been conducted there, and then being retrieved using the newly developed Fulton Skyhook Aero-retriever, everyone up the chain of command, from his civilian boss up to and including the Chief of Naval Operations for Air, all derisively exclaimed to him, "Whadaya want to be, the American James Bond??!!"

Well, perhaps he did! Despite the derision of his superior officers in 1961, LeSchack knew he could "pull it off" if he received their support! Concomitantly, he increasingly began to believe he just might have not only the same espionage skills, but also some of the same attractiveness to desirable women as did Ian Fleming's fictional character: He happily remembered the sloe-eyed Giselle, his first real love; then, on his way to the Antarctic— New Zealand was the U.S. staging area—where he met and enjoyed the voluptuous Pamela, followed soon after by the equally voluptuous and most vigorous Maisie, who fortified him for 14 months of Antarctic celibacy; then on his return to the U.S. aboard the USS ARNEB, which anchored at Valparaiso, Chile, to re-fuel and re-provision, where when ashore, he met and thoroughly enjoyed the most voluptuous, demanding and experienced Elsa. Upon returning to U. S. soil, and becoming a commissioned officer, his experience now also included an extended love affair with the enigmatic, but highly energetic lover, the French-speaking Simone, while he was stationed in Boston. It was a vibrant affair that had endured from 1960 until May, 1962, and the onset of Project Coldfeet. His affair with Simone, like the one with Giselle, were ones that he never forgot!

However, despite the derisive comments by his Navy superiors, by continuing to push and agitate, eventually both the CIA which had then the only serious Skyhook aircraft capability and the Defense Intelligence Agency (DIA) which didn't want to see the Navy Project Coldfeet die, together came to the rescue with both funds and aircraft! And LeSchack's James Bond-like espionage operation went forward and turned into a brilliant success!

As well, too, it appears so did his Bond-like attractiveness to desirable women!

All that was *before* the U.S. overtly committed itself to Viet Nam. Released from active duty in 1963, LeSchack embraced academic studies and contract research in "far away places, with strange-sounding names" — but he returned to active duty again and again, at the convenience of the Government, until he retired, a Navy captain, as the Cold War ended.

Now, his services to the Government, both on and off active duty, had been in the shadowy, often dangerous, sub-rosa world of intelligence and espionage. For LeSchack, this world included two more trips to Soviet territory for clandestine activities during the height of the Cold War, both such excursions harrowing in the extreme for him. He suspected — from secret sources — that the Soviets had found out about his 1962 Arctic operation shortly thereafter; he just didn't know on his subsequent forays to the Soviet Union in 1965 as the Polar Regions Project Officer for the 1967 Canadian World's Fair, and a 1973 trip to Siberia (that was directly funded by CIA!) whether they — the ubiquitous KGB — were aware that *he* had been the instigator of that earlier Coldfeet espionage. And that was a ghastly, nagging fear for him on those forays: *was he known and now targeted by the KGB?* He knew what excruciating ordeals awaited the likes of Francis Gary Powers and Professor Barghoorn of Yale University that had occurred a few years earlier *when they showed up* in the Soviet Union. Then a young man and still a junior naval officer, LeSchack had his suspicions. Later after the end of the Cold War and as a retired Navy captain, he was to have those earlier suspicions positively confirmed by a retired CIA officer: the Soviets *had known* about the secret mission to their drifting station in the Arctic in 1962. However, he still doesn't know whether the KGB had been aware of *his* starring role in that 1962 espionage during his later visits to the USSR.

When we say both such excursions were harrowing in the extreme for him, this is no understatement. In wartime spies are shot! And this Cold War at this time in history was a real war. When LeSchack represented the Canadian 1967 World's Fair he felt the Soviets would likely refrain from perpetrating an incident because he knew how much they wanted to show off at that event; nonetheless, he felt while in Leningrad a "Honey Trap" had definitely been set to co-opt him with the good-looking Anya, the interpreter assigned to him in Leningrad's Arctic and Antarctic Institute . And during this time he very much wished to get into her pants, but knew he had to ignore her overtures!

In the case of the Siberia trip, although he was there as a guest of the Soviet Academy of Sciences to attend the Second International Permafrost Conference, considering his CIA involvement he knew he would, if found out, be considered a spy!

On both trips back to the USSR, after the conclusion of Project Coldfeet, LeSchack felt he had been in serious danger!

In the book "Goodbye Darkness," a Memoir of the Pacific War, by historian William Manchester, a former Marine, he observed that "Desire is the sequel to danger." LeSchack certainly believed this from his experience and he observed this for himself!

Because so many of his projects during this Cold War period were conducted in dangerous venues, his level of "sexual desire" throughout this entire period, accordingly, was extraordinarily high!

****

As a commander in the Navy, owing to his knowledge of French (learned as a student in Paris) and Spanish (learned as the U.S. Official Representative to the 1962-63 Argentine Antarctic Expedition and serving on board ships of the Argentine Navy) , the Navy now called him back to Active Duty to become the "Coordinator"—the "Colonel Klink"—of the Cuban-Haitian Refugee Center—a concentration camp—

established in Puerto Rico by Jimmy Carter just months prior to his bid for re-election. All because Castro, in one of his cutest Cold War pranks, released Cuban asylum inmates and emptied his jails of their prisoners to float them ashore to South Florida aboard the 1980 Mariel Boat Lift. Just to cause mischief and tweak Uncle Sam's nose because there was already a surfeit of illegal Cubans and Haitians at U.S. detention camps in Miami, a political liability for Carter in Florida. Although LeSchack had been a long-time student of political terrorism—testifying before the Senate Judiciary Committee four years earlier on this subject—it was on this assignment in Puerto Rico that he got his first real taste of terrorism: There were terrorist bombs meant to kill planted in his own backyard.

Then there was a strange tour, on assignment as a Navy captain in intelligence, from the highest levels of the Defense Intelligence Agency, to Noriega's Panamá. It was 1981. That was the turbulent time just after the U.S. agreed to return the Canal—for 66 years a U.S. fiefdom—back to Panamá. He was there to investigate the potential for political terrorism against the Canal during a period of multiple Central American wars, arms smuggling, drug dealing, and double-dealing—all orchestrated from Panamá—but he would encounter strange, inexplicable resistance from the people he was sent to assist, the U.S. Southern Command.

Could that resistance have been because someone in Panamá was fearful that LeSchack was uncovering U. S. clandestine operations not authorized by Congress—the forerunner to Iran-Contra? Or could he have been bureaucratically confused or conflated with another American who had recently lived in Panamá named *LeSchack*? It happens there had been one there—A. L. LeSchack, Captain LeSchack's cousin, same initials, only transposed. His cousin had met for official reasons with Manuel Antonio Noriega, Chief of Panamanian Intelligence, shortly before LeSchack was assigned there, (and therefore Noriega had a file on LeSchack's cousin). The Southern Command likely too had a file on LeSchack's cousin since he also had inadvertently been responsible for having a senior U.S. Army intelligence officer summarily thrown out of Panamá for conduct absolutely "unbecoming."

Or could it be owing to Len LeSchack's frequent travel to Panamá, and from there to other parts of Latin America? In those days, the U.S. Southern Command certainly had numerous entry-exit files on LeSchack, himself—its "Travelers in Panamá" program—owing to the many Cold War-funded scientific research projects he mounted as a civilian researcher both in Panamá, and from Panamá. In Panamá, LeSchack was conducting research in the jungle areas of the Darién. On Barro Colorado Island in the Gatún Lake in the center of the strategic Panama Canal, he also had established a long-term research program. From Panamá LeSchack traveled several times to Colombia, and once to Perú, to jungle areas in those countries that just coincidentally were known to be locales for violent political terrorist factions as well as unfettered coca growing. Accordingly, there was an abundance of LeSchack's peripatetic history for the Southern Command to consider, along with the rumors of his connection to CIA—rumors that were not without some foundation!

Moreover, the U.S. and Noriega were known to share files during this period, so the name "LeSchack" might well have been under scrutiny from both intelligence services. Or could the resistance to LeSchack's mission have been due to *all* of the above circumstances in some combination? Taken altogether by a suspicious bureaucracy unlikely to have been aware of all the facts and which may have mistakenly conflated LeSchack with his cousin owing to the close similarity of names, this might well have set off alarm bells. Whatever the case, one thing seems clear: a senior U.S. SOUTHCOM intelligence officer, within a few days of LeSchack's arrival at the US Naval Station Panama Canal , gratuitously introduced him to a bright and gorgeous Panamanian woman—one with whom LeSchack enjoyed instant rapport. The circumstances surrounding their meeting, however, suggest this was a classic set-up; she was probably put in place, whether she knew it or not, to compromise LeSchack, the now senior intelligence officer with Top Secret clearances and accesses. Just *the appearance* of compromise—in the usual way—with this voluptuous Panamanian woman would be enough for establishing grounds for someone in Panamá desirous of so doing, to send him promptly packing, and thus abort his DIA mission!

At the conclusion of his strange mission to Panamá and his release from active duty, LeSchack moved his private scientific research office from the Washington Beltway to the Florida Keys so he could continue his work in the open water with his midget oceanographic research submarine. Just as he did so, by coincidence, the Department of Defense established the Joint Command, U.S. Forces Caribbean, at the Naval Station at Key West. The Navy, aware of his expertise in the Caribbean and knowing he was now living in the Keys and still in the active reserve, tasked him with setting up a Naval Reserve Intelligence Unit to support that new Joint Command, and to become its first commanding officer. So, in addition to his civilian research, LeSchack was now often at COMUSFORCARIB. He was there at the time of the Grenada Rescue mission and the heating up of the dirty little wars then playing out in Central America just before the Iran-Contra scandal broke — and frequently enough now, he was serving as the Acting- or Deputy- Chief of Intelligence for that Command.

What he *had* intended to be as a child was a scientist and an explorer. He certainly accomplished those goals during the Cold War, contributing in some small measure to the scientific advances to which Robert Mann alludes. These goals were largely facilitated by Cold War politics and funding.

But LeSchack's story is a romance in the truest sense. Despite his occasional diffidence and maverick-like behavior both as a scientist and naval officer, he was an incurable romantic and adored women, as earlier observed — and there were many in his life until eventually, he found his perfect lover. Or perhaps she found him.

Len LeSchack, the Cold Warrior and intelligence briefer to congressmen in the autumn of 1962, knew more than most folks ever would, how close the world came to nuclear holocaust during the Cuban Missile Crisis. This knowledge chastened him for the remainder of his days. Although he was clearly born before the "flower-child" generation that became boisterously famous during the promiscuous 1960s and 1970s, he increasingly became partial to that later generation's slogan, "make love, not war." Accordingly, many of the women who grace the pages of this memoir mutually chose, with LeSchack, to know one another in the biblical sense, and both he and they thoroughly enjoyed gaining that knowledge. They all added immensely to his adventure and to the fullness of his life, and add much to this saga. He hopes, in some way, his pleasure with them has contributed to *their* enrichment and enjoyment of life also.

As well, he had many, many adventures in the old-fashioned geographical sense known to earlier explorers — all as a result of the Cold War:

In the Antarctic from 1957 to 1959 conducting geophysical studies during the International Geophysical Year (IGY): Then, traveling across the continent in a tractor train traverse, he explored, recorded seismic soundings, and gathered gravity and magnetic data. This major Antarctic program that the United States launched was more designed for geopolitics than for science. It needed to equal or surpass the massive IGY program undertaken there by the Soviet Union. LeSchack spent fourteen continuous months in Antarctica. He has a mountain named for him there.

In the Arctic Ocean on drifting ice stations (ours and theirs), and working with nuclear submarines on secret patrols beneath the ice: This was driven by recognition that any attack on the United States by the USSR would be launched over the North Pole, or from the Arctic Ocean. And with the Soviet's ever increasing fleet of nuclear submarines stationed in the Arctic Ocean, and capable of launching ballistic missiles, this became an increasingly dangerous threat from the mid-1960s to the end of the Cold War, a threat far more dangerous than the buildup of missiles in Cuba in 1962 ever was;

In South and Central American jungles conducting environmental research from 1967 to 1973 to correlate the tropical vegetation as seen from the air and in aerial photography with engineering and logistics problems associated with moving men and machinery through the tropical forest: Those jungle programs of LeSchack's were directly related to, and in aid of operations in Viet Nam, and funded by the Department of Defense;

And in California's deserts, hunting for geothermal energy resources in the mid-1970s, a direct result of the 1973 pre-emptive war launched by Egypt and Syria, with Soviet support, against Israel. Then as a result of United States military support for Israel, allowing the Israelis to beat back the Egyptians and Syrians, Arab countries retaliated by embargoing further shipments of oil to the U.S. This caused the U.S. Department of Energy, in alarm, to belatedly fund all sorts of alternative energy research, and a geothermal energy exploration program designed by LeSchack in 1976 was one such program. That program lasted for several years thereafter.

This Cold War saga is American in its point of view. The discerning reader will see that the historical framework has been carefully presented, and is believed to be accurate. LeSchack's adventures during the Cold War are real. Owing to the tricks the author's memory may have played on him over time, exact timing of events may be slightly off, and dialog of any sort represents the author's best efforts at recalling what was actually said—it certainly conveys the author's sense of what the speakers likely intended. Poetic license has been used occasionally in this regard. Except for historical characters, and persons whose actions so positively added to this memoir that they *should be identified for history*, most people's names have been changed to respect their privacy, and that of their families.

Len LeSchack was a man who, throughout his life, heard a different drummer, a drummer who beat a Cold War tattoo. He stepped to the music he heard. This is his Cold War story.

Leonard A. LeSchack

Foreword

A review of "He Heard a Different Drummer," as published in the Calgary Sun on Sunday March 19, 2006, and written by former Sun political columnist, Paul Jackson (now retired)

Oilman's real life spy exploits more thrilling than fiction

Calgary oilman Len LeSchack handed over the manuscript of his memoirs as a globe-trotting intelligence officer in the United States Naval Reserve (USNR) and then preceded to uncork a bottle of the finest wine. And I mean the finest wine.

For Len is a most cultured fellow. LeSchack, now 71, is an erudite and patrician figure, somewhat reminiscent of Conservative guru William F. Buckley.

The difference is that while Buckley pens novels about his fictional spy Blackford Oakes for amusement, LeSchack actually lived the real life espionage game. Here I should also add the New York City-born LeSchack, president of Calgary-based oil exploration company Hectori Inc., also passed to me photographs of the many ravishing female companions he had around the world during his more adventurous days on intelligence assignments.

While his wide-ranging memoirs, tentatively titled He Heard a Different Drummer are stirring, derring-do stuff, I had known about Len from the 1996 book Project Coldfeet: Secret Mission to a Soviet Ice Station, published by the Naval Institute Press, based in Annapolis, Maryland, which he co-authored with William M. Leary, whose many claims to fame include the 1996-'97 Charles A. Lindbergh professor of aero-space history at the National Air and Space Museum in Washington, D.C.

The book was cleared to use hitherto classified information to inform the public of one of the most successful espionage coups of the Cold War.

It tells of how in 1962, the Office of Naval Research (ONR) and the Central Intelligence Agency (CIA) launched one of the most audacious spy missions of the era. LeSchack and fellow officer and Russian linguist James F. Smith parachuted onto a hastily abandoned Soviet drift station on a deteriorating Arctic ice pack to poke through any data and assess any eavesdropping equipment the Soviets had left behind when the drift station began to break up.

If you saw the 1968 blockbuster movie Ice Station Zebra with Rock Hudson and Ernest Borgnine, you'll get the drift, if you'll pardon the pun. Back in those days, both the Soviets and the U.S. set up monitoring and communication bases on 'ice islands' to track each others submarines—this was in the age when nuclear subs were first appearing—and when the U.S. and Canada knew an air attack on their nations would almost certainly come over the Pole.

The ice islands, some several miles in diameter and several hundred feet thick, often had to be abandoned quickly when they appeared to be breaking up. LeSchack, a petroleum geologist and an oceanographer, then doing his stint with the U.S. naval reserve, heard about the sudden evacuation of one Soviet ice island code-named NP-8.

He proposed landing a team on the island before it disintegrated and scout out what the Soviets had left behind. A dangerous mission by any measure.

But even more dangerous since in those days—now four decades and more ago—helicopters couldn't operate in those extreme temperatures and Arctic storms. "We would have to parachute in, but how to get off?"

That was solved by a brilliant engineer called Robert Edison Fulton who conceived and designed the "Fulton Skyhook" which, carried on a CIA-owned B-17 aircraft, would be lowered over the ice island and lift men and equipment aloft. He adds: "Being snatched from the ice on 500-ft balloon-lifted line and then reeled up into a specially outfitted B-17 bomber travelling at 125-knots is not for the faint of heart."

Whatever, the operation was a huge success, and is now a textbook case of ingenuity in the spy world of the Cold War.

"What we found was astounding. We discovered the onset of a program that would support the massive build-up of Soviet nuclear missile submarines beneath the Arctic Ocean that, in the late 1980s, would threaten North America more than any missiles in Cuba ever would."

Len, just 27 at the time, was awarded, amongst other honours, the Legion of Merit, for this and other missions.

At one point, someone assessing the mission, said to LeSchack: "Len, you're a real live James Bond." To which, LeSchack replied:" No, I'm just a scientist with a good imagination."

For sure, LeSchack's complete memoirs are going to be edge-of-the-seat and a nail-biting read.

Author's Note

This Cold War saga is American in its point of view. The discerning reader will see that the historical framework has been carefully presented, and is believed to be accurate. LeSchack's adventures during the Cold War are real. Owing to the tricks the author's memory may have played on him over time, exact timing of events may be slightly off, and dialog of any sort represents the author's best efforts at recalling what was actually said—it certainly conveys the author's sense of what the speakers likely intended. Poetic license has been used occasionally in this regard. Except for historical characters, and persons whose actions so positively added to this memoir that they *should be identified for history*, most people's names have been changed to respect their privacy, and that of their families.

Leonard A. LeSchack, Captain USNR(Ret.)

TABLE OF CONTENTS

VOLUME I

Era of the Cuban Missiles; the *cold* Cold War Years/coming of age of a young and eager intelligence officer, explorer and scientist in the conduct of research and diplomacy, as well as espionage against the Soviet Union -1946-1966

He Heard a Different Drummer

This is to acknowledge Ms. Susan Lucas, the first editor of my manuscript, "He Heard a Different Drummer," my memoirs of the Cold War. She was a Canadian Army Brat, growing up in Cold War Germany where her Dad, a professional soldier, was often stationed, and during the period when the Soviets were regularly threatening to surge through the Fulda Gap into West Germany and clash with NATO forces at any provocation. She quickly began to learn real history, and eventually became an historical researcher, and editor. She was the first to edit my manuscript. I also acknowledge, Paul Conrad Jackson, a former political columnist for the Calgary Sun, now retired, who reviewed my original manuscript and published his review in the March 19, 2006 issue of that newspaper. He has graciously allowed me to use that review as the Foreword to my book. Also to be acknowledged is Tom Ullappa, former Navy man and talented wordsmith who reviewed my final draft, and Nancy Gerth, a professional "Indexer," who created the extensive Index for these memoirs.

Finally, I acknowledge Karla Keller, my secretary and office manager who meticulously put this manuscript into a format suitable for publication. The talented artists of "99-Design" created the book covers based upon my cold War Tales.

Götterdamerung-Soviet Style, and the Captain's Revelation: an Introduction

> *If a man does not keep pace with his*
> *companions, perhaps it is because he hears a*
> *different drummer. Let him step to the*
> *music he hears, however measured or far*
> *away —Henry David Thoreau*

Captain Len LeSchack, USNR (ret), was born a Pisces. He had a strong affinity for the ocean. He loved adventure of almost any sort, both physical and intellectual, and adored brilliant, sexy women of all ages. He was a retired naval officer and decorated. But he was also a scientist, an adventurer in the old fashioned geographical sense, and an author. Occasionally, he fancied himself a poet. At this moment, sitting alone on the veranda of a beach cottage, he was the poet, contemplating the majestic Pacific Ocean. He was enjoying a desperately needed vacation at the US Navy's Pacific Missile Range Facility in Kauai. Voluptuous, swirling, multi-colored images of oceans he had sailed, flown over or swam in danced through his head. Often he sat alone and contemplated the ocean. This night not only did he contemplate the ocean, but his life, his loves and that all throughout that life, and in all things, it seems that "he hears a different drummer." And steps accordingly.

As a youth he was a lifeguard during his summers away from high school and university. From high school days onwards, he was often paid to stare at the ocean. As a junior naval officer on watch he would stare at the sea. Before the Panama Canal Zone was returned to Panamá he was stationed at the U.S. Naval Station in Panama. His office at Fort Amador faced out to the sea and he could watch not only the water, but a dozen ships at anchor, anxiously awaiting their turn to pass through the Canal. And while stationed at the US Caribbean Command at Key West, with his own boat he could slip out to sea in off duty hours. Although he would often go out alone, he preferred boating with friends or lovers. Either way, he enjoyed the time to contemplate the ever-changing waters of the Florida Keys. Now, long since retired from the Navy, he had had to return to the sea again. He had too long been away. Captain LeSchack had rented a beach cottage at this Navy base to once again stare out at the sea, and quietly contemplate not only the water, but now more urgently, and for the first time, what was left of his life and what had gone before.

All alone each day during his short vacation at the Base—known familiarly by the name of its famous beach, Barking Sands—Captain LeSchack had morning coffee on the veranda. Then he walked along the length of the long and often deserted beach. A bit later, he entered the water. Upon regaining the beach after a long, meditative swim in the warm tropical waters, he would then dry off by walking the beach yet again. Some days he did it the other way around. He enjoyed not having to exercise his creative mind for a while, and cruise through these precious few lazy vacation days with his brain in neutral. He left his biggest decision of the day for the early evening: should he have gin and tonic or rum and tonic?

Now at age 66, 12 years after he had retired from the Navy, he had a revelation. It was the year of the 11 September terrorist attack. The city in which he was born had been attacked by terrorists. Also, Washington, D.C., the city where he frequently lived during his military career. The terrorists attacked the very building at which he often worked while serving the Nation—the country to which his Ukrainian father immigrated in 1906. This attack, in the Captain's mind, was the "first shot fired" of the next 50-year's war and, he mused, the second time there was " a shot heard round the world."

His entire civilian and military life, spanning youth to late middle age, had been governed and formed by the just-concluded last 50-year's war—the Cold War. That was a period beginning in 1945 and ending in 1990 with the destruction of the Berlin Wall, the declarations of Perestroika and Glasnost—*Götterdamerung* for the Soviet, and the disbanding of the USSR by Yeltsin. It was a time when the United States was pitted in a life or death struggle against the Soviet Union. Captain Len LeSchack took part in that struggle.

In the book, <u>The Cold War</u>, journalist Robert T. Mann wrote:

"The Cold War continues to profoundly impact the lives of everyday Americans in all sorts of ways. Its legacy still impacts our politics, military strategy, and national diplomacy. Our culture bears its scars and influences. And the fields of medicine and technology continue to benefit from its scientific advances. As much as World War II—perhaps even more so—the Cold War shapes what we are as a people and as a nation. The war may be over, but we still live in its enormous shadow."

The Cold War had a seminal impact on Len LeSchack, and it continues to do so. Inchoate inklings of how his life had been shaped by the Cold War began early in his life. The final revelation came to him because fifty years of accumulated bits of history had reached a critical mass in his brain. He now finally had both the time and the maturity to allow these bits to dance around his head until they assembled themselves into a coherent and meaningful whole. They had popped up again and again over the course of his life, only now to coalesce and become clearly visible to him in his aloneness, staring out to sea. The revelation occurred while the Captain patiently (and hopefully) awaited the final spectacular green flash, as the fading sun would extinguish itself in the ocean. Perhaps the rum acted as a catalyst; it occurred while he was sipping a rum and tonic as the sun was setting over the Pacific. And the sun did set in a glorious display of colors in one overwhelming and revealing instant.

For fifty years the Cold War was an intense and continuous intelligence war, both active and passive, with spies and counterspies, both human and electronic. For most of his naval career, Captain Len LeSchack lived in that world. He had been a naval intelligence officer. There was not active combat, in the usual WWII sense, over that period of time, although there clearly were intervals of hot war; the Korean War and the Viet Nam War being the notable examples for Americans. Of course, there were also uncounted mini-wars all over the world that were spawned by the Free World-Communist World confrontation and exacerbated by civil unrest in the Third World.

The Captain could see that in the world that now surrounded him there was little understanding of the motives for, and the dynamics of, the Cold War. This was especially true for that period from the late 1940s to the late 1960s, which did so much to shape the Captain's life. Most people now living were not yet born at the height of the Cold War. Certainly he saw no understanding in his own children who had inherited his keen intellect. They had no sense of this history.

The Captain thought of this when reviewing a paper on "U.S. Nuclear Strategy and Diplomacy," co-authored by an old Navy colleague, Captain Ken Hagan, USNR (ret), Professor Emeritus of History from the U.S. Naval Academy. With regard to undoubtedly the most dangerous period of the Cold War, the Cuban Missile Crisis, cited in that paper, the Captain wrote to his colleague:

> *"I suspect that I am one of the few people you know who recognized how close we actually came to the 'nuclear Armageddon' you expressed in your paper: On two occasions in the autumn of 1962 I was on The Hill briefing congressmen about our clandestine intelligence project, "Project Coldfeet," our Cold War spy operation. I was allowed to stay and listen to the other briefings, which concerned the missiles in Cuba. Scary. It was with considerable foreknowledge and trepidation that I turned on the TV to listen to Kennedy talk frankly to the Nation on 22 October." I then thought a devastating nuclear exchange was a serious possibility—with Washington a likely target."*

The Cuban Missile Crisis ended on 28 October 1962. Three days later LeSchack—then a lieutenant (jg)—received his first decoration, the presidential Legion of Merit for his role in Project Coldfeet. Project Coldfeet was a spy mission conducted in the spring of 1962. He and Air Force Major James F. Smith clandestinely parachuted onto Soviet territory to conduct an intelligence-gathering mission. Upon completion of their data gathering, they were retrieved by the Fulton Skyhook system, a system designed to extricate personnel from denied or inaccessible terrain. The Captain had been the first person to have used the Skyhook on an operational mission (Some years later James Bond used it in the movie, "Thunderball"). LeSchack often mused whether the President, himself, wouldn't have pinned the decoration on him instead of the Secretary of the Navy had it not been just hours after the conclusion of the Missile Crisis. "Project Coldfeet" would have been the kind of operation John Kennedy, a naval hero in his own right, would likely have enjoyed," thought the Captain, knowing from CIA sources that the President was briefed on Coldfeet. "He might have wanted to personally present it to me," the Captain mused, "but opted instead for a bit of a vacation after the Missile Crisis ended."

It should be pointed out at this juncture that the Captain had never intended, in the early years of his life, to join the military. Born a first generation American during the height of the Great Depression, this son of liberal Jewish pacifists of Ukaninian descent wanted only to grow up and become a scientist and explorer. His childhood desires, fired by reading accounts of the great explorers, scientists and inventors, however, were pushed well into the future. This resulted from the onset of WWII, and his childhood reactions to this catastrophic event.

As a youth, the Captain—LeSchack —had become aware that his aunt and uncle escaped from Germany just before the onset of war. He saw all around him young men going to war, and a steady stream of military aircraft taking off from Mitchell Field on Long Island, close by where he lived as a child. He saw his own father, too young for WWI and too old for WWII, learning to be a civilian aircraft spotter, perched like some raptor atop tall buildings in his hometown, searching the sky with binoculars. During the War, he noted the incongruity of hearing, in a religious setting, the admonition his Sunday school teacher expounded at nearly every session: "Remember, children, the only good German is a dead German." The Sunday school teacher had not long before returned from Spain as a scarred veteran of the Abraham Lincoln Brigade, fighting alongside the Republicans in that country's civil war. He had *seen* the Stukas dive-bombing innocent Spanish civilians at Guernica, testing out their tactics for the war to come immediately thereafter!

Most devastating of all to the young LeSchack was the anti-Semitic behavior that seemed to visit his neighborhood during this wartime period, and how often he felt it was directed personally at him. His next door neighbor, a boy a few years older, taunted him with racial epithets, as did some children at elementary school. He also heard with irritating frequency that old canard of the time that, " Jewish boys couldn't or didn't fight," while the "other" boys did; and the inexperienced boy had no way of verifying the falsity of this. And then, a childhood fury developed within him from stories of the concentration camps that began trickling out of Europe, stories which were verified as the war ended.

Although LeSchack's mother, a teacher of high school history in the New York City school system, never belabored these wartime horrors that so tormented her young son, she did force him to learn history because "it was necessary, just to be a good citizen." And it was in a history class early on in high school, just after the war had ended, that he saw that a girl classmate, a European refugee, had a concentration camp number tattooed on her forearm. She sat across the aisle from him and, while involuntarily stretching at her desk, inadvertently pulled the sleeve of her blouse up her arm and revealed this horrible disfiguration. In one blinding instant the horrors of WWII became personalized to the young and basically sheltered LeSchack. He saw an otherwise pretty, young teenage girl with an indelible "Nazi license plate," carved upon her, from her wrist to her elbow. This, LeSchack thought to himself, was real history being taught in history class. He never told his mother of this history lesson, because it set in train events in his life that were not approved of by his pacifist parents.

It was during this period that a prescient, but horrible, thought began to occur to LeSchack that, perhaps, Americans were not all that different from Germans and Japanese despite his current WWII-based perceptions; he wondered, could this all happen here? Or could Americans perpetrate similar disasters upon other peoples? It was at this point that LeSchack began to think, just *as a personal precaution*, he had better learn military skills, along with his science. This was not only to prove to himself that Jews, and he in particular, could fight if need be, but to be in a position to keep his eyes and ears open as to what his own government was doing, well before most of his fellow citizens became aware. Accordingly, acquisition of military skills became a part of his long-term "life" plan.

After graduation from college, to deal with his childhood concerns, it eventually turned out that he joined the military. But true to his early childhood dreams, he also became a scientist and explorer as well. LeSchack found a way of interspersing his science and his exploring, side by side, with his military career. This was thanks to the Navy's Cold

War policy of allowing, and in fact, encouraging, certain reserve officers to leave temporarily their civilian endeavors to return to active duty from time to time, as the service's need arose. And it arose on several occasions throughout LeSchack's life because he had acquired some combination of science, language, foreign travel and intelligence skills that were most unusual, and from the Navy's point of view, desirable to be able to tap.

Sitting comfortably, feet up on the beach cottage's veranda railing, all alone, he began another rum and tonic and watched the sea and sky darken. He contemplated his life. He contemplated how his lust for learning, his lust for adventure, and his lust for women had shaped his life. He attributed the first two lusts to his brain and soul, but the latter to an over abundance of raging hormones (now blessedly diminished). All these diverse desires, together with external world events, had formed that life.

With regard to those hormones, he knew for example, that his own persona had been shaped significantly throughout much of his life by those chemicals that his body so gratuitously produced. Whether other men or women were so affected, he never clearly understood. He did note, however, that the accounts, histories or biographies of unusual men and women, people who were driven, as LeSchack was, often contained cryptic references to extraordinary and frequent amorous adventures. He sensed from their context that these literary asides, although not necessarily germane to the specific story, related directly to these people's lives, power and achievements. LeSchack thought there was a direct chemical connection. As an illustration, he remembered years later, that President John Kennedy was reputed to have told British Prime Minister Harold Macmillan "that if he went without sex for three days he got a terrible headache." Whether or not that story is true, LeSchack had no difficulty in believing such a physical reaction was possible. He had frequently experienced similar reactions as a younger man.

LeSchack contemplated this, and all of his travels, his adventures, his writings of which there are many, and his science, much of it paid for with Cold War dollars from the Department of Defense and other governmental agencies. Finally, he contemplated what he had learned about power and Cold War politics throughout a career in military intelligence. He contemplated, yet again, who he was. He was a loner, an adventurer, a bit of a poet, a lover of brilliant and sexually active women—women who significantly shaped his perceptions and enjoyment of life—a Pisces who adored the water, and a man who often adopted the contrarian's positions in both his science and his interpretation of world events and international power politics. He frequently was correct, he recognized, in his evaluations of people, events and historical outcomes, often to the dismay of others.

In this Navy setting, a venue at which even though all alone, he felt comfortable, he contemplated, yet again, his detachment Fitness Report from Panamá, "FITREP" in Navy jargon. It so well described his entire life as well as the reporting period, many years earlier, for which it covered. It was written in 1981 by his reporting senior at the U.S. Naval Station Panama Canal. His reporting senior, the Commanding Officer of the Naval Station, and the United States Southern Command's (SOUTHCOM) Navy Component Commander, was a Navy captain also. He was a bit older than LeSchack, and was an extremely astute man. He captured, in one succinct paragraph (succinct, that is, for military people familiar with its wonderful acronyms), Captain LeSchack's service in Panamá, as well as, the Captain thought, a concise exposition of him, both as a naval officer and as a man:

ENERGETIC; AGGRESSIVE; INNOVATIVE; IMAGINATIVE; PHYSICALLY FIT AND ACTIVE; SCHOLARLY; AMBITIOUS; ABRASIVE; LOQUACIOUS; OPINIONATED - AND QUITE OFTEN AND QUITE OBVIOUSLY RIGHT. CAPTAIN LESCHACK DISPLAYS A REMARKABLE BLEND OF THESE QUALITIES CONFIDENTLY TO PROCEED TO HIS GOALS. DURING THIS PERIOD OF TEMAC, SPONSORED BY COMNAVAIRLANT, CAPTAIN LESCHACK HAS PRODUCED A HIGH-QUALITY COMPREHENSIVE STUDY OF THE POTENTIAL FOR POLITICAL TERRORISM AGAINST THE PANAMA CANAL AND LOCAL NAVAL FACILITIES. THE STUDY MEETS THE HIGHEST STANDARDS OF

SCHOLARSHIP AND HAS DIRECT AND IMMEDIATE
APPLICABILITY. HE ALSO FUNCTIONED AS
COORDINATOR FOR NAVY CONTROLLERS DURING
THE MAJOR JCS EXERCISE BLACKHAWK IV
CONDUCTED IN THE PANAMA CANAL AREA BY
USCINCSO AND COMPONENT FORCES. HE VERY
SUCCESSFULLY MELDED HIS STUDY AND HIS
EXERCISE ROLE TO DEVELOP EXCEPTIONALLY
EFFECTIVE TESTS OF CANAL DEFENSE AND HIS
THESES ABOUT ITS VULNERABILITY TO
TERRORISM. HE ALSO DEVELOPED THIS
COMMAND'S INPUT TO USCINCSO FOR THE "DOD
PLAN FOR INTELLIGENCE SUPPORT TO
OPERATIONAL COMMANDERS," AND DEVELOPED
A SOUND AND COMPREHENSIVE PROPOSAL FOR
REORGANIZING RESERVE UNITS ASSIGNED TO
THIS COMMAND. THOUGH NOT LACKING IN
TACT OR DIPLOMACY CAPTAIN LESCHACK'S
RELENTLESS PURSUIT OF INFORMATION AND
LOGICAL ANALYSIS PROVED PARTICULARLY
IRKSOME TO SOME INDIVIDUALS WITH DIFFERENT
PERCEPTIONS, MAKING IT OCCASIONALLY
NECESSARY FOR THIS EVALUATOR TO MEDIATE
DIFFERENCES. HE WAS SELECTED AND FROCKED
TO CAPTAIN DURING THIS TEMAC PERIOD, AND
IMMEDIATELY FUNCTIONED COMFORTABLY AND
EFFECTIVELY IN THAT RANK. HE HAS BEEN AN
ACTIVE PARTICIPANT IN NAVAL COMMUNITY
ACTIVITIES, HAD SEVERAL EFFECTIVE CONTACTS
WITH THE DIPLOMATIC AND FOREIGN NAVAL
COMMUNITIES IN PANAMA AND WAS A WELL-
RECEIVED GUEST SPEAKER AT A LOCAL NAVY
LEAGUE COUNCIL LUNCHEON. HE IS VERY
HIGHLY RECOMMENDED FOR RETENTION IN THE
NAVAL RESERVE AND FOR FURTHER PROMOTION.
HE IS MOST SPECIFICALLY RECOMMENDED FOR
TEMAC OR RECALL FOR FURTHER DEVELOPMENT
OF HIS TERRORISM STUDY AT THIS LEVEL, IN

OTHER COMMANDS, OR IN HIGHER ECHELONS.
THIS STATION AND THE U.S. NAVY HAVE
RECEIVED GREAT BENEFIT FROM HIS TEMAC.

LeSchack mused that many of these characteristics applied equally well
(or poorly) in the conduct of his many torrid love affairs throughout his
life, as well as with his interactions among the scientists, writers, military
men, and fools with whom he came in contact. His was not an
innocuous life. He was not universally admired nor loved, to be sure,
"but people who make a difference and Navy captains in particular,
rarely are," thought LeSchack.

As the moon came up to gently kiss the waves with sparkling diamonds,
he continued to stare at the beach called Barking Sands, unable to look
away. He recalled vividly, through his now alcohol-induced
mellowness, other beaches that he knew, and that were forever captured
in his Piscean memory:

The beach at Curiche, Colombia, to which he, alone in 1967, waded
ashore after jumping off the lowered ramp of a Navy LST: As opposed
to the fond memories of many other beaches, this was an ignominious
scene for him. He had waited too long before debarking, and the more
rapidly than he predicted incoming tide had assured that instead of
wading to shore in knee-deep water, upon jumping off the ramp, he
went straight to the bottom with his heavy pack. The water below the
ramp had reached a depth of a foot or so more than his six-foot height,
and he nearly drowned. Fortunately, he was then a strong and capable
swimmer, and thanks to years of life-guarding experience, able to avoid
panicking. He held his breath and bounced and walked along the
bottom until the water was shallow enough so that his head emerged
and he could breathe, and he then waded ashore.

Fortunately, his destination was an Army Corps of Engineers
construction camp built on the beach to support the Inter-Oceanic Canal
Studies program. It was not wartime, so no one was shooting at him
from the beach, but more importantly, no one on the LST saw him
commit such a silly, albeit, life-threatening blunder.

Each afternoon, after returning from explorations of the Colombian jungle with his Army colleagues, he bathed in the gentle waves rolling up on the gorgeous beach. As he luxuriated in the warm Pacific waters, he thought the only thing now missing was a complaisant lover to share this beautiful scene. Curiche Beach was a beautiful tropical beach, and one he will always remember. He expects that now, this very same perfect beach, because of its geography is a FARC or ELN rendezvous point for drug- and arms-related exchanges in support of their respective terrorist activities. They might even be using the same camp building on this beach and left by the Corps of Engineers, if it is still there.

The moonlit beach at Miami in 1969: Alone, LeSchack viewed it for many melancholy hours from the balcony of the room in a luxury hotel where he was vacationing. Here too, he wished he had been accompanied by a vibrant lover. Instead, he was accompanied by his beautiful, but emotionally unresponsive wife, Virginia. She slept blissfully away, uninterested, in the adjoining bedroom. At that sad time, he considered leaving her, then and there. However, he didn't for another ten years.

Sand Dollar Beach on the Big Sur in 1975: There, after a night of magnificent lovemaking, LeSchack and the beautiful Heidi spent the day lying on the beach listening to Beethoven played on an eight-track tape machine. The beach was deserted and the sun was warm. They laid out a large beach towel and watched the waves roll ashore and splash on the isolated rock outliers that dotted the shoreline. Heidi had been a young teenager in Austria at the time of *Anschluss*, and told him that adults around her remembered it not unkindly. Long since an American citizen, she had been a photographer's model—a voluptuous one. She and LeSchack loved Mozart and Beethoven and Schumann, and often talked of WWII history and Heidi's teenage memories of it. On this day, as Beethoven's "Ode to Joy" was majestically rolling toward the waves from their beach blanket, a lone jogger ran by along the strand. Hearing the glorious sounds as he jogged by, he began "conducting" with his arms until he ran out of earshot. Sensing, rather than actually seeing the clearly implied intimacy on the blanket, he did not visually intrude on them.

LeSchack's affair with Heidi, beginning thirteen years after he first married Virginia, was the first truly lusty relationship he had since before that emotionally disappointing marriage. LeSchack and Heidi's tryst that began at the Big Sur, endured for several years thereafter and restored his enthusiasm for life, for not only was their lovemaking glorious, but so were their conversations about history, music, politics and ways for enhancing lovemaking itself.

The beach along the Fort Amador Causeway in 1980, near Flamenco Island, Panamá: There, one night he and Dorothy, the flighty but very pretty Naval Station Administration Officer, a lieutenant commander, decided to become lovers. They watched the twinkling lights of ships at anchor awaiting their turn to transit the Canal. Their amorous decision catapulted them into a short-lived but intense and satisfying affair immediately thereafter.

The beach at Punta Chame, Panamá in 1981: There, he and the worldly Roberta, a senior Army nurse from Fort Clayton, a lieutenant colonel, made glorious love in broad daylight on the beautiful, deserted beach, and then, hand-in-hand, went swimming together. They often went to this beach on weekends to be alone together, and they thoroughly enjoyed the beach and each other. Roberta had served two tours as a MASH nurse in Viet Nam. Upon returning, she retrained as a public health nurse. LeSchack overheard her tell another nurse that after serving in Southeast Asia, she vowed never again to deal with "red blanket" stretcher cases. She served thereafter, until she retired from the Army, in well-baby clinics.

The deserted beach in the Florida Keys in 1982: There, he and the extraordinarily passionate and voluptuous Barbara often swam together. Barbara was LeSchack's only true love. They were soulmates. He has a vision of Barbara that is etched indelibly into his memory — she is standing up straight, walking from the water onto their beach, proudly carrying a branch of coral for him to inspect. She is a veritable Venus from the sea, wearing only her bikini bottom. As she walks toward LeSchack, the wind blowing her long hair, her narrow waist and magnificent bare breasts call for him to jump up and enfold her in yet another loving embrace. They made love on the beach, on their boat, in every room in their home, and under a full moon. Again and again, they praised the Moon Goddess, making love outdoors in the moonlight.

They remained passionate lovers for many years thereafter. And they spent memorable times together on such wonderful beaches, there and elsewhere in the world. Always with enormous pleasure, not only for each other, but for the water and their beaches. They were both good swimmers, LeSchack, the Pisces and Barbara, the Scorpio.

******

There are two other beaches that are etched indelibly in LeSchack's brain and psyche—the beaches called Omaha and Utah. He was only nine years old on 6 June 1944 when his countrymen stormed ashore from thousands of landing craft onto the shores of Normandy, but he knew as much about them as any nine-year old boy would know and could learn from newspapers and radio broadcasts at that time. He also knew that that just to the east of Utah and Omaha, there were Gold and Sword beaches, where British forces landed, and Juno Beach where Canadian forces came ashore. He knew that those men storming ashore were fighting LeSchack's battle from the coast of France to the gates of Berlin to expunge the Nazis from the face of the earth. His nine-year old spirit was with those men. Years later as a student in France, he had walked the American beaches one summer's day. He saw a profusion of scarlet poppies desperately trying to hide the hideous rusted barbed wire entanglements and crumbling and decaying bunkers and gun emplacements, all still there, that slowed but did not stop American, British and Canadian men, really just boys, perhaps ten years older than he was at that time, from accomplishing their heroic mission.

And finally one last beach for LeSchack, the Pisces, came into focus. It is an allegorical one, to be sure, but nonetheless it made a most powerful and long-lasting, many-dimensional impression on him: that allegorical beach represented the ever-present specter of the Cold War's greatest threat to mankind—nuclear holocaust.

Within weeks of his being commissioned an officer in the United States Navy in 1959, Hollywood released a film, "On the Beach," based on Neville Shute's novel of the same name. The story is about *how the world came to an end*. That disaster occurred as a result of an inadvertent accident or mistake that initiated an ever-expanding nuclear exchange between the United States and the Soviet Union. The 1959 movie postulated that it took place four years later, in 1964. Mass annihilation resulted because of that mythical war which released a poisonous radioactive cloud that quickly encircled the world. The story focuses on the only immediate survivors—yet to succumb to the ever-spreading radiation cloud—the residents of Australia, and the officers and men of the U.S. nuclear submarine, SAWFISH. The SAWFISH happened to be submerged, and on patrol in the Pacific Ocean at the time of the short, devastating mythical U.S.-Soviet nuclear war; the submarine and its crew survived only because it had been shielded by seawater, and Australia simply because the deadly cloud had not yet arrived.

LeSchack knew that ever since the Soviets detonated their first atomic bomb in 1949, followed in 1953 by their first hydrogen bomb, every knowledgeable person in the world knew the potential for such a disaster was there. People, if they could afford to, built and stocked atom bomb shelters, and school children learned to perform essentially useless drills to shield themselves from atomic blasts. But for most of these people, such a calamity was a fearful, but intangible concern. Not for LeSchack. For him, it was incredibly real. At 24 years of age and a newly commissioned naval officer, that movie presented to him a believable representation of the devastating results that could occur owing to miscalculation by any number of personnel on either side. And the older he grew, the more he learned about the real "almost disasters" that were kept secret and never made the news. Of course, there were a number of disasters, based on miscalculation, that did make the news; however, despite the loss of life, one side or the other chose not to make an issue of it, just to avoid a confrontation with which neither was ready to deal.

Most of the scenes of this exceedingly disturbing movie either took place aboard the submarine, SAWFISH, or in Australia. *None of those scenes was far-fetched or alien to LeSchack; on the contrary, they all seemed absolutely real.* Six months before his commissioning, he had sailed on two U.S. Navy ships, one to New Zealand from Antarctica, and one home to the U.S. from Sydney, Australia; he had spent a number of weeks "on the beach," Navy slang for "off the ship and on shore," in Australia. He knew and swam at many of the beaches on the east coast of Australia where the movie was filmed. He had dated young girls there. Now, a naval officer himself, and one who shortly after commissioning *had cruised on a U.S. Navy submarine*, LeSchack had strongly identified with the doomed young Royal Australian Navy officer—a man his own age—who had met his pretty, young wife, as he said, "on the beach" and where he fell in love with her. LeSchack saw that movie in 1959 in the company of another young girl, in New York City, just as pretty as the young wife in the movie, and he could easily see himself and this girlfriend in the same situation.

The musical score of the film was based on that quintessentially Australian song, "Waltzing Matilda," a song that was played endlessly in the messes aboard the USS ARNEB, the ship LeSchack boarded in Sydney Harbor and sailed home on in the spring of 1959. It was clear that song was played largely for the benefit of the now melancholy officers and sailors of the ARNEB who had to leave the women they had met "on the beach," downunder. LeSchack, too, had been sad to leave. As the movie progressed, it became clear to all living in Australia, and all officers and men of the USS SAWFISH, now berthed there—and of course, to the movie audience—that it would only be a matter of weeks before they all would perish from radiation sickness. These people, the last survivors of Planet Earth, would shortly all be gone. There were plaintive scenes of preparations for their coming doom as orchestrated by the music and prayers of the Salvation Army in open-air prayer meetings in downtown Melbourne. It was hard for LeSchack, now a Navy officer himself, to see any of this as make-believe. He had walked those very streets of Melbourne, six months earlier. He had stayed at a Salvation Army hostel in Sydney, while on leave.

And the final scene for LeSchack, particularly as he grew older and increased in rank in the Navy and became more knowledgeable of both the Cold War, and love, and duty, was one last view from the beach. The CO of the SAWFISH, a commander who had lost his wife and two children in America to the nuclear holocaust, had reluctantly fallen in love one last time in Australia. He bid a sad, passionate farewell to the beautiful Australian woman with whom he had fallen in love. But most of the remaining officers and men of the SAWFISH—his ultimate responsibility—had voted to sail back home to America to die in their own, now barren country, rather than remain in Australia. It was that last scene that so haunted LeSchack, the Pisces, for the remainder of the Cold War. He and the audience saw that one beautiful woman, standing on a dune, on their beach, watching her new and last lover, the US Navy Commander—which 15 years later, LeSchack was destined to become— sail resolutely past out into the open reaches before her. And in plain view of that desperately sad woman, the Commander began submerging in his nuclear submarine, to sail home to oblivion.

It was only three years after the debut of "On the Beach," that LeSchack in 1962, now a lieutenant (jg), learned while briefing congressmen on Capitol Hill how close the world would come to just such a nuclear nightmare during the Cuban Missile Crisis. As he grew older and rose in rank during the Cold War, becoming exposed to more and more classified information, and information of greater and greater secrecy, the specter of "On the Beach," became to LeSchack less and less unrealistic. Till the end of the Cold War, the last scene of that beautiful woman sadly watching—from the beach—haunted him; standing alone, a gentle, radioactive wind blowing through her hair, she saw her last lover, the captain of the submarine who chose duty over love, sail home to America one last time. *Because that was his duty.*

Then, before retiring to a fitful slumber, all the other significant events from high school on to the present moment, fast-forwarded through LeSchack's mind. This video-like display of his time on this earth provided him an opportunity to see how much of that life was involuntarily related to, and formed and financed by, the then apparently never-ending Cold War—LeSchack's "different drummer." From the many beach scenes that just flitted through his mind, he could also not escape the conclusion that despite his tendency to be a loner, the love of women was essential to his life and his creativity. One of his beach lovers, Barbara, who knew him extremely well, astutely observed that despite all his adrenaline-filled physical adventures, parachuting, scuba diving, working with midget submarines, and engaging in all sorts of exciting espionage activities on behalf of his government, he seemed to be alive—truly alive—only entwined with an eager woman, and in the midst of orgasm. LeSchack had to admit that she was right.

Well, largely right; for him, listening to a Beethoven symphony could come close.

The LST USS CHURCHILL COUNTY at Curiche Beach Colombia 1967.

Now at age 66, Captain Leonard LeSchack, 12 years after he had retired from the Navy, had a revelation. It was the year of the 11 September terrorist attack. He was sitting on the veranda of the beach cottage at the Navy's Pacific Missile Range Facility on Kauai staring at the beautiful beach, "Barking Sands," waiting for the sunset and drinking rum. He could not help but remember other beautiful and important beaches vividly implanted in his brain: The magnificent beach at Curiche, Colombia where he debarked from the LST USS CHURCHILL COUNTY, the beach on the Big Sur, the beaches in Panama' and in Long Key, Florida, all accompanied by astounding lovers, and other beaches of geopolitical importance to the Captain.

LCDR Dorothy at Ft. Amador where they became lovers in 1981

LCOL Roberta, Punta Chame, Panama'. They, too were lovers, 1981

Barbara, LeSchack's Soulmate Long Key, Florida, 1984

Heidi at Big Sur, a lover LeSchack will always remember

Formative Years: The Making of an Adventurer, Naval Officer and Maverick Scientist

Far away places with strange-sounding names, far away over the sea
Those far away places with strange-sounding names, are callin', callin' me.

Goin' to China or maybe Siam, I wanna see for myself,
Those far away places I've been readin' about, in a book I took from the shelf.

I start getting restless whenever I hear the whistle of a train,
I pray for the day I can get underway, and look for those castles in Spain.

They call me a dreamer, well, maybe I am, but I know that I'm burning to see,
Those far away places with strange-sounding names, callin', callin' me.

Bing Crosby's 1949 hit song.

LeSchack could hardly remember a time when he could not read nor swim—or wished to visit faraway places. He assuredly could not remember when he began to talk or walk. He learned to read when he was in nursery school. His parents read to him every night before he went to sleep. His mother was a high school history teacher and his father an attorney. Although the bedtime stories they read to LeSchack included the usual nursery rhymes and children's stories, they also included stories from "The Book of Knowledge." His favorite stories were about scientists, explorers and adventurers. This was largely, because he fancied himself pursuing one or all of these professions.

Although born during the height of the Great Depression, LeSchack seemed to have escaped the worst of that financial disaster, owing to his parents each earning their own professional incomes. While not being particularly over-indulged, he did receive "educational toys," usually as birthday presents, that helped shape the young LeSchack. An "erector set," a tool box, a chemistry set, toys that helped him think and design, and a two-wheel bicycle that gave him mobility and set him free.

He was six years old when Pearl Harbor was bombed. Although he heard President Roosevelt's Declaration of War speech on 8 December, he didn't know what this all meant, except that he saw the horrified reactions of the adults around him. He soon became a participant in elementary school air raid drills, and learned some of the World War II songs, like "White Cliffs of Dover." To this day, when LeSchack hears the song "God Bless America," the movie image and voice of Kate Smith pops up into his consciousness and tears come to his eyes. World War II had a major, life-shaping affect on the impressionable LeSchack. It colored his perception of the world for the remainder of his life.

LeSchack's father was too young for World War I and too old for World War II. Nonetheless, he thought that if the government decided it would draft older men, lawyers would not be what were needed, but radiomen might be. And he thought he was, in fact, too old for the infantry, which was the usual destination for draftees. So shortly after the US entered the war, LeSchack's father began taking courses in radio theory, radio repair, and Morse code. Just in case. As a result, LeSchack's dad had, at one time or another, taken apart and "repaired" every radio in the house. Additionally, radio paraphernalia, radio chassis', tools, earphones and the like, were frequently scattered about for the curious LeSchack to use as sophisticated toys. For example, he clamped the earphones over a child's Army Air Corps cap and ran around the house pretending to shoot Messerschmidts and zeros from the top turret of a B-17.

During the World War II-period LeSchack's favorite reading was the "Hardy Boys" series about teen-aged boy detectives who had lots of wonderful adventures, and the "Flying Cadet," a comic book series. Although available on newsstands, Flying Cadet was, in fact, a training aid used by the Army Air Corps for its flight cadets. In addition to complementing the official training manuals, it provided stories of air combat, as well as elementary flight theory and mechanics. It was the former that interested LeSchack, for he also fancied himself a fighter pilot.

LeSchack's bicycle set him free. He was able to begin to visit, *on his own,* "far away places" of great romantic interest to him. There were such places nearby where he lived during these wartime years in Freeport, New York, on Long Island. These included dense forests, open meadows and deserted beaches. In places like these, he could easily picture himself as an explorer. In the family basement rumpus room he set up his chemistry set where he could "experiment" with all manner of colorful and smelly concoctions that intrigued him. While he did so, his faithful "bunny," a stuffed animal and a constant companion, watched over him, close by, from a nearby shelf. The shelf was filled with a variety of his erector set constructions—he also thought of becoming a construction engineer.

While LeSchack did not consider himself particularly asocial, his mother told him that she was often called to school by his elementary school teachers or principal to discuss some of LeSchack's "problems." This infuriated his mother, because, after all, she was a teacher too, and "children of teachers" were supposed to behave better. Frankly, LeSchack remembered none of this, and never thought of himself as asocial at school. A daydreamer—as in the song, most assuredly—but not asocial. However, he was mostly a loner, constructing adventurous scenarios with himself as the hero, be it explorer, adventurer or scientist; in his daydreams he often surrounded himself with the prettiest little girls of his acquaintance. Occasionally, he even had real dreams that involved some of these same girls. No doubt, there were latent sexual connotations involved in such dreams, but LeSchack knew nothing about anything in a sexual context. Sex was not a topic of discussion in his family. Politics was.

LeSchack knew very little about girls; only that they grew up to be women. None of the books he read said much about girls. LeSchack, the child scientist, did take note of the fact that little girls in the classroom smelled pleasantly different from the way boys did. Something in their hair, LeSchack thought.

Some of his childhood adventures with little girls, however, were neither dreams nor daydreams. They actually occurred, and clearly had latent sexual connotations. He certainly remembered them vividly as individual events, but was not able to evaluate properly these adventures at that time. Not till he was way beyond puberty could the effect of these experiences be meaningful. Nonetheless, as a budding young scientist, he dutifully cataloged in his memory these adventures for future evaluation.

Let's start with Taffy, a girl a bit older and bigger than LeSchack, and one who had fascinated him. They were no more than seven or eight years old and, as children do, became involved in a fight over some issue. In the ensuing tussle, she overpowered him, knocked him to the ground and sat on top of him, pinning his shoulders to the ground with her knees. In the process of losing the tussle with her he observed, with both horror as well as latent delight, that when she pinned him down on the ground, her dress billowed up and her panty-covered crotch slid extraordinarily close to his face. Not only was the loss of the fight to this girl mortifying to LeSchack, it was also magnificently exciting. Even at that young age, it was arousing to have his face forced to be so close to that secret and damp space between a female's thighs.

During this same time-period, there was also the irrepressible Velma, a girl LeSchack's age, who lived a few houses away. She seemed to have had no inhibitions at all. One day she took LeSchack to a secluded spot in his backyard and calmly and deliberately proceeded to lift up her dress, drop her panties and, while squatting, let loose a steaming golden stream into the garden. She had absolutely no reservations about providing LeSchack with an unobstructed, close-up frontal view of her young, hairless cicatrice spurting its liquid onto the ground.

Complementing these strange, crypto-sexual experiences with Taffy and Velma was the even stranger childhood experience of being invited by Richard, the young teen-aged boy next door, to watch a display of masturbation. It was conducted in the back seat of that boy's family automobile, parked in their garage. LeSchack was the only spectator in attendance. He had no idea till then that a penis had any other purpose than being a urine spigot. He soon recognized however, that whatever the mechanics or other uses for the penis were, the process of expelling semen all over the interior of the car was giving Richard extraordinary pleasure. The accompanying commentary by Richard that this procedure, in conjunction with a woman's vagina, was directly related to the birth of babies was, for LeSchack, simply beyond comprehension. He was not prepared to believe his parents could have indulged in such a procedure. As with the unusual events involving Taffy and Velma, LeSchack simply mentally cataloged, for future reference, this event also. It would be nearly a decade hence before LeSchack even began to consider boys and girls in any sexual context.

World War II was clearly the seminal event in LeSchack's early youth. It introduced him to building model airplanes, and radio as a means of communication, and it introduced him to the concept of military operations. He became aware from the reading of biographies of his favorite explorers, Admiral Byrd, Admiral Peary, Lewis and Clark and others, that military training and experience seemed to be a common denominator.

As the War entered its final year, LeSchack's family moved to a suburban community closer to New York City. He enrolled in a new elementary school. As far as LeSchack could see, the only difference in his new school, part of the New York City school system, was that the teachers were older and uglier. Not better. Basically, LeSchack learned what he wanted to learn, not specifically what the curricula wanted to teach him. And mostly by reading on his own. Sometimes he did well, other times, not. He did fall in with a group of boys in the fifth grade who played baseball. That changed his life for the year. Because he batted left-handed, he regularly hit the ball into right field where opposing players never seemed to be. Although they eventually would learn that that was where LeSchack would hit the ball, by the time they had done so, he had become a minor baseball hero in his class. And that meant he was invited to parties that were thrown by his class' most popular girls; this was because his gang of ballplayers were the most popular boys.

That didn't last long, however. Soon after, a burst of academic energy on LeSchack's part resulted in his being skipped a grade forward. One could do this then in the New York City system. While this higher grade did not pose an academic problem for LeSchack, it did pose a social one: he was now the youngest in the class and no longer in the "popular group." His new classmates not only were older, but looked older. LeSchack retreated to science. By the age of ten, just as the War was coming to an end, he had built his first one-tube radio and began using his chemistry set to make bombs. Because his new home was nearby the

New York City subway system, he was able to walk to the subway and, for a nickel, visit the Museum of Science and Industry and the American Museum of Natural History; both were in Manhattan, and both of which he thoroughly enjoyed.

His interests began to grow: gasoline-powered model airplanes, photography, and geographical exploration of any place that could be classified as "rural," that is, not chock-a-block with human beings. At this point in his life, such were the "far away places with strange-sounding names." Young girls, even pretty ones, were still low on his list of priorities. Afternoons, upon returning from school he often retired to his workshop in the attic where he built his model airplanes. In those days, the afternoon airwaves were filled with 15-minute serial adventure stories on the radio. He listened avidly to them as he constructed his models, and his imagination soared. In the early evening his parents let him listen to some radio programs that they deemed suitable for a young boy, such as the "Lone Ranger." For reasons not entirely clear to LeSchack then, his parents forbade him to listen to radio programs later on in the evening.

That's when the one-tube radio he built came in. It received all the standard radio stations available in his area, but instead of a loudspeaker, it used earphones. That allowed LeSchack to listen to programs, unbeknownst to his parents, while under the covers in bed — with his earphones on. A whole new adult world opened to LeSchack, a world where sometimes, he learned, clandestine behavior paid off.

During the summers of LeSchack's youth, he led a much different life. His parents owned a cottage in what were then the wilds of Connecticut. The cottage was located on a one-acre plot of wooded land that bordered the Aspetuck River. There were some fifty other families with cottages in the same area, most of whom were professionals of about the same age as LeSchack's parents. A number of these families had children LeSchack's age. Each summer while he was growing up LeSchack played with these children. They hiked together, swam together, took day trips and had picnics together, all under the supervision of an adult counselor. While LeSchack noted that all the girls in his gang were pretty, more or less, only two of the boys his age had any interest in "exploring or adventuring." He spent most of his time with these two boys.

Even though the summers were the most enjoyable time of year for LeSchack, he continued to spend much of his time alone, building things, conducting chemistry experiments and taking photographs. Several of his little girl friends began referring to him as a "mad scientist." He recognized this *was not* a compliment. On one occasion, the group was having an evening picnic around a campfire, cooking hot dogs, burgers and baked beans. On little girl placed an unopened can of beans onto the burning logs so as to heat the beans. LeSchack made the observation to her that she had best puncture the can before it got too hot.......°or there would be trouble." The little girl turned to a nearby counselor for advice as to whether to heed the "mad scientist."

The counselor dismissed young LeSchack's cautionary observation, implying that grownups don't take much heed to 10-year old boys' concerns based on theories of physical chemistry. LeSchack quietly backed away from the fire to the periphery of the assembled adults and children to await the inevitable catastrophe to follow. It did. The bean can exploded, frightening everybody except LeSchack. The explosion scattered baked beans all over the area and into the little girl's hair, face and onto her clothes. The same fate befell all others, including the counselor, who happened to be near the detonation. Asocial or not, LeSchack had the good grace not to say, "I told you so!"

****

By the time he became thirteen, to LeSchack's way of retrospective thinking, several momentous events occurred: he had entered high school; he was absolved from further practice of the violin; he began serious study toward earning an amateur radio license; and he was entering, and not gently, puberty! It only was years later, and only after being around the world a couple of times, that he sensed that these all were truly significant, life-altering events.

In 1948, LeSchack entered Forest Hills High School, at that time known to be one of New York City's finest secondary schools for general academic excellence. This was the first time in LeSchack's academic career that there were a number of men who would be his teachers.

Most of them seemed to LeSchack to be recently discharged veterans, the War having ended just three years earlier. And they were not just in the physical education department. Hell! His music appreciation teacher was a former Marine! LeSchack, still basically a child, was a bit overwhelmed by some three thousand classmates who were already "big boys," and girls who were not only pretty, but were beginning to look to him like real women.

The high school not only had many good teachers, it also had excellent facilities for conducting science experiments of the type LeSchack could not perform in his own basement. It also had good gymnastic facilities in the physical education department. Although LeSchack was not particularly interested in team sports, he did enjoy gymnastics at the school's facilities. Frequently, after classes, he would practice tumbling routines on the mats and work out on the high bar and parallel bars. He learned a fascinating lesson just after one such gym session. He was in the locker room getting dressed to leave when a minor pogrom broke out!

Forest Hills High School was largely populated by the progeny of upper middle-class New York professional families. There were, however, a small percentage of working-class New York City ethnics who attended the school. A much larger percentage of the latter folks visited the gym after school than did the former. For whatever reason, on that particular day, a group of rough and tumble guys, all bigger than LeSchack, came screaming down the rows of lockers, yelling and whooping, slamming open locker doors and harassing and punching any boys in their path. Although LeSchack heard the oncoming horde of hoodlums, he did not have adequate time to get out of their way. Just as three guys were about to beat the shit out of LeSchack, one of the attackers yelled, "Hey, don't touch that guy. He can do standing back flips!" That was a fact. LeSchack could do these and other tumbling routines. And the horde just ran around the frightened LeSchack to harass the next guy that they chanced upon. "How bizarre," thought LeSchack, surprised that his ability at tumbling had saved his ass from the cretin mob. It also made him think more about serendipity and random events, and how they impinged on his life.

From the age of five LeSchack had essentially been coerced by his father to play the violin. His father was an amateur violinist, playing in local orchestras, as well as for his own enjoyment. His advice to his son, "you can't be popular at parties or with girls unless you play the violin, Son." This sounded ridiculous to LeSchack. Certainly between the age of five, when he started and thirteen when he quit, he rarely went to parties nor was interested in girls. LeSchack's uncle was a violin-maker, and he was commissioned to make a three-quarter-size violin for the child. Along with the mandatory elementary school education, LeSchack took mandatory violin lessons. Sometimes he liked it but most of the time he didn't. He hated to practice. It detracted from his science and baseball time. By the time he entered high school, he was able to convince his father that he was unlikely to become a concert violinist, and needed to devote his attentions to academic pursuits. LeSchack's father relented, but with sadness. Although the violin and music lessons never brought LeSchack pretty girls or life-of-the-party status, it did give him an appreciation for violin music, and classical music in general, that were to enrich the remainder of his life.

LeSchack's interest in radio and specifically, two-way communication by means of radio only blossomed upon his success in building his own one-tube radio set. Some of his relatives and friends had radios that also permitted reception of short-wave frequencies. LeSchack began avidly listening to radio broadcasts in English from around the world whenever he had access to someone's short-wave radio. In the process of tuning across the radio spectrum, LeSchack became aware that not only was radio used for transmitting "formal programming," there were private radio operators all over the world who spoke to one another "just for fun." They were known as "amateur radio" operators, otherwise known as "hams." To LeSchack, listening in on their conversations, it sounded like they were having great fun. He wanted to learn more. He decided to do so, and this became a clear and unequivocal turning point in his life.

The first wireless "radio" signals were transmitted across the Atlantic Ocean in 1901 by Marconi, using the Morse code, a system of long and short signals invented earlier by Samuel Morse to be transmitted over a wire network for message communications. By the time of the First World War in 1914, wireless radio was becoming an increasingly important form of communication. Shortly after that war, a number of national governments recognized the value of this form of communication and agreed to set aside certain radio frequencies for citizens to use for "amateur" radio communication. This was not altruistic on the part of governments. The art and science of radio was arcane. Not many people then either knew it or knew how to use it effectively. And it was particularly valuable to governments, especially during wartime, to have available for military service, people who were already trained in this new technology. Accordingly, international agreements were put in place that encouraged citizens to learn, and become proficient in radio communication. These agreements set aside certain specified radio frequency bandwidths for private citizens to use, at no cost to them. However, in return, the agreements also required such citizens to pass rigorous government tests to obtain a license to use the airwaves legally. LeSchack decided at age thirteen to obtain such a license from the Government of the United States of America.

In those days, just after the conclusion of World War II, the Federal Government's test for obtaining a free amateur radio license consisted of three parts: knowledge of federal communication laws; knowledge of theory of radio transmission and reception; and a working knowledge of the Morse code. It was the practice then for potential hams to purchase a commercially available radio communications receiver, to build their own transmitter, often from inexpensive surplus military aircraft command sets, and become proficient in Morse code simply by practice, and more practice. LeSchack did all this, over a period of two years, his first two years in high school. While his parents thought this two-year period of extracurricular activity was a detriment to his high school studies, it wasn't. But ham radio opened up major opportunities for LeSchack in the following decade. In 1950, when he was fifteen years old and just after the Korean War started, he received his license from the Federal Communications Commission in Washington, D.C.

At the outset, his license permitted LeSchack to talk, for free, using AM voice communication, to people all over the country and the world. Not only was this exciting, it gave LeSchack training in speaking "blind" to adults, on adult topics. In those days, radio communication was "one way." First, one party talks, then says "over," then the second party talks, and so on. Over time, ham radio was a remarkable confidence-builder for the young LeSchack. It required him to organize his thoughts quickly and give miniature speeches during the time slots allotted between "overs." It also required him to listen carefully to what the other ham was saying to him during that person's allotted time. Quite different thought LeSchack, from the usual way of conducting conversations.

Seven years later, he obtained his first job upon graduation from college as a geologist, largely as a result of his ham radio license. After the fact, one of his college professors told LeSchack explicitly that he had gotten the job as a result of the radio and electronics experience. The professor had a close relationship with the recruiters from Shell Oil, the company that hired LeSchack. The recruiters told him that they intended on placing LeSchack in the geophysical trainee program, and the practical electronics experience made the difference. It certainly made the difference, shortly thereafter, in LeSchack's selection for the U.S. Antarctic Expedition that would form in 1957. LeSchack was chosen for its over-ice exploration traverse program during the International Geophysical Year. Not only was his practical electronic experience valued then, but so was his ability to communicate using Morse code. And the Antarctic Program launched LeSchack's career in real science, real geographical exploration of "far away places" and ultimately, real adventures in the United States Navy. But we get ahead of our story.

LeSchack's high school years—compared with the rest of his life—were basically uneventful. He studied. He spent, according to his parents, an inordinate amount of time on ham radio; he excelled in science and English, as well as eventually, history. But that was largely because LeSchack's mother, a history teacher at another high school in the New York City school system, force-fed him on history each evening at home. She taught from the same curriculum so she knew what LeSchack needed to know on exams. He also learned a bit of real history. The Korean War was now underway and some of his older classmates enlisted. One who rode the same school bus as LeSchack had enlisted in the Marines. He didn't come back.

Also, he was inducted into the "Captains' Corps," an organization run by the physical education department. The "captains" were leaders of squads of students during the "phys-ed" periods. The squads were largely organizational units set up by the phys-ed teachers, all of whom were ex-military, for rapid taking of attendance. However, the "captains" were invited and, in fact, were encouraged to attend after-school sessions to practice sports and gymnastic routines in the gym. It was the latter that interested LeSchack. As an added benefit, captains were issued distinctive and exclusive "Captains' Corps" T-shirts for use during gym periods; occasionally they might be worn to classes and used as girl-bait.

By the time LeSchack was sixteen he had achieved a man's body—six feet tall with broad shoulders. He had passed his Red Cross Senior Lifesaving test that qualified him to be employed as a lifeguard during the summers, and he received his badge for his bathing suit. Also, he had what could be called his first "date" with a girl. Her name was Micaëla, presumably named by her parents after the cigarette girl in the opera, "Carmen." Frankly, LeSchack thought she looked more like the exotic Carmen, herself. It was hard for the young LeSchack to believe a fourteen-year old girl could look so sultry! It was during the summer, in Connecticut, and they were walking along a back-country road, holding hands. LeSchack's knees turned to jelly. He could hardly walk. Eventually they kissed and necked, which completely disrupted LeSchack's equilibrium. "So this is what girls do to you," he mused as his bloodstream was inundated with an overdose of endocrine chemicals.

The first three events, high school, violin lessons, and amateur radio, were clearly fork-in-the-road turning points in LeSchack's life. The last, the onset of puberty, a puzzler for him, was not specifically an event, but it certainly introduced to him an era of increasing change, a change that appeared to color powerfully LeSchack's perceptions of life and the "life force," as well as to fuel his drive for adventure of all sorts. And it certainly colored the perceptions of him by others, just as did his six-foot height, broad shoulders and "command presence," as they call it in the military. Just as did his left-handedness and strong right-brained thinking. Whether or not it was a puberty-driven hormonal imbalance, a vivid imagination, his early experience with women, or just a plain abundance of biblical lust, he observed that increasingly as life progressed, he enjoyed frequent and vibrant female companionship. While LeSchack knew that less charitable people might invoke that eighteenth century word, "womanizer," to describe him, he preferred to think of his propensities as "the natural order of things."

******

For LeSchack, high school was essentially a non-event in his life. It seemed only to be a holding tank for him to metamorphose from a child of thirteen to a gangling teenager of seventeen—all while being pumped full of learning. Well, at least enough to continue on to engineering school. He made a few male friends with whom he sporadically made contact after graduation, but no female friends, although he flirted a bit with some girls in his classes. Basically, he was completely unsure of himself as far as girls were concerned, but this did not seem to pose a major problem for him.

That uncertainty towards dealing with girls was reduced substantially when, during his senior year, Joyce appeared on the scene. Joyce, who also attended the same high school, was in none of LeSchack's classes. She contributed to the teen social column of a local newspaper, and for reasons unknown to LeSchack, "discovered" him. Then, she decided she liked him, and commenced an aggressive pursuit. And she wrote about the otherwise diffident LeSchack! But as one wag said, "good publicity or bad publicity—it doesn't matter—it's publicity!" At this point, any publicity seemed helpful to LeSchack. But probably more important to LeSchack's well-being and future growth was that Joyce enjoyed "necking and petting," and taught LeSchack how to also enjoy these pleasures. She certainly knew how, and LeSchack was a quick learner. And then he graduated from Forest Hills High School.

High school graduation was also a non-event. The "Senior Prom" was cancelled owing to one of the periodic teachers' strikes, and for LeSchack, the mid-year graduation ceremony was completely forgettable. He began working for an electronics firm between February and September, 1952, when he started college. The electronics firm, located on the seedy west side of mid-town Manhattan, near the docks, was a useful experience for LeSchack. It was his first real work experience, and in electronics, and the first time he was exposed to the less-than genteel aspects of blue-collar life. That was a real and necessary education for LeSchack. Especially so in later years, when he joined the Navy.

*****

In September 1952, the second year of the Korean War, LeSchack entered Rensselaer Polytechnic Institute in Troy, New York. Rensselaer, or RPI as it was known, was an old and well-known engineering school, the students of which were about 99% boys. LeSchack had enrolled in the electrical engineering department, thinking this would be a course in "advanced ham radio." It wasn't, but that didn't much matter, since the first two years worth of courses were largely the same for all students: mathematics, physics, and chemistry. The school's curriculum was extraordinarily rigorous, but the school administration had a laissez-faire attitude about studies. You were told early on that statistically only two-thirds of any entering class would graduate. The individual student was left with the responsibility for determining for himself which group he would fall into.

In addition to an excellent academic program, there was a diverse athletic program and a social life that revolved substantially around some fifty national Greek-letter fraternities. There was also a quasi-military air about the school, not only because of the on-going Korean War, but for historical reasons. RPI had been an important source of naval officers (the V-12 Program) during the Second World War, less than ten years earlier. All three services maintained an active ROTC program on campus, and most students, all of draft age, were well aware that a federal college student draft deferment program allowed them to be at school rather than in Korea. And a sizeable number of students were already veterans.

In many ways, college was just another "holding tank" for force-fed learning as far a LeSchack was concerned. He knew that a college degree was necessary, but it seemed to LeSchack that this was simply putting off, further into the future, the real adventures that he sought in "far away places with strange-sounding names." But he plugged on. He enrolled in the Air Force ROTC program. He joined a fraternity, largely because the fraternity houses typically had far better food service than the student mess hall did. And he decided he no longer wanted to be anonymous, as he largely had been in high school. He decided to join the cheerleading squad!

LeSchack made the deliberate decision in his freshman year to become a cheerleader because in that way he could be noticed by everybody who attended sports events. Not surprisingly, the cheerleaders were all boys. Their routines, particularly at football, soccer and lacrosse games, were heavily weighted toward somersaults, handsprings, back flips and the type of tumbling that LeSchack was good at doing. He tried out and was accepted. He learned the cheers, received a pair of bright red pants, and a white sweater. These were the school colors. And he performed, along with the rest of the squad. Well, LeSchack was noticed. By nearly everybody, including the dates his classmates brought to sports events. This was what LeSchack had wanted and, for what it was worth, he was successful. If being called "cute" by desirable girls was a mark of success. However, the red-headed LeSchack did not find "cute" quite the appellation he had hoped for. But both girls and his fellow students *did* know who he was. Aside from this, he remained a loner.

LeSchack's first two years at RPI were life altering. He learned that electrical engineering was not what he wanted to do as a career. It would not lead, he felt, to a sufficiently adventurous life. He switched to geology instead. That, thought LeSchack, would likely lead to a more out-of-doors life, like that which his childhood heroes had lived. He certainly would be proven correct there! He learned from ROTC that: saturation bombing was counter-productive, based on World War II experience; that the U.S. should never again get involved in a land war in Asia—this based on the experience of that military genius General Douglas MacArthur. He made admonitions to that effect; and that LeSchack was not Air Force officer material, based on the wisdom of his Air Force instructors. That organization threw him out after two years. While a disappointment, the Korean War had ended and there was less chance of being drafted. So LeSchack just counted on a student deferment to hold him until graduation. Finally, at age eighteen, he met Giselle, a pretty Canadian girl with whom he would soon fall in love. His first real love.

Giselle lived in Montréal, a six-hour drive north of Troy, New York. She often visited her cousin who lived in Albany, just across the Hudson River from Troy. That cousin, a girlfriend of one of LeSchack's fraternity brothers, brought Giselle to a weekend fraternity party where they met. LeSchack liked her. At the time they met, she was a tall, skinny girl, quiet, bright, demure, and pretty. She seemed more knowledgeable of the world than most of the young girls LeSchack had known. In addition to English, her native tongue, she also spoke French. This, along with the fact that she was "foreign," intrigued LeSchack.

The two teenagers decided that they would like to keep in contact and continue seeing each other. They began writing, phoning and visiting. LeSchack would drive up to Montréal about once a month and Giselle would occasionally come to visit LeSchack. At first LeSchack stayed with a classmate from Montréal when visiting Giselle, and she would stay with her cousin while visiting LeSchack. Their relationship matured rapidly.

Shortly thereafter when Giselle visited LeSchack to attend a school dance with him, they were simply too frantic after the dance *not* to consummate their bubbling passions any longer. At the time, LeSchack was living in the school dormitory, but he had his own private room. Although it was strictly forbidden to take a girl there, they were prepared to take the chance now and they snuck stealthily into the room together. It was well past midnight when LeSchack and Giselle entered the dorm. No one was in sight and it was completely quiet. Giselle removed her high heels and, as stealthily as possible for two teen-agers bubbling with passion, they climbed the two flights of stairs to reach LeSchack's room. Fortunately, they met nobody on the stairs. Entering his room and locking the door, they threw themselves on the bed. And really alone for the first time ever, this was the first time LeSchack had ever made love to a woman.

It seemed that once LeSchack and Giselle began making love to each other, they both developed quickly, physically and emotionally. It became more quickly apparent with Giselle, for it seemed that the instant she lost her virginity, her breasts blossomed to a deliciously large and enjoyable size, and the rest of her body also became appropriately curvaceous. She also became more at ease with her body and the world. LeSchack became a lot more comfortable with his maleness and happy that he had such a pretty partner for a friend and lover. She enjoyed lying on top of him in bed, slowly sliding her naked body across his, until her now very womanly breasts brushed across the top of LeSchack's mouth. As lovers do, they taught each other the things that made each other happy. And each time now when they had the privacy to do so, they made love and became better and better at pleasing one another.

Shortly after that milestone event with Giselle in his dorm room, he was approached by one of his dormitory mates. "Hey Len," he asked casually, "Did you have a girl in your room the night of the mid-winter school dance?" "What makes you ask?" LeSchack responded carefully. "Well, *we know* there was a girl in the dorm late that night. We asked everyone else we thought she might be with, and they all denied having a girl with them. That leaves you. Was it?" LeSchack was most uncomfortable with the question. Whether he was uncomfortable because he was the last to be asked, or because he was asked at all, LeSchack was not quite sure. "Hey, buddy, your secret is safe with us. We just wanted to know." LeSchack smiled cautiously, recalling that delicious clandestine encounter with Giselle, a genuine co-mingling of spirits that, for the first time in his life, made him feel whole. He also smiled because intuitively *he did know* his secret would indeed *be safe* with them. The "we" who were making this unsettling inquiry were his dorm mates who were all World War II veterans. Intuitively, he knew they, of all his classmates, wouldn't squeal. Nonetheless, he wondered how they knew.

LeSchack also recognized that the time had now come for him to rent his own private room in downtown Troy, away from the rules and regulations of the school. With LeSchack's and Giselle's passions now un-bottled and bubbling over, he knew that he could not take any further chances that could compromise the two lovers. It turns out that one of his classmates, Victor, who also came from Montréal, had just the solution. That classmate lived in a disreputable house at the edge of the Troy slums; it had a room available, and cheaply. Its most recent occupant, another student, was moving elsewhere. LeSchack took the room. It was a good choice. Not only could LeSchack have privacy when Giselle came to visit, he had a built-in travel partner to share expenses whenever the two had both the time and the money to drive to Montréal. For his Canadian classmate *also* had a girlfriend in Montréal.

Each summer since he had reached the age of sixteen and earned his Red Cross senior lifesaving badge, LeSchack worked as a lifeguard. He enjoyed the sun and water, and he was a good swimmer. At age eighteen, just after college had ended for the summer, he enrolled at the Red Cross' two-week training course for becoming certified as a "Water Safety Instructor." He enjoyed using summer breaks for life-guarding. Specifically, he enjoyed putting his brain in neutral for two months and concentrating only on whether his charges were swimming comfortably or were drowning. As an added benefit, he also enjoyed watching young women in bathing suits. By the time these non-intellectually rigorous summer days were over, he was both mentally and physically able to, once again, dive into his academic work.

After completing the first two years of schooling in electrical engineering, LeSchack had, in fact, switched majors and began studying geology. The geology curriculum better suited both his intellect and his thirst for "real exploration." Increasingly, he recognized that applying science to work out in the field would offer the most satisfying work environment for him. He enjoyed working in the out-of-doors. And there was plenty of geological interest in the Troy area for LeSchack and his fellow students to examine. Also, since his trips from Troy to Montréal passed through the Adirondack Mountains, he had plenty of roadside geologic outcrops to visit and study.

Once LeSchack and Giselle became lovers, they recognized they had unleashed an enormously powerful, almost cosmic force within themselves. When LeSchack went to Montréal, he began staying at Giselle's family's apartment. When she came to Troy, she now stayed with LeSchack in his room. She also now joined LeSchack at his parents' homes, either in New York or in Connecticut over long school vacations. Both families assumed by now that LeSchack and Giselle were intending to get married. That certainly *was* their intention. On LeSchack's twenty-first birthday, during his senior year, Giselle spent LeSchack's birthday night, along with a bottle of champagne, in his Troy bedroom. That evening was most memorable.

In LeSchack's senior year he began to wonder what life in the real world might have in store. He expected that he likely might be employed by an oil company since that was the usual destination for graduating geologists. He also wondered about the possibility of joining the soon to be launched U.S. Antarctic Expedition. He found out about this expedition from a classmate who showed LeSchack a letter of rejection from that expedition's director. The rejection was based solely on the fact that Harry, LeSchack's classmate, had not yet graduated. The director urged Harry to finish his schoolwork and re-apply. LeSchack was fascinated by the potential adventure that such an expedition could create. He asked Harry whether he would mind if he could write the author of the rejection letter and see if *he* would have better luck.

Harry gave LeSchack the address of Dr. Albert P. Crary, the expedition's director. And LeSchack began what turned out to be lengthy correspondence with Crary and the U.S. National Committee for the International Geophysical Year (IGY). This correspondence led, two years later, to a truly life-changing experience for LeSchack. But in the meantime, LeSchack continued studying, and continued visiting with Giselle as often as he could afford—in both time and money.

As the year progressed, it became ever clearer to both LeSchack and Giselle that a genuine conflict was developing. It was between a life of adventures in the oil fields or in areas yet unknown for him, and a life of settling into her own career and a marriage and family for Giselle. That semester, Giselle had enrolled at McGill University in the physical therapy program. She would have at least another three years of study ahead of her. As lovers do, both of them put these thoughts of likely separation back in the recesses of their consciousness as LeSchack's college days became numbered and Giselle's had just begun. Eventually, over the next months the sadness of the inevitability of going their separate ways eclipsed the enormous pleasure of their past enjoyment of each other. Most reluctantly, and with much anguish, they separated, each suspecting in their heart of hearts, this would be for the best. It was an extraordinary sadness for LeSchack. Despite later extraordinarily pleasurable encounters with other women, it took years before Giselle disappeared from his dreams.

LeSchack's graduation from RPI, like high school, was a non-event. And for the same reasons. By switching majors, LeSchack added an extra semester to his curriculum and again, graduated in January when, at RPI, there were no mid-year graduation ceremonies. He simply packed up and left Troy, and by February 1957 had driven to Baton Rouge, Louisiana to begin working for the Shell Oil Company. Although graduating as a petroleum geologist, he had been accepted into Shell's geophysical training program, reputed to have been the best in the industry. Because the RPI curriculum was heavy on physics and math, and because LeSchack, as a result of his ham radio, had already demonstrated proficiency in electronics, he was hired as a potential geophysicist, rather than a geologist. This would be just fine for LeSchack, since young exploration geophysicists were often out in the field.

Although life in Baton Rouge was a bit strange for LeSchack—basically a product of the Northeastern "intelligentsia"—he gradually adapted to the "good ole boys" and the "Cajun" milieu of field work in Southern Louisiana and the Mississippi Delta. That was where much of Shell's geophysical exploration was occurring. And these were the people who populated this "fieldwork" scene. The Shell training program involved six months of being an apprentice to a variety of seismic and other geophysical exploration crews, both in the office as well as in the field, followed by a formal academic program at Shell's laboratories in Houston, Texas. LeSchack rented a small apartment in Baton Rouge and began enjoying the freedom of having a regular paycheck. He was on his own at last, and he enjoyed this freedom. At last, he had an opportunity to apply the arcane technologies he had learned about at school, and make money.

LeSchack was twenty-two years old at this time, but he looked much younger. He found that there never was any problem in his passing for under eighteen, if that were of value, as it was for getting into the city's municipal swimming pool at the under eighteen ticket rate. Where this was a drawback was out in the field. The field hands on the various seismic crews to which he became apprenticed enjoyed hazing the young LeSchack. Take, as an example, the almost nightly ritual in the mess hall of the quarter boat in the Mississippi Delta. After a day in the shallow waters and marshes of the Delta, the seismic crews of roustabouts and roughnecks would gather for their evening meal. Sometime during the meal, a cracker would stand up and yell to all, "Hey podners, what's the difference between a 'Yankee' and a 'Damned Yankee'?" While the question was directed to all assembled, the only northerner in sight was the young LeSchack. The response to the interlocutor's question was a thunderous and unanimous cry, "The Yankee stays up North!" Other examples occurred with the seismic crews on land. For example, when there was a fenced-in pasture with a ferocious-looking bull in the center of it, LeSchack was always the one who was called upon to string shot wire or phone line wire across the field. It always appeared that the path that the party chief chose for LeSchack was as close to the bull as possible, and across as many gooey cow patties as they could find for him to traverse.

Actually, LeSchack was just fine with all of this. He enjoyed the fieldwork as well as the work in the offices in Baton Rouge and New Orleans. He enjoyed getting paid. He learned much about the practice of geophysical exploration for hydrocarbons both ashore and at sea. With regard to offshore exploration, he sought and obtained permission to board Shell's ships exploring in the Gulf of Mexico using seismic as well as gravity surveys.

During one such offshore seismic survey, he had a most harrowing experience. The survey was being conducted from a converted U.S. Navy minesweeper. A sudden squall materialized that was absolutely frightening. It occurred about two in the morning and the ship suddenly heeled over in the face of the storm. LeSchack had been awakened before the full force of the gale descended, and had made his way to the wheelhouse to see what was happening. When the ship heeled over, the starboard railing slipped under water and remained so. Rain, driven horizontally, was forcing its way around the dogged hatches and into the wheelhouse. The wind tore off the radar and other antennae, and boxes of seismic explosives heretofore neatly tied in rows on the after deck, now were dancing and skittering loose all over that deck. Intellectually LeSchack knew that, because the explosives had not been fused, no disaster was likely to occur. However, it was as if depth charges, as yet unarmed, which that ship used to carry, and which packed about the same amount of punch as the seismic charges, were rolling loose on deck. It scares the shit out of you!

The storm lasted about an hour before it abated. When the sun came up and the damage was surveyed, it was determined that the ship needed to return to port in Morgan City, Louisiana for repairs prior to returning to exploration duties. LeSchack learned what he needed to know, and was happy to leave the ship when it docked. In fact, in a later career in the

U.S. Navy, LeSchack never experienced a storm at sea like that one in the Gulf of Mexico. The closest depiction of what happened that night at sea as far as LeSchack was concerned was presented in that scene in the movie, "Caine Mutiny," when the USS CAINE was about to founder in the typhoon.

During this period in Louisiana, several things of note occurred in LeSchack's life: he had begun to gain practical experience in the science that he had studied at RPI. He had learned to deal with, and frankly enjoy some of the practitioners of this science, the rough and tumble, beer-swilling crews who implemented the technology. These were not the type of people his parents would invite to join them for their genteel dinner parties. A year after the onset of his correspondence and submission of an application to join the US Antarctic Expedition, he received a response. With yet more forms to fill out. His application for the Antarctic adventure was still alive! And his draft board in New York, that ever present Cold War albatross, inquired after him. A response from LeSchack announcing he was no longer in that draft board's purview resulted in an invitation, not to be turned down, to go directly to the Army induction center in New Orleans to take a qualifying physical and written exam. And finally, despite occasional dates in both Baton Rouge and New Orleans, there were no young women who filled the emotional void left by his lover, Giselle.

On the appointed day set by the Selective Service System, LeSchack joined a busload of young men being escorted from Baton Rouge to New Orleans for their pre-induction exams. LeSchack knew it was inevitable that he, sooner or later, would become a part of the U.S. Armed Forces. He was not averse to this, but the budding young maverick that LeSchack was now becoming wanted to go when *he wanted to go.* Not before. Nonetheless, he took the physical and written exams.

After they were complete an Army captain took LeSchack aside to cajole him into enlisting, rather than waiting to be drafted. "Listen, LeSchack," the Captain said, "Your scores are high enough so that I can enlist you right now into any one of the Army specialties that you might like. Better enlist now. Your Draft Board will be calling you pretty soon, I'm sure." LeSchack had no reason to doubt him. The decision that LeSchack had to make was, "do I take a chance that I am invited to join the Antarctic expedition, sponsored by a U.S. Federal Agency, before the Draft Board, another U.S. Federal Agency calls? If so, I could likely get military service put off yet again, because another governmental agency so requested it." He knew, however, that should the Draft Board call first, he would have been better off enlisting *now* in a specialty he preferred, rather than arbitrarily being placed in the infantry. He mentally tossed a coin. He told the Army recruiter that he opted to wait and take his chances with the Antarctic expedition.

After six months of serving as an apprentice geophysicist in Baton Rouge, Shell sent LeSchack to Houston where the formal academic portion of the training program was given. It was just like going back to school. There were daily classes in geophysical exploration theory. During that period, there was increasing correspondence from the U. S. National Committee of the International Geophysical Year directed to LeSchack. He knew at this point that he was seriously being considered for the Antarctic Expedition. But he also knew it was just a matter of time before the Draft Board would act. Who would win—or rather, would LeSchack lose? He hung tight, afraid to talk to anybody, especially Shell, about the Antarctic possibility, lest he jinx it. Shell already knew about the Army possibility, since in those Cold War days, induction into the Army was a fact of life for not only all healthy young men, but for their employers as well.

At the end of August 1957, the Antarctic Expedition and LeSchack had won! He was asked to join as an assistant seismologist in the Antarctic over ice traverse program. With official notification of his acceptance, LeSchack immediately got the U. S. National Committee to write his Draft Board to cease and desist, at least for the time being. Actually for nearly eighteen months—fourteen of which would, in fact be spent in Antarctica. He got Shell to release him from his employment commitment, and he began preparations for commencing what would be the start of a lifetime full of adventures—the type of adventures LeSchack had always dreamed and fantasized about, in "far away places with strange-sounding names." And what he now had the training to do competently. Especially so, after his experience as a geophysical trainee with Shell Oil Company.

At this point in LeSchack's life he now had knowledge enough to know how to gain more knowledge; training enough to know how to gain more training; experienced enough passion with women to know that he wanted and, in fact, needed more and even greater passion with other women; and adventures enough to want to seek even more adventures. And Antarctica would be his next adventure– truly a *Cold* War adventure—one that satisfied all of these requirements!

LeSchack at right, with fellow lifeguards, 1956

LeSchack and Giselle, 1954

LeSchack's College years were spent grinding away at academics most of the year, lifeguarding during the summers, and playing with his first lover, Giselle, of Montreal, whenever he could

Antarctica and the International Geophysical Year-The Cold, Cold War Years

> *The biggest impact of the IGY (International Geophysical*
> *Year) on mankind was not new scientific discovery, but rather*
> *the start of the "space race." Once the tiny beep of Sputnik-I,*
> *the initial Soviet IGY satellite, was heard circling the world on*
> *4 October 1957, President Eisenhower had the delicate task of*
> *assuring his nervous nation that a Soviet basketball in orbit*
> *was nothing to be alarmed about. But when the Navy's rocket*
> *failed to get the IGY Vanguard satellite into orbit and the*
> *Russians launched an even larger IGY satellite with the dog,*
> *Laika, on board, news commentators did not treat the situation*
> *lightly.*
>
> *L.C. Lawyer, Charles C. Bates and Robert B. Rice, authors of*
> *"Geophysics in the Affairs of Mankind," published by the*
> *Society of Exploration Geophysicists.*

The first week of October 1957 was momentous for both Len LeSchack and for the Free World. The long anticipated International Geophysical Year, or IGY as it was known, had just begun. IGY was a multi-national, multi-disciplinary study of the earth's geophysical characteristics, a study that was designed to benefit mankind. Many years of planning by the international scientific community and their members' host governments had gone into developing the IGY program. Although nominally a year in duration, it began in mid-1957 and terminated at the end of 1958.

IGY was initiated formally that week by LeSchack when he boarded a Navy aircraft at the Naval Air Station at Anacostia, in Washington, D.C. It would shortly be on its way to New Zealand. From there, he would leave for Antarctica. He was now, finally, a member of the U.S. Antarctic Expedition which was a part of the IGY program. It was the beginning of his first major adventure to "far away places with strange-sounding names," the kind of physical and scientific adventure he had always dreamed about as a child.

In stark contrast to LeSchack's modest fashion of initiating the onset of IGY, the IGY was spectacularly initiated by the Union of Soviet Socialist Republics; during that same week the USSR launched into space a geophysical instrument called "SPUTNIK I." The USSR was the first country to ever launch an orbiting space vehicle. The timing of their launch was impeccable. It was dramatic. A Soviet vehicle, circling the globe *all alone* in outer space, and transmitting beeping radio signals back to earth. While most of the world applauded the Soviet's astounding scientific feat, it scared the shit out of the U.S. Government. The U.S. suddenly came face to face with the fact that if the USSR had a rocket that could launch a geophysical package into space, it might also be able to launch an intercontinental ballistic missile. The U.S. had not yet achieved this same capability. It prompted G. Mennen Williams, then governor of Michigan, to pen these politically incorrect lines:

Oh little Sputnik
With made-in-Moscow beep,
You tell the world it's a Commie sky
And Uncle Sam's asleep.

Just to make a point, and to see if the world had caught the significance of their last act, the Soviets' launched "SPUTNIK II", a much heavier satellite, into space a month later. Sputnik II contained a dog named Laika, which had medical instruments attached to its body. These two events that announced the USSR's entry into the IGY affected more than merely the geophysical literature of that year; it shaped U.S. domestic and foreign policy for the next several decades, and significantly altered the course of LeSchack's life, as well as the lives of many others. Journalist Robert T. Mann wrote:

> The Soviet's success with both Sputniks shocked the American people. They asked how such a seemingly backward, unsophisticated nation could develop something so technologically advanced. But the more important question was: Did Sputnik signal that Khrushchev was truthful the previous year when he boasted that his nation had also developed an intercontinental ballistic missile? To many, it was

plausible.

Government-sponsored reports quickly recommended a number of responses. One, commissioned by the National Security Council, called for a large increase in military spending and for development of bomb shelters. Another report more ominously suggested that the Soviet Union had pulled ahead of the United States in the development of nuclear missiles.

The U. S. Congress did what it always does when it encounters an unanticipated embarrassment like this: it appropriates huge sums of money to throw at the problem that it should have addressed much earlier with a better conceived long-term, and overall likely less expensive, program. Naturally, more money was appropriated for military programs. More money for teaching and conducting advanced science and advanced mathematics was also appropriated. More money for major new programs in the Antarctic and in the Arctic was made available. In the Antarctic, because the Soviets had planned a major ongoing exploration program there that now needed to be at least matched for political, not scientific reasons; in the Arctic because military planners now recognized that any possible attack on America by the USSR, either with conventional bombers or now, intercontinental ballistic missiles, would be launched from the Soviet landmass, directly over the North Pole. All of this was to have a direct and long-lasting impact on LeSchack. It would strongly influence his military career, yet to come. It would strongly influence his earth science research business yet to be established. And it would facilitate the ease with which he could bounce back and forth between these two, in many ways, mutually supportive careers throughout the remaining thirty-three years of the Cold War.

LeSchack knew that the jump-off point for Antarctica was New Zealand, and he would likely spend some time there and possibly also, in Australia. He had been an avid reader of James A. Michener's early novels, "Tales of the South Pacific," and "Return to Paradise," both providing a palatable history of the region. He read and re-read these stories, till he felt he knew something about these people and especially their recent history during the Second World War and directly afterwards. After all, when LeSchack would be visiting, it was just a bit over a decade since War's end.

Christchurch, New Zealand would be the departure point for the Antarctic continent. But to get there from Washington, D.C. in 1957, in a four-engine prop Navy aircraft, was not a simple flight. The plane, an R6D, flew first to Alameda Naval Air Station in the San Francisco Bay area, where LeSchack and his new Antarctic comrades would overnight. The following day they flew on to the Barbers Point Naval Air Station on Oahu where they would spend the night also. Well LeSchack and his new friends would *spend* the night in Oahu, but most of it was actually spent at Waikiki. There they ate at the "Waikiki Sands," a nightclub featuring hula dancers, after which they took a nighttime swim at the beach.

The swim for LeSchack and his new colleagues, most in their early twenties, was performed largely so they could say that "they had done so." It was dark by the time they got there, and there were no girls on the beach that our intrepid Antarctic heroes could see. Or who could see them. For LeSchack, however, the highlight of the evening was watching the enthusiasm of one these men for the hula dancers. Although all watched with enthusiasm, Jack Long, in particular, was carried away by voluptuous young Polynesian women performing the Tahitian hula, an especially vigorous dance. Jack hooted and clapped his hands and banged the dinner table until his wristwatch literally fell apart. Springs and gears bounced and rolled all over the table and into the food. Although Jack was chagrined, everyone else seemed highly amused. Jack would be the tractor mechanic on the over-ice traverse party to which LeSchack was assigned. He was a young man who would become LeSchack's life-long friend and share in some of his later adventures.

This gang eventually returned to Barbers Point for a few hours sleep, but soon they were aboard the R6D again, winging their way across the Pacific. After hours of flying over the empty ocean, they put down at Canton Island, a tiny, lonely coral atoll, in the Phoenix Islands. It is 1,850 miles south of Hawaii and was used by Pan American Airways as a refueling stop. Shortly thereafter, they were on there way again for another refueling stop at Nadi, in the Fiji Islands. When it seemed to LeSchack that they had been flying forever, they finally landed at the airport in Christchurch, a city in the South Island of New Zealand. The IGY authorities stationed at Christchurch had pre-arranged accommodations for the exhausted passengers and, in short order, LeSchack and his new colleagues were whisked off to their new temporary homes. Temporary, that is, until they were scheduled to depart for Antarctica, or as was the saying, " to go *on the ice"*. Usually, that would be only a matter of days. Not so for LeSchack.

It turned out that, for reasons not entirely clear to him, the IGY was not quite ready to place LeSchack on the ice where he was intended to be assigned. Accordingly, he was told to just hang around, on salary and per diem, until he was, in fact, called. On no other occasion in his life had a travel foul-up ever worked to LeSchack's advantage like this one did! He, most wonderfully, had the opportunity to spend six weeks in New Zealand, on his own, with expenses paid. Within a week of his arrival, he chanced to meet a free-lance photographer from Gisborne, on the North Island. The photographer was planning on spending several weeks driving around the South Island to complete the photo-essay book he had started earlier on the North Island. When LeSchack inquired as to whether the photographer would care for a companion who would share expenses for the next few weeks, he received an unqualified "yes." And so, LeSchack's Antarctic adventures began in New Zealand. The only constraints that the Christchurch IGY office placed on LeSchack were to phone them every few days to ascertain a likely departure date. Not at all onerous

The photographer, Dick Crone, had as an itinerary, a trip across the Canterbury Plain on which Christchurch was situated, across Otago, the desert region, over the Alps, the South Island's mountain spine, and down the cloudy, grey west coast from Greymouth to Franz Josef Glacier. This suited LeSchack perfectly. Dick had a wealth of information not only about photography, a subject that keenly interested LeSchack, but about New Zealand's history and geography. Although LeSchack had traveled in Québec and learned a bit about Canada from Giselle, this was the first time in his 22 years that he was away from North America, learning about another country that he had only read about before.

It was a glorious experience for him. There, in New Zealand, and later upon his return from Antarctica when he visited Australia, the impressionable LeSchack was to learn that at that time, just a bit more than a decade after the Second World War had concluded, most New Zealanders and Australians genuinely did appreciate Americans. The U.S. Navy had stopped the Japanese fleet at the Battle of the Coral Sea at a time when Japan was bombing Darwin at will, and was threatening and, in fact, had plans to invade both northern Australia and the North Island of New Zealand. This was the only time in LeSchack's life when he recognized that other peoples truly appreciated the efforts of the American generation that preceded his. And, no matter where he traveled thereafter in the world, he never saw that kind of genuine, heartfelt appreciation for his countrymen ever again.

LeSchack also discovered another form of appreciation when Dick and he stayed at the wonderful old hotel at Franz Josef Glacier. They spent several days there, photographing the scenery, flying in a light plane directly over the glacier, and just talking and eating. The "appreciation" that so pleased LeSchack was courtesy of Pamela, a hotel staff member. She was a few years older than LeSchack and, he thought not only pretty, but knowledgeable and politically savvy. Through her Maori friends, she introduced him to the indigenous and fascinating Maori culture of New Zealand. Gratefully, from LeSchack's point of view, the voluptuous Pamela also introduced LeSchack to her bed in the hotel. This was the first time that he had made love to a woman since he and Giselle had sadly gone their separate ways over a year earlier. Also the first time he made love to a large-breasted woman with a narrow waist. "What a magnificent experience," the young LeSchack thought. Now, it was LeSchack's turn to be appreciative. And he was.

LeSchack spent several weeks traveling about the South Island, getting to know the astounding geography of that island, its history and its people. Every other day he would phone the IGY office in Christchurch to keep abreast of departure schedules for the Antarctic. As long as his departure was not imminent, he could continue this marvelous odyssey with Dick, taking photographs under that master's tutelage, and writing notes. After three weeks, Dick had made a complete cycle about much of the South Island and returned to Christchurch. Upon their return, LeSchack decided it was close enough to his likely departure time to feel comfortable in taking up an earlier offer by a family there to remain with them until he was scheduled to leave. He bade goodbye to Dick, promising to visit him in Gisborne upon his return from Antarctica in about fourteen months. And then he joined the hospitable family of Isaac and Jade, and their two young children at their comfortable home in the suburbs.

Isaac was an ex-Australian soldier who had moved to New Zealand and now owned a restaurant in Christchurch, a good one LeSchack thought. During his stay at their home, there were frequent parties that Jade and her friends held, and to which LeSchack was always invited. LeSchack's connection with Isaac was clear: Isaac and his brother, born German Jews, had managed to escape Nazi Germany before the War, just like LeSchack's Uncle Walter and Aunt Alice had done. Isaac had immigrated to Australia and joined the Australian Army when the War began. He fought in the South Pacific and had obviously survived, although not unscarred. Isaac's brother, LeSchack was told, had joined the RAF and he had become a flyer. The brother, shot down over Berlin, had recognized he could neither bail out nor land anywhere safely. Having once lived in Berlin, he also recognized the municipal gas and power works below during his last few minutes in the air. Heroically, he guided his flaming aircraft down into that flammable target, creating his own pyre.

LeSchack's connection with the New Zealand-born Jade was pleasurable and interesting, but more tenuous. A good-looking woman and free spirit ten years younger than Isaac, but eight years older than LeSchack, she was a party girl and incredibly sexy. Jade and her friends were the New Zealand version of what Jack Kerouac called "the beat generation," or "beatniks." LeSchack got to know her during the three weeks that he remained at their home in Christchurch prior to shipping out. It was summer down under, and she and her two young children, some friends, and LeSchack would frequently drive to nearby Brighton Beach for a swim and picnic. Isaac could never join them owing to the requirements of his restaurant business. She certainly appeared to be a warm and loving mother to her children, and delightful to her adult friends. And particularly so to LeSchack who she was trying to seduce. He found that most troubling. He could not deny his attraction to her. It was a terrible temptation and a complication that he wished to avoid.

The temptation, fortuitously, was rendered moot at one of the many parties that LeSchack attended. Conjured up by Joyce, one of Jade's friends, the event was a costumed affair, billed as a "back to childhood" party. It took place at Joyce's on the Saturday before LeSchack finally shipped out. Dressed in shorts, suspenders and a T-shirt LeSchack, now 22, looked maybe fifteen. By arrangement, LeSchack was picked up in front of Isaac's restaurant by a vehicle that was already packed with party-going humanity. He recognized no one in this vehicle, and to gain passage he had to, in fact, jam himself tightly into the front seat. As it happened, he had to share what normally would have been a single place with Maisie, a most voluptuous and sexy woman, dressed only in shorts and a child's sweater. She was already quite high, and had the largest breasts LeSchack had ever yet seen on a woman. She clearly did not object to LeSchack sharing the same space with her in the car; in fact, she rather enjoyed doing so, and was literally, "in his face" with her pulchritude.

He had been to Jade's and Jade's friends' parties before; the beverage of choice, or perhaps just the one most affordable, was parsnip wine. LeSchack had tasted it, and as a result, chose to bring his own beverage — a bottle of "Canadian Club" — a whiskey he had taken a fancy to as a result of his many trips to visit Giselle in Montréal. While the parsnip wine was flowing freely, LeSchack made up some whiskey sours for himself and for Jade, as he had promised her he would. He wandered around the pulsating humanity at the party till he found her. She was dressed in a teeny little-girl dress and looked fetching. Upon handing her the whiskey sour, she smiled sweetly at LeSchack, thanked him, and swished away into the swirling crowd.

Living in the same house as Jade for three weeks and resisting her blandishments had created an enormous tension in the young LeSchack. This was assuredly heightened as a result of LeSchack and Maisie sharing, for all intents and purposes, the same physical space during the jostling automobile ride to this party. Finally, the knowledge that he momentarily would disappear into fourteen months of celibacy on the

Antarctic Continent had sharply focused LeSchack's attention to the need for assuaging his desires, now at the boiling point. To this end, he began searching for Maisie in the expansive house that was the venue for this costume party. Eventually he found her drinking parsnip wine and sprawled insouciantly across a wing-backed chair in a room off the party's beaten path. A bit tipsy, she welcomed LeSchack and invited him, as if he were a courtier and she a queen, to sit down before her. Only she, most assuredly, was not sitting in a queenly fashion on her throne—she was drunkenly sitting in her tight shorts and teeny sweater cross-wise on an ordinary chair. And frankly, there was not another spot near her in the room that she could have invited LeSchack to join her to have a convenient conversation. But as high as they both were, a conversation they, indeed, had. She was a musician and worked in a music store. So they talked about music.

Sitting thus, they talked together much of the evening in that gradually emptying room. They talked of Beethoven as LeSchack began stroking her bare thighs. LeSchack noted they were soft, very soft, and alabaster-white. They talked of Brahms and Maisie began tightening her thighs around LeSchack's gently moving hand. He noted her thighs were now also damp. When they began to talk of Mozart, Maisie's thighs became downright wet; at this point they then decided that they should return to Maisie's apartment for the remainder of the night—and much of the following day. It was glorious for LeSchack. Probably for Maisie also. Because each time after they slept a bit, she would ask him upon awakening, "Do you feel strong enough to continue?" And they did. Several more delicious times. And once again, the relatively inexperienced LeSchack observed to himself, "voluptuousness in a woman can sure make for a magnificent love-making experience. First Pamela, now Maisie. Just marvelous!" Thanks to these two women so early on in his life, he was forever hooked on those special visual and tactile sensations that are the hallmark of love-making with well-endowed women.

He was now spiritually refreshed and ready to leave for, and take on, the Antarctic.

****

A few days later LeSchack was embarked on an Air Force C-124 Globemaster winging its way south to the IGY base at McMurdo Sound on the Antarctic continent. The cavernous cabin of the Globemaster was configured much as a hospital aircraft might be: there were racks not unlike those aboard a troop ship for men to sleep on. LeSchack was quick to notice this, and since there was no assigned seating, he just chose a convenient rack, climbed into it, hoping no one in authority would challenge him, and promptly fell asleep. He slept soundly for nearly the entire flight, twelve hours in length. He was finally awakened when the aircraft began to circle the IGY base at McMurdo Sound in preparation for landing on the sea ice runway. As the plane circled, not only could the base be clearly seen in the icy-cold summer air, but so could Mt. Erebus, the nearby volcano, gently smoking away.

The United States Navy was the logistics and engineering agent for all support activities for U.S. IGY science programs on the ice in Antarctica. The base at McMurdo was the "port of entry" for most U.S. scientists and military people arriving in the Antarctic during the IGY, as it had been for many years. One of its most famous early visitors was Captain Robert F. Scott, RN. During the first decade of the Twentieth Century Scott had launched two expeditions into Antarctica from his base at McMurdo. The second was his ill-fated trek to the South Pole, which he reached on 17 January 1912, five weeks *after* the Norwegian explorer, Roald Amundsen had achieved that same goal. Scott and his entire crew perished on their return trip to their McMurdo base—a base that, owing to the cold, arid environment, still stood. While he was there, LeSchack would visit Scott's perfectly preserved shelter, now a shrine of polar history.

LeSchack remained at McMurdo for several days waiting for transportation to Little America V, the next stop on his way to Byrd Station. Byrd was the base at which he would live, and operate from, for the next fourteen months. During his time at McMurdo he walked around the station which was built on the shore of the Ross Sea, at the foot of Mt. Erebus. For most of the year the sea is frozen and the landing strip is prepared anew on this sea ice for each new season. D-8 tractors and graders are used for this preparation. The station itself was comprised of numerous permanent structures: mess hall, sleeping quarters, working and storage spaces. At the time LeSchack was there, electrical power was provided by diesel generators. A few years later, a nuclear reactor was established there to provide power. Not many miles away, over a big hill, the New Zealanders maintained there own IGY station, Scott Base. LeSchack and some colleagues walked there to visit and talk with the New Zealand scientists.

While LeSchack was at McMurdo, he noted that all the gear he had shipped from Christchurch had arrived with him, except his technical books. They were missing. He brought this to the attention of the Camp Commander and his executive officer. They asked LeSchack for a description of the package of books. "Well," LeSchack replied, "I packed the books in a carton, clearly marked for "Leonard LeSchack, Byrd Station--Technical Books." The officers then asked LeSchack, "Is there anything else you can tell us? Can you describe the Box?" LeSchack thought a bit, "Well, I think the box was a packing carton used for whiskey—yes, I believe it said "King George IV Scotch Whiskey," a box I got in Christchurch." Silly little smiles flitted across the officers' faces. They opined the box would soon show up. "We would sure like to see the look on the face of the sailor that unloaded the Globemaster and 'misplaced' that box—when he finally opens it!"

In mid-November when LeSchack arrived on the Antarctic Continent it was summertime. It was perpetual daylight. The sun was up in the sky 24 hours a day, just circling around the horizon. And it was cold. A number of the men stationed in the Antarctic reacted negatively to the perpetual daylight, and were afflicted with a malady known as "the big eye." This was a general disorientation that resulted from no clearly defined daytime and nighttime, such as can be found everywhere else, except for at the North and South Poles. It made some men irritable, uncomfortable and sometimes zombie-like. The big eye did not strike LeSchack. He was awake when he wished to be, and fell asleep when he so desired.

A few days later he flew from McMurdo to the station at Little America, his next stop on his way to Byrd. The aircraft used was a twin-engine R4D, the Navy equivalent of the DC-3, also called a "Dakota," or C-47. All passengers scheduled for Little America boarded the R4D. Except for three canvas seats used by VIPs, LeSchack and other personnel enroute to Little America arranged themselves, bobsled-style, along the length of the fuselage. Forward in the cabin was an extra fuel tank; in the Antarctic, the wing tanks alone did not provide an adequate safety margin for the typical distances flown. Also, strapped to the wheels were skis, since ice runways are rarely smooth enough for a wheeled landing or take off. The R4D warmed up on the ice strip, the pilot gunned the engines, and then released the brakes. The plane slowly, ever so slowly, began to gain speed and bump down the rough, sea ice runway. When the two engines were screaming and it appeared that the old bird just could not possibly reach take-off speed, a horrendous roar surrounded the aircraft. LeSchack nearly jumped out of his skin. He thought the tail gear had collapsed and the tail of the aircraft was scraping across the ice. One of the VIPs, a grizzled old Navy captain who was sitting next to LeSchack, gently placed his hand on his shoulder: "Son, every time I hear those JATO bottles go off, it scares the shit out of me too." It was Captain E. H. Maher, Commander of U.S. Naval Units Antarctica, as well as Commander U.S. Naval Support Activity, Antarctica.

JATO, jet-assisted take off, was essential to get those aircraft airborne in the Antarctic. They are bomb-shaped canisters filled with a slow-burning gunpowder that is ignited electrically from the cockpit at — with skill and luck — just the proper moment. Typically, four such bottles are strapped around the waist of the aircraft. With the thirty seconds of thrust that these rockets, firing in unison provide, the under-powered aircraft limps into the sky. And so, this one did also.

It should be pointed out that LeSchack and the captain were not the only ones scared by these R4D takeoffs. In those early days of the IGY when all this Antarctic exploration was not only new, but newsworthy, large pools of print reporters and TV journalists descended upon McMurdo and Little America. Three such journalists composed a song to this venerable aircraft. It became quite popular with those scientists and Navy men stationed there. Sung to the tune of the "Wabash Cannonball," it was called, "Cannonball R4D," and went:

> *I*
> *Now listen all my shipmates, a tale I'll tell to you*

> *About some Navy pilots and of the planes they flew*
> *They flew down to McMurdo for Task Force forty three*
> *They didn't fly an airplane, they flew an R4D.*

Chorus

> *Now listen to the rattle, the rumble and the roar*
> *Going down the runway in a beat up ole R4*
> *Feel the airframe shaking, see the pilot's trembling hand*
> *If he don't get her airborne, we'll see the Promised Land.*

II

> *A-bucking and a-sliding as down the ice we go*
> *Every one sit forward —good Lord —we're awfully slow*
> *Throttles to the firewall. JATO trails you see*
> *There's eighteen tons a-riding in this beat up R4D.*

III

> *Now looking down the runway, what do my poor eyes see*
> *Ten thousand correspondents and that dad burn NBC*
> *They've heard about this aircraft, and all expect the worst*
> *But if it's going to happen, then they wanna get it first.*

> *By: Pat Treese, Jack Donovan, and Bill Morgan Cumbie*

Little America V was constructed on the Ross Ice Shelf just as were the previous Little America stations over the years that were established in this area. The Ross Ice Shelf is an enormous tongue of fresh-water ice slowly sliding off the Antarctic landmass into the sea. Large chunks of the shelf ice, when it reached the edge, would "calve" and fall off into the sea. At the time LeSchack arrived, Little America V was perhaps a mile away from the "barrier," which was the name given the line of demarcation between the "shelf ice" on which Little America V was situated, and the seasonal sea ice. Eventually that station built on the shelf ice and perceptibly moving, but ever so slowly would, in fact, become part of the barrier and then fall off and disappear into the sea.

LeSchack spent about a week at Little America V awaiting a final flight that would take him to Byrd Station. During that time he acclimatized himself to the Antarctic weather as well as the routine of living in an all-male society made up of scientists, technicians and U. S. Navy men. He met and renewed acquaintances with some of the men with whom he flew down to New Zealand on his way from Washington, D.C. Since LeSchack had signed on as the assistant seismologist for the Byrd Station exploration traverse, he had nothing much to do until he actually reached Byrd and joined that traverse. He therefore occupied himself with seeing the scenery, learning the ropes, and meeting and getting to know many of the cast of characters in this first of many major adventures in his life during those Cold War years.

The first Little America was established by Admiral Richard E. Byrd in the 1930s, and the shelter that he lived in, all alone, for a year was still standing nearby the current station. LeSchack visited it as if it were a shrine; it was for LeSchack, since Admiral Byrd had been one of his childhood heroes. He walked from Little America down to the barrier— then about a mile from the station—and onto the sea ice of the Ross Sea. Looking up at the barrier from sea level he could discern a towering cliff of shelf ice, extending endlessly in both directions as far as the eye could see; it abruptly met the sea ice on which he was standing. Also, along with his colleagues who were viewing this extravaganza of nature, was an entire rookery of penguins tolerantly watching them stare up at the awe-inspiring ice interface. The penguins were not the least bit frightened by the interlopers in their domain. Nor was an Antarctic seal sunning itself, all alone, on the sea ice.

LeSchack spent time wandering about the base, examining all. He noticed the station's rolling stock: a variety of Caterpillar tractors which were kept running all the time. They were diesel powered and, in this frigid weather, it was easier to keep them running rather than starting them up each day, a time-consuming and aggravating job in the cold. Also the M-29 "Weasels;" they were gasoline-powered, tracked personnel carriers, originally designed for the Army. Throughout what would turn out to be an extensive career in the Polar Regions for LeSchack, he often encountered these vehicles, and they were often inoperable. They were high maintenance vehicles that required devoted mechanical care. Nonetheless, they could be found everywhere the U.S. conducted polar operations, and frequently in an immovable condition. But they sure were useful when they did work.

He also noticed that the station kept Alaskan Husky sled dogs, but they were there as pets, not as working dogs. He visited many of the various scientific laboratories established at the station for measuring many aspects of the earth's geophysical environment, such as its magnetism, seismicity, and ionosphere. And of course, he ate and ate in the mess hall, which was open 24 hours per day, and engaged in endless bull sessions with all comers often—but not exclusively—about nubile women whose absence was already noticed.

While still at Little America awaiting transportation for Byrd Station, his box of technical books appeared, and with a most unusual story attached. The books in the King George IV scotch whiskey carton had apparently been found at McMurdo, and despite clear instructions that it was destined for Byrd, it was placed on an aircraft bound for the Amundson-Scott South Pole Station. There, it was para-dropped along with other supplies. If that was so, it looked, thought LeSchack, like the parachute never opened. The box was badly mangled. Obviously it had been found at the pole and been returned, this time well marked by some intellectual wise-ass at Pole Station, noting, not only in English, but in Russian, Arabic and Chinese, that its true destination was Byrd. It also had a picture of Kilroy painted on the mangled box.

Finally, the day came for all those bound for Byrd Station, 500 miles inland, to board a Navy aircraft flying them there. All passengers scheduled for Byrd boarded and fastened themselves into canvas seats that ran the length of the fuselage. Byrd station was located hundreds of miles inland on a basically flat, but occasionally gently rolling plain of ice, about 600 miles north of the geographical South Pole. Closely clustered in what appeared from the air to be just a random blob on this endless ice, were the buildings that comprise the base at Byrd Station, situated at 80E South Latitude, 120E West Longitude. From the air it looked a bit like a few lumps of coal scattered on a white tablecloth. As the R4D circled lower and lower over the base, a somewhat smoother but arbitrary stretch of ice was seen that had been smoothed further by tractors so that aircraft could land and take off with minimum catastrophe. Landing a ski-equipped aircraft on the Antarctic ice was not really a landing at all—at the best of times it was a controlled crash! It was just a bit safer, and less jarring if the ice strip had been first smoothed by tractors and graders. And the veteran R4D did, once again, arrive safely on the ice, amidst a great noise and much blowing snow and ice crystals. Everyone was able to descend from the aircraft uninjured, although, as usual it turns out, a trifle shaken.

Along with LeSchack on the plane were several senior naval officers, scientists, a distinguished visitor, the Australian polar explorer, Sir Hubert Wilkins, now quite aged, all of whom came on an inspection tour. For them, this was a turnaround flight and they would be gone in a few hours. LeSchack and a few other personnel who were assigned there would remain at Byrd for the next year. One by one they descended and stepped onto solid ice. Because on these aircraft, which have inadequate heating for polar climes, the relief tube is invariably frozen; just about everybody needs to urinate immediately upon debarking. And so they do. No need for modesty in the Antarctic with no women around. All the needy men simply put their backs to the wind (and there rarely is a day without wind), unzip the many layers of polar clothing, and relieve themselves on the ice. No need either to be embarrassed by the yellow stain left on the ice. It will soon be covered up by more ice—blowing ice crystals. LeSchack debarked from the R4D along with several sea bags containing all the clothing, and other personal possessions that official weight limitations allowed.

A weasel was waiting at the ice strip to carry the sea bags of the wintering-over personnel to their quarters. Do you know the weasel? Officially designated the M-29C, this small, tracked, amphibious vehicle was made only during World War II and not in great quantity. As exasperating as this vehicle was to handle and maintain, it was only until much later the best personnel carrier for the Polar Regions. Clambering into, and onto the weasel (for there is not much space inside), that tracked relic slowly wheezed and clanked toward the encampment.

Although now only mid-summer 1957, LeSchack would be required to spend the entire frigid Antarctic winter at Byrd so that he would be in place, ready to join at its outset, the 1958 traverse expedition the following year. In those days both the aircraft and the navigation systems available were unsafe to depend on for flying in the six-month winter cold and darkness. As a result, all air transportation was constrained to the warmest, brightest austral summer months, November through February. The implications for LeSchack were clear: although IGY intended that he join the already deployed 1957 traverse sometime yet that summer, it was its intent that he would definitely be ready for the 1958 traverse that would sortie again from Byrd before that summer's flights had commenced. Well, at last, he had now definitely arrived in the frigid wasteland called Byrd. This would be his home for quite some time.

The Byrd Station camp had been constructed the previous year on the ice by the Navy's construction battalion, or "Seabees,"as they were called (a spelling out of C.B., for construction battalion). The basic units of construction for many of the buildings were the "Jamesway huts," developed during World War II. These huts were made of semi-circular wood frames over which an insulated, water-proofed "Blanket" was stretched. These buildings looked, for all the world, like steel 55-gallon fuel barrels split length-wise with the open end on the ground, only much larger. The top and bottom ends of the split barrels were flat semicircular walls of the same material with a door, and sometimes a window. These Jamesways were complemented by standard, build-them-yourself, construction-site trailers. This combination of buildings was constructed on the ice surface during the summer months; the buildings were laid out closely together in an arrangement that would remain permanently for the rest of its life. Then, a framework of 2 by 4s, covered by chicken-wire, and then parachute silk, would be constructed to make tunnels for inter-connecting all camp buildings. By the end of summer, the almost constant wind and blowing ice crystals would pile up a huge, low mound of ice around and over all buildings and chicken-wire-parachute-silk tunnels. By winter, the entire inter-connected complex was buried "underground"—one huge ice mound that covered the entire camp. One entered the complex through an entrance tunnel that was kept open by bulldozers.

Oh, and there was an endless supply of parachute silk. Most of the camp's supplies were air-dropped by the Air Forces' C-124

"Globemasters," the largest cargo aircraft at the time, and each air-dropped palette was attached to usually three T-10 cargo parachutes. It was not practical to collect, clean, re-pack and then reuse the parachutes for further air-drops, so the silk was available for construction use.

The "permanent," that is, wintering-over, contingent of men at Byrd Station was comprised of twenty-four men—twelve civilian "IGY" people, performing and administering the science, and twelve Navy men who provided logistical support for the scientists and technicians. When LeSchack arrived at Byrd there were also summer visitors working there on various projects. They would leave on the last aircraft flights out at the end of the summer season in January. The personnel, both Navy and technical people, were mostly young, in their twenties and thirties. The technical folks were largely employees of government agencies, the Weather Bureau, the Coast and Geodetic Survey, the Geological Survey, the National Science Foundation and a variety of governmental research laboratories. The over-ice traverse program to which LeSchack was assigned was composed of university scientists and employees of the Arctic Institute of North America, a contractor for the U.S. National Committee for the IGY. LeSchack was one of those.

The Navy personnel were commanded by the only naval officer assigned to Byrd, a medical doctor. The rest of the naval personnel were enlisted men; either radiomen and their electronic technician, or Seabees—carpenter, plumber, electrician, mechanic and construction drivers. As it turned out, this wintering-over group was congenial; a half-dozen of the civilian technical people had already served in the Armed Forces and this, along with, fortuitously, most of the personalities now assembled there, made for a mutually supportive atmosphere. This is not always the case at these types of remote bases, as LeSchack was to learn. In fact, the last crowd at Byrd was both surly and back-biting toward one another and, he was told, it had been a dreadful year for all of them.

The Byrd Station traverse party, a geographical, glaciological and geophysical survey team, was already out in the field exploring; LeSchack would not join them for another six weeks. He, therefore, settled into Byrd, determined to meet and get to know the others at this remote outpost, and learn as much as he could about the operations and the various scientific disciplines represented there. Almost immediately, he was taken under the wing of George Toney, nominally the Byrd Station scientific leader. Nominally, because George was neither a scientist nor technical person; but he was, in his forties, one of the oldest civilians there. He had been an English teacher and was now a bureaucrat in the IGY office in Washington. A strapping and robust fellow, he enjoyed vicariously the associations with the young adventurers pursuing science on this expedition. He announced to LeSchack that Charlie Bentley, the leader of the traverse party, had assigned him a surveying task several miles away from the base; it was to be conducted by LeSchack prior to his leaving to join the already ongoing traverse. George also observed that he would be available to assist LeSchack in the conduct of such a survey.

Soon after becoming settled into Byrd Station and its daily routine, LeSchack examined Charlie's instructions for the desired survey. The object of the survey was to compare the topography of a large area of ice surface with the topography of the underlying rock, thousands of feet below. This could be accomplished by first mapping the hills and valleys of the ice surface using standard surveying methods, methods that LeSchack had learned in engineering school. Using a surveyor's transit, he would locate some 36 points, each a kilometer apart, to form a grid 4 by 9 kilometers in size. At each point he would leave a flag that many weeks later would be re-occupied so that seismic depth-sounding and other geophysical studies could be conducted at each such location. The exercise for LeSchack was to choose an arbitrary area that was well away from any of the modifying effects on the ice surface caused by proximity to the base, or the drifting ice around it. The assignment was to choose and map a virgin ice surface. Once LeSchack chose such a location, he would then map its topography. And virgin ice surface is an appropriate term; it would be highly unlikely that *any human being* ever despoiled or even walked this expanse of the Antarctic continent ever before in the world's history. LeSchack and his team would be the first.

The ice mapping exercise assigned by Charlie was a valuable introduction for LeSchack not only into Antarctic exploration, but into bonding with older men and working with young Navy enlisted men; both of those experiences served LeSchack well in years to come.

Each day that the weather was clear enough for mapping with a surveyor's transit, the team—LeSchack, the surveyor, George, LeSchack's assistant who held the survey rod, and Ken Johnson, the Navy construction driver who drove the M29 weasel—packed their lunches in the Byrd Station galley. They then chugged and bounced out across the ice to the survey location LeSchack had chosen. The ride took about a half hour each way. It was not easy talking in the noisy, clanking weasel, so they drove back and forth in silent contemplation. For LeSchack, who since childhood had dreamed of being an explorer, each survey day was an opportunity for "treading where no man went before."

When LeSchack's team returned to base at the end of the working day— one can hardly call it evening, when the sun is up all summer—it was usually dinnertime. All at the base descended upon the mess hall for this major culinary and social event of the day. This cooking and dining facility occupied an entire Jamesway hut. The cook—really a chef—was a senior Navy man, a man from the U.S. Navy's submarine service. Cooks in the submarine service are reputed to be the best in the Navy, if not in all the services. Food aboard a submarine, with its cramped quarters, is about the only morale-builder there is for the submariners; food has to be good otherwise the men become cranky at one end of the spectrum or consider mutinous activities at the other end. In many ways, life at Byrd Station was similar to the cramped life aboard a submarine. The cook, William "Tommy" Thompson, was excellent. And his specialties were breads, cakes and pastries. The Navy had sent him for a six-week internship with the kitchen staff of the Waldorf Astoria Hotel in New York City to polish up not only his culinary skills, but for polishing up skills in dealing with civilians, skills often lacking in military cooks. By the time he reached Byrd, both of these skills were more than acceptable.

Food was served in that cafeteria style well known to enlisted men. The difference here was that with only a total of 24 men the atmosphere was more congenial than usually found in such mess halls, whether military or university freshmen dining halls. The men, both military and civilian scientists and technicians, took turns at "mess-cooking," the term used for bussing tables and washing dishes. Tommy, the only cooking staff that the base had, was rarely relieved, had no weekends off, and typically, was always on duty, except for eight hours sleep each night. It required considerable skill and endurance for Tommy to maintain such a schedule for over a year but he was able to do so with equanimity.......and alcohol.

Yes, alcohol. Those who have served in the U.S. Navy know that alcohol is absolutely forbidden aboard ships. From the Navy's point of view all U.S. Antarctic stations were "ships." Never mind that in the case of Byrd Station, the nearest open water was 600 miles away. Whether it was the fact that half the station's complement was comprised of civilians, or that duty in the Antarctic was considered an exceptional circumstance, all of the U.S. Antarctic stations had special dispensation; beer and liquor were allowed aboard Antarctic stations. There were, of course, rules. No drinking during duty hours, and don't show up in the morning drunk or with a hangover. As far as LeSchack could determine, this policy was never abused. It should be pointed out, however, the Navy screened, with psychologists and their tests, personnel assigned to winter-over in the Antarctic. Those deemed by the psychologists as unable to withstand any of the deprivations resulting from extended living in the Antarctic environment, or who would abuse alcohol, were not sent there.

Day after day, for a period of several weeks, LeSchack, George, Ken and the weasel chugged out to the survey site. Starting at the last survey flag they planted the day before, they began the new day's survey. LeSchack would set up his transit at that flag, and Ken, George and the weasel would drive a kilometer, according to the weasel's odometer, in the appropriate direction, and then stop. In those days prior to GPS navigation, the best Ken could do was come within a quarter-mile of where he was directed to go. Although the ice surface was not without features, it was hard not to lose one's sense of direction in that vast expanse of ice. There was nothing at which to aim. It was like sailing on an ocean without a compass. When the weasel stopped, George would get out and LeSchack, using his portable two-way radio, or walkie-talkie as they were then called, would direct him where to plant the next flag. Looking through the telescope on his transit, and arm out pointing in one direction or the other, he would let George know in which direction to move. When George was properly lined up, LeSchack would take those measurements that would allow him to compute the values for preparing his map. And then the weasel would return, pick up

61

LeSchack, and they all would return to that last point just surveyed and repeat the process, until eventually it was time to return to base so as not to miss the evening meal.

*****

The survey continued, on and off, depending on the weather, for several more weeks. Occasionally there were welcome breaks in this, sometimes tedious survey regime. One such break occurred, unexpectedly, as LeSchack, George, Ken and the weasel were heading out for a survey day. An airdrop of much-needed supplies suddenly materialized, literally out of thin air—and the air was thin at Byrd Station! Airdrops were, in those days in the late 1950s, the most efficient way of quickly moving a large of volume of supplies.

Today, the Navy's C-130 Hercules has little difficulty landing on any ice runway. It is even being done in darkness during the six-month polar winter. The C-130 can load up with tons and tons of bulky equipment and supplies at McMurdo, take-off from that base's prepared sea-ice runway, and fly the 900 miles to supply Byrd, or other lonely outposts. But when LeSchack was there, it was not this easy. During the International Geophysical Year, a large part of the goods needed at Byrd Station, or at the Arctic drift stations at the other end of the world, could only be delivered by parachute. The C-124 Globemaster, available at that time, was capable of carrying the volume of supplies needed at either Pole but was not able to land safely on the ice runway at Byrd or Arctic Drift Stations Alpha or Charlie, for example. Therefore, polar programs at either end of the world used the air-drop, and such programs were the culmination of a vast logistic effort. If you have never seen an air-drop, you should know that this is a marvelous spectator sport, especially in the Polar Regions; but only if you are not responsible for cleaning up afterwards.

During the month of November 1957, the huge Globemasters would lumber off the erratic sea-ice runway at McMurdo Sound, laden with supplies for Byrd. They usually arrived overhead at midnight local time, much to the annoyance of the personnel who retrieved the air-dropped supplies. The Globemasters' pilots, you see, were on McMurdo time, which was many hours earlier. The fact that it was midnight at Byrd made no difference to them, for this was summertime and there were 24 hours of daylight.

An air-drop in the Antarctic is quite spectacular. First, visualize a vast, boundless sea of ice, mostly flat, but rough, frequently hard, and yet, sometimes soft; now place a few small buildings large enough to house 24 men in the center of all this. That's the setting. One person described it as "miles and miles of nothing but miles and miles." The closest thing that approaches this desolation is the view from the bow of a ship, alone, in the middle of the ocean. Now imagine an aircraft arriving, seemingly from nowhere, circling around your minute outpost at the bottom of the globe, its engines shattering the pristine silence of your icy world. It is your only tangible proof that a world *does exist* elsewhere. And then the aircraft begins dropping food, mail and equipment to you by parachute. It's quite a sight.

Picture it: The Globemaster makes one or two passes over the station as the pilot picks out the marked drop-zone. On its next pass, at an altitude of a few hundred feet above the surface, the cargo door is opened. And then it starts. First you see tiny specks leave the plane trailing nylon and ice crystals. Then the billowing canopies stretch out the nylon risers attached to each load. In three seconds, one, two, or even three chutes blossom over the rapidly falling loads. The chutes are colorful. Red, blue, green and white are usually used, and these are brilliant, almost iridescent. The supplies, packed securely on steel pallets, oscillate gently at the end of the risers as they descend. Upon hitting the ice, the loads make a splash of ice powder that looks similar to an impact on water. The canopies appear stunned by the sudden shock and hang motionless above their loads, and then slowly settle to the ice. Back and forth the Globemaster goes, dropping one or two more loads each time it crosses the drop-zone. The last package to be dropped is the one that few eyes leave from the moment it passes out of the cargo door till it reaches the ice, for this small bag of international orange suspended on a solitary white chute contains the mail.

On this particular day at the height of the air-drop season, LeSchack, George, a Navy man named Bruno, and Ken had prepared to go surveying. They had the weasel all set to go out the Little America-Byrd trail when a Globemaster circled the station and commenced dropping supplies. While waiting at the end of the runway till the drop was over, they noticed that one of the chutes had not collapsed after landing and was billowing in the wind. A sudden gust filled the chute and within a few seconds, the pallet was under way. Once moving, this windblown sled maintained a disconcerting ten knots. They started up the weasel and took off after it, hoping to catch and salvage the pallet, any supplies that might have remained on it, and the chute.

Although it was said that the weasel was the workhorse of the Arctic and Antarctic, this one was ready for the proverbial glue factory. Poor maintenance, careless usage and a general disregard by the previous station personnel for the special care needed by machinery when operated under rigorous polar conditions left this weasel in a rather anemic condition for the chase. And so, fussing and fuming like a cantankerous old man, the weasel clanked off toward the rapidly diminishing parachute, on four cylinders, with fouled plugs, trying to ignite fuel fed through a clogged carburetor.

After ten minutes of hard driving in first—the gears wouldn't shift—the engine overheated and stalled. That was not surprising—just disgusting. There was a sudden lull in the wind and the chute stopped some thousand yards away. On the slim chance that the wind might hold off for a few minutes, LeSchack jumped out the weasel and started for the slowly sagging chute. The plane commander of the Globemaster must have seen the supplies getting away for he attempted to help. What that man did showed pure genius and LeSchack felt that he would sure like to meet him and shake his hand in gratitude. You know what he did? He brought that flying freight train down till he could have dragged his feet on the deck if he had stuck them out. In the wake of his slipstream there was a swirling cloud of ice crystals that formed a thick fog along the ice surface. He held it at this height and headed straight for the chute. At the instant when LeSchack expected to see him wrap the canopy around his two starboard engines, he pulled up and roared over the gently billowing chute. Like a sudden blow to the solar plexus, the Globemaster's slipstream hit the chute and it buckled over and collapsed.

During this time, the weasel driver managed to restart the engine and he soon caught up with LeSchack. LeSchack jumped on to the weasel's running board and hung on to the roof ski carrier. From this position, he hoped to jump on to the pallet, should they be able to reach it before the engine overheated again.

The weasel's bucking, wheezing and clanking as it clawed over the ice gave one the sense of breakneck speed that the eye, having no point of reference on the featureless ice expanse, found hard to believe. Actually, they were traveling no faster than five knots. On and on they rumbled and each time they got close enough to think they had it, a coquettish gust of wind pulled their goal just a little bit further away, enticing them on like the man whose hat is blown to the sidewalk by a March wind. However, after being knocked flat by the Globemaster's slipstream, the chute and pallet never picked up their original speed and they soon were abreast of the pallet. At this close range they saw that the pallet was dragging two other chutes which must have collapsed upon landing. LeSchack poised himself for the jump and noticed that George, too, had climbed from inside the weasel to the other running board. LeSchack waited for the right moment ....steady ....steady....go! He leaped toward the bright red steel pallet, suddenly aware, to his disgust, that the pallet was empty. It had scattered its contents along the way after landing. But no matter, they could at least save the pallet after coming this far.

He landed with his head well forward and his thermal boots dug in simultaneously in preparation for the sprint to the pallet. And then he felt a crushing weight on his back which brought him right to the ice. It was Bruno. He, too, had jumped. However, he must have made some miscalculation of his forward motion or wind velocity (or maybe even Coriolis acceleration which is opposite in direction in the southern hemisphere). Nevertheless, there they were—a mass of arms and legs. This was LeSchack's introduction to Bruno's uncanny knack of being clumsy at the most inappropriate times. He was later to find that Bruno's ineptitude with his two feet was exceeded only by his bland sense of humor and his capacity for hard liquor.

LeSchack quickly untangled himself and jumped up in time to see the last of the trailing parachutes go by. George, who had jumped from the other side of the weasel, had reached the pallet and jumped on. LeSchack sprinted to the collapsed canopy and dove on it. Pulling himself hand over hand, he laboriously made his way along the risers, his belly buffeted by surface bumps and his face stung with flying ice, until he reached the pallet. George already had his knife unsheathed and was cutting the risers of the wind-filled chute. The wind had gained strength somewhat, and the pallet was plowing through the ice at a good ten knots, spraying ice shavings over the front, much like the water over the prow of a boat. Grabbing his knife, he started cutting the risers nearest him. They were prone on the pallet, head and arms over the front, squinting into the ice spray as the last line parted. The pallet stopped dead. The chute, freed of its load, sailed off toward the South Pole. LeSchack and George looked at each other and laughed. Upon looking back, they saw that they had rapidly outstripped the weasel and it was now easily a quarter of a mile behind them. Well, they had saved the steel pallet. It would be used for heavy construction back at the station where there was a scarcity of building materials.

While waiting for the weasel to catch up to them they noticed another pallet, its canopies billowing, on its way toward them. This had been dropped after they had left the station and had not been retrieved in time. A strong gust had caught both chutes before they could collapse and it was off. Closer examination showed that this pallet was fully loaded and definitely worth stopping. And it was coming towards them quickly!

The weasel rumbled up to them and they jumped in. Bruno was already inside. He had been picked up by the weasel driver at the spot where he and LeSchack had collided on the ice. Now, they thought, let's try to head this one off. The oncoming pallet followed every caprice of the wind. Zigzagging as it came towards them, their weasel followed its movements like a mirror image, trying always to meet it head on. Their apprehension mounted rapidly as the pallet drew closer. It was big. About five feet cubed and coming fast. If one of its zigs or zags should fake them out, they might lose it completely. If it should pass them, they would never be able to catch it. Closer and closer it came. At a hundred yards away the three men jumped out, each landing on their feet this time.

LeSchack was downwind of the starboard chute, directly in front of the rapidly oncoming heavily laden pallet. All he had to do, or so he thought, was to grab and spill the canopy. That would slow down the load. What an *idiotic* thought that was. Years later during jump training, and still later when he was involved in "Project Coldfeet," he learned that a fair amount of skill and strength are required to spill the air out of even a small personnel chute, and this one was a 60-foot cargo chute. And he had tried to spill it with heavy mittens on. The canopy hit him full in the face and gently flowed over him, a fluid motion. It was like trying to catch a puff of smoke.

Then he thought that he could catch on to the risers that were now all around him, and hang on and cut while hanging on. Parachutists everywhere will recognize that this decision was hardly more sensible than the last. As the risers went by, he hooked his elbow around them and hung on, his legs dragging lightly over the ice. The chute, pulling a load of what they later found to be 3500 pounds of frozen food, held the risers taut. LeSchack had his knife out and started hacking away. One by one the lines fell, allowing more and more air to spill out of the canopy, thus reducing the wind's pull on the load. He saw that George and Bruno had approached the pallet from behind and had climbed on. So far, so good. Suddenly, the wind that had been toying with them all afternoon, shifted, something LeSchack had not counted on. There was a change in acceleration and the lines slackened. He stumbled and tripped. And, just as quickly, the wind picked up again and the lines snapped taut, out of reach. LeSchack looked back and there was the oncoming pallet, plowing through the snow at the fastest ten knots he ever hoped to see, spraying ice like a speedboat cutting water. He had always thought that if it ever came to a showdown when speed, quick thinking, faster action and his safety were concerned, he would be able to take care of himself. This was an erroneous assumption. "Roll! Roll, you ass..." something inside him shouted. Lord knows, he tried. George was on top of the food box. He was shouting, "Get up! Get up! Get up!" but LeSchack, exhausted by now, could not. He was sure that *this* was it. He was certain that he would be crushed by the pallet against the hard ice.

A swoosh, a mass flashing by and icy cold fingers down his back. LeSchack looked up. There ahead of him was the pallet moving away fast. George and Bruno, aghast, were looking back. LeSchack managed a weak, "I think I'm OK" wave to them.

Without being entirely sure, LeSchack supposed that the square front end of the oncoming pallet pushed a triangular pile of ice ahead of it, much like a snowplow, and cowcatcher style, must have pushed him aside, unhurt. He didn't escape his stupidity unscathed, however. His parka hood opened and like a funnel, it scooped a pile of ice shavings and forced them down his back, but at that moment he was thankful that he was able just to feel that minor discomfort. After all, this was little enough penalty to pay for attempting such a stunt, for just seconds prior to this he had had visions of being completely mangled under the pallet.

The weasel was coming back to pick LeSchack up. He could see the driver shaking his head slowly. LeSchack's face was soaking wet; melted ice shavings, he supposed. Since the temperature was a few degrees below zero, it couldn't have been sweat. But then again, maybe it was.

Was the chase worth it? Well, the pallet with a locker containing 3500 pounds of frozen meat *was* saved. Bruno and George stayed with it and finally cut all the lines. The weasel caught up with them a quarter of a mile farther on. As they headed back to the station, they saw the D-8 tractor lumbering out to meet them and tow the pallet back.

Some months later, long after the airdrop season was over and winter darkness had fallen upon them, they were enjoying a particularly tender sirloin in the mess hall and reflecting upon the chase of the air-dropped frozen meat locker. Had they not intercepted it, perhaps the men at the South Pole station, 600 miles away, would be enjoying this steak and the Byrd Station dinner would have been that delectable military staple, canned spam. At the time, that sirloin seemed awfully important. However, thinking about it years later as he was preparing for Project Coldfeet, LeSchack couldn't help but think how lucky he was learning earlier the power and capriciousness of a parachute that has not collapsed when its load hits the ice.

LeSchack's survey continued, on and off, depending on the weather, for several more weeks. But there were other breaks in this routine. On one Sunday morning, early in December 1957, George came into LeSchack's sleeping quarters and rudely awakened him from a deep slumber. "No surveying for us today. Come on along on our recon flight!" Two R4D's landed the day before with personnel and fuel for the traverse team. It was a beautiful day. LeSchack, George, Steve Barnes—George's replacement as Scientific Leader—and Fred Darling, a meteorologist from the U.S. Weather Bureau, all piled into one of the R4Ds. This plane had a name, as military aircraft often do: "Que Será Será." That wistful, poetic name may have been taken from the then popular Doris Day song, but equally likely, may have reflected the philosophy of the Navy aviators who recognized the inherent dangers of frequently flying in this extreme environment—"*Que Será Será.*"—what will be, will be. On this flight, it was piloted by Lieutenant commander Frank Wasko and Lieutenant Frank Dandrea.

The R4D taxied up to the empty fuel barrels that marked the end of the ice runway, and as it revved up, it was observed that the pitch control of the port engine wasn't working properly. The aviation mechanics worked an hour on it before the engine was declared fit to use. LeSchack and the gang jammed themselves, bobsled-style, on the port side of the in-fuselage fuel tank for the take off. Wasko wound up the engines and almost immediately, fired his four JATOs. The R4D bounced several times on the ice before becoming airborne. Once aloft, the aircraft followed the proposed triangular traverse route. They flew the third leg first.

LeSchack sat at the port window and made notes of the ice surface. He recorded the size and frequency of occurrence of potentially life-threatening crevasses, and the "*sastrugi,*" a Japanese word for the wind-formed erosional shapes of the ice. These statistics of the ice surface suggested the level of difficulty the traverse team would have in navigating across the frozen wastes. Charlie, the traverse leader, in particular was concerned that there may be dangerous crevasses ahead that were associated with the Sentinel Mountain Range. Crevasses, as opposed to sastrugi, are fissures in the ice, often covered with snow so as to be to undetectable from the ice surface. Such crevasses are frequently large enough to swallow a tractor if it should break through the snow cover. Those crevasses while often invisible from the ground, however, can often be seen from the air. And it was LeSchack's job to map them and take photographs of the Sentinel Mountains as they flew through that mountain range.

He recorded his notes every five minutes of the more than seven-hour flight. They flew through the Sentinel Range and believed they were the first people to see as much of these mountains as they did. The Sentinels were first seen, and from a distance, by Lincoln Ellsworth in 1936 and were named by him. The Que Será Será flew down a narrow pass and around behind part of the range and back out again. Both pilots were most edgy about this portion of the flight. The winds were turbulent in this range. The base of the Sentinels was at about 11,000 feet with an estimated altitude of 18,000 feet for the mountain peaks.

LeSchack had noted several rock outcroppings of what appeared to be a sedimentary section. These outcrops were the bare faces of the mountains through which they flew. Examination with binoculars suggested the rocks were intensely folded. One outcrop that they passed by at eye-level—as they flew dangerously close by—seemed to exhibit alternating bands of brown and black rock—coal seams, perhaps. Alpine glaciation appeared prevalent. These scenes were starkly magnificent, the type of scenes that so inspired Ansel Adams, the nature photographer. But Adams viewed his mountains only from a distance, while LeSchack experienced them, it seemed, within inches of the aircraft's wingtips. As seen on the aircraft's radar screen, the Sentinel Range appeared to extend 80 miles in length.

When they reached the end of that traverse leg, the aircraft turned and flew over the second of the traverse's legs, territory that to their knowledge had never been seen before, even by Ellsworth. LeSchack continued to record crevasse and sastrugi data for the traverse party. They flew along the second leg until they reached "Corner Mountain" so called because it had been selected from Ellsworth's 1936 map as the intersecting point for Legs 1 and 2. The aircraft flew around Corner Mountain, an almost completely ice-covered dome, and took many photos of this mountain and the surrounding ice. These photos were for the benefit of the traverse party that was then only a few days from reaching this mountain. LeSchack continued recording ice surface data as they flew along that leg. He also spotted outcrops of a dark brown-black color, which because of their jagged angularity, LeSchack expected to be volcanics. It was hard for LeSchack to imagine fiery volcanoes and lava flows amidst all that ice and snow!

Flying along this leg, the plane eventually reached the traverse party.
The R4D circled once, low over the party, and wagged its wings to the
wildly waving crew below. This was the crew that LeSchack would
shortly join. The aircraft then continued on home to Byrd. LeSchack,
who had scanned the ice with his binoculars as the plane circled, spotted
Bill Long, the traverse glaciologist below, in his red parka. Bill was the
only one of the crew that LeSchack could recognize. The aircraft would
land back at Byrd Station at 1920 hours local time after eight hours in the
air, and after covering 1020 miles of barren ice.

It was not until the R4D landed that the significance of what he had just
done dawned on him: LeSchack and his colleagues had just flown over
completely unexplored territory and flew through the Sentinel Range.
More than Lincoln Ellsworth had done in 1936 — and he had been the
only other person that history records had ever been there at all. It was
nearly a year later — September 1958 — that LeSchack began to realize not
only the significance of that flight but of the photographs of the Sentinel
Range that he had taken and processed immediately thereafter. By then,
mail had begun arriving again and with that mail came a clipping from
the New York Times of 10 March 1958: There, on page 25c, was one of
his photographs of the Sentinel Range. In his haste to process the photos,
nearly a year earlier, and pass them on to those who needed them and
who would be leaving Byrd that next day, LeSchack had neglected to
write his name — as the photographer — on the photos. By default, the
photo in the Times had been credited to the National Academy of
Sciences. But LeSchack, then 22, was proud that he had taken that
particular photo, and that it was published in the New York Times.
Smugly, he knew that if he ever had to prove this, he had the negative
(and still does), taken on infrared film using a 4x5 Speed Graphic, from
the co-pilot's seat of a Navy R4D-5, Bureau Number 12418, *Que Será Será*.

As for the Que Será Será, a year earlier, in October 1956, that aircraft had
been the first plane ever to land precisely on the geographical South
Pole. Although LeSchack knew this in a general way when he had flown
aboard her on that traverse recon mission, he would not realize then, nor
for decades thereafter, that during the IGY he had been flying in an
aircraft that was a genuine piece of aviation history. Eventually, the Que

71

Será Será was displayed in the Smithsonian Air and Space Museum in Washington, along with Charles Lindbergh's "Spirit of Saint Louis." In his later years, LeSchack had occasion to visit her there. Alone, in front of the suspended Que Será Será, amidst a museum full of visitors, he stopped starring at the old bird and closed his eyes. From the twilight of his memory he could hear a chorus of alcoholic sailors singing the old refrain: "Now listen to the rattle, the rumble and the roar; going down the runway in a beat up ole R4; feel the airframe shaking, see the pilot's trembling hand; if he don't get her airborne, we'll see the Promised Land."

******

It was January, 1958, the latter part of the austral summer, when LeSchack joined the Byrd Station Traverse Party. It began and ultimately ended at Byrd. The party was composed of six men and three Tucker 743 Sno-Cats. A Sno-Cat was a tractor that, instead of having four wheels, had four separate tracks on steerable pontoons. It had a large, rectangular cab, looking a bit like a van, mounted on the tractor chassis. In short, it looked like an RV for the Polar Regions. In many ways, it was. Minus bath and toilet facilities, so bodily needs were all dealt with *al fresco*, that is, outside on the ice, with the frigid wind blowing up your pants. Each tractor slept two men, and contained much of the sensitive scientific equipment needed for the over-ice research program.

Also, each tractor towed a sled on which were loaded all the food, tools, fuel and supplies needed for independent operation in the field. One of the sleds had constructed a shed on it. It was used as a cook-house and dining hall. On the lead tractor was mounted an ungainly apparatus for detecting crevasses. It had four sensors that made contact with the ice, well forward of the advancing tractor. In theory, it was designed to detect crevasses by analyzing variations in an electric field transmitted through the ice. Variations could indicate a gaping, dangerous void beneath a thin layer of snow or ice. If the apparatus detected a crevasse, it would so signal to the tractor driver who presumably would then have opportunity to stop safely, prior to his slow-moving tractor overrunning the crevasse with its full weight.

The core of the traverse party was comprised of two geophysicists, two glaciologists, one tractor mechanic, and another scientist or technical person. From time to time the traverse party would also have a visitor, usually someone from the press or media, who would travel with the team for a week or so. Once it was Phillip Benjamin of the New York Times; on another occasion it was Emil Schulthess, a well-known Swiss travel photographer and the author of many splendid books of photographs from all over the world. With the standard six-man contingent, two men slept in each of the tractors, but not, alas thought LeSchack, for more than six hours per day. The occasional guest would be squeezed uncomfortably amongst them of the unwashed multitudes. This last is not a literary metaphor; once out on traverse, there were simply no bathing facilities for the several summer months you're on the trail. It is bearable only because the frigidly cold environment inhibits bacteria that generate body odor. Just barely.

LeSchack found that there were two types of days on traverse—a travel day, and a station day. They occurred alternately. And occasionally, there was a "storm day," when it was impossible to travel at all. A travel day began with the lead tractor, named "Carole" heading off into the Antarctic wilderness following the chosen track along a course that, in a general way, was held by a gyroscopic compass. Travel speed rarely exceeded three knots. You can run faster than that! When Carole traveled three miles according to the tractor odometer, it radioed to the second and third tractors that it had reached the first measurement point. In the second tractor in the entourage, "Hectori," now three miles behind the first, there was a barometric altimeter that matched the one carried in Carole. They were both read at the same instant as coordinated by radio. By assuring calibration of the two altimeters and by computing the altimeter differences over each three-mile separation during simultaneous readings, differences of elevation along the track could be computed and surface elevations of the Antarctic ice cap could be mapped.

Once altimeter readings were complete, Carole left a flag in its track, and commenced driving the next three-mile leg. Hectori and the third tractor, "Buttons," then proceeded to follow Carole's clearly visible track in the snow until they reached the flag left by that lead tractor. At that point, Hectori radioed Carole that it was ready to read again and, when the lead tractor was ready to do so, they both read simultaneously, once again. At this point, one of the geophysicists read a gravity meter mounted inside Hectori, while the other read a magnetometer on the ice away from the magnetic field of the tractors. This procedure was followed for every three-mile leg until the end of the travel day.

Typically, thirty miles over the ice could be made in a day. Usually the greatest hazard one faced on travel days was falling asleep at the wheel. And that wasn't much of a hazard since there was usually nothing much you could run into, except when you were in crevasse country, which was infrequently. "Falling asleep at the wheel" did happen from time to time though, and then one of the more alert tractor drivers radioed frantically to the wayward tractor to "wake up and return to our track!" When this happened, it usually was a driver from one of the other tractors who called. That is because it also usually happened that if one driver fell asleep, the other man with him in the same tractor would have nodded off also, so one had to depend on more alert drivers from another tractor for the wake-up call. Other than embarrassment, however, no one was the worse for such a lapse of consciousness.

At the end of the travel day, the three tractors with their sleds would form a triangle of sorts, somewhat like "circling the wagons," and for much the same reason—safety. Not against marauders, but against the wind and blowing snow and ice. From time to time the wind would suddenly pick up, blowing ice crystals that would create a low visibility environment in which one could easily lose one's way if he were not within the confined space afforded by the triangular array of tractors. Wandering blind in an Antarctic ice storm is life threatening. You can easily lose your way and be unable to return to safety—and so likely freeze to death.

In the center of this enclosed space, the glaciologists would dig a square pit in the ice, about six feet on a side, and ten feet deep. After they carefully cleaned the vertical walls of the pit, they could see clear layers of ice and snow—the stratigraphy—that could be measured, described, and correlated from pit to pit, over the entire traverse. That was the job of the glaciologists. They would begin the pit-digging as soon as a camp site was chosen for the "night."

One or the other of the Hectori drivers, LeSchack the assistant geophysicist, or Jack Long, the traverse mechanic, would take turns making the evening meal in the cook shack on travel days. In those days, well before GPS navigation, Charlie, the chief geophysicist and traverse leader, would set up a theodolite and begin to take "sunshots." Sunshots permitted calculation of lines of position of the sun as it circled the heavens. And circle it did. The sun did not rise and set each day as it does in temperate zones; it merely circles around you at slightly different elevations each day as the summer progresses. With three or more lines of position, taken over a twenty-four-hour period, one can calculate, to within a mile or two, your location on the face of the earth. This was how the traverse crew plotted their daily position; it was exactly the same procedure then used by ships at sea for navigation.

The following day—the station day—the glaciologists finished digging their pit, and began measuring the ice strata. The geophysicists set up a seismic array, in much the same way oil exploration is conducted, and measure the depth from the ice surface to the rock basement below them. It was LeSchack's job to lay out two, one-thousand-foot long seismic lines in the shape of an "L", then connect the geophones, and drill ten-foot deep holes in which he placed dynamite charges. The basic theory of seismic exploration is simple. You set off an explosion beneath the surface, and measure the time it takes for the sound energy so generated to bounce off the ice-rock boundary and return to the surface. This return is recorded at each of the geophones spread out along the length of the seismic lines. The geophones, actually, earth microphones, sense the returning seismic echoes and feed them to a seismograph that then recorded the echoes on photographic paper. From such recordings, LeSchack and Charlie could not only measure the depth to the rock of the Antarctic continent, but could estimate which way the rock surface was sloping.

While the scientists were making their measurements, Jack, the mechanic, would service the tractors and make whatever repairs to the mechanical equipment required. To service the underside of the tractors, Jack would use that old method used by automobile mechanics early in the Twentieth Century—driving the vehicle over a pit, a pit into which he could descend and service the underside of the tractor. So, like the glaciologists, he too would dig a pit in the ice, only his was long, rectangular, and deep enough so that he could stand up in it, and narrow enough so that it could be straddled by the Sno-Cat's tracks when he drove over it.

That's it. Those were the two types of days the traverse crew experienced, over and over again. It would have been boring, except for the occasional frightful blizzards, life-threatening crevasses, extraordinary mountain scenery, odd quirks of nature, and of course, food, lots of food.

Basically, time allowed only one meal a day on travel days, and only a breakfast and a dinner meal on station days. Frankly, the logistics of preparing a meal and, in fact eating it that tiny, crowded and icy-cold cook shack on the sled pulled by Buttons, went beyond the pale. The cook shack, called a "wannigan," an American Indian word, took up about half of a two and a half-ton sled. It measured eight feet by seven feet and was seven feet high. It was built of plywood, canvas and assorted odds and ends. It was the only enclosed space the traverse crew had within which they could stand erect. It was not heated except from that heat thrown off by the Coleman Stove used for cooking. There was a table in the center and two benches on either side. Because it was cold inside, all six men left there parkas on and sat three to a bench. It was a tight fit for everybody. And convivial as well as smelly!

Food generally was good and there was plenty of it. Obviously, in Antarctic temperatures, even in summertime, it was below freezing and there never was any problem in storing frozen food. Huge quantities were cooked, boiled, fried or broiled at any one time. The wannigan was the crew's place, their clubhouse and restaurant, and the only daily meeting place out of the wind that they had. And once everyone jammed themselves in, no one moved or got up to leave until everyone was finished and *ready* to leave. And you had to stand up, one at a time and exit the wannigan door before the next man in line could get up and leave. Be it ever so humble!

The scenery that this crew encountered along the traverse was often spectacular. LeSchack observed that the mountains, whenever there were any in sight, were unlike anything he had ever seen before. They all had been carved by glaciation and are sharp and craggy. LeSchack wrote in his notes that they were like the surface of the moon, as he then imagined it to be. But of course this was in 1957, well before we had satellites that actually took photographs of the moon! On the windward side of the mountains the ice had been blown off, usually displaying a sizeable area of eroded rock outcrop. But when there are no mountains, there is nothing. You can look until your eyes drop out, but still there is nothing. The ice goes on forever and ever. It is bearable and, in fact, quite beautiful on a bright sunny day, but highly depressing during a "whiteout." Then the gray ice meets the gray sky and there is no horizon and you see nothing. That doesn't mean there is no visibility; there may well be. You could see the tractor ahead of you even if it were a half-mile away, but it simply looks suspended in space, a ghostly, disembodied shape, with nothing else to define it in that space. Whiteout conditions made for difficult traveling.

LeSchack wrote in his traverse notes:

"I have noticed some unusual optical phenomena down here. Temperature inversion immediately above the ice surface causes a peculiar refraction of light. Thus, I have seen the desert wanderer's "lake" in the middle of an otherwise homogeneous ice field. I have seen mountains, when some are actually in sight, with their mirror-image of those same mountains, one atop one another; a normally conical-shaped mountain, for example, has appeared to me (and my colleagues also) as an hour-glass shape. I have also seen peculiar distortions of objects, such as elongation in the vertical plane yet not in the horizontal plane. For example, the tractor, Carole, three-miles ahead of me would appear through binoculars to be three or four times as tall as it really was compared to its width.

"Also, I have noticed on one occasion this type of refraction, or channeling, also occurs with sound waves. It was -45F outside (at this temperature, degrees Fahrenheit and Celsius are essentially equal). I was at one end of the 1000-foot seismic spread, working and cursing the cold, and Charlie was at the other end. Hearing me curse, he noticed that we could talk to each other over such a distance, something we had never before (or afterwards) been able to do. "No need to shout at me, Len," the acerbic Charlie said to me, in mock condescension, in what to me clearly was hardly more than a whisper. "I can hear you." We were able to conduct a normal conversation over that thousand-foot distance. Also, the sound did not appear to come from the direction of the speaker as you would expect, but from a point in the air, halfway between us.

There were many things in LeSchack's life, out with the traverse party, which were completely different from the life experiences that he heretofore had. And other things, that while otherwise normal, were simply so *incongruous* in context with the everyday realities of traverse life. For example, washing the day's seismic records, recorded on photographic paper, in an old plastic bucket and, at the same time, listening to Beethoven. It had become LeSchack's habit to turn on the short wave receiver in Hectori and try to get some music while he was engaged in washing the chemicals off the records. The radio was an Army ANGRC-9 command set installed in each Sno-Cat for two-way communications. The receiver also covered the commercial short-wave bands of the world. The music broadcasts helped LeSchack relieve the tedium of an otherwise cold and horrid job, and the occasional melancholy of the extended separation from his other, more cosmopolitan world.

The seismic records were in the last rinse; he leaned over the receiver and started tuning...the usual hisses, squeals, an occasional brrrrrrrr, like a noise maker at the height of a children's party. This last was the "Voice of America" being jammed; that time, 1957, was after all, the height of the Cold War, and the Soviets electronically blocked, i.e. "jammed," from the ears of the Soviet and Soviet Bloc people, international broadcasts from the Free World that contained any reportage of a "political nature." The electronic jamming signals, however, were not content to remain within Soviet Bloc borders, and like any radio signals, propagated wherever the ether let them go—so LeSchack heard them in Antarctica. And then, finally he found what he was searching for—a touch of civilization, now so remote; Radio Cologne, the Berlin Symphony Orchestra, playing Beethoven's Seventh, one of LeSchack's favorites. He sat transfixed. His eyes closed and, in spite of the radio's static, his mind wandered off...to a lovely concert hall, to an orchestra all dressed in black, and to an audience of neatly cleaned and perfumed women and freshly clean and shaven men.... These were the only times on traverse when he *even* had the opportunity, or space in his twenty-two year old brain, to think lovingly and longingly about women and cosmopolitan pleasures.

His eyes opened with a start and he looked out the windows to see the ice stretching endlessly off in all directions. The midnight sun came streaming in the windows and made the ice a desert of sequins, all sparkling. And his hands were cold. The record rinse water had cooled off. The inside of the tractor also, was cooling off to a steady and frigid twenty degrees F. Outside, Jack was brushing his teeth with a toothpaste-ice mixture. He scrubbed and spat and then stuck his tongue out to examine it over the tip of his nose. Apparently satisfied, he tightened his parka and went back to Buttons, the cat in which he slept. He knocked a few icicles off the door as he got in.

Charlie, working in the back of Hectori presently looked up. He pushed aside the Nautical Almanac and, as the Fourth Movement of Beethoven's magnificent Seventh Symphony was coming to its climactic crescendo, he announced, "85 degrees 03 minutes South." He had just computed the current traverse position, and he had just announced that they were within 300 miles of the Geographical South Pole of the earth! As the Berlin Symphony Orchestra faded into the ether, LeSchack looked out the Sno-Cat's window and at the endless ice glistening under that midnight sun. *Three hundred miles from the South Pole; that was the information that now pertained to LeSchack's world, and it was indisputable! The incongruous vision of the concert hall, like a will o'the wisp, sadly disappeared.*

LeSchack's experience with Shell Oil's training program in Louisiana and Texas had prepared him for the geophysical field work he was now conducting. Ned Ostenso, who was finishing his tour as Charlie's assistant geophysicist, trained LeSchack in the practical aspects of exploration in the Polar Regions. Aspects like how to handle the explosives safely in freezing weather—a misstep here could be fatal. For LeSchack, the difference between a Shell seismic crew and the traverse seismic crew was amazing: Shell's crew had about twenty people, including drillers, explosives handlers, surveyors and instrument recorders. Two people did all that on the traverse; of course, on the traverse they didn't have to commute to work! But they also had far less sleep, far less to drink and, of course, no weekends, ever!

There were two types of seismic exploration that LeSchack and Charlie conducted: reflection seismology, the most common form that bounces seismic energy off the rocks below, and refraction seismology which measures the sound energy that is channeled at various depths within the transmitting media—rock in the usual case—but ice in Antarctica. There is a significant difference in the logistics required for these two seismic methods. In the case of reflection seismology, the explosive shot is set off at the apex of the L-shaped array of seismic lines. That shot point is just a few hundred feet from the Sno-Cat encampment. However, in the case of refraction seismology, the shot points are located at increasing distances from the encampment where the recordings are made. For LeSchack, refraction seismology was a special adventure.

Although the traverse party was indeed an operation remote from civilization, LeSchack occasionally found the civilization that he was now a part of—six very grungy men, and enforced 24-hour per day togetherness—was a bit too much. A refraction seismology survey, conducted about once every two weeks during the traverse, was a refreshing opportunity for him to get away from all this; as assistant seismologist, it was his task to travel alone in Buttons to a distance of 15 miles away from the encampment, shooting explosives—Nitramon and C-4—all along the way. It took a full day to do this. All alone on a refraction day, he would drive away from the camp, stopping at pre-determined distances to set off his explosions.

LeSchack and Charlie would choose a station day when the weather was clear, there was relatively little wind, and both of those conditions appeared likely to remain that way for a day. Fortified with plenty of water, food, fuel and explosives, he would set off at the beginning of the day for an adventure in exploration and solitude. For LeSchack it was most exhilarating. He was traveling over terrain that nobody else had seen or likely would ever see. At predetermined intervals, and using the Sno-Cat's odometer, he would stop, drill a hole in the ice with a hand auger, and insert an explosive charge down the hole. He would then radio Charlie that the charge was ready, and with the seismograph set to record, LeSchack would set off his charge. He would wait until Charlie confirmed that he had recorded the blast, and then LeSchack would proceed to the next shot point.

The further away from the camp that LeSchack traveled, the larger the amount of explosives he had to drop down the ice-hole to create sufficient energy to be recorded back at the camp. By the time he had reached the furthest refraction shot point, he needed 250 pounds of explosives to create a sufficient explosion to be "heard" by Charlie. But to physically place that volume of explosive in the ice, LeSchack first had to auger a 26-foot hole and then explode a one-pound charge at the bottom of this hole to create an under-ice cavern of sufficient volume to now accept so much explosive. The scene created by that next explosion was something to behold! When Charlie was ready, and LeSchack detonated the 250 pounds of C-4 explosive, the ice and the tractor shook and smoke and ice blew up into the sky like a geyser. Quite a spectacle. When that last blast was successfully recorded back at camp, LeSchack would pack up, turn the Sno-Cat around, and follow his track on the ice back to the camp.

LeSchack enjoyed his refraction survey days and their solitude. He had the time, inclination and opportunity to commune with nature. Alone, to face nature in its rawest form. Not only scientifically, but spiritually. And from time to time he would experience nature in a way that would be difficult if he were working at Camp. Take the case of the near-surface collapse of the ice, for example. On one of his refraction runs LeSchack was at the end of a refraction survey day and had just descended from the Sno-Cat. As he was walking to an area away from the tractor at which to auger his ice hole, he felt the ice surface literally drop from under his boots! Not far, but clearly noticeable and disconcerting. Perhaps four inches. And it was not just under his boots. It felt as if a substantial plate of surface ice all around him had simultaneously dropped. And with a significant noise. Frankly, it was frightening for him. As he gathered up his wits and walked on to reach his chosen location for augering, yet another ice plate dropped, then another. All no more than four inches but, nonetheless, unsettling. It was clear that, for whatever reason of nature, there was a void between the upper crust of the ice surface and some more stable layer below, and his weight had triggered the collapse. He had never experienced this before.

LeSchack proceeded to his location for augering his hole, and eventually filled it with 250 pounds of C-4. He radioed Charlie that he was ready. Charlie readied his recorder, and as was the usual procedure during seismic shooting, he alerted everyone in camp to stop work and stand still to avoid creating any noise that would interfere with his recordings. Everyone at camp stood stock-still at Charlie's signal, a signal he also transmitted to LeSchack. LeSchack detonated the blast from inside his Sno-Cat. To his horror, that blast triggered a major collapse of the ice surface for what appeared to be miles around. It sounded like a freight train roaring past. He felt the ice beneath the tractor drop. He heard the collapse perpetuating itself as a dull roar in outward concentric circles around the Sno-Cat, with the sound of the collapse gradually diminishing in all directions. LeSchack was certainly startled, but otherwise nothing appeared amiss. That, however, was not the case with the glaciologists working in their ice pit fifteen miles away at the camp. When he returned several hours later to this camp, the glaciologists reported to him that within instants of his detonating his refraction shot, what sounded like an earthquake, and clearly advancing speedily toward them from LeSchack's shot location was a general collapse of the ice for miles around. While Charlie felt it in Hectori, for the two glaciologists down in their pit and surrounded by ice, it sounded like their days were over—it scared the shit out of them.

Traverse days continued into February 1958. They were exhausting days of endless sunlight, hard physical labor in the cold, and with never enough sleep unless the traverse party ran into a storm. A storm in the Antarctic is mostly high winds. The Antarctic interior is a desert and there is rarely precipitation. But the wind can whip up ice crystals that not only obscure visibility, but create so much acoustic noise that it is impossible to make useful seismic recordings. On such occasions, the order is given to stop and circle the tractors to wait out the storm. Such wind storms often last several days and traverse members use this time to catch up on sleep, often spending twelve hours at a stretch in their sleeping bags. LeSchack found such occasional storms a blessing.

During such wind storms not only was visibility obscured and too much seismic noise created to work effectively, but radio communication, especially with Byrd Station, was difficult. Each day the traverse party attempted to radio their position, the weather, and their need for supplies to the Navy radio operators at Byrd. Usually they got through. During wind storms, however, the high velocity wind-blown ice crystals against the whip antennae of the Sno-Cats created a static electricity charge on each antenna that made radio communication nearly impossible. During one such windstorm, LeSchack decided to measure the electrostatic charge on Hectori's antenna. Putting on gloves, he unfastened the radio's lead-in wire from the antenna terminal inside the tractor and brought a screwdriver close to the bare terminal. He was surprised to see that he could draw a *continuous* spark of at least one-quarter inch in length from the terminal to the screwdriver blade. It was like watching a Van de Graaf generator experiment at work in his high school science class. Such a spark represented a literally shocking voltage—one that could easily, and inadvertently, set off a blasting cap, the kind LeSchack used for seismic work. This was just another reason to avoid working—and sleep—during such storms!

About every two weeks when the weather was good, the traverse party would be re-supplied. A Navy R4D with food, mail and fuel would fly out and land on the ice nearby the waiting traverse party. Although the R4D was ski-equipped, the traverse party would attempt to choose an area with a relatively smooth expanse of ice for its landing. At the best of times, landing on an un-graded ice surface is a rough landing. The traverse crew therefore made every effort to find the best landing spot with the least amount of rough sastrugi to reduce the likelihood of damaging the landing gear. Generally, the most pressing need by the traverse crew was gasoline for the Sno-Cats. A large tank was installed in the R4D's fuselage to permit rapid pumping of gasoline out of the airplane and into the sled-mounted 55-gallon drums that the traverse party used.

The R4D crew did everything, in fact, as rapidly as possible to re-supply the traverse so that the aircraft could soon become airborne again. The flight crew was rightfully concerned about the weather closing in on them. Except when the trail party had just left Byrd at the beginning of summer, or was close to Byrd as the summer was coming to its end, they were invariably hundreds of miles away from any safe base for a re-supply aircraft to return and land.

The Navy's re-supply flights, even as brief as they were, provided an important boost to traverse morale. Often, by the time the airborne re-supply could occur, the traverse party was nearly out of gasoline. On a few occasions, during the two traverse seasons with which LeSchack was involved, the party actually ran out of gasoline and had to remain stationary where they ran out until a re-supply flight could reach them. The periodic arrival of these re-supply flights reinforced the occasionally flagging feeling that someone from the real world was actually looking out for them. From LeSchack's point of view, it also gave him yet another opportunity to evaluate the Navy (as opposed to the other military services) for his next career move. He knew that this Antarctic excursion would be the last time that he would be able to outfox his persistent Draft Board, and that he would need to enter the military soon after he returned to the United States. And for LeSchack, there were few things that could then inspire as much awe for the Navy as an R4D re-supply plane, on skis, taking off, after its ever-so-short visit to his icy world, dramatically firing all its JATO bottles in doing so. He would watch and listen to the thrilling takeoff of the aircraft that, moments ago had just been on the ice with him, and now was back in the sky, trailing billowing clouds of ice crystals and JATO exhaust. "Yes, sooner or later, it will be the Navy for me," LeSchack mused.

The 1957 Byrd Traverse was triangular in shape and more than a thousand miles in length. LeSchack joined it when the traverse party had started its last leg and was returning to Byrd Station. And, eventually toward the end of February 1958 the traverse party did return, recording glaciological, geological and geophysical data all the way back. They arrived at Byrd without much fanfare and parked their Sno-Cats. Before entering their old home and heading for the showers that they all desperately needed, the six traverse party members, all disgustingly filthy and smelly, posed for a photograph together in front of one of their tractors. They were all smiling, not so much because they had just completed a Herculean adventure, but in anticipation of the showers that they shortly would enjoy.

Ned and Vern Anderson, the senior glaciologist, would shortly leave Antarctica, departing on the tractor-train returning to Little America before the winter closed in. LeSchack, Charlie, Jack and Bill would remain, spending eight months at Byrd, working on their data, planning for the following season's traverse, and just thinking, before setting out once again on the 1958-1959 Traverse for new adventures in polar exploration. But now, they had another adventure to face: living together amicably and productively in frigid isolation for an extended period of time with eighteen other men, some of whom were late-arriving replacements whom they had yet to meet.

The transition for LeSchack was relatively easy. In his nearly two months-absence from Byrd, the Seabees had made major improvements to the station. New quarters had been constructed and life was relatively easy compared to life on traverse. LeSchack, Bill, Jack and Marion Todd, the aurora observer, shared a trailer with two double-decker beds. LeSchack and Marion shared one double-decker and Bill and Jack shared the other. A double-wide trailer served as the office for the traverse people, as well as the ionosphere people from the National Bureau of Standards. The U.S. Weather Bureau had their own office and an outdoor facility from which they could inflate and release weather balloons. The Navy maintained the radio station.

The Seabees had sensibly built the diesel generator facility in such a fashion that it served several purposes beyond generating power. The exhaust pipes provided heat for a "snow-melter" that was the source of fresh water for the camp. There was no end of raw material for the snow-melter, except that it became a camp rule: no one takes a shower without first going outside and shoveling ice and snow into the melter. The Seabees, with remarkable forethought, connected a duct to allow the hot air moved by the cooling fans to flow between the generator shed and the head. The head, or bathroom facilities, were all combined; sinks, showers, and commodes, all in one building. The commodes were simply a line of open holes cut in a long bench built over a deep pit. This was the construction style used at all of the U.S. Antarctic stations. The Seabees at Byrd recognized that at all other similar facilities, there was a problem that troubled the more fastidious—the endless Antarctic winds blowing over the ice create a higher than ambient air pressure in the porous, near-surface layer of ice. When a large pit is excavated into this ice to be used as a holding tank, there is often a not-so-gentle breeze that blows up from the bottom and sides of this pit, a breeze resulting from the outside wind blowing over the ice surface. The usual end result— words chosen carefully here—is that it is difficult to delicately dispose of used toilet paper; a wad, even a heavy one, is caught up on the air column below and refuses to easily drop to the bottom of the pit.

At the other stations, these aerodynamic phenomena were the source of great scatological humor. At Byrd the Seabees addressed this problem with their conduit from the generator shed that provided sufficient air pressure to neutralize the natural upward flow from the deep pit. In addition to over-pressuring the head, it provided a continuous stream of warm air out of the overheated generator space into the head where it was welcomed by all hands.

All of the individual spaces, offices, sleeping quarters, mess hall, recreation hall and storage areas, were connected by the chicken-wire-parachute-silk-tunnels that by now were completely covered by wind-blown ice. Thus, it was possible to remain "underground" for days at a time without stepping into the frigid Antarctic winds. And for many of the station personnel—referred to snidely as "tunnel rats"—who had no reason to venture outside into the increasingly frigid Antarctic winter, that's what they did—remain inside.

LeSchack and Charlie, however, continued to work outside for most of the Antarctic autumn. Each day that weather permitted, they drove Hectori out to the survey site LeSchack and George had prepared earlier in the summer. At each marker flag that LeSchack had planted, he and Charlie laid out the seismic lines and recorded the depths to the rock below, and therefore, the thickness of the Antarctic ice cap. In addition, they recorded gravity and magnetic readings as they had done on traverse, and the glaciologists eventually joined them to dig five pits and collect cores there. The main difference between this work and traverse operations was that the sun no longer just circled the heavens. It was noticeably darker in the mornings when they left Byrd, and when they returned in the evenings. And, of course, colder. On 17 April, the sun set permanently until 25 August, when it momentarily peeked back over the horizon.

The major difference now, as compared to surveying on traverse, was that LeSchack and Charlie ate a proper breakfast before leaving Byrd each morning, and could expect a proper dinner when they returned. Also they could shower and watch movies in the evenings. The Navy had provided a 16mm motion picture projector and some 400 movies for a year's worth of entertainment. Movie time occurred shortly after the completion of the evening meal. It was the key social event each day for the 24 station members. As the winter wore on, it became clear that with the increasing intimacy and knowledge of each other that these men developed resulting from the enforced togetherness, the movies triggered some fascinating observations on the life that they all shared. Mostly during movie time, and mostly when they were drinking. For LeSchack, movie-watching at Byrd was a fascinating experience. Largely because of his family upbringing and the consuming nature of his own projects, he had rarely watched movies *of any sort* until he settled in at Byrd Station.

Naturally enough, the movies the Navy shipped down had been produced before 1957, the year IGY commenced; some movies had been produced considerably before that, in the late thirties and forties; movies then were quite different from those produced today. Movie producers then recognized that, absent television which only became generally available in the 1950s, their product was often the major form of entertainment for North American families during that period. Accordingly, movies were often structured to be enjoyed at several different levels, from that of sophisticated adults, to unsophisticated adults, and down to and including the children of all the movie-going families; they had to cater to a whole spectrum of human understanding and life experiences. The 24 men at Byrd, however, were not your usual distribution of moviegoers of the period. The IGY personnel although many quite young, were all well educated, in the formal sense. The Navy personnel may have been less well educated formally, but all were well-traveled, many having already been stationed all over the world. This was particularly true of the Seabees; they were typically older and more worldly than that of most Navy enlisted men. They certainly had a broader view of the world than many, and certainly had a wide range of amorous adventures that they chose to share—vividly, with little left to the imagination! The result was that nearly each movie elicited substantial commentary during its showing, often profound, but always profane!

As winter set in and it became perpetually dark outside, more and more of everyone's activities became focused indoors. Everyone had indoor projects of their own to work on, either ones of their own choosing or assigned by their superiors. LeSchack, having finished his outside survey, worked on his data, studied celestial navigation, built equipment to make traverse work easier the next season, and read and wrote his observations. For the first time in his young life, he had both the time and the inclination to take stock of his life up till then, and to ponder what, after all, was life all about. "Being immersed with 23 other men, mostly older than I, and being a part of the nightly movie experience with them is a valuable social education," he thought to himself.

Movies were shown in the recreation hall, another Jamesway hut. There were also ping-pong and pool tables, and a record player in that Jamesway. Because alcoholic beverages were permitted during off-duty time, movies were often accompanied by beer-drinking. Beer in the Antarctic was Budweiser, or more properly had, at least, begun life as Budweiser. What it was at Byrd was something dreadfully different; imagine this: a case of beer starts off by being loaded into the hold of a Navy ship at a port somewhere in the U.S. The typically non-air-conditioned ship crosses the Equator, bringing the beer close to a boil. The ship eventually crosses below the Antarctic Circle and the beer freezes. It is then off-loaded at McMurdo and placed in a warehouse where it thaws. It is then transshipped to Little America during which process it freezes again. Then it thaws again at Little America, only to freeze again when it is shipped by annual tractor train to Byrd Station. Once again it thaws in storage at Byrd. Do you suppose the liquid now in the Budweiser can is the same liquid Anheuser-Busch originally shipped? It wasn't, but it didn't much matter to most Navy men at Byrd, men who were known to drink unadulterated torpedo alcohol.

The metamorphoses of the beverage drunk while watching movies at Byrd is relevant to our tale; as much of the conversation in the movie hall centered around that liquid being drunk as it did about the finer points of the movie being viewed. Mostly, "finer points," was simply a discussion of the attributes of the leading lady in the movie—and, of course, how she would likely behave if magically thrust into the Byrd environment.

What was now in the Budweiser can was a transformed substance: (1) a clear, pale insipid liquid with hardly any beer taste, and (2) a gelatinous substance that had separated out and was dubbed, "goobers," by the Navy men. Not because it had any relation to peanuts, but simply because of the disgusting euphoniousness of that word—"Goooober!" While some might punch open the can and drink as usual, excepting that their drinking noises were punctuated by what sounded like a raw oyster or two inadvertently going down with the liquid, others opened the can and then filtered the contents through a handkerchief. That procedure detained the goobers, allowing only liquid into a glass below, and so no slimy goobers were swallowed. Imagine this scene every night in the movie hall, along with the discussions of the film while still in progress, by men who all fancied themselves proper movie critics! Goober beer was not the only unorthodox beverage the Byrd crew drank. The Navy had made, under special contract, a bourbon by the name of "Old Methusalem." It was as bad as you could imagine. It was not even clear to LeSchack why they even sent it to Byrd, since the station also had pure grain alcohol for medicinal use, liberally provided by Dr. Peter Ruseski, the Navy doctor, as appropriate for health and welfare. Usually, with orange juice. But the strangest drink of all that they had at Byrd was courtesy of the Army Corps of Engineers.

The Engineers were responsible for drilling a thousand-foot vertical hole through the ice at Byrd to collect continuous ice cores for scientific analysis. Ice cores in polar regions contain indications of climate changes, variation in atmospheric gases and temperature regimes, that all can be dated through the stratigraphy of the ice. For example, the eruption of the Krakatoa volcano in Indonesia in 1883 could easily be seen by the volcanic ash inclusions in the ice laid down at that time. Before they had left Byrd for the winter, the Army had drilled to a depth of 1013 feet. They used the last few feet of ice (beyond that required under its orders) for throwing a party. There was something awe-inspiring about pouring Old Methusalem into a glass with pieces of ice thousands of years old. The ice had inclusions of gas from the time of deposition that were dramatically released when the ice was melted by the bourbon. The ice shattered and continued to shatter vigorously in the glass until it all disappeared as the high gas pressure within the ice was released by the warm liquid poured over it. It was exciting, both intellectually and romantically, to drink this bubbling, frothing history in a glass, even though the ice imparted a bitter taste to the drink. That did not, however, detract from the intrinsic cheap taste of the Old Methusalem.

Some of the movies shown in the recreation hall, particularly the good ones, had intense affects on the men; like "Camille," or the "Lady of the Camellias," the story by Dumas about a courtesan who gave up the man she loved to save his family's honor. That story was the basis for the opera, *"La Traviata."* As the movie came to its tearful conclusion, Mutt, a worldly Navy Chief and senior mechanic, sadly observed that while the do-gooders in the story were all now happy, everyone else was miserable because a passionate love has been unrequited. Shortly thereafter, when the movie hall emptied out, Fred, the meteorologist, found phonograph records of *La Traviata*, and began playing it—and began crying.

Surprisingly, there was not an abundance of military or service-related movies for this audience. And if services other than the Navy were depicted, there were often hoots of mock derision from the moviegoers. Because there were only 400 movies provided for the whole year, and two movies were shown on weekend nights, it was clear that the Byrd crew would likely have the opportunity to see the same movie twice or more over the course of the year. One movie was so bad that *everyone insisted* on seeing it many times. It involved the "star," John Agar, a dreadful actor, and an actress, Rosemary Bow; her only redeeming virtue was that she looked splendidly in bathing suits. The film involved scuba diving, so there was plenty of opportunity for her to show off her swimsuit wardrobe. But the dialog was beyond dreadful. The Byrd crew insisted that they see it so many times that they began to memorize that painfully trite dialog. The last time LeSchack saw it, the projectionist was instructed to turn off the sound, while various members of the Byrd crew took turns in mouthing their version of the dialog. Because of the amount of goober beer drunk that night, as well as that of the more effective spirits, that movie night was absolutely hilarious. The score: Navy won, John Agar, zero. Rosemary Bow, however, received many offers to play the upcoming season.

The 24 men confined to Byrd for a year all knew, at some level, that they simply had to get along together, whether they liked each other or not. For LeSchack, a whole new male behavior pattern emerged that he had never seen before. It became *unmanly* to get involved in a serious argument or a fight. Throwing a punch at another guy was an indication that "you couldn't take it!" That you couldn't hold up under the strain. As a result, there were no fights. Occasionally you saw a hole or two, about the size of a fist, in the wall or a door, and you knew someone had been seriously angry, but there were no fights!

The whole range of human emotion was on display at Byrd that winter. Reports from home of family joys and catastrophes, girlfriends or wives moving on and sending Dear-John letters or messages, babies being born, family members dying, all had to be accepted passively. The people at Byrd were unable to do anything about it, like being with family. They could send short radio messages, or use the ham radio with phone-patch connections, but this was rarely a satisfying or private way of sharing the emotions of grief or joy.

Sven, a geophysical technician with the Coast and Geodetic Survey, a big bull of a man and former Marine, learned that his brother, a Marine aviator stationed in Hawaii, had been killed in a plane crash. Sven was grief-stricken and angered at it all; unable to leave Byrd to attend the funeral, unable—as a former-Marine himself—to get a satisfactory report from the Marine Corps as to the cause of the crash, unable to be with his family. It took Sven months to come to grips with this. The only thing possible at Byrd was to talk to one another. To this end, it became the practice for the men to post "Dear John" letters and radio messages on the communal bulletin board, just so these men wouldn't have to bear their grief privately.

Despite the strongly felt absence of women in the confined all-male milieu of Byrd, everyone, from senior scientist to lowest enlisted man, recognized that in such a hermetically-sealed environment, the presence of women would be a disaster. That would add a dynamic that all understood in such a closed male society would create intolerable strains, strains that all wished to avoid. That doesn't mean that they didn't *think* often of women, though.

LeSchack certainly did. One night during the winter, he abruptly awoke after having a vivid dream of Giselle, his first lover. He had neither seen nor thought of her for the past two years, but this was more than a dream—it appeared to be an apparition. He felt that she had just been in bed with him, in his top bunk, in the same room as Bill, Jack and Marion! Bolting upright in his bunk, he looked warily about the room, but everyone was sound asleep, and his lovely apparition was gone.

He wrote in his notes in mid winter, June, 1958:

> "Lately, I have found that I can't seem to keep my mind off of girls. I often think of Giselle and the wonderful times I have spent with her. I shall never forget the first time I crawled into bed with her. I couldn't have been older than nineteen at the time.... I really don't know when it was exactly. It was at her house in Montréal. She slipped out of her clothes in the dark; I could barely see her, just beautiful outlines and fluid shadows as she moved. I heard the bed creak just a little, and then her quiet, lilting voice. I had removed all of my clothes and slid between the crisp, cool sheets, and then my body touched hers. It was the most delicious sensation I had ever felt. She was so smooth and warm. Every part of her was in dynamic motion, a symphony of movement.

She had an exciting, intoxicating fragrance that I thoroughly enjoyed; it was a delicious feminine odor. Her mouth had a clean, very wet taste. Her tongue and lips were vibrant, demanding. Her firm breasts were cushions for my chest, her nipples were hard against me....my hands, my tongue. Her stomach was smooth and flat and was tight against mine, a marked contrast from the undulating mass of soft hair pushing and rubbing my loins. Her legs were smooth and were wrapped around mine.

This was the first time I was ever in bed with a girl, and I was deeply in love with her. I knew then we would soon become lovers."

On another occasion during that mid-winter he would write:

"At times, the days seems to drag terribly. Although there is always something to do, there seems to be little reason to do it. Bad moods or depressions appear to be brought on by the movie the previous night. Girls, mostly. At times they provoke the most intense desires which I somehow have difficulty in sublimating by picking records, slide rule work, or building my newest project, a SHORAN set. My temper has been very even; not even an occasional snarl. The petty annoyances seem to leave me unscathed, but the sum total is the cause for my occasional black moods.

"I find myself looking quite frequently at such magazines as the "New Yorker" and "Esquire" with much interest. I find that I have a desire to wear new clothes; in a word, to dress up, go out dining and dancing. I wonder whether this is a phase, due to the particular conditions of the Byrd Station environment, or something which will be permanent. It might also be due, in part, to my last stateside remembrances; the very pleasant urban delights that I experienced in New Orleans with Ellen.

> "I think I have changed somewhat. That is, with respect
> to people back home. Exactly what change has taken
> place, it is hard to say. It is sort of a feeling I have."

In mid-winter women seemed to be on everyone's mind at Byrd. Take for
example the story of LeSchack's calendar. Sometime before the last mail
came to Byrd, LeSchack received a pin-up calendar from his brother. It
was his brother's contention that such an item might brighten up the
otherwise female-less lives at Byrd. He obviously meant well and
couldn't have possibly imagined the controversy which that calendar
created there. In the real world, this calendar would have been just the
thing for a boys' dormitory or for hanging over a workbench at the
corner garage, but somehow it was remarkably disturbing at Byrd.
LeSchack didn't propose to set himself up as a connoisseur of calendar
art but he had seen a lot more daring poses on dozens of other calendars
that were a lot less annoying than this one was. Yes, that was the correct
word—annoying. Mind you now, there was nothing obviously wrong
with this calendar; it would not have any difficulty in complying with
the 1957 postal regulations. You could have picked it up with no trouble
at your favorite news stand, thumbed through from January to
December, smirked, and then would probably have just put it back
without buying it. Well, the reaction was just the same at Byrd—at first.

Mail call was generally held in building six, right near LeSchack's desk.
When he received his mail, he left the milling crowd and sat down at his
desk to examine it. The large manila envelope caught his eye so he
opened it first. And there it was. Before he got as far as March, the
crowd began to gather at his desk. And so they all looked through it
together. Then, of course, the differences of opinion that characterize
the American male were displayed to best advantage.

> "Jeez, what a build!"
> "Ugh! Such a pig!"
> "Now she is a whore!"
> "That's O.K., I'll take a dozen of them."

The dialogue no doubt is familiar. And so it was. The calendar went up on the wall by the desk. That occurred in December, toward the end of summer. Hardly a day went by throughout most of the winter, however, when someone didn't stop at the calendar to check the date.

As we mentioned, there was nothing particularly obvious about the pictures, but nonetheless, there was something rather insidious about them; something which became more and more noticed as the months dragged by. Make no mistake; these were the same dull-eyed, voluptuous women, who beckon you from girly calendars everywhere. There was the same insipid prose underneath. The girls, perhaps younger than you would expect, rather than being artfully clothed, were merely partially undressed. Instead of getting the feeling that they were posing seductively for you, you felt as if you barged in unannounced and unnoticed. And here is where the insidiousness lay. The pictures were photographs, but with distracting backgrounds. The discerning eyes of the men, sharpened by months of living in a female-less society, picked out obscure details that annoyed them. It was much like the psychologists' ink-blots and picture tests. The men's desires, frustrations and backgrounds seemed to determine what they saw. Within narrow limits, of course, for there was no mistaking the primary overtone of the pictures... Sex.

Perhaps an illustration can be made. Nearly all of the men had their last fling in New Zealand. This was the last place they had the things that one usually takes for granted. Fresh milk, vegetables (what the Byrd inhabitants would have given for a tossed salad), women. Then down to the ice and months of constant sunlight, an obviously alien environment, and the big eye. Just when you believe that you are getting used to this, the last plane leaves, and it starts to get progressively darker. You have the feeling of complete abandonment. There was nobody, nothing, within six hundred miles of them; and these were, after all, men. The nearest women...two thousand miles away. It was then the middle of winter, and pitch black out all day.

And so, they looked at the calendar, to check off the passing days; to check the girls. Each one saw something different in each picture. There was some agreement, of course, but never unanimous. Miss March was a good example. Here was a sweet young blonde in a blue negligee standing by a window, with her hands behind her head. She said

95

nothing. She was neither sexy nor did she have any aesthetic value, as far as LeSchack was concerned. Everyone else liked her. Nearly everyone asked for Miss March as the end of the month approached. Since LeSchack's roommates expressed the desire to have her also, he decided to pin her up in their room. It was not long, however before Miss March, who obviously was coveted by someone else at Byrd, was gone. Yes, coveted, as in the biblical sense. As harmless as it might seem elsewhere, in the Byrd environment, the purloining of this picture of a woman was coveting!

******

The timing for the IGY, 1957-1958, was chosen because that period was the time when the 11-year sunspot cycle was at its maximum. That period is associated with intense electromagnetic bombardment of the earth's ionosphere, and that, in turn, is associated with a maximum of auroral activity. Auroras—Aurora Borealis near the North Pole and Aurora Australis near the South Pole—are literally awe-inspiring natural phenomena. Only people living in the far north or the far south ever have much opportunity to watch these spectacular natural displays. In mid-winter at Byrd Station where the sky was absolutely black, and there was no interference from city lights, in fact, no outside artificial lights at all, one could watch the aurora at its most dramatic. LeSchack would often watch these fantastic displays as part of his weekly shower ritual.

Because of the rule requiring shower-takers to fill the snow-melter prior to indulging in their ablutions, most personnel limited the shower taking event to once a week. For those like LeSchack who learned to endure months on traverse without a shower, showering once a week was no hardship at all. And considering the effort of first, fully dressing to go out of doors in 40 below weather, then shoveling for half an hour to fill the snow-melter, a shower once a week was quite adequate. But LeSchack added to the shower ritual by also watching, while he was outside, nature's polar extravaganza, the aurora. After working up a sweat (under all his polar gear) by shoveling, and if it were a clear night, LeSchack would find a nearby open space, and lie on his back on the ice and look at the sky. In that way he had an unobstructed view of the entire sky and the dancing, waving lights called aurora.

For those who have never seen an aurora, it is difficult to describe adequately; for those who have never lain on their backs in the Polar Regions on a black night during a sunspot maximum, it is nearly impossible to create a word picture that does it justice. An aurora is a living thing. It glows, it moves, it shimmers. Like sheets and waves and curtains of colored lights. It is usually yellow-green in color. The more intense the electromagnetic storm, the redder the lights get. Within a period of five to ten minutes, these curtains of light can cross back and forth across the sky. It is one of nature's true extravaganzas. During the winter, when he needed a shower, LeSchack would treat himself to this extraordinary show of dancing lights before he bathed.

Eventually the need for shower-takers to fill the snow-melter first was superceded. The Navy radiomen had continually complained about all the electronic "noise" generated by Byrd Station machinery and equipment that plagued reception of radio signals. They had wished the radio shack had been built further away from the hub of the base and all its electronic noise. Dr. Ruseski, who was the perfect combination of medical man and military officer, decided to combine the military's well-known need to keep its men busy at all times, with the radiomen's perceived need to separate the radio shack further from the station. Also, by mid winter Dr. Ruseski had recognized that his men were getting a bit restive with six-month's darkness, and a general lack of diversity of things to do and people to see. While traditionally for make-work projects the Army digs foxholes and the Navy chips paint and then repaints, what fit for his men at Byrd Station was digging a seemingly endless tunnel in the ice from the center of Byrd Station to what turned out to be a mythical location for a new radio shack.

Perhaps Dr. Ruseski recognized that a new radio station three hundred or so feet away from Byrd would never be achieved, but everyone else thought it would be, and that it was a good idea. And it certainly made sense to the Navy men. Their radiomen colleagues had long complained about the station's electronic interference. LeSchack and Steve, the new station scientific leader, both of whom were ham radio operators, recognized the Navy radiomen's concern as being legitimate. And no one thought it would be safe for the radiomen to walk back and forth three hundred feet outside at 40 below in the dark and wind, several times each day, to reach a new radio station elsewhere. Accordingly,

Dr. Ruseski's order to start work on the tunnel for the new radio station was well received by everyone. It was made high enough and sufficiently wide to walk comfortably through. Years later, in retrospect LeSchack, the retired Navy captain, recognized the brilliance of the tunnel plan ordered by Dr. Ruseski, then only a junior naval officer. In addition to keeping the men busy—Dr. Ruseski's intention—there was another benefit: each day's worth of ice from the tunnel-to-nowhere was hauled by sled back to the station; it was then thrown into that snow-melter. Everyone now had their showers without the pain of first going outside to feed that snow-melter.

Eventually, as the tour at Byrd Station was coming to an end and, for whatever reason, no new radio station was built at its terminus, the tunnel still served a purpose. All the camp's garbage, instead of laboriously being carted out of doors and then buried, was merely hauled by sled to the end of the tunnel and stored there where it froze solid, until the Antarctic became a tropical paradise once again, as it had been hundreds of millions of years earlier.

LeSchack observed that morale at Byrd was generally good over the winter. He also knew from stories he had heard before arriving at Byrd and through the Navy grapevine, that the previous winter had been quite dreadful as far as morale was concerned, not only at Byrd, but at several other of the U.S. Antarctic stations. While he wanted to know why, as an academic matter, he sensed, rather than knew, that it would be valuable in his future endeavors, whatever they might be, if he could divine what, or who it was that made twenty-four men of diverse backgrounds want to work together harmoniously for the common good. LeSchack suspected that it was largely due to the quiet leadership of one person, Steve, the IGY station leader. Steve likely was the oldest man at the station, probably in his mid-forties. He ran the ionospheric sounding station for the National Bureau of Standards, a Department of Commerce office. He had run such stations in a number of remote locations throughout the world for many years, and was technically competent in his discipline. He had served in the Navy during WWII, and was therefore familiar with the Navy's folderol, and its arcane behaviors. With regard to that service, one of the young men at the Station once asked Steve, "what did *you get out* of the Navy, Steve?" Steve's bland answer, "What did I get out of the Navy? Well, I *got out of the Navy!*"

While Steve looked and acted most fatherly to all the men, his direct counterpart at Byrd was Dr. Ruseski, a boyish but athletic-looking Navy lieutenant just out of med school. Although freshly-minted young Navy doctors rarely have what the military calls "command presence," Dr. Ruseski had it. He looked like a naval officer. And Dr. Ruseski had several experienced and highly competent non-commissioned officers in his Navy group who were prepared to support him.

Shortly after the summer had ended and the period of winter isolation began, Steve and Dr. Ruseski called an all-hands meeting. They jointly and clearly stated that the purpose of Byrd Station was for the conduct of IGY science. It was clearly acknowledged that without the Navy's logistic support, none of this could happen. It was recognized, and then ordered, that neither group was, in any way to look down upon or disparage the work of the other group, but that they must plan to work together as necessary to assure that the common goal be achieved. It was also recognized that inevitably there would be disputes. A protocol for dealing with such disputes was agreed upon and was always adhered to thereafter. Everyone left that meeting with the understanding that a harmonious atmosphere would greatly enhance the chances for a scientifically productive year, as well as for achieving more enjoyment of the experience for all concerned.

From LeSchack's point of view, Steve's quiet fatherly manner was the catalyst for making this happen. While Steve may have been fatherly, he had other attributes that commanded unexpected respect. During one communal mealtime, for example, a heated discussion broke out about, of all things, some of the finer points and batting averages of certain baseball players. To gain the argumentative advantage, one of the Byrd men boldly stated, "I could bat better than he did." Several other station members booed and denounced the speaker.

The scientific leader quietly looked up at the arguers and softly announced that he could pitch three strikes over the plate to each and all of the arguers, that none of them could hit! This seemingly absurd statement from the rotund, middle-aged Steve just flabbergasted all of those young men around the table. Until, that is, he diffidently observed that for a number of seasons he had been a pitcher for the Philadelphia A's farm team before he joined the National Bureau of Standards!

Steve was also responsible for providing and maintaining the best ham radio station in the Antarctic that year. Steve, an avid ham radio operator, recognized how great a morale-builder was regular communication with family and friends back home. To this end, and as part of his overall program of ionospheric research, Steve brought some extra equipment of his own as well as from the National Bureau of Standards that strongly enhanced Byrd's ability to communicate around the globe using the amateur radio wave bands. It was a good thing he did, because it turned out that the Navy's ham radio transmitter was found to be inoperable, and not repairable with the electronic equipment available at Byrd.

Ham radio allowed communications with other ham radio operators around the United States who willingly provided *pro bono* phone patch service to the homes of Byrd Station personnel. Normally, those who wished to do so had an opportunity to use the ham radio-phone patch service about once a week. This service had enormous morale-building value to the completely isolated Byrd people, as well as to their loved ones back home.

LeSchack learned two valuable lessons from the ham radio experience at Byrd. He learned that when intending to conduct remote area operations, if a particular tool or piece of equipment is absolutely necessary in the conduct of those operations, *bring it yourself.* Do not depend on anyone else to have it for you. In the case of Byrd Station, had Steve not been experienced enough to know to bring his own radio equipment, station personnel would have not had the morale-building opportunity for communications with home that they had. Also, LeSchack began to recognize that he was a "loner," not wanting nor requiring constant communications with everybody. He learned that he was comfortable most of the time with his own company. As a ham radio operator himself, LeSchack was allowed to use Steve's radio equipment whenever Steve, himself, was not using it. Nonetheless, LeSchack only used it about once a month, occasionally to talk with his parents, and to talk with other ham radio operators around the world—

simply because they were strangers outside of his confined polar milieu.

LeSchack also had at Byrd Station his first lesson in "leading by example," a lesson that was to be increasingly valuable at later times of his life. The essence of that lesson is that it is easier to teach a concept by "doing *as I do,* rather than by doing *as I say.*"

That lesson was learned as a result of an interesting behavior pattern he observed during the dinner meals. The men, both scientists and military, basically hurried through their meals as if there were always something more important to do than to eat for enjoyment, and socialize while doing so. This was contrary to the fashion in which LeSchack was brought up; meal times were times to socialize and discuss the events of the day. While a case might be made for rushing during the breakfast and lunch meals, it was rarely necessary to hurriedly eat the evening meal (as it might be in the enlisted mess aboard ship where there were consecutive sittings). This was not the case at Byrd. The only thing of importance afterwards would be the evening movie, and that of course was simply more socializing. LeSchack's particular observation, both on eating rapidly, and on leading by example, occurred whenever it was his turn to mess-cook, that is, to buss all the dirty dishes.

On LeSchack's duty days he would chose *not to eat hurriedly,* since after all, the dirty dishes would wait for *him* to remove them. This was particularly true if the meal went better with a beer.....and LeSchack had one. He would eat slowly and enjoy chatting with the guys next to him at the table. Eventually over the winter months, LeSchack was to note that whenever he had mess-cook duty, like he, himself, nobody else rushed through that dinner. They all lingered over their meals until LeSchack finally got up from the table and began to clear his own dishes first. In short, LeSchack learned that by setting an example by "doing," the men would follow (especially, he recognized, if it was to their advantage to do so). And the movie would start a half-hour later and nobody, including the projectionist ever complained. LeSchack was to learn later on in life, however, that leading by example was somewhat more difficult to do when the men were less inclined to follow!

The men of Byrd found much to occupy their spare time. The doctor gave medical presentations, Jack gave judo lessons, another guy gave dancing lessons and there were lay church services given each Sunday. Holidays and birthday parties were always a cause for celebration. The Winter Solstice and the Fourth of July parties were especially lively. Seminars were given in a variety of subjects throughout the winter.

July 1958 was particularly noteworthy for its weather; an outdoor temperature of -81.7 degrees was achieved. Also, a wind velocity of 83 mph was observed. While it was a good time to remain indoors, many did briefly go outside, just to be able to say they had done so under such horrible conditions!

By October it was now completely light outside again, and the beginning of the summer. Markers were placed along the ice runway, now graded to reduce bumpy landings of soon-to-be- arriving aircraft. A new drop zone for airdrops was also delineated by marker flags. On 7 October 1958 the eight-month isolation period at Byrd was broken when the first Air Force C-124 Globemaster arrived overhead and proceeded to drop needed supplies and mail. Unfortunately, the surface winds were high, and while the Byrd crew made a heroic scramble to retrieve successfully the international orange airdropped bag that contained the first mail in eight months, many tons of other supplies got away. The parachutes did not collapse and the loads were carried downwind at an awesome rate.

The Navy at Byrd mounted a major operation with the station's D-8 tractors to follow the tracks of the wayward pallets and retrieve what they could. In the end, they retrieved about 85% of the supplies that had gotten away. They were found at various distances from Byrd, with the parachutes lying collapsed around the pallets. A heavy 30KW Caterpillar generator, and desperately needed at Byrd, was found 94 miles downwind of the station and brought back.

On Halloween, 1958, Byrd Station threw a magnificent party for the 1958-59-Byrd Station Traverse Party. Tommy baked a magnificent cake on which he had written in icing, "Good Luck, Byrd Station Traverse." As an afterthought, additional icing was added at the bottom of the cake, "Get Lost." It was a huge party, and one at which LeSchack, for the first and last time in his life, drank way too much. He drank himself into the "Hall of Shame." And he was sorry the next day.

******

On 1 November 1958, a day that will live in infamy in LeSchack's head, the 1958-59-Byrd Station Antarctic Traverse to the Horlick Mountains got underway. It was a bright, clear day and the temperature was -40 degrees Fahrenheit; it was also -40 degrees Celsius, the only point on the temperature scale where both dreadfully cold temperatures are exactly the same. For LeSchack, this was a blessing. It was only when, bareheaded, he stepped outside into that temperature environment that his splitting headache subsided and could be tolerated. Apparently, the cold air froze his aching brains. But driving in the tractor was another story.

The lead Sno-Cat, the erstwhile "Carole," was now dubbed, "Sallie-Jeanne" honoring both Bill's wife and that of Fred, who joined the traverse as an assistant glaciologist. Hectori and Buttons, followed three miles behind as before. The original planned outgoing traverse track had been modified after the catastrophically poor airdrop of the previous month. The track was now oriented downwind of Byrd for the first several travel days so that the remaining errant pallets might possibly be located and their locations radioed back to Byrd. What was not modified was the same mode of travel, three miles at a time of bumping across the ice at an excruciatingly slow pace. For LeSchack, "excruciating" was the operative word here. Each bump made LeSchack feel like his brain was loose and rattling around in his skull.

The only mercy Charlie allowed was that he would drive, something that would be intolerable for LeSchack to do physically with his headache, and that he gave LeSchack the momentary pleasure to leave the tractor at every three-mile stop so that he could carry the magnetometer outside and freeze the pain in his head for the duration of the reading. And from time to time, retch. In normal circumstances, reading the gravimeter from inside the tractor was the preferred travel-day geophysical task on such days as cold as this one was. Fortunately, by the end of this icy cold travel day LeSchack's headache had finally disappeared. He vowed to himself that he would never drink like that again—and he never did.

For the next few days of travel, all eyes were searching the horizon for the wayward airdropped supplies. Several loads were actually found. The traverse party would steer towards them, flag them with international orange, and note their positions for radioing back to Byrd. If there were any indication that a parachute would come to life again causing further movement, the shroud lines would be cut to avoid such resurrection. On one occasion crew members saw the oddest thing on the horizon—a complete Sno-Cat rear axle with transfer case standing on its end in the snow. Painted international orange like the Sno-Cats themselves, it looked strange and forlorn in the middle of an endless field of ice, with an attached parachute, mostly collapsed, waving desultorily in the breeze. Jack had urgently needed that axle to replace a badly worn one on one of the Sno-Cats. The traverse crew simply hoisted the axle up on to one of the sleds, and Jack used it to replace the worn one at his first opportunity.

The first several weeks of the traverse continued to be icy cold and uneventful. LeSchack and Charlie found that the severe cold had a deleterious affect on seismic recording; for whatever reason, the unusually cold ice surface caused excessive acoustic noise that degraded the seismic signals recorded. Eventually, however, things changed. It warmed up, the traverse approached the beautiful Horlick Mountain Range, and visitors and new crew members began showing up with re-supply flights. First to arrive was Bill Chapman, from the U.S. Geological Survey. He was a cartographer, and joined the traverse to map the locations of the mountains that came into view as the traverse passed in front of the Horlick Range. He also relieved Charlie of the task of locating the traverse stations by recording the sunshots himself.

Next to arrive for a visit was Philip Benjamin, a reporter from the New York Times. LeSchack, himself a New Yorker, was impressed that the Times should send one of their reporters to spend a week with the traverse team. It was clear to all traverse members, however, that the urbanite that they sent was ill-prepared for the traverse life style. While LeSchack was delighted to have the urbane visitor to talk to for the period of time that he was there he, as well as the other traverse members, couldn't resist the temptation to dramatize the daily workings of traverse life—like taking a bumpy ride together with reporter Benjamin on a sled filled with explosives.

That event occurred on one of the station days that Charlie wanted to shoot a refraction survey. Since this involved moving progressively further away from camp and the seismic spread, shooting charges all the way, LeSchack determined to do this in the most theatrical way possible. That, of course, was having a Sno-Cat, driven by Jack, tow a sled, called an akio, with a few boxes of Nitramon, a seismic explosive, atop of which LeSchack and Benjamin would ride from one shot point to another. LeSchack, with a straight face, pointed out that this was always the way that task was done! While the ride was wonderfully uncomfortable, there was no chance of a mishap, save falling off the slow-moving sled to the ice surface, perhaps six inches away. Nitramon is an explosive that simply can not be detonated except by another explosion, such as that caused by an electrically fired cap. But the total scene, and the intrepid behavior of that Times correspondent were duly reported in the great newspaper some weeks hence!

Sometime later, after the Times correspondent had departed, a then well-known Swiss photographer, Emil Schulthess, joined the team. He was middle aged and well experienced in the rigors of field expeditions. Before he arrived with the traverse, he had visited and photographed a number of other Navy and IGY activities in the Antarctic. He quickly became a well-regarded member of the traverse for the period during which he stayed. One of his more famous photographs was that of Bill Chapman, standing naked on an empty Nitramon box, taking a makeshift shower in the middle of the night.

It had been observed by the traverse crew that if you could avoid taking a shower for two to three weeks, and learn to live with yourself, you could continue forever that way without bathing. The pain is in living with yourself for the *first two weeks*. Well, Bill Chapman, new to the traverse, couldn't stand himself after two weeks and decided to take a shower while everyone else in the crew—and all filthy dirty—was sound asleep. Because he was shooting the sun at least once every six hours so that he could record the sun's lines of position as it completely circumnavigated the summer sky, there was a period of time at "night" when everyone was sound asleep. That was the time he chose to cleanse himself without risking derision from his colleagues who had, by now, gone well past that two-week cut-off and were quite happy with the way they smelled and felt. So Bill Chapman filled a huge aluminum pot with hot water, the one used for boiling water and making spaghetti, and began his ablutions in privacy. Privacy that is, until Emil had to crawl out of his sleeping bag in his Sno-Cat and go out of doors to relieve himself in the middle of the night.

Because of the way the traverse crew circles the tractors at a work station, there was no possible way for Emil *not to have missed* Bill Chapman ladling hot water over his head. Forgetting his original mission, Emil, with the experience of a veteran press photographer—and like one of the paparazzi—ducked back into his cat, grabbed his Leica, and quickly snapped a few wonderful photographs in blinding color, of the now clean, but highly embarrassed Bill Chapman. The photograph, published in Emil's book, "Antarctica," shows a buck-naked Bill Chapman, standing on an empty explosives box, pouring water all over himself!

You could see the Horlick Mountain Range from miles away. That means at the rate of traverse travel, one could see them from afar for many days before you actually got close to them. The one thing the traverse crew did know about the approach was that they would be assuredly running into crevasse country. Crevasses often form in association with mountains. Both Bill and Fred, driving in the lead Sno-Cat, Sallie-Jeanne, were now constantly scanning the horizon in front of them and carefully watching the chart recorder attached to the electronic crevasse detector. On and on they went, slowly, carefully approaching the mountains, and with no adverse warnings from the crevasse detector.

At one point LeSchack, driving Hectori, the usual three miles behind the lead Sno-Cat, stopped abruptly. It is not difficult to stop short in a Sno-Cat tractor. All you do is take your foot off the gas. At 3 miles per hour there is no coasting. You stop right there! "Bill!' LeSchack exclaimed over the radio, "You've just got to turn Sallie-Jeanne around and come back to where I am. You've gotta see this." Bill radioed back, "But I am already at my 3-mile altimeter reading site." LeSchack exclaimed, "Just leave a flag there, Bill. We'll get it another time. I'm not yet at your last flag. But you've just got to turn around and meet me here."

Bill turned Sallie-Jeanne around and retraced his track to where Hectori and Buttons were now waiting. What they saw was frightening. Sallie-Jeanne had crossed a large crevasse; the weight of the Sno-Cat and its towed sled had broken the snow bridge that had obscured the crevasse, and there was no longer a track across the ice at that point, just a gaping chasm. As luck (and only luck) would have it, the Sno-Cat and sled had crossed at such an angle with respect to the linear-shaped crevasse that the left forward pontoon and the right rear pontoon had both been on solid ice at the same time, while the other two pontoons had been left dangling over empty space when the tractor crossed. Apparently, also the front tip of the left sled runner and the rear tip of the right runner were adequate to keep the sled from falling in. The track pattern on the solid ice unequivocally identified this as what had happened.

Bill and Fred said they had felt nothing unusual when they had crossed; but now they said they felt, "throw-up, and shit-in-your-pants sick," when they saw the chasm they had just run over. Obviously, the Sno-Cat was well-balanced on only the two opposing pontoons for that moment when it broke through the ice. Had the tractor crossed at a slightly different angle it would still, to this day be at the bottom of the crevasse, with its sled, likely on top of it. Talk about the fear of God! And the efficacy of the crevasse detector! Charlie sighed, and sensibly declared that moment to be the end of the travel day. The traverse crew camped, regrouped, and examined and climbed down into the crevasse to inspect it. And Bill dismantled the cumbersome crevasse detector that, for the past year, he had confidently depended upon, and packed it back on his sled, never again to be used.

When the crew finally got underway again, they fell back on that old, low-tech methodology used by mountain climbers and polar explorers of yore for moving safely across crevasse fields; one man, tied to a long rope attached to the lead Sno-Cat, walked ahead of it, poking holes every few steps with a mountain-climber's ice axe. If he were about to step into a crevasse, the pointed end of the ice axe would usually break through the snow bridge hiding the crevasse, thus providing warning of danger below. If a crevasse was revealed, he would motion the tractor to advance in a different direction to avoid falling through. In the worst case, should the lead man accidentally break through a snow bridge and fall into the crevasse, he would not fall far since the rope wrapped around his waist and tied to the Sno-Cat behind him would minimize his fall.

And so the crew moved onward along the front of the Horlick Mountains. They were visually astoundingly beautiful, rising as they did, straight up through the ice; actually, you were really seeing the tops of these mountains. And when the tractors came close enough so that the crew members could walk or ski up to the rock faces of these mountains and touch them, that was like an epiphany. Visualize the city of Denver now covered with a mile-thick layer of snow and ice that begins at the Mississippi River and butts up against the Rocky Mountains. You are driving your tractors across the top of the ice sheet and you know Denver is a mile below you from your seismic soundings. As you travel west, you reach the highest peaks of the Rockies poking through this ice sheet. That's the picture. And the traverse crew had now reached these peaks, the Horlicks, which had risen above the ice sheet.

LeSchack and Bill Long, both of whom were trained as geologists, were awestruck. Using geologist's hammers, the two began gathering rock samples. It was New Year's Day, 1959. As LeSchack was examining his samples, he found some fossils in the sedimentary rock, fossils of shell fish known only to grow in tropical water. An eerie feeling came over him—a bit like he was caught in a time warp. Here he was, freezing his ass in the coldest weather known on earth, and in his mittens he held incontrovertible proof that this was once a tropical sea!

It was good for the crew to travel in and through the mountains. After traveling for so long over essentially flat, seemingly endless ice, unbroken by features larger than sastrugi, it was refreshing to travel amongst these mountains. And so, on they traveled. One day travel, the next day a station day. As they did the previous year, Jack and LeSchack alternated as cooks at the end of travel days while the others got a head start on the glaciological and seismic work that would be continued the following station day. At the end of one such travel day that he had cook duty, LeSchack wrote in his notes:

"With some trepidation, I opened up the door of the tiny

cook shack and peered out into the blinding Antarctic whiteness. I always felt a trifle nervous when I called the boys in for their first meal in twelve hours; they were always starved after a day's travel and I knew there was nothing quite so disappointing at this time than an inadequate meal.

"'Chow down!' I yelled, after my eyes accustomed themselves to the brilliance. For a moment nothing moved. Then Bill Chapman, the navigator, squinting into his theodolite not ten feet away, turned his head slowly. He looked at me rather quizzically, adjusted his woolen cap that was invariably askew, closed his chronometer, and ambled forward.

"Jack was next to appear, emerging from under a Sno-Cat tractor with a huge wrench in his hand. He was indescribably filthy. When looking at Jack after he had been wrestling with one of his cats, the offended eye would trace a path from the tip of his greasy-black field cap, down his grimy face, pausing an instant at the unusual blob of grease hanging from his straggly beard, and then race down his torn, black field pants. Automatically the eye turned to the clear, clean ice in the distance for relief. Jack stroked his beard, came across the grease blob and, straining his beard through his thumb and forefinger, much like clothes through the old Bendix wringer, dislodged the offending lump and tossed it into the snow with a wry smile. He, too, started for the cook shack door.

"Off to the right, two frosty-looking creatures grunted as they pulled themselves out of a deep pit in the ice, gopher-style. Fred, assistant glaciologist, was first to climb out. Tall and somber looking, he had a magnificent ginger beard that sparkled in the sun, the ice crystals in it reflecting the sun like so many sequins. Bill, the chief glaciologist and Jack's older brother, followed Fred out of the pit. He was wearing the usual

perplexed look he reserved for any occasion when he
stroked his thin, rather nondescript beard, which he was
now doing. They both proceeded to shake the
accumulated ice crystals off themselves, the result of
their pit-digging.

"Charlie was the one remaining member of the party not
present and after a brief look around, I spotted him
some thousand feet away at the far end of the seismic
line. I dashed over to the Sno-Cat, hopped in and
sounded the loud air horn. Charlie looked up and
waved acknowledgment.

"As I walked back to the cook shack, I couldn't help but
smile. With the exception of Charlie, who was walking
back now, everyone was already inside waiting for
dinner. For over two months now, six of us would pile
into that tiny cubicle for our meals. And it was tiny.
The cook shack, which we called the wannigan, when
filled with the six of us was crowded. Holy smokes!
"With everybody inside, and the table set, you'd have to
come to attention and do an eyes right in order for
anyone to leave. Needless to say, notwithstanding the
undoubted degree of accuracy attained in the scientific
study of statistics, it was always the man furthest from
the door who, out of biological necessity, had to leave
most frequently."

That night LeSchack remembers was a spaghetti and meat sauce night.
He had made enough for twenty normal men. When the dinner was
over, it was all gone. It is amazing how much one can eat, and not get
fat, when conducting hard physical labor in an extremely cold
environment; your body burns a whole lot of calories!

And on and on the summer went. A day of travel, a day on station. An
R4D re-supply flight every ten days or so, an event that was always
welcome. In addition to fuel and food, it usually brought accumulated
mail. One time it brought a Navy dentist from Little America. It seems

that at some point during the summer Bill Long had bitten on a frozen jellybean, forgetting that this was the Antarctic, and normally soft candies gain a bit more resiliency when frozen, while teeth do not. He split a molar, damage that eventually required the service of a dentist. You didn't know dentists make house calls? Well, Dr. Denton flew 600 miles with a re-supply R4D to extract Bill's broken tooth. Converting Buttons into a dental office, the doctor, with Jack's assistance, performed the operation, and relieved Bill of his agony, but not necessarily of his chagrin.

As February 1959 and the summer were drawing to a close, one of the last R4D re-supply missions brought replacements for LeSchack, Charlie, Jack and Bill. There was enough overlap time so that the veteran crew could impart some of its field wisdom to those who would take over and eventually bring the tractors back to Byrd, well after the last flights of the season had ended. Finally, the veterans hopped aboard the last re-supply flight and returned to Byrd. They left the party they had spent four months with and boarded the R4D at the conclusion of its traverse re-supply. It remained at Byrd long enough to allow them to gather up any belongings left there. And shower.

It was fascinating. None of the old guys were at Byrd to greet the returning traverse personnel. They had long since departed. The new Byrd Station crew unceremoniously showed the four traverse members directly to the showers, holding their noses as they did so. Apparently, upon warming up once inside Byrd Station, the gathering aromas of four months of un-cleanliness, heretofore frozen into submission, burst forth in olfactory hideousness! When LeSchack stripped off his polar gear down to the skivvy level, he found that his chest hairs had grown through the weave of his T-shirt. This was horrible, he thought. What pain in removing a T-shirt with ingrown hairs—like tearing off a plaster bandage from his hairy body. No, not so. The T-shirt had become so rotten after remaining on him, unchanged and unwashed, that with a slight tug, it merely disintegrated around him!

Cleansed and refreshed, the four traverse veterans boarded the now refueled R4D and took off for Little America, where the ship, the USS WYANDOTTE, AKA 92, was moored at the Barrier. That ship would take them back to Christchurch, New Zealand. After fourteen continuous months on the Antarctic continent, in just a matter of hours they found themselves aboard a ship that, hardly had they boarded, singled up its lines from the edge of the Ross Shelf, and was underway, plowing north through the ice-infested Ross Sea.

An AKA is the Navy designation for a cargo ship. It is a large ship. LeSchack and his gang were just a few of the many bodies that the AKA brought back to New Zealand from the Antarctic. They were assigned bunks below decks in a huge dormitory compartment. There were row upon row of bunks, stacked four high. Nothing elegant about this at all. But for LeSchack, this was the real Navy. He had a week aboard with nothing to do except eat in the mess, go up on deck and watch the ice floes drift past, and think about what was next in his life. And talk Jack out of abandoning ship!

LeSchack knew that Jack was a sleepwalker. It seemed like this was simply part of his experience growing up. Along with the many silly stories they told one another during the endless hours driving Hectori, he had learned of Jack's childhood propensity toward sleepwalking. It seemed to LeSchack that it would be brought on by some stressful experience that occurred to Jack earlier in the day. For example, during the past winter Dr. Ruseski trained the traverse crew in being able to give injections (morphine, saline IV's), should such be needed, after an accident on traverse. The entire concept of needles and injections was extremely unsettling to Jack. That night in their room at Byrd, Jack jumped out of his upper bunk and began wandering about the room, eyes closed, mumbling about injections and IV's. LeSchack awakened him and told him to return to his sack. Aboard the WYANDOTTE, LeSchack awoke one night to the spectacle of Jack running up and down the narrow aisles between the bunks mumbling loudly that "we should all abandon ship! The ship is sinking!" LeSchack, who had a top bunk, was able to reach down and catch Jack on the chest as he ran up the aisle past his bunk, eyes closed, with his warning of an imminent watery doom. "Jack, you're sleepwalking again! It's okay, the ship is fine; it is not sinking," LeSchack reassured Jack, who was now awakened from his sleepwalking state. Jack, a bit chastened, returned to his sack.

During the past winter, LeSchack had figured that joining the military would likely his next step in life after leaving the Antarctic, owing to the persistence of his Draft Board. To this end, he told Dr. Ruseski, and a few of the chiefs at Byrd, as well as Captain E.H.(Pat) Maher, who had been Commander, U.S. Naval Units, Antarctica, that it was his intention of applying for a commission in the Navy upon his return to the United States. He requested that these gentlemen, who all knew him, would consider writing letters of recommendation for him, should the Navy Department eventually request such references. Spending a week on the WYANDOTTE, although much of it spent in his bunk was, in LeSchack's mind, a bit more mental preparation for that next step.

Within only a few days of sailing north, the cold weather began to fade and the ice floes disappeared from the sea surface. Within a few more days the WYANDOTTE was docking in the Port of Lyttelton, Christchurch's harbor. It was understood by the IGY personnel aboard the WYANDOTTE that the IGY office in Christchurch had arranged for the first available military air transportation back to the U.S. for its people. In this case, it seemed like first available air transportation meant within the next day or two, and this was being confirmed on the ship's quarterdeck by Eddy Goodale, the senior IGY representative in Christchurch. He was talking with each of the debarking civilians and confirming their return reservations to the United States.

When LeSchack met Goodale on the quarterdeck, he specifically stated that he would prefer to return home on a U. S. Navy ship if such arrangements could be made. LeSchack indicated that as opposed to the other IGY personnel, he was in no rush to return—no girlfriend or wife was waiting for him, only his Draft Board. Eddy, a senior and fatherly civil servant who LeSchack had known before, simply observed that, "I will see whether there is a Navy ship soon to depart for the U.S., and whether, in fact, the Navy would agree to allow you aboard. Nobody has asked me before to do this," he observed. "I'll find out for you. Where can I reach you?" LeSchack gave Eddy the phone number for Isaac's home in Christchurch, the place that he had stayed just prior to embarking for the Antarctic over a year earlier. LeSchack thanked Eddy Goodale in advance, and with all his Antarctic gear, staggered down the gangplank to make contact with Isaac.

Within the next few days Goodale made contact with LeSchack. He would be allowed to ride home on the USS ARNEB, AKA56. He would have to board that ship in Sydney, Australia six weeks from then, and pay all his expenses to get himself there. Eddy had implied then, "That was an unusual request from an IGY person, but the Navy agreed." It was only some forty years later that LeSchack, now a retired Navy captain, began to consider that maybe Captain Maher might have intervened on LeSchack's request. Maher, then Commander US Naval Support Activity, Antarctica, a man who LeSchack had known on the ice, and who knew LeSchack was planning to go for a commission in the Navy after returning home, would likely have seen Eddy Goodale's request cross his desk. And likely approved it. The kind of thing LeSchack would do years later as a senior Navy officer for people he was mentoring. But in 1959 LeSchack, now 24, knew nothing about mentoring and just put it down to "good fortune."

LeSchack would spend three weeks in New Zealand and the next three weeks in Australia before boarding the ARNEB. He visited a few days with Isaac first. LeSchack had left his temperate climate clothes at Isaac's home, rather than have more things to lug around Antarctica. He found that in the intervening months Isaac and Jade had broken up, leaving the children with Isaac. He then traveled some more on the South Island with IGY colleagues who had opted to travel on their own expense and remain in the South Pacific, rather than use pre-paid government transportation but have to go home immediately.

It was the end of the austral summer and LeSchack enjoyed visiting places on the South Island that he had not previously seen with Dick Crone. Later, he took the ferry to the North Island and visited Wellington and then Gisborne, where he stayed a few days to visit with Crone. He then flew to Rotorua on a single-engine private plane arranged by Dick. The cargo hold of the plane was filled with fresh strawberries destined for an ice cream manufacturer in a small town near Rotorua. LeSchack was fascinated by the communication system the pilot used for the delivery of the strawberries. When he reached the town to which they were to be delivered, the pilot buzzed the town and then circled a few times until he saw a taxi that recognized the pilot's pre-arranged signal head from the small town out to the airstrip. The pilot then landed, off-loaded the strawberries and immediately took off again. LeSchack disembarked shortly thereafter at Rotorua, the world-famous geothermal and geysers region of the North Island. LeSchack, the geologist, was fascinated with the whole concept of superheated underground rock that provided the energy for the spectacular geyser displays.

In fact, after 14 months of isolation, LeSchack seemed fascinated with *everything*, the foreign surroundings, including the geography, the history, and after living so long in an all-male society, most certainly the women. The truth is though that LeSchack was experiencing a renaissance, literally, a rebirth, a re-evaluation of himself and the world around him. For the first time in his life he had time enough and money to leisurely wander about a part of the world that had always fascinated him, and in an un-pressured environment where he could begin to think in more worldly terms.

He continued on to Auckland where he visited museums, ate in quiet, pleasant restaurants, and then flew on to Sydney, Australia, where he would have three more weeks to wander before boarding the ARNEB. He spent a week in Sydney, during which time he began to get some sense of that city. For a bit of adventure he hitchhiked from Sydney to Brisbane. It was on that trip, thumbing his way north into Queensland, that LeSchack first got any real sense of what the U.S. Navy had done at the Battle of the Coral Sea in 1942, just 17 years earlier. The northeast coast of Queensland is bordered by the Coral Sea. James Michener, in his Pulitzer Prize-winning book, "Tales of the South Pacific" began his chapter on the Coral Sea:

> I am always astonished when an American says, "The Coral Sea" Where is that? I never heard of the Coral Sea." Believe me, Australians and New Zealanders know all about it. The battle we fought there will be in their history books for some time to come.

Well, the middle-aged Australian men—traveling salesmen, truck drivers and other motorists—that picked LeSchack up on the highway into Queensland from Sydney certainly knew about it. And they had every reason to believe that the young man they had just picked up, clearly from his accent, a Yank, *was a sailor*. For after returning from the

Antarctic, LeSchack typically wore the best, most comfortable clothes he had with him. These were the Navy khaki trousers and blouses that were issued to the IGY people, along with their heavy Antarctic gear. While these clothes bore no insignia or rank, they were clearly military issue; the fact that LeSchack mentioned that he shortly would need to meet his ship at Garden Island, the Royal Australian Navy mooring in Sydney Harbor, clinched that minor deception, one that he did not disabuse them of. LeSchack happily let them believe that he was a U.S. Navy man, for in his own mind, he would soon truly be a U.S. Navy officer. Of this, he now had no doubt.

Whoever these Australian men thought LeSchack was, they all treated him with a special kindness. They were buying him drinks, treating him to dinner, taking him home for the family to meet, and helping him get rides along his way, simply because 17 years earlier the U.S. Navy, in a colossal battle, turned from their shores a most certain invasion, an invasion the Imperial Japanese forces made no secret about intending to conduct. He was deeply touched, and he never forgot those kindnesses. LeSchack stopped at the beaches along the Gold Coast, Surfers Paradise and Coolangatta, both tiny towns then, and went swimming in warm subtropical waters and walked the beaches at night. He went night clubbing in Brisbane and pub-crawling back in Sydney. As he began to rejoin polite society again, he met, and had long conversations with fascinating women; an exotic-looking woman who was half Aboriginal-half Italian, and a gorgeous brunette who emigrated to Australia after surviving the London Blitz. And a woman named Primrose in Kings Cross, Sydney.

By now, LeSchack's mind was adjusting to a return to civilization; his young hormones too, were beginning to remind him of a fourteen-month deprivation of their satisfactory expression. Primrose solved that. She was the first woman LeSchack had made love to in fourteen months. Never before in his life, nor afterwards, did his body respond to a complaisant woman in just such a manner as it did with Primrose. As he embraced and entered this willing woman, he sighed deeply and gently fondled her. And eventually he exploded violently in relief. They smiled at each other and whispered to one another. However, to their astonishment, instead of disentangling and languidly sliding out owing to detumescence, he continued to remain ram-rod hard inside of her. He continued to massage gently her warm, pliant breasts while embracing her, and they continued to talk. And then, most surprising to both of them, within just a few minutes, his whole body involuntarily stiffened and, with renewed undulatory vigor, he suddenly exploded again inside of her, even more powerfully than he had the first time. Now out of breath and just beginning to soften, they remained entwined thus for a long time, whispering and fondling, finally drifting off into slumber, deliciously entwined.

It's not clear what Primrose thought of this voluptuous circumstance; LeSchack thought that he should not again go without luscious lovemaking for fourteen months at a time.

A few days later, orders in hand, LeSchack climbed the gangway and crossed the quarterdeck of the USS ARNEB, moored at Garden Island. He showed his orders to the Officer of the Deck and was shown his stateroom. And this was indeed a stateroom! It was Admiral Dufek's when he was aboard. As opposed to the hordes aboard the WYANDOTTE, LeSchack and two other men were the only IGY personnel to return home on the ARNEB. One, Mario Giovinetti, an Argentine glaciologist, was returning this way because the ARNEB was planning a port call in Valparaiso, Chile, a point at which the Argentine would debark and board a train across the Andes to return to Buenos Aires, the least expensive way for the U.S. Government to get him home. The other man, Hugo Neuburg, another glaciologist, shared with LeSchack the Admiral's cabin, for there were two bunks in it.

Did Hugo merely request passage as LeSchack had, and had no other IGY people so requested? Or had a number of other IGY people requested passage and were turned down, and the stateroom made available for LeSchack only at Captain Maher's request, and the one other bunk given to Hugo, simply known to be one of LeSchack's colleagues? LeSchack wondered. But he chose to think that this was Captain Maher's way of mentoring. If so, it surely worked. He thought that Captain Maher would have been proud, were he to be ultimately made aware of LeSchack's naval career, thirty years later. LeSchack's experience on the nearly month-long passage back to Newport, Rhode Island, with a port call in Chile, and a passage through the Panama

Canal, was a most important introduction to the naval career he was intending to embark upon once he returned to the U.S.

A day later, the USS ARNEB singled up it lines and, with three powerful and mournful blasts of its whistle, backed away from Garden Island and into what may be the best natural harbor in the world, Sydney Harbor. And then set course out to sea.

LeSchack's voyage home aboard the ARNEB was, in retrospect, another seminal event in his life. It was a month long. He had nothing to do aboard ship but think and assimilate all his life experiences into a whole story, and begin to plan for the future. Few people have the luxury to do this during their lives, and fewer still in an environment so conducive for thinking and planning for the future. The voyage across the South Pacific was calm and uneventful. He often went out on the prow and simply watched the ship cut through the sea. During the daytime, he could look down and watch the bow wave and the flying fish that jumped before it. At night, that bow wave was all brilliantly phosphorescent. And when he tired of watching the sea, he would look up at the sky and watch the Southern Cross, and all the other stars.

He ate in the officer's mess, the wardroom. There were a number of junior officers there that were about LeSchack's age, and he got to know them. They would have graduated from the Naval Academy a few years earlier, and this would be there first tour at sea. He peripherally got to know the Executive Officer—XO—a lieutenant commander, who was president of the wardroom mess, and the captain of the ship, a Navy captain, who traditionally, ate alone in his own cabin. LeSchack got to know them only because he had purchased in a Melbourne book store a marvelous historical book about the sea that these two officers both wished to read. The book was a limited edition: Bligh's Narrative of the Mutiny On Board H.M. Ship Bounty, and the Minutes of the Court Martial. When LeSchack casually mentioned to the captain and the XO that he had such a book, they both expressed interest in borrowing it so that they could read it during the voyage. And they later had a chance to discuss it together. But mostly, because of their common experiences in Antarctica, which the Navy men did not share, LeSchack spoke only with his two IGY colleagues. And this was not at all a surprise to him. Even then, LeSchack knew that bonding amongst men was based upon intense and shared experiences—such as occurred to them in the Antarctic.

After cruising for two weeks, the ARNEB anchored at the port of Valparaiso, Chile. The ship would remain in the harbor for a week, refueling and re-provisioning, and providing liberty for the ship's company. LeSchack and Hugo took advantage of the ship's stay at Valparaiso to go adventuring ashore for several days. They arranged a train trip from Valparaiso, through Santiago and across the Andes to Las Cuevas, the first village in Argentina through which a cross-continent rail line passed. There the two disembarked, purchased some groceries, and began a hike back to Chile over the Uspallata Pass. LeSchack could hardly remember a hiking trip as glorious as this one. It was a bright, clear, cool autumn day. LeSchack and Hugo followed a narrow, graded road that wended its way back and forth up the mountainside. Occasionally a vehicle passed them on the way up, but mostly they were all alone enjoying the spectacular scenery of the Andes.

Eventually the two reached the summit, some 12,500 feet high. From there they could see Mount Aconcagua in the distance. The summit was the dividing line between Argentina and Chile, and directly straddling the border was the "Christ of the Andes" statue commemorating the 1902 peaceful settlement of a border dispute between the two countries. Next to the statue was an Argentine meteorological station, which also sold souvenirs and was open to the public. LeSchack and Hugo went into the station and to their surprise, found that the meteorologist-in-charge had spent the previous year at one of the Argentine Antarctic stations. With that unusual experience in common, the three began fascinating conversations, LeSchack and Hugo using high school Spanish and the Argentine using the best English he could muster. It was fun, instructive and hilarious.

LeSchack's and Hugo's original plan was continue the hike and descend from the summit to Portillo, Chile, the ski resort on the other side where they would catch a train back to Valparaiso. To have accomplished this, and reach Portillo before nightfall, they would have to keep hiking and not dally. But as our three Antarctic heroes found more and more in common, it became clear that LeSchack and Hugo could not possibly reach Portillo while it was still light—and hiking on a desolate mountain road at night is not pleasurable. Nor is it safe. LeSchack expressed his concern to the Argentine. *"No hay problema, señor.* You will stay with us for the night."

With that settled, the Argentine announced they would have a party to honor the gringos from Antarctica, and they invited their Chilean meteorological colleagues, who manned the Chilean weather station, perhaps 300 yards across the border, to come join them. The Chilenos brought the wine, and the Argentines supplied the steaks. It was a wonderful party for LeSchack and Hugo. They partied most of the night, and late the following morning they made their goodbyes and began the hike down the Chilean side of the Andes. Again, it was a beautiful day for hiking. They boarded a train after they reached Portillo, and returned to Valparaiso. It was an exquisite adventure for LeSchack; but most importantly, it made him realize the value of learning languages other than his native English. And high school Spanish was not enough.

Soon enough, the ARNEB weighed anchor and cruised north until about a week later, it reached Panamá. The ship docked at Rodman, at the U.S. Naval Station Panama Canal, and a few days later transited the Canal. A week later the ship arrived at Newport, Rhode Island, where LeSchack debarked. Although he left for home in New York City within hours of debarking, he expected he would soon be returning in a more official capacity.

The voyage home on the ARNEB was valuable for LeSchack in a number of ways. It gave him an opportunity, in an unhurried atmosphere, to digest and assimilate all that he learned and all that happened to him over what were to be the eighteen months that changed the course of his life. In that same unhurried and benign atmosphere, he was able to learn much about the seagoing Navy that midshipmen must learn in a highly stressful atmosphere. Not only about the routine of Navy life, but about the arcane and sometimes incomprehensible way that the Navy does things. This knowledge was to be enormously valuable during the upcoming months when he was accepted into the Navy's Officer Candidate School at Newport. And lastly, as a result of all this travel, he recognized the need to understand more world geography and history, and that his knowledge of the English language alone was not sufficient.

He knew he had to improve his Spanish, and learn at least another language after that. French? Russian? All he knew is he had to begin.

There is an epilogue to this story. Let us begin with the full quote with which we commenced this chapter. It was from L.C. Lawyer, Charles C. Bates and Robert B. Rice, authors of "Geophysics in the Affairs of Mankind," published by the Society of Exploration Geophysicists, in their chapter on geophysics in the 1950s and the International Geophysical Year:

> "The biggest impact of the IGY on mankind was not new scientific discovery, but rather the start of the 'space race.' Once the tiny beep of Sputnik-I, the initial Soviet IGY satellite, was heard circling the world on 4 October 1957, President Eisenhower had the delicate task of assuring his nervous nation that a Soviet 'basketball' in orbit was nothing to be alarmed about. But when the Navy's rocket failed to get the IGY Vanguard satellite into orbit and the Russians launched an even larger IGY satellite with the dog, Laika, on board, news commentators did not treat the situation lightly. To dampen this concern, Eisenhower appointed Dr. James R. Killian, the president of MIT, as his Special Assistant for Science and Technology on 7 November 1957. However, it eventually took some $40 billion before America could counterbalance the lost lead in satellite technology by finally landing a man on the moon (20 July 1969) and by flying the first space shuttle, Columbia, capable of repeatedly orbiting the earth and then making a wheels-down landing (April, 1981)"

Although the Iron Curtain descended across Europe in 1946, the Cold War itself approached its most frightening to the United States beginning in 1957 with the launching of Sputnik, and culminating in the Cuban Missile Crisis just five years later. That was the period during which time LeSchack came of age, not only as a man, as an explorer, and as a scientist, but also as a Cold Warrior. In addition to the funds provided for advancing space technology, there was a massive increase of funding for basic and applied research in many other areas deemed by government to be necessary now "to catch up with the Soviets." Both as a private businessman-scientist, and as an active duty naval officer, many of LeSchack's research projects and adventures would be sponsored, approved and funded as a result of these public monies now unleashed and lavishly being doled out from 1957 on to the late 1970s.

From this point on until 1990 when the Cold War ended, LeSchack's life, research, adventures, and his perception of the world would be governed by an event lasting nearly fifty years, an episode of world history that most of the world's people have never heard of, or they have long since forgotten. Nonetheless, it was likely that during this period, the world would come as close as it ever will to the onset of total holocaust, with officials from both sides having their fingers on the nuclear button. That was the time period LeSchack had now entered. And IGY, the International Geophysical Year, was his introduction to that way of life.

LeSchack setting off seismic blast, 1958

1957 Byrd Traverse, Mt Johns, Antarctica, 1957

LeSchack surveying, Byrd Station,Antarctica, 1957

Voluptous Pamela, New Zealand, 1957

The last few months of 1957 were momentous for both LeSchack and the Free World. During that time LeSchack began the adventures he had long sought (both scientific, and with complaisant women) by joining the U.S. Antarctic Expedition's over-ice traverse program during the International Geophysical Year (IGY). To show its scientific prowess during the IGY, the USSR successfully launched Sputnik 1 and then Sputnik 2, the first ever rocket-launched space vehicles. This mightily frightened the U.S.Government, and began the true Cold War.

Chapter 3

The U.S. Antarctic Expedition was mounted from New Zealand, where LeSchack spent six weeks waiting, not impatiently, to begin his Antarctic tour. This lack of impatience was due to dalliance with the voluptuous Pamela, followed by a similar dalliance with the equally voluptuous Maisie, both of whom made him forget his longing for his first lover, Giselle. Antarctica hooked him on a life of physical and scientific adventures; Pamela and Maisie hooked him on the pleasures of making love with voluptuous women. Both kind of adventures were physically and emotionally satisfying for him! And remained so for the rest of his life.

The U. S. Navy and the Cold, Cold War Years-Officer Candidate School

"It is by no means enough that an officer of the Navy should be a capable mariner. He must be that, of course, but also a good deal more. He should be, as well a gentleman of liberal education, refined manner, punctilious courtesy and the nicest sense of personal honor. He should not only be able to express himself clearly and with force in his own language both with tongue and pen, but he should be versed in French and Spanish. He should be the soul of tact, patience, justice, firmness and charity. No meritorious act of a subordinate should escape his attention or to be left to pass without its reward, if even the reward be only one word of approval. Conversely, he should not be blind to a single fault in any subordinate, though at the same time he should be quick and unfailing to distinguish error from malice, thoughtlessness from incompetency, and well-meant shortcoming from heedless or stupid blunder. As he should be universal and impartial in his rewards and approval of merit so should he be judicial and unbending in his punishment or reproof of misconduct."

Code of a Naval Officer — John Paul Jones

With the IGY over, Len LeSchack planned that his next adventure would be enlisting in the Navy, and quickly becoming a commissioned officer. And an extraordinary adventure it would turn out to be, forever changing the course of his life. In those days, there were three main ways of obtaining a commission in the U.S. Navy: The Naval Academy at Annapolis, the Navy's Reserve Officers Training Corps administered as a four-year series of elective Navy courses at a variety of universities, and the Navy's Officer Candidate School at Newport Rhode Island, a four-month training program. At this point in LeSchack's life, the latter was the only option. LeSchack knew this as he disembarked at Newport from his month-long cruise aboard the USS ARNEB. Therefore, he expected to be returning here soon, if he could beat his Draft Board to the draw!

He returned to a warm welcome at his parent's apartment in New York City, and announced his plans. This was not a surprise for his father, an attorney in the City, for he had been keeping track of mail to LeSchack from his increasingly, and annoyingly persistent Draft Board. Within a few days of arriving, LeSchack took, what year by year became, in his mind, an increasingly unpleasant, noisy, crowd-packed journey on the dirty, graffiti-festooned subway, to the Navy Recruiting Office in downtown Manhattan. There he obtained all the papers and application forms needed. And he began to fill them out. In those days, one could apply directly to Officer Candidate School (OCS), if you had a college degree in almost anything, could pass the physical exam, as well as pass a variety of intelligence tests. LeSchack met all those qualifications. Finally, he had an interview with the CO of the recruiting station, a lieutenant commander. Having, during the past eighteen months on his Antarctic adventure, met an admiral—Rear Admiral George Dufek, USN—spoken with captains and flown regularly with lieutenant commanders, LeSchack was not in awe of military officers and was quite at ease during his interview.

"I see you've spent fourteen months during Operation Deep Freeze in the Antarctic with the Navy, the interviewing officer observed. You are a true adventurer, LeSchack. The Navy doesn't get many of those these days." The officer, a World War II veteran, seemed to be harkening back to the previous century and the early part of the Twentieth Century when classical explorers often *were* naval officers. Now, he seemed to be implying, young men only seem to join the Navy to avoid being drafted into the Army. "Now," the recruiting officer stated, "we send these completed forms to the Bureau of Naval Personnel in Washington. It will take three months before you know whether you will be accepted." LeSchack didn't have that long.

LeSchack's Draft Board, located in Jamaica, New York, was known by the young men in that community to be insensitive, bureaucratic, irascible and vindictive in the extreme. It appeared less concerned with the good of the Nation, than of fulfilling its monthly quota of bodies. Shortly after he submitted his application for OCS, LeSchack received an ominous postcard from that Draft Board: "If you have legitimate reason *for not being drafted,* tell us now—otherwise you will soon receive your official draft notice." LeSchack anticipated this, and while at the Navy Recruiting Office, had requested a letter stating that his application for Navy OCS had been forwarded to Washington for approval. LeSchack's reasoning had been that such a letter on U. S. Navy Recruiting Station letterhead would clearly indicate his intention to serve on active military duty with the Navy, and that he was in no way attempting to avoid serving his country.

In response to the Draft Board, he immediately visited his Board to show them the Navy's letter. The letter read,

> *"Mr. LeSchack instituted processing for appointment to a program leading to commissioned grade in the Naval Service on 4 May 1959. At least 90 days will be needed to process his application. Since he possesses unusual experience which we feel will be of value to the Navy, any consideration which may be given to him to allow processing will be appreciated."*

LeSchack thought that would be a "legitimate enough reason" for his Draft Board to delay the final draft notice. To his dismay, it then became clear that from this Draft Board's point of view, their job was simply a numbers game—it had nothing to do with serving the best interests of the country! LeSchack was just another number, a number that had successfully remained beyond its reach for far too long!

"This letter means nothing to us," stated the rotund and thoroughly unpleasant middle-aged man, a non-salaried volunteer, who LeSchack spoke with at the Draft Board office. In those days, it should be pointed out, draft boards had some paid federal civil service clerks for administration but, at that Board, at least, it was non-paid old curmudgeons from the community who determined the fate of its young men coming before the Board. "And LeSchack, what does the Navy mean by referring to you as "*Mr.* LeSchack in this letter?"

What an odd question, thought LeSchack. "The man appears to be affronted by the commonly accepted form of letter-writing courtesy, likely preferring reference being made to the potential draftee by his last name only." Instead, he replied looking at the man coldly, "Mister," is the form of address applied to junior officers in the United States Navy, and as you can plainly see from the letter, the people who wrote it expect me soon to become one!" "Well," replied the Draft Board adjudicator, equally coldly, "this letter won't stop us from sending out your Final Notice within the next few days. "It's the Army for you, son!" "Misguided, overstuffed old fart," thought LeSchack, as he stomped out of that office.

LeSchack returned home and told his father of the day's proceedings. His father, who was too young for World War I and too old for World War II, had none of the sense of the military experience. Nonetheless, he did understand that the trauma of World War II and its aftermath, and the harrowing experiences in Germany related by LeSchack's Uncle Walter and Aunt Alice, and how they ultimately escaped in 1938, were the root of his personal and patriotic need to serve. Also, his father had frequently observed that if *one were going to serve*, the Navy was the service in which to do it. Something about clean sheets to sleep on aboard ship, and decent food. He said, "Well, let's talk with my friend, Harry. He is a member of a draft board in Manhattan. Perhaps he can offer you some advice." Harry was a businessman of the same age as his dad, and LeSchack knew and had, as a child, played with Harry's children. A meeting was soon arranged, and LeSchack showed Harry the Navy Recruiting Office's letter. It was clear then to LeSchack that Harry had often been approached by sons of other friends who were looking for a way to *avoid* serving in the armed forces. But when Harry saw LeSchack's letter, he recognized that this was an entirely different situation; LeSchack was a man who wanted to serve, but in the military service of his choice. With that in mind, Harry was willing to use bureaucratic chicanery, the positive results of which became a lesson that LeSchack was quick to learn and remember throughout his career. "Len," Harry announced, "Our only legal recourse is to request an official review of your Selective Service Classification of 1-A. That was the designation given to men physically and mentally fit for service. "You are legally able to request such a review. It will take six weeks or so for that adjudication. You will buy time. But, of course, when they finally get around to you, they will, with rightful irritation, observe that you were properly classified all along. Get the Navy to act quickly, my boy!" Harry then showed LeSchack the words to use on an official request for a review. He thanked Harry profusely.

Having taken Harry's advice, LeSchack expected that he would have at least six weeks during which nothing of consequence would happen. So he visited old girlfriends and old haunts in the New York City that he grew up with. He noted that both had changed. But then he reflected, he too must have changed, perhaps more than anyone or anything else as a result of his intense experiences of the last eighteen months. It was now the summer of 1959. Eisenhower was president. And the U.S. Government was nervously watching the continuance of the Chinese civil war, particularly the shelling of the islands of Quemoy and Matsu between the mainland and the U.S. client, Taiwan. LeSchack and his younger brother, Peter, decided this would be just the time then to get away from it all and go camping for a few weeks. This would, of course, be the time events would move swiftly to their denouement—without LeSchack! Everything considered, however, this all turned out for the best.

It seems, according to LeSchack's dad, that during this period, the final draft notice warning did show up in the family mailbox, for as Harry predicted, there would be no reason to re-evaluate LeSchack's Selective Service designation. Fortunately, his dad opened it and, fortunately too, his law office was just a few blocks away, on Broadway, from the downtown Navy Recruiting Office. It was a quick walk for him, so he took time from his busy schedule to do so. Upon entering the Recruiting Office, he saw a bunch of sailors, mostly yeomen, at their respective desks, or just wandering about. Scanning this group, and with a voice that only trial lawyers have, he requested to see the chief of this office. LeSchack's dad, of course, wouldn't have known that a "chief" in the Navy is a senior non-commissioned officer, but not the chief or CEO of that outfit. One look at the Navy chief that soon appeared, and LeSchack's dad recognized that there must be a more senior man with whom he wished to speak. With the insistence and "command presence" with which he went before judges of the City of New York, he got to see the same lieutenant commander that had interviewed LeSchack a few months earlier.

Again, according to his dad, he stuck the advice of an imminent draft notice under the recruiting officer's nose. "My son, for I know not what

127

reason, wishes to join the Navy. He tells me he has fulfilled all the requirements for enrollment in your Officers Candidate School and that his paperwork has been in Washington for some time now. If you want this man, you need to enlist him now!" The recruiting officer looked at the card from the Draft Board and recognized LeSchack's name. He also recognized that, to the lawyer standing before him, "now" meant now! "Sir," the recruiting officer asked, "is your son the man who spent over a year in the Antarctic with the Navy on Operation Deepfreeze?" "Why yes," LeSchack's father said, "That would be he. And I'm not sure why he did that either!"

With that, the recruiting officer picked up the phone and called the Bureau in Washington and, using what LeSchack would eventually discover to be one of the most efficient networking systems in the entire world, asked to speak with a classmate of his at the Bureau of Personnel. According to LeSchack's dad, the conversation between the two naval officers was brief. "Lieutenant Commander Johnson, please........Hey Skinny, it's Jim...346 Broadway. I need a favor. OCS application for Leonard A. LeSchack...4 May 1959...I need to enlist him now or lose him. Can you speed it up? Yeah, I'll wait...... It's done? Tomorrow? Wonderful! Yes, okay, and thanks, Skinny. I owe you one," and the recruiting officer hung up. "Mr. LeSchack, your son's just been approved. I have the authority to enlist him tomorrow morning. Get him here."

Fortunately, LeSchack who was still camping with his brother chose to call home that evening. His father relayed to LeSchack the proceedings at the Recruiting Office, and recommended that he waste no time in returning home for your "Draft Board is hard on your heels, young man!" Driving all night to get home, LeSchack showed up the next morning at the Navy Recruiting Office for the formal enlistment and pledge to "defend the Constitution of the United States of America against all enemies, foreign or domestic....." The recruiting officer told LeSchack that he would begin his officer candidate training the following month—July 1959—in Class 45 at Newport.

With his official Navy enlistment papers in hand, it was with some glee that LeSchack phoned his Draft Board from the Navy Recruiting Office.

The voice on the other end was not so pleased. "Prove to us that you are legally enlisted in the Navy," the unhappy voice at the other end said. "I can mail you a copy today," said LeSchack blithely. "That won't do. Your draft notice is due to go out tomorrow. Bring your enlistment papers to me by close of business today, or your notice *will go out* tomorrow."

Now it was LeSchack's turn to be displeased. In 1959, before the general availability of fax machines, LeSchack knew he would have get on, once again the dirty, depressing New York City subway system which increasingly he disliked doing, and hand-carry his enlistment papers to an office at the other end of the City to satisfy some low-level bureaucrat. But now, physically and emotionally exhausted, he did just that. LeSchack knew that even though the Navy had beaten the Army—by less than 24 hours—he didn't wish to be a pawn in a pissing match between those two agencies, as to which had legal rights to LeSchack. However, at the end of the day, he smiled to himself; LeSchack, now 24, had distinguished himself by eluding his Draft Board since he was 18— six straight years of legally outfoxing a system that, at least, thought LeSchack, as far as that Board was concerned, had dishonored its mandated purpose!

In due course LeSchack received a set of orders to Newport. On the day in July set forth in his orders for reporting, he took the train from Grand Central Station and arrived in Newport, Rhode Island a few hours later. He already knew the School's procedure: sections of about 30 men apiece would be formed for some thousand men descending on the base during the proscribed arrival day. Once the men set foot within the base, they were immediately gathered by active duty sailors into individual sections, on a first come, first serve basis, until each section was filled. Then the entire section was marched off to its assigned barracks. Each section would, in fact be a "class," marching to lectures, study halls, mess halls, parade field... marching together to all prescribed activities.

LeSchack knew that there was no way of learning before hand anything about his potential section mates with whom he would spend the next four months of intense togetherness. That information was unavailable to anyone, including the OCS itself. It all depended on when, during the entrance day, the men showed up at the base. LeSchack decided to devise his own scheme for determining, as best as possible, the make up of his section mates so that he could be a member of a congenial crew.

From his college days, and from his IGY experiences where many men were involved, he felt men fell in to three general categories: the "grinds" as they were called in engineering school, the middle-of-the-roaders, or "B" students who were less "intense," but still bright and more amiable, and finally the laggards and fuck-offs. LeSchack reasoned that the grinds would show up first to form the early sections, the " B" students would arrive around noontime and the laggards would show up as close to the end of the day as possible. Although LeSchack arrived outside the base mid-morning, he dawdled outside the gate until a bit after noon before physically walking on to the base. At which point he was immediately grabbed to become a member of Section K-4, in KILO Company, the company he anticipated would be the "B" group, and he began marching. To this day, LeSchack thinks that was the correct decision for him to have made. The "sword-winner" for Class 45 came from Section K-4, and history shows that three members of K-4, LeSchack and two others, made captain.

It is the intent of the officer candidate schools for all the military services to place their candidates under the maximum pressure possible during their training. The clear purpose of this was to see as early as possible how the men would perform their military tasks under the pressures of combat or other highly stressful conditions. As opposed to the Marine Corps Officer Candidate School, that deliberately places their recruits under intense physical pressure and the well-known tutelage of hardened and crusty drill instructors, the Navy puts its officer candidates under intense *academic* pressure. And the Navy system seems to work for the Navy—at least ten percent who would likely crumple under the pressures of stressful situations aboard ship did, in fact, flunk out of OCS.

Most officer candidates, like LeSchack, entered the Navy officially with the rate, "Officer Candidate Seaman Apprentice," or OCSA. A small percentage of LeSchack's classmates, however, came directly from the Fleet. They were highly qualified and motivated sailors who had been specially selected from the ranks after having served a number of years on active duty. In practice, an OCSA wore a sailor's uniform with two slashes signifying he was a "seaman apprentice," an enlisted sailor, but he also wore a small "OC" patch on his shoulder. Only another officer candidate knew what the OC signified—and, of course the young girls in Newport searching for husbands who likely would soon become naval officers. The SA part meant you were the lowliest sailor in the United States Navy, and you would remain in that status for essentially your entire enlistment if you flunked out of OCS and were obliged to join the Fleet.

There were two parts to the Navy curriculum: military training and academics. The military training was basically a boot camp; marching, formations, inspections, standing forever on the parade ground—all things to make one feel like he was really in the military service. For LeSchack the academics felt much the same as they did back at engineering school. The courses were engineering, navigation, operations, orientation (to make one think and behave like a naval officer), seamanship and weapons. Frankly, this program was little different from the Navy V-7 program that Willie Keith of "Caine Mutiny" fame entered 16 years earlier. The only difference appeared to be that Willie Keith's Officers Candidate School was located at Columbia University in New York City, and Willie lived comfortably in a dorm room, three men to a room. LeSchack lived cheek-by-jowl with sixty other men in a barrack, one of many at the school in Newport. An excellent description of what LeSchack's OCS "campus" looked like, was described succinctly by R.L Johnson, Jr., in an article, "Weariest Sailors in the Navy," published five years earlier in the "Saturday Evening Post:"

> "OCS occupies some two dozen depressingly uniform, overage wooden buildings spaced along the hardtop roads of Coddington Point, a turtle-backed promontory jutting northeast into Narragansett Bay. Half of these U-shaped, two-storied, white structures are fitted out as barracks; the rest house classrooms, administrative offices and the like. There is no glamour to OCS."

Nothing had changed since 1954 when Johnson's piece was published, except that the buildings were five years older!

Except for the officer candidates that entered directly from the fleet, LeSchack was likely one of the officer candidates best prepared for the OCS routine. As opposed to the vast majority of the candidates, with no previous military experience who entered directly after graduating from liberal arts schools, LeSchack had eighteen months of living with the Navy and also, viewing that experience from an officer's point of view. His engineering school experience and his study of celestial navigation at Byrd Station were also of considerable benefit in the conduct of the prescribed curriculum. To his detriment, however, he rarely did a good job on the daily shining of his boots. And even in those days of his youth, he did not suffer fools gladly. And there were enough to go around, mostly among the junior officer level of the teaching staff.

The various academic departments had both very junior officers and very senior non-commissioned officers as instructors. The chief and first class petty officers, most of whom had served during the Second World War, and who were instructors, taught the subject that they had spent their entire Navy career in performing. They were professionals. However, the junior officers in these departments, with few exceptions, were no older than LeSchack and were soon destined to leave the Navy. The Navy knew this and, in its wisdom, decided they would do less harm teaching, than being left out in the fleet on operations where they could cause serious harm. LeSchack thought this policy was debatable. It was with this junior officer level that LeSchack had greatest difficulty in disguising his occasional displeasure for those young officers who, like substitute teachers in the New York City school system, were usually just one lesson ahead of their students. Barely.

Early on during his four-month training period, LeSchack was to learn the value of the Navy's network system. The Assistant Company Officer of Kilo Company was Chief Boatswain's Mate Edwin H. Todd. Just prior to assignment to the School, he had served on icebreakers in Operation Deepfreeze in the Antarctic. As the Assistant Company Officer, he would have read the paperwork of all OC's in Kilo Company, and would have recognized that LeSchack not only had been in the Antarctic when Todd, himself was, but was requesting to go back there on active duty. That would have, in the Navy network system, marked LeSchack for "special attention" by Chief Todd. And, at exactly the appropriate time,

LeSchack got that attention.

Chief Quartermaster Douglas Dunn was LeSchack's instructor in Navigation. LeSchack caught Dunn's attention on two counts: Dunn was particularly enamored of the romance, and utility of celestial navigation. He was a genuine Yankee seaman of the old school. Before GPS navigation, celestial navigation was the only sure way of determining one's position anywhere on the face of the earth. And it is romantic; shooting the stars and sun with a sextant in conjunction with an accurate chronometer, a quartermaster can mystify his fellow seamen by applying the arcane mathematics of spherical trigonometry to locate one's ship with relative accuracy. LeSchack had learned and used this science in the Antarctic and, not surprisingly, was the Chief's best student in this subject. Secondly, during the War Dunn had served on submarines based in Australia, and apparently had enjoyed his shore leaves there. In early conversations with him, LeSchack observed that he too, had just spent time "down-under," also enjoying his leave there (and probably for the same reasons), and had just returned from Sydney aboard the USS ARNEB prior to enlisting into OCS.

It was Chief Dunn, who explained to LeSchack what he called the "sea-pappy" networking system of the Navy. That system had evolved as a strategy by both officers and enlisted men, alike, to get around the Navy's stultifying bureaucracy, and involved keeping track of commanding officers, classmates, and others with whom you have served, and were in a position to help. In short order it turns out, both Chiefs Dunn and Todd helped LeSchack.

The OCS barracks were large, long, white two-storey high buildings. On the top floor there was one large dormitory room with the head at one end, and on the bottom, the study hall. The head was a completely communal affair—personal modesty was inappropriate here—with commodes, washbasins, urinals and sinks all in one open space. And in no way would it be possible to accommodate all the barracks' sailors at one time. In the center of the dormitory, there were banks of lockers, back to back for the OC's to store a minimum of their belongings. Sleeping facilities were double-decker cots similar to those seen in the movie, Stalag 17. Bunks were assigned by alphabetical order, and so Len LeSchack and Paul Hurley—whose name was alphabetically the closest—lived in one double-decker with LeSchack having the top bunk.

Although LeSchack had long since lost the uncomfortable-ness of using wide-open bathroom facilities after a year at Byrd Station, the one thing he did not have to do at Byrd was shave, for he grew a beard within weeks of arriving in the Antarctic. Navy OCS was a different story. A clean shave every day was mandatory to pass inspection! Not only did he not enjoy standing in line before a washbasin at which to shave, the washbasins were too close together and LeSchack was left-handed. Statistics say that his neighbor at the next basin would be right-handed. Neither LeSchack nor his shaving neighbor would be pleased by banging elbows during this unavoidably rushed process, exacerbated by jostling lines of cranky men behind each of them. Accordingly, LeSchack very quickly evolved a scheme: he learned to set his biological alarm clock to five minutes before the 0600 reveille. He learned to creep out of his bunk without disturbing either Paul or 58 other dormitory dwellers. Then, he had learned to open the combination lock on his locker, in a room illuminated only by a red emergency lamp at the far end of the room. Finally, he had learned to shave and shower in the dark—for he dared not turn on the light and alert the hordes before reveille. He would complete his ablutions before the sounding of reveille and the madding crowd burst in!

The well-known bed-making process—can you bounce a quarter on it?— was solved by LeSchack with a simple expedient, for he was not proficient in, nor did he enjoy making beds. He used safety pins, carefully hidden from inspecting eyes, to keep his sack always tight as a drum. He slept on top, under a raw blanket. After four months on traverse in the Antarctic, sleeping in a greasy, smelly sleeping bag, and never bathing, LeSchack had forgotten about any fastidiousness he ever had! But now, he was always clean and ready for inspection-- although he did it his way.

From July to November, the routine for LeSchack and his OC classmates was much the same: reveille at 0600, fall out for inspection, march to the mess hall, march to the parade ground (known, without much exaggeration as the "grinder"), march to classes, march to lunch, march to classes, march to dinner then march back to the barracks. Back at the barracks, the OC's attended to the all-important task of shining their boots and attending to any other business screaming for their attention, and that could be accomplished within fifteen minutes or less. Promptly at 1900, everyone descended to the study hall on the bottom floor of the barracks until 2200. And studied!

Most of the OC's had graduated from liberal arts colleges and universities. The Navy's heavy emphasis on technical and engineering subjects was a challenge for many of these men. In many ways LeSchack was far better prepared to manage OCS than the others. Not only had he spent time on U.S. Navy warships, which only those few OC's who came directly from the fleet had done, but his years at engineering school had prepared him for more easily understanding the Navy's technically-oriented curricula. The one thing his previous 24 years of life experience had not well prepared him for was being self-effacing before assholes who out-ranked him! And, sure enough, he ran into some who caused him grief!

In all classes, a week would not go by without at least one small quiz per subject. While most quizzes were of the well-known multiple-choice type, in Navigation and Operations many of the quizzes involved drawing and making calculations. Such was the case in Operations class one day. The class was given a maneuvering board problem. Today, warships have computers that solve these problems. But in those days they were done on polar coordinate paper where your ship was plotted at the center, or pole, and other ships, either yours or the enemy's were plotted based on their azimuth and distance from your ship. The point is—and in LeSchack's case, both literally and figuratively—one needs a divider with *sharp points* for solving correctly these maneuvering board problems.

A divider is a simple instrument, in many ways like the compass used by schoolchildren for drawing perfect circles; only instead of one steel point and one pencil lead, a divider has a second steel point, replacing the lead. The divider is a tool for measuring distances on a chart, and transferring quickly that distance to another part of the chart. Officers using maneuvering boards on operations need to be able to do this, and quickly and accurately. So here are the origins of LeSchack's problem. The operations instructor announces, "Okay officer candidates, here's what you've been waiting for—a maneuvering board quiz," and with that, amidst the groans of anguish from the liberal arts majors, the instructor begins to pass out polar coordinate paper and dividers to the class. One sheet of paper, and a pair of dividers to each OC.

In this classroom, LeSchack occupied the last seat in his row. He gets his sheet of polar coordinate paper and a pair of dividers just as does everyone else in the class, only both steel points on the dividers he receives *are broken*. He raises his hand. The operations instructor acknowledges him. "Officer Candidate LeSchack, **Sir**! Sir, I have received a pair of dividers with two broken points! May I request another pair, **Sir**!"

"Well LeSchack," replied the instructor, "you can't very well get an accurate answer...." at which point he looked around at all the OC's in the class, "and you will all be graded on accuracy......if you don't use proper tools. LeSchack, I have no more dividers. Go downstairs to the Operations Office and ask Lieutenant (jg) Crow for another pair with proper points. Tell Lieutenant Crow I sent you and I am holding up giving this quiz until you return. Hurry right back, LeSchack!" "Yes Sir!" LeSchack replied as he got up from his seat and double-timed it to the Operations Office.

A moment later LeSchack was standing at attention before Lieutenant (jg) Crow. He handed the lieutenant his broken dividers and requested another pair, saying that, "My Operations instructor, Lieutenant (jg) Napoli, has ordered me to request another pair from this office, Sir! And he is holding up giving a maneuvering board quiz, until I return, Sir!" Officer Candidate LeSchack, six-feet tall and standing at attention, made the shorter Lieutenant (jg) Crow appear shrimp-like by comparison. "What's wrong with these, Officer Candidate LeSchack" replied Crow, appearing to be at eye-level with the name tag pinned to LeSchack's chest. "Well, can't you see, **Sir**, the points of the dividers are broken, and the quiz is to be graded on accuracy, **Sir**!" and then LeSchack added, "And, you see, **Sir**, I'm a perfectionist."

The conversation went downhill from there. Lieutenant (jg)—(jg standing for junior grade)—Crow, now appearing to LeSchack like a Little Napoleon, then said, "Use them anyhow, they'll do." LeSchack looked at him thinking, "Two years ago this pipsqueak was a liberal-arts major who never learned how to do maneuvering board problems properly while at sea. So the Navy dumped him here!"

That did it! While LeSchack did not *think* he was foolish enough to have *mouthed those words out loud,* his body language must have needed little translation! And in what appeared to LeSchack to be the next instant, he was on report! For insubordination of a superior officer! Dumbfounded, he skulked back upstairs and took the operations quiz anyhow, and did the best he could with his defective tools.

Within 24 hours he was standing at attention before the Kilo Company Officer, Lieutenant Jane, and Chief Todd, the Kilo Assistant Company Officer. Lieutenant Jane, a naval aviator, was perhaps five years older than LeSchack and was seated insouciantly—and deliberately, thought LeSchack—with his feet propped up on his desk, with the <u>Manual of Courts Martial</u> clearly visible for LeSchack to see. And he began reading out loud what he believed to be the pertinent articles related to insubordination to a superior officer. Finally, and only as an afterthought, he requested that LeSchack provide *his side* of the story. LeSchack provided the two presiding officers with his version of what he thought had happened, knowing full well that none of this was a court-martial offense as implied so theatrically by the naval aviator. LeSchack had met with enough of them in the Antarctic assigned to the VX-6 Squadron, and flew with a number of them. He had become well aware of their propensity for drama.

As Lieutenant Jane continued intoning, chapter and verse, from the Manual, Chief Todd began quietly, but nervously pacing back and forth in the Company office. Finally, the Chief, who was twice as old as LeSchack, and knew better than LeSchack did, that the current proceedings were a bit overblown, spoke up. "Lieutenant, let me deal with this case. I know just how to take care of this man. *I know his type.*"

Outside, and away from the Company office, the Chief shook his head sadly, looked at LeSchack in a way that said, "I can just picture what really happened." He actually said, "Son, I know you've put in for icebreakers and want to go back to Task Force 43. I want to see you get back there. Maybe you'll be assigned to my old ship, the GLACIER. Don't fuck up now, son. You're almost there!" Finally, shaking his head even more slowly, he said to LeSchack, "But I've got to give you some punishment. Four hours of EMI this Saturday."

EMI is one of those wonderful Navy euphemisms. It stands for "Extra Military Instruction." What it means, however, is marching back and forth on the main street in front of all the barracks with a rifle on your shoulder. On Saturday afternoon, when everyone else has liberty and is drinking in downtown Newport. Although LeSchack would have preferred drinking beer with his section-mates, four hours of EMI was endurable, he thought, under the circumstances. LeSchack *knew* how to march with a rifle on his shoulder. And well! He had performed with the Air Force ROTC Drill Team during his foreshortened tenure with that organization at engineering school. He had been kicked out for what Air Force officers perceived then as "bad attitude," not for lack of ability to march and perform the manual of arms! Perhaps they might have been right—five years earlier.

On Saturday when the EMI list was posted as part of the "Orders of the Day," He noted that his four hours of EMI had been reduced to two, and that the charge of "insubordination to an officer" had been downgraded to "frivolous comment to an officer." Perhaps LeSchack's first "seapappy" had wanted him to spend at least a little bit of Saturday afternoon, after EMI, drinking with his shipmates.

About half-way through OCS, the autumn of 1959, two things occurred that energized LeSchack. First, the shelling of the islands, Quemoy and Matsu, between mainland China and Taiwan, began to increase. The United States Government, headed by Dwight Eisenhower, made threatening gestures to Mao Tse Tung if this shelling presaged an attack on these islands or on Taiwan. The Navy was put on alert. LeSchack and his OCS classmates wondered if this would be where their first services as officers would be utilized. Secondly, LeSchack received a telegram from the Arctic Institute of North America.

The Arctic Institute of North America (AINA) asked him whether he would be interested and available to do a tour as a geophysicist on the

Air Force Arctic Drift Station T-3. Interested, most assuredly, LeSchack responded to the AINA from a phone booth just outside the OCS barracks; available well, only if the Institute could pull some strings for, as LeSchack explained, "I am a Navy man now, and could only do things under proper Navy orders."

The AINA had been the contractor for the U.S. National Committee for the IGY, and it was the AINA, which had paid LeSchack's salary in the Antarctic. The AINA, he knew, was also a contractor for both the Air Force and the Navy and, in his youthful naiveté about such things, he blithely suggested that an arrangement could sensibly be made between both services to have him assigned directly to the Air Force upon his completion of OCS and his commissioning as an officer. Having told them this, he left it in the hands of the AINA, and returned from the phone booth to address a more immediate concern — polishing his boots to a high luster. Nonetheless, LeSchack was intrigued. There were now two exciting possibilities before him after commissioning: returning to the Antarctic, likely aboard an icebreaker, or being ordered to a scientific, as well as military adventure in the Arctic Ocean on a drifting ice station.

In LeSchack's OCS status, there was little for him to do other than leave his fate in the hands of others, and he spent little time thinking about AINA's request. However, the AINA officer to whom LeSchack spoke, Bob Mason, broached the subject with Col. Lou DeGoes, USAF, at the Air Force Cambridge Research Center (AFCRC), who administered the science programs aboard the Air Force Arctic drift stations, and to Dr. Max E. Britton of the Arctic Program of the Office of Naval Research (ONR). Col. DeGoes said such a scheme as LeSchack proposed could work if the Air Force didn't have to pay for LeSchack. Max Britton said it sounded like a fine idea having a Navy presence on an Air Force drift station, and that ONR would pay the expenses, "so let's try and do it." Max, a scientist and senior bureaucrat, however, had little time or inclination to mess with the Navy bureaucracy. He promptly turned this interesting bureaucratic exercise over to Professor Jess Walker, from Louisiana State University, who fortuitously was on a year's sabbatical at Max's ONR Arctic Program at just that moment. Jess was a former U.S. Marine, well familiar with the Navy's arcane procedures, as well as with the Arctic. And so for LeSchack, matters sat for another two months while he presumed, the bureaucracy churned. The OCS routine was simply too busy for him to think much about potential bureaucratic actions in Washington that could affect his life. And, therefore, he didn't.

Also, halfway through the OCS curriculum, most of those officer candidates who couldn't cope with either the academics or the military regimen, had flunked out and had been dispatched to the fleet. Those who remained had a sense that they would make it. LeSchack certainly had that sense. And so did Paul, LeSchack's bunk-mate. Paul, largely by virtue of his proximity, was one of the few men LeSchack got to know well. Paul was a lawyer and, upon graduation, would be assigned directly to the Navy's Judge Advocate General or JAG. He and Paul were both about two years older and had more worldly experience than most of their section mates. Both had lived in southern Louisiana and both enjoyed New Orleans. When Saturday afternoon liberty was granted, as it now was more frequently in the final weeks of OCS, LeSchack and Paul would go to downtown Newport for their relaxation. They, like most of the other OCs granted liberty, would head for the boisterous, overly smoke-filled beer hall in the basement of the Viking Hotel.

By tradition, the Viking was always the OC's starting point for liberty, and a place to grouse about the Navy folderol and foibles of their instructors. However, after an hour or so, the beer hall became too noisy, and far too smoky for Len and Paul to enjoy, and so they would leave for a nice, quiet restaurant where civilized conversation was possible. In addition to discussing the events of the week at OCS, they often talked about New Orleans. Paul's wife was living there awaiting his graduation and their subsequent assignment, likely Washington. LeSchack had a girlfriend, Ellen, in New Orleans, whom he had met while working for Shell Oil before his Antarctic adventure. He had kept in touch with her and had visited her upon his return from the Antarctic a few months earlier.

On this particular Saturday evening, LeSchack asked Paul why the Navy forced a lawyer who had passed the bar to endure the physical and emotional stress of OCS. Paul smiled wryly and said, "The Navy told us that every lawyer should get to know his client; this is the Navy's way of giving us that intimate familiarity." Although Paul grimaced as he said that, LeSchack thought that, in truth, this was not a bad way to accomplish that aim. "A bit hard on the lawyers perhaps, but they would clearly better serve the Navy for this rigorous experience."

That was the way these two typically spent Saturday afternoon liberty. They had to be back on base and checked in with the OOD, the Officer of the Day, prior to midnight Saturday night. So there was little motivation for either of them to do much more than have a leisurely dinner and return to base. And Sunday was a catch-up day, church for those inclined, and study hall for those who needed it. But Sunday or not, if you were on base, it was reveille at 0600!

The weeks marched on with a stressful tediousness. As graduation and commissioning began to loom into view, LeSchack took care to heed Chief Todd's advice not to screw up, and to watch his body language when speaking with junior officers. LeSchack literally "sailed through" his navigation course, while it confounded many others. Once a week, the course instructor conducted a practical test in Navigation, known as, "P-Works." P-Works was a weekly test to see if you could successfully navigate from one part of the world to another part, usually some foreign port that few had heard of. It included guiding your ship safely out of harbor and across the ocean, where celestial navigation was required. One's answers were cumulative, rather than individual, as would be the case on a real ocean voyage. This meant if you made an error early on, and made your next calculations based on that error, you might end up in Djibouti, rather than, say Cherbourg. Some did. Depending on the OC, the results could be extreme. One story, perhaps apocryphal, has it that an OC who simply had to pass a certain P-works, or flunk out—his marks were so borderline—found he had sailed to Djibouti, when Cherbourg was the destination, and time ran out on the quiz! As the story goes, the blood drained from his face, he went rigid, and collapsed onto the floor.

LeSchack faced a similar situation in one of the last P-works sessions. It would not have been catastrophic, since his early grades were sufficient to compensate for the failure this time. However, he had made an error at the onset that invalidated the remainder of his work. When he received his test back at the next session, rather than seeing a "big failure" grade, he saw that the proper answers had all been written in over his incorrect ones; Chief Dunn, who by now knew LeSchack, and knew from his previous work that he *could navigate,* simply "helped him out." Now that's Navy networking!

In the midst of all the class work, the marching, the inspections, the harassment, LeSchack who in engineering school had been known as practical joker, was scrupulously careful to avoid bringing attention to himself by so doing at OCS. Nonetheless, he succumbed to the temptation when it came to Officer Candidate Bray, one of his fellow OCs. Officer Candidate Bray, a sailor in LeSchack's Section K-4, and the Section Leader, was simply overbearing and offensive to LeSchack, and to many in the section. Bray, a recent graduate from Yale University, had a father who was an admiral. He never forgot to remind his section mates of these two facts—Yale, my alma mater, and Admiral, my daddy! And as section leader, he often had to report to seniors—with his section in tow….. "Officer Candidate Bray, **Sir,** reporting **Sir!** Officer Candidate Bray-**Sir**…this, and Officer Candidate Bray-**Sir**…that"… that one could not help but notice a silly euphoniousness to it…Bray-**Sir,** Bray-**Sir,** so that there was much mimicry behind his back.

As graduation was approaching and graduation photographs of individual OCs in uniform became available, LeSchack managed to purloin one of the loathsome Officer Candidate Bray-Sir. Moments before Section K-4 was to assemble for marching to class, LeSchack slipped away to the study hall with an 8x10 photo of Bray-Sir. He went directly to the large wall-mounted table of organization for the entire Officer Candidate School, headed by Captain Lauteret, USN, whose photograph was at the top of the chart, and he quickly and deftly inserted Bray-Sir's photo on top of Captain Lauteret's. LeSchack noticed there were a few stragglers remaining in the study hall; they saw him do this, but at this point, he didn't care. LeSchack acted as though he was performing an official task, duly ordered! And then, he quickly fell in to formation.

In most normal situations, LeSchack's prank would be almost meaningless. In a military organization where position is everything, Officer Candidate Seaman Apprentice Bray-Sir's photograph substituted in the most senior slot on the table of organization display, and replacing that of a Navy captain, could be considered a serious effrontery.

Section K-4 had marched and had nearly reached its first class at the far side of the base. Then LeSchack, at the rear of the squad, noticed that when the Section was rounding a corner and out of view of officers, one of the marchers leaned over to Bray-Sir. He whispered into Bray-Sir's ear—something forbidden while in formation—and Bray-Sir got a shocked look on his face and bolted from the marching formation— something even more forbidden—and began running back to the barracks. LeSchack smiled to himself, but not surprisingly, nothing was ever said to him about his prank.

With only a few weeks left to go before graduation, the feeling by OCs was palpable that they would soon become commissioned officers in the United States Navy. As a matter of numbers, there was a point past which a failure on one or two more tests would not depress one's overall average sufficiently—below 2.5 on a 4.0 scale—to cause him to flunk, or bilge out, as the saying went. In general this set the stage for a somewhat more relaxed atmosphere overall.

The case of Officer Candidate Blogs is a fine example. Blogs, a practical joker in his own right, received his comeuppance when his section mates found him taking a shower when he should have been shining his boots. Several of his mates seized him from the shower and threw him outside, stark naked, and then locked the doors to the barracks. Nakedness, per se, in this all-male environment was by now, not a concern for Blogs, nor was the weather cold enough to be a distress. However, Blogs panicked when he spied the Officer of the Day walking briskly towards the barracks area. Unable to re-enter the barracks, Blogs jumped through the open door of a nearby Dempsey Dumpster, a garbage storage bin, and closed the door behind him, just as the OOD rounded the corner. But not quite soon enough! The OOD knew something was amiss as he saw, for the briefest instant, Blogs' bare ass sail into the dumpster. Upon marching up to the dumpster and opening the door, the OOD was surprised to see Blogs, standing at attention, saluting, and blurting out, "Dempsey Dumpster all secure! **Sir!**"

A week before graduation, the OCs were granted liberty for the entire weekend! Also, LeSchack received his first set of official Navy orders. Upon commissioning, he was to be assigned as "Deck Officer" on the USS EDISTO, an icebreaker attached to Task Force 43 in the Antarctic. Clearly, this was the work of Chief Todd, who was looking out for LeSchack's interests. But LeSchack was less interested in that assignment now, with the recently offered potential of being assigned to the Arctic aboard an Air Force drifting station in the Arctic Ocean. But all he kept hearing from Bob Mason at the Arctic Institute was... "the Navy and the Air Force are still working out the details....." Both were exciting assignments, but at that point, LeSchack was hoping to go to the Arctic, reasoning to himself that, "he had already been to the Antarctic. It's time to try the other Pole."

With the prospect of a weekend liberty — Saturday afternoon to midnight on Sunday — Section K-4 decided to throw a party at a restaurant in downtown Newport. LeSchack and Paul reserved a hotel room for themselves in a quaint, old-fashioned Newport hotel so they could sleep late on Sunday morning. Their plan was to get a bottle of whiskey, drink and carouse all afternoon at the Viking, and then go to their section party that evening. Upon checking into their hotel room, they each had one small drink, and then decided a short nap, rather than joining the other OCs at the Viking, might be worthwhile. In fact, so physically and emotionally exhausted were they that they both slept through until it was time to join the Section party at the restaurant. A number of their instructors had been invited to that party so, for the first time, they began to know, socially, the people who held the OCs fate in their hands. It was at that party where LeSchack really got to know Chief Dunn, and learn about his wartime duty in the South Pacific.

A week later, on 20 November 1959, approximately 90 percent of the OCs that entered Class 45, graduated. The graduation ceremony was a formality that ended the training of Class 45. The previous day, however, was the day that the OCs were formally commissioned officers in the United States Naval Reserve and were awarded a single gold stripe. On the day he was commissioned, LeSchack had not received notification of any change of orders to his icebreaker. It was only then that LeSchack recognized how much he wished for that Arctic drift station assignment with the Air Force at the North Pole, rather than the one aboard the EDISTO.

After commissioning, the entire Section K-4, with the exception of LeSchack, headed to the Viking and a good party. LeSchack, saddened by lack of an order change at this late date, and now completely emotionally exhausted, crawled into his bunk in the completely empty barracks and fell into a disturbed, dream-filled sleep. It was sometime later that afternoon—LeSchack couldn't tell how much time had passed—that he was awakened by an OC unknown to him. Surveying the empty barracks, the OC came up to LeSchack's bunk and shook him gently. "Excuse me Sir...I'm looking for Ensign LeSchack. Are you Ensign LeSchack?"

LeSchack was completely startled, not only from his restless sleep, but because for the first time in four months at OCS, he was addressed by his new commissioned officer rank, **ensign**! "Yes, yes, that's me," he replied, much disoriented. "Sir," the OC said, "the OOD has sent me here to tell you that you have just received a change of orders from the Bureau of Personnel in Washington. Your new orders are at the Administration Office."

LeSchack startled not only the OC standing by his upper bunk, but himself. Without pause, he leapt from that top bunk, landing solidly with both feet squarely on the floor, all in one fluid motion. Suddenly LeSchack was highly energized! "Thank you, thank you very much," Officer Candidate.....Jackson." LeSchack breathed, as he squinted at the OC's name tag to discern his name. "May I go now, sir?" the OC then requested. "Of course, and thank you again..." and as an afterthought LeSchack uttered, "good luck in Class 46!" "Yes sir! And thank you, sir!" LeSchack hastily donned his uniform, trotted up to the Admin Office to check his orders, and verifying that his assignment had indeed, been changed to the Air Force Arctic Drift Station T-3, grabbed a cab and went directly downtown to the Viking to begin partying!

As this important episode in LeSchack's life was drawing to a close, it is appropriate to place the time, 1959, into its contemporary context. Certainly, the United States was entering into the coldest part of the Cold War. Only six years earlier the U.S. and its allies were fighting in Korea. Only fourteen years earlier the U.S. and its allies were fighting Nazi

Germany and Imperial Japan. LeSchack and his OCS classmates had all lived through this. Most of the senior officers and non-commissioned officers at OCS had served on active duty in one or both theaters of war. LeSchack and his classmates knew this. But for the officer candidates, most between the ages of 22 to 25, the music and movies of the day also set the stage, and became an integral part of their time at OCS.

The song, "When you walk through a storm..." from the Broadway musical "Carousel" was used as the sign-off music for a local Newport radio station that needed to cease broadcasting at sunset. Even today, that music has a spiritual quality that is well recognized. But for the OCs in Section K-4, who all shined their boots out on the second floor balcony of their barrack at the sunset hour, that music, played on someone's portable radio had, and to this day, has a special meaning that links them with their shoe-shining OCS days, the days of their youth, their patriotism, and their spirituality. They can still remember those days, humming or singing along as the radio station prepared to leave the air.

The 1957 movie, "The Bridge on the River Kwai," which won seven Academy Awards that year, was also well-known to LeSchack and his OCS classmates. The fate of British POWs at the hands of their Japanese captors in Burma too, was well known, at least its history, and occurred to men now the same age as the senior instructors at OCS. The music that is most remembered from that movie is the "Colonel Bogey March" an old British World War I march past. This march past, as well as "Stars and Stripes Forever" and other John Philip Souza marches, were played as part of the daily morning ceremony on the Grinder. Every morning, rain or shine, the entire Class 45 marched to this music and assembled in formation on the parade ground in preparation for the 0800 flag-raising ceremony. Promptly at 0800 sailors hoisted the flag to the bugler's call to the colors, as the entire class saluted the flag. They held that salute for the playing of the National Anthem.

And then came the administrative procedures, all accomplished with exaggerated military precision, and all done by fellow OCs. There was the Regimental Adjutant that did a stiff military waddle-march up to the Assistant Regimental Commander. He reported that "all companies are present and accounted for, **Sir!**" And they stiffly saluted one another.

Then the Assistant Regimental Commander marched over to the Regimental Commander, reported, and they too, stiffly saluted one another. All in front of the entire Battalion—Class 45. Much of this marching, and all of the saluting and reporting, took place on a long, wide, raised veranda, part of another barracks building, in plain view of all the OCs. This was military ceremony, pure and simple, played out each day, and taken most seriously by everyone present. Except off duty in the barracks where self-styled military comedians enjoyed mimicking, like marionettes, that "regimental martinet strut."

The crux of this story, and why it is so fixed in memory of that time, is that the Regimental Commander was *clearly Oriental*. From California, he was likely a Nisei, an American born of Japanese, or Japanese-American parents, who likely also suffered internment during the War. On the last Battalion formation day before their commissioning, Class 45, standing rigidly at attention, watched their last "regimental martinet strut." Then the Regimental Commander, instead of dismissing the battalion as he always did at this point, turned and slowly walked over to the veranda railing and faced the Battalion. He then leaned over the railing. At that moment, by what now appeared to be clear pre-arrangement, the beginning bars of the "Colonel Bogey March" blared over the loudspeakers that surrounded the grinder. As the music died, the Regimental Commander smiled the evilest oriental grin he could conjure up and announced, as Sessue Hayakawa had done in the movie, *"Gentlemen, today we will begin to build the bridge."*

For a long moment the Battalion was stunned! That dramatic scene was right out of the movie. All the men had seen it. It was the same scene as in the prison camp! And to many, standing rigidly at attention on the grinder that day, OCS itself appeared to be a bit like a prison camp! World War II was still too close to these men standing in formation. The knowledge of Japanese wartime barbarity had been learned during their childhood. Many of the OCs had fathers in that war. But a moment later, almost simultaneously, the entire Battalion recognized the excruciating irony of the Regimental Commander's shocking performance, and recognized that he too would be commissioned an officer in the United States Navy, just as would they, the following day. With one spontaneous roar, the entire Battalion jumped up and down and cheered, first the Regimental Commander, then the Officer

Candidate School, the U.S. Navy, and finally each other, and on that parade ground, all sense of military decorum vanished. And, OCS was coming to an end.

The following day it had come to an end. LeSchack, and those of the original Class 45 who had stayed the course, were commissioned ensigns in the United States Naval Reserve. In a mass ceremony, all the OCs, on cue, tossed their white sailor hats into the sky, signifying the end of their enlisted status. They were now all officers, and would serve in that status for at least three years. For LeSchack, some major adventures were about to begin.

After the commissioning ceremony, LeSchack and the rest of Section K-4 returned to their barracks to clean out their lockers for the last time. Waiting at the barracks door, as expected, was Chief Todd. In Navy tradition, the first enlisted man that gives a newly-minted officer a salute, receives a crisp dollar bill from that officer. The Chief *was waiting* at the barracks to receive his due from his troops as they entered, one-by-one. As Ensign Leonard A. LeSchack, USNR approached the Chief, he received his first salute from his first seapappy, another Antarctic man, a man twice his age, and returned it smartly, and the two, for just an instant, winked at one another while shaking hands goodbye.

Chapter 4

Ensign Leonard A. LeSchack, USNR graduates from Officer Candidate School in Newport, Rhode Island in November, 1959, and is prepared to take on the world—and as many adventures and complaisant young women as possible! He eventually is highly decorated and makes captain!

The U. S. Navy and the Cold, Cold War Years-Arctic Drifting Station T-3

> *In an era of Cold War between the world's two great*
> *superpowers, the Arctic region became an area of crucial*
> *geopolitical significance. "Study your globe," observed*
> *General Henry H. (Hap) Arnold, retired chief of the Army Air*
> *Forces to the graduating class of the U.S. Military Academy*
> *in 1946, "and you will see the most direct routes [between the*
> *United States and the Soviet Union] are not across the*
> *Atlantic or Pacific, but through the Arctic." If a third world*
> *war breaks out, he warned, "its strategic center will be the*
> *North Pole."*
>
> *Project Coldfeet: Secret Mission to a Soviet Ice Station,*
> *William M. Leary and Leonard A. LeSchack*

Ensign Leonard LeSchack took ten-day's leave to decompress from the OCS experience. He visited Ellen, his old girlfriend from New Orleans. While he had a pleasant visit with Ellen, now living in Houston where he had once worked for Shell Oil, and he was able to relax with her, LeSchack recognized that Ellen would remain *just an old girlfriend*. Their relationship had no future, he realized. They had grown too far apart in the past two years while he had been away from her. He flew to Washington when his leave came to an end, and he never saw her again.

His new orders, as Office of Naval Research (ONR) Representative to the Air Force Cambridge Research Center (AFCRC), required him first to visit ONR in Washington, D.C., before reporting to the Air Force in Boston. At ONR LeSchack met Dr. Max Britton and Dr. Jess Walker at the ONR Arctic Program Office for the first time. They told LeSchack about the overall U.S. Arctic drift station program, part of which was operated by the Navy, and part by the Air Force. They also told LeSchack about the Arctic Research Laboratory (ARL) at Barrow, Alaska, which was largely funded by ONR.

Gratuitously, they also told LeSchack that no one in Washington had ever expected his "ridiculous" request to AINA to succeed, least of all, them. Nonetheless, much to the surprise of everyone concerned (except for LeSchack, of course, who knew no better), Jess and Max had bludgeoned the request through the Navy bureaucracy, and so his orders were changed—and at the last possible moment.

At AFCRC he met with Dr. Albert P. (Bert) Crary, LeSchack's Antarctic mentor, who was now working for AFCRC, and learned about the geophysical research program that he was assigned to continue aboard T-3. Bert had also offered some suggestions about what research LeSchack might pursue. In these days at the height of the Cold War, LeSchack saw nothing incongruous about mixing pure science with military operations. In fact, it seemed to him a most appropriate thing to do. And now, having credentials as both a scientist and military officer, he felt he was in a good position to assist in the conduct of such dual operations. For LeSchack, this was a correct judgment. From that time on until the end of the Cold War, he would be involved in both science and military operations, flip-flopping back and forth, as was needed, to accomplish the task But it began with his assignment to the Air Force's Arctic drifting station T-3.

LeSchack did not stay long in Boston. Within days of his checking in and becoming oriented with the Air Force program on T-3, he received a set of orders and airline tickets to fly to Fairbanks, Alaska, and Ladd Air Force Base. At Ladd, LeSchack would check in with Air Force Captain James F. Smith who headed the "Project Ice Skate" office, the office that managed the logistics of operating Drifting Station T-3. Although LeSchack and Captain Smith only talked over the phone that day, they would meet a few months later, and ultimately become partners in a most unusual and daring mission, Project Coldfeet.

T-3 was simply an abbreviation for "Target-3." It was an ice island and these were, in fact, radar targets as seen from Air Force reconnaissance planes. The ice island, T-3, was actually a good radar target. It was about nine miles long and three miles wide. It was a good target because it was an ice "island," a large chunk of glacial, or fresh-water ice that had broken off from the Ellesmere Ice Shelf in the Canadian Arctic and got caught up in the slowly moving sea ice. As opposed to the sea ice— frozen seawater—that, on average is ten feet thick, the island of glacial ice was 160 feet thick and floated higher than the surrounding sea ice.

Ice islands, therefore, make good radar targets. And they make excellent floating platforms for recording a variety of meteorological, geophysical and oceanographic measurements. They also make excellent electronic eavesdropping stations, as was the case during the Cold War, located so close to the Soviet land mass.

By the beginning of December 1959, LeSchack was aboard T-3. He flew directly there from Ladd AFB on a C-123 twin-engine cargo plane, over the Brooks Range, over the North Slope and over the Arctic pack ice until T-3 was reached. At first glance, the station at T-3 looked much like Byrd Station—trailers, tractors, Jamesway huts, an ice runway for flight operations, and of course, lots of ice. But there were differences. During the summer months, the ice melted and formed rivers and lakes, and puddles of meltwater, resulting in significant changes in the camp's morphology. Whereas in the Antarctic, blowing ice would tend to bury manmade structures, in the Arctic ice, summer melt-water would ablate the ice, tending to raise all structures with respect to the ice surface that had melted and flowed away. The trailers that served as living quarters, mess hall, head, recreation hall and radio shack had survived several summer melt seasons. Because the ice beneath these structures did not melt, while the ice around them did, all structures would find themselves higher above the surface ice each succeeding season. To reach the doors of these structures you had to climb up a ladder! Otherwise, the life style at Air Force ice stations was similar to that in the Antarctic.

Shortly after LeSchack landed on T-3, he became familiar with camp routine, set up his own research program, and continued programs that had been ongoing. Although LeSchack was then the most junior of junior military officers aboard T-3 (or anywhere, for that matter), there was only one other officer there, the base commander, Lieutenant Colonel. Marshall, USAF. The remaining personnel were mostly Air Force enlisted men. There were not many scientific personnel aboard for the four months LeSchack was at T-3.

It was the best of all possible worlds for LeSchack: the usual hazing period that enlisted men visit upon newly-minted officers was dispensed with in his case. Fourteen months in the Antarctic had given him credibility in this Arctic world with both the enlisted men and the C.O.

His officer status, he found, was enormously valuable in the pursuit of his scientific work. He did not need to beg and cajole the enlisted men, as he had to do as a civilian in the Antarctic, for the logistic assistance needed to conduct his research. He also enjoyed that special aura, known only to Navy navigators, of knowing how to locate, by celestial navigation, the whereabouts of the drifting station as it moved slowly around the Arctic Ocean.

Every other day, in the winter cold and darkness, LeSchack would shoot the stars with a theodolite to be able to calculate the station's geographical position, information of value for pilots of aircraft bringing food, mail and replacement personnel. At his request, Air Force enlisted men built an open-topped canvas shelter for him so that he could be shielded from the frigid Arctic wind while recording his star shots. Also from this same star shot data, LeSchack could calculate the azimuth of the rotating ice station by comparing azimuths of the stars with the azimuth of a distant fixed point on T-3. The point LeSchack chose was the vertical portion of the tail of a downed and damaged Air Force DC-3 at T-3, looking more forlorn by the day as the ablating ice raised this sad bird higher and higher on its glacial pedestal. And for LeSchack, every time he sighted on this forlorn aircraft, he was reminded of the hazards of flying in the polar regions.

LeSchack soon recognized that the special "sight forms" that the Navigation staff at OCS had designed for P-Works, would be a most valuable tool for quickly calculating T-3's positions. At his request, the Air Force radio operators at T-3 sent a message to Chief Douglas Dunn at the Navigation Department at Navy OCS, requesting a stack of these forms for him. Navy networking worked! In short order, LeSchack received a package of these forms from the Chief, with the admonition to "not make any more foolish mistakes in your calculations....this time it counts. Your comrades-in-arms will be depending on you, Ensign LeSchack!"

LeSchack expected, in fact, that he was one of the few OCS graduates that promptly upon graduation, had the task of navigating, exactly as he had been taught at OCS.

In this Air Force Arctic world, LeSchack continually heard stories about the Navy's "Arctic Research Lab" that Max and Jess told him about in Washington. However, he was only dimly aware of what it was until one winter's day when, with only a few hours of daylight, two Cessna 180s from ARL landed on T-3 for refueling. At that time, T-3 was north of Barter Island, drifting in a westerly direction. The pilots of each aircraft, Bobby Fischer and Bobby Main, had been returning from the evacuation of the crumbling joint Navy-Air force Drift Station "Charlie." They left their aircraft on the mile-long T-3 ice runway and went to the mess trailer for coffee. LeSchack chatted with them there, and then returned with them to the ice runway to wave them farewell.

In the short interval of their stay on T-3 for refueling and coffee, an Arctic "williwaw," a powerful wind-storm, came up, the wind shifting 90 degrees from the prevailing direction to which the ice runway was oriented. It was clear to LeSchack they could not take off from the ice runway in such a cross wind. It was obviously clear to the pilots also. They went into a huddle and made their decision: they positioned their Cessnas on one side of the runway, perpendicular to its length, facing into the ever-increasing wind. The runway could not have been more than 250 feet wide at this point. They set their brakes and revved up their engines to the maximum the aircraft could tolerate and, together, they released their brakes. LeSchack watched in awe as the two Cessnas roared across the *width* of the runway and were airborne before they could collide with the hummocks and ridges on the other side. This was LeSchack's *real* introduction to the Arctic Research Laboratory.

During the 1959-1960 Winter, LeSchack regularly made vertical seismic soundings from the pack ice off T-3 at a location known as Colby Bay. He also made frequent measurements with a gravimeter, similar to the one he used in the Antarctic, to record not only the gravitational field at any given point in the Arctic Ocean over which he drifted, but to measure the oscillations of this gravity field due to ocean waves and tides beneath the ice.

As at Byrd Station, there was an adequate supply of movies to have one shown in the recreation trailer each evening after dinner. The CO being a senior officer from SAC, and a bit more punctilious about military protocol than had Dr. Ruseski at Byrd, had set aside two "assigned seats" for officers in the movie hall. At that point in his military life, such a distinction, among some 24 men, and only two officers, seemed to be a bit unnecessary, but LeSchack went along with the system. On occasion, LeSchack, even as junior an officer as he was, could poke a bit of fun at the system: One night the featured movie was, "Run Silent, Run Deep," released just the year before. It was, and is, a classic Navy film about submarine warfare in the Pacific, featuring Clark Gable and Burt Lancaster. That exciting story was written by Captain Ned Beach, USN. LeSchack waited until just the last minute, when everyone including the Colonel was seated, and he then strode in wearing the same non-descript military fatigues that everyone else was wearing, with one exception—LeSchack was wearing the distinctive peaked cap of a naval officer. "No need to rise, gentlemen, simply because a *U.S. Navy officer* is coming aboard!" That act did cause much merriment; even the Colonel smiled—faintly.

In February 1960, a more senior naval officer arrived on T-3. Lieutenant Commander "Cock" Cockerel, USN, of ONR came with a crew from the Navy's Underwater Sound Laboratory. They were aboard to conduct a highly classified acoustic experiment with USS SARGO (SSN 583) which would shortly be cruising beneath the ice in T-3's vicinity. From the Navy's point of view, this was an important experiment since it had only been two years earlier that the nuclear submarine, USS NAUTILUS (SSN 571) became the first submarine to traverse the Arctic Ocean beneath the ice. The Navy knew it would not be long before the Soviets also would be cruising their own nuclear submarines beneath the ice and it wanted to learn how to efficiently track them. This would be the first time that the Navy would have an opportunity to track acoustically, in real time, a nuclear submarine— a cooperative one—cruising beneath the ice, and learn how to best do it!

Commander Cockerel guardedly approached LeSchack. As the only other naval officer on the island, Cockerel wished to determine if he would feel comfortable in discussing the secret under-ice acoustic project with LeSchack who to him, was an unknown and a most junior officer. From LeSchack's experience in seismic work—that is the study of acoustics in the earth—and his knowledge of surveying, gained at engineering school, Cockerel felt that LeSchack was well qualified to understand the requirements of Cockerel's program. Accordingly, he was quickly pressed into service by Cockerel as a surveyor to help identify locations for drilling holes in the pack ice for emplacing a circular array of hydrophones.

After the array was set in the ice, it was necessary to orient it with respect to true north. This, like orienting T-3 itself, was an exercise in computing the azimuth of the array with respect to a star's azimuth. This needed to be done in the dead of night (not difficult in mid-winter in the high Arctic) with LeSchack manning the theodolite in the centre of the array and Cockerel, waving a flashlight, moving from location to location until the azimuth of true north was reached. At one point during this exercise, Cockerel yelled out in terror: "Don't shoot! It's me." It was just amazing how much the sound of thermal cracking of the ice in mid-winter resembles the sound of the bolt action of the M-1 rifles they were ordered to carry to protect themselves against marauding polar bears.

Once the array was in place, the USS SARGO, a nuclear attack submarine, made numerous passes, at a variety of speeds, and on a variety of courses beneath T-3. This was the first of the serious submarine "war games" under the Arctic ice cap. But this would not be a game for much longer. In short order, the USSR would build nuclear attack as well as nuclear ballistic missile-launching submarines that were capable of cruising beneath the pack ice in the Arctic Ocean.

The significance of this should not be lost to the reader. A ballistic missile submarine can hide under the pack ice and can be found and neutralized only with great difficulty and only with an opposing nuclear attack submarine. And a ballistic missile submarine can leave its hiding place and find thin ice or open water to launch missiles when so ordered. This fact alone meant that starting from the time LeSchack arrived at T-3 and participated in the sonar array experiment with the SARGO, and continuing for the next 30 years, U.S. foreign policy *vis à vis* the USSR was seriously influenced by the capabilities of nuclear submarines under the Arctic ice.

One night while LeSchack and Cockerel were both in the head, Cockerel asked LeSchack how, on T-3, he got away with growing a beard when the other military personnel would, at most, be permitted to grow moustaches. LeSchack's response was that when comment had been made at the outset about his advancing stubble, he observed (correctly at that time) that the Navy always grew beards while on polar duty. And the base commander had the good grace not to press this point with LeSchack. Cockerel promptly began growing his own beard.

Although LeSchack was assigned to T-3 as a military officer, his chief duties were those of a geophysicist. He regularly recorded seismic and gravimetric data as the ice island slowly drifted westward with the slowly moving Arctic ice pack. He did the navigation, not because he was assigned to do so, but only because it was valuable for all programs, both scientific and military, and because he was the only one who knew how. Most of the time, he worked alone. The gravimeter was located in his office, a warm trailer. Seismic data, by necessity, were recorded at a place called Colby Bay, about two miles away from the main base, not only to be away from the machinery noise of the camp, but also to be off the glacial ice and on the sea ice. Being there also had the psychological advantage as far as camp members were concerned, of keeping the dynamite that LeSchack needed, away from camp. On most days that LeSchack went to Colby Bay, he walked, not only for the exercise, but because he enjoyed the icy solitude.

LeSchack had only worked a few weeks with Commander Cockerel on his under-ice acoustic project, but even in that short period of time he gained an understanding of the enormous strategic and foreign policy implications of super power nuclear ballistic missile submarines cruising, with impunity, beneath the Arctic pack ice. He also gained an understanding of the potential for Arctic Ocean drifting stations being used as clandestine listening stations in the increasingly ominous confrontation developing between the US and the USSR—with only the Arctic Ocean separating them. He also sensed that with the introduction of the nuclear submarine capable of launching nuclear ballistic missiles—like the then recently successful Polaris missiles—the Air Force interest in the Arctic, as espoused 15 years earlier by General Arnold— using long-range bombers—was now bound to be replaced by an ascending Navy interest. The Navy could now cruise, essentially undetected beneath the Arctic ice with nuclear submarines capable of launching ballistic missiles, if a Third World War were ever to be launched.

Having completed his assignment on T-3 at the end of March 1960, LeSchack began his return back to AFCRC in Bedford, Massachusetts to reduce the large volume of data he had collected. On the way, as a matter of courtesy, he stopped briefly at the Project Ice Skate office at Ladd Air Force Base (now Fort Wainwright), in Fairbanks, Alaska. It was there that LeSchack met Captain James F. Smith, USAF, who ran this office and who had earlier been the base commander for the U.S. Ice Stations Alpha and Charlie. Although neither LeSchack nor Captain Smith could have known it at the time, they were destined to play significant roles in each other's lives in a high Arctic adventure launched two years later.

LeSchack's tour with the Air Force had another three months to go. He returned to develop his data into a useful form for AFCRC. Although that laboratory was co-located with Hanscom Field, an Air Force Base in Bedford, he wished to avoid staying at the BOQ on base. He did so by taking advantage of the opportunity to share an apartment in nearby downtown Boston with David Doman, a high school friend who now worked for a computer firm in that city. This, and the downtown ambiance of Boston in springtime, was just what LeSchack needed after four months on an Arctic drifting station. That ambiance very quickly included Simone, a French speaking lady of indeterminate age and profession, who quickly became LeSchack's first long-term lover since Giselle, some four years earlier. And Simone lived within walking distance of David's apartment.

Back in civilization and off base, LeSchack typically had weekends to himself. Shortly after he settled into David's apartment and his regime of data analysis at AFCRC, he decided to fly to New York City to visit his family. Simone happened to be seated next to him on the flight. They struck up a conversation on the way to New York that resulted in his obtaining her address and phone number. That resulted in LeSchack's taking her to dinner the following week when they had both returned to Boston—and not long after that, becoming lovers.

LeSchack was then 25 years old. It was hard to tell how old Simone was.

LeSchack guessed she could have been anywhere between 25 and 45 years old. She was bright and sexy in an enigmatic sort of way. And she *was enigmatic,* and drank whiskey like a man. She said she was from Grasse, on the French-Italian border, and was an architectural student at MIT. While she spoke with a slight French accent—although not Parisian French—she did not have any of the architect's paraphernalia around her ample apartment in Boston. LeSchack's cousin was an architect, and there had been many architectural students at his engineering school, whom he knew. They had their entire environment littered with the tools of their trade, the drafting board, T-square, triangles and drawing instruments. LeSchack saw nothing of that in her apartment. And in the three months he remained in Boston, he got to know her apartment thoroughly.

What he did see in her apartment were books. Books on history and politics, mostly in English, but some in French. She seemed to know a lot about European history, and particularly of the French interests in Algeria; those interests were angrily being debated in 1960 by both political left and right—both verbally and through political terrorism mounted from both sides—but nonetheless, France's hegemony would shortly be coming to an end. LeSchack could not be sure, which side Simone took in this argument; sometimes it appeared as though she were on the far left, other times on the far right siding with the Pied Noirs. They were the reactionary French settlers in Algeria who were strongly opposing French President De Gaulle's move to disentangle France from its old colony. De Gaulle, however, did not wish France to be faced with an Algerian Dien Bien Phu, less than ten years after France was ignominiously forced out of Indo-China.

Simone also had a book translated from the original French about the infamous Alfred Dreyfus case. This, during the 1890s, like the battle for Algiers in the 1960s, completely polarized the French people, far left through far right. It is the story of a Jewish captain in the French Army wrongfully convicted of treason. The case generated extraordinary political and social controversy, pitting every shade of leftist against every shade on the right. While LeSchack already knew the story because it is a classic case of anti-Semitism, it seemed that Simone had it because she was a classic political activist. And he still wasn't clear on which side.

Frankly, LeSchack doubted that Simone was an architecture student at MIT. The only thing LeSchack was certain of is that, whatever Simone's politics, and whatever else she was doing, she seemed to enjoy making love with him, and as frequently as he wished to do so. And she was experienced! Furthermore, he enjoyed being with her, and being seen with her. In LeSchack's present circumstances, he was able to sleepover with Simone several times a week, for nearly a full three months. This certainly was a new, refreshing, and life-shaping experience for him. LeSchack found this far more fulfilling than the one-night stands with which he had become familiar on his Antarctic trip, or the sporadic, but intense, passion he had shared with Giselle whenever they could manage to get together alone. But it also introduced him to a new and life-altering experience—that of becoming high on his own hormones. That is the only way he could explain it.

Making love two, three, and sometimes four times a night, over a period of days, as was now possible with the complaisant Simone had left not only a perpetual and delicious ache in his groin, it must have unleashed an unusually high concentration of his own body chemicals into his bloodstream that left him magnificently disoriented all-day long. In that state, all he seemed to want is more and more, just to maintain this wonderful high. Also, LeSchack sensed another feeling, equally wonderful, but far more subtle. They slept on a narrow, single bed, essentially a cot . To avoid one of them falling on to the floor, they learned to sleep together, all night long, thoroughly entwined. LeSchack thought this was just wonderful! So entwined, he felt continually bathed in an aura, perhaps even a miasma, of exquisite passion and female energy. LeSchack simply adored that new feeling also.

In addition to this sustained passion, however, Simone had also introduced LeSchack to French history, language and culture, all interests that he pursued long after he and Simone parted ways. He continued to meet with, and thoroughly enjoy Simone for another year, even after he left Boston. Although it would be another few years before LeSchack began training as an intelligence officer, he could already see inconsistencies in Simone's behavior that suggested she was other than who she presented herself to be. But who, and why? Of that, he was never to be sure.

His three months at AFCRC were valuable to LeSchack, both as scientist, and increasingly as a Cold Warrior. He was able to receive detailed guidance from Bert Crary on the analysis of his geophysical data. Bert arranged for the Air Force to hire an assistant for LeSchack to help in reducing his T-3 data. He also met with scientists and mathematicians working on the Vela Uniform program for the Department of Defense. These people were working on a methodology for detecting and monitoring clandestine nuclear blasts.

As spring wore on and the Boston weather improved, the drive from David's apartment to the AFCRC became increasingly enjoyable. During his drive he would often listen to a commuter-time radio program of music that signed on and off with the rousing Glazunov "Autumn," from the "Four Seasons". He would always turn up the volume when this music played. On one glorious spring day, LeSchack was particularly inspired by the music, by the warm sunshine, the budding trees, and the way his data analysis was going. As he walked past the office of the Arctic Institute of North America (AINA) representative, who managed many of the Air Force's Arctic research contracts with AINA directly from AFCRC, LeSchack stopped, and peeked in. Patricia, who ran that office for AINA, and whom LeSchack knew peripherally because of previous AINA contacts, was in her office. She was a single young woman with a convertible.

"How would you like to take me for a drive through the countryside this afternoon, with your top down?" LeSchack inquired with a broad smile, suggesting he had enjoyed his *double entendre*. Patricia looked up from her work and eyed him in his khaki uniform. You remember the beautiful tan uniform that was so well-tailored and form-fitting? That uniform now is no longer part of the officers' wardrobe because, allegedly, some fat Chief of Naval Operations banned it; he couldn't fit inside! Well LeSchack was wearing that uniform because it *was* then the uniform of the day in Boston—and it fit him perfectly. Patricia appraisingly, looked him up and down several times, then said tentatively, and with a bright smile, "It could be arranged. How would *you* like to take me to a nice place for dinner, Len?"

And so a social arrangement was struck, and that afternoon Patricia put the convertible top down and they hopped in. She had correctly gauged the young warrior with whom she agreed to dine; she said simply, "I understand you've never been to this area before. Well, before it gets dark, there is a place we should drive to first." She put the convertible in gear and began driving. The warm spring breezes blew through Patricia's hair and seemed to make her feel not only comfortable, but joyous. LeSchack was just pleased because it was springtime, and he was with a young woman.

Patricia drove south from their office in Bedford through what in 1960 was still countryside and rolling fields. LeSchack was more interested in the convertible experience that day, with wind wildly blowing Patricia's hair, then where they were going, but he enjoyed the countryside. Eventually Patricia pulled into an empty parking lot and stopped. "Let's get out here, Len." LeSchack, who had removed his cap in the open convertible, now replaced it on his head and followed Patricia out of the car. They walked in what appeared to be a large park with a stream running through it. The two of them walked together quietly along the path. As they approached a small bridge that crossed the stream, Patricia dropped back. "Go to the bridge Len."

In the late afternoon sunshine, he leisurely strolled up to the small bridge by which there was a simple plaque. As LeSchack saw the writing on the plaque, his body involuntary straightened up and he came to attention. He read:

> By the rude bridge that arched the flood,
> Their flag to April's breeze unfurled,
> Here once the embattled farmers stood,
> And fired the shot heard round the world.

LeSchack, the first generation American, read again the lines of the poem by Ralph Waldo Emerson that commemorated the first significant move toward U.S. independence. He had memorized those lines as a child. After standing thus for a few moments, he soberly did an about face and walked back to Patricia quietly waiting for him. "Thank you, Patricia," he said softly. "Thank you very much for taking me here. That plaque commemorated another fine April day, oh so long ago," he opined. And together they walked back to the car and drove away from Concord, to a fine restaurant.

By the end of June 1960, his assignment with the Air Force had come to an end. He had analyzed enough of his geophysical data to provide a useful contribution to the Air Force's Arctic drifting station program, as well as to write a few technical papers for publication. From a military point of view, he had learned, as an ensign in the Navy, proper military behavior and had earned respect from both officers and enlisted men alike. It was clear that his earlier Antarctic experience had largely been the basis for that respect. The most important concept that he was introduced to during his time on T-3 was the growing strategic and tactical importance of nuclear submarines in the Arctic. This was a direct result of assisting Commander Cockerel set up a hydrophone array to track the USS SARGO. That knowledge was to grow and influence his perceptions of the world, as well as his career as the years went by.

With respect to that career, his next step was to visit his detailer at the Bureau of Navy Personnel in Washington. Detailers are officers whose responsibility is keeping track of personnel and attempting to provide them with the best assignments, commensurate with the needs of the Navy and the capabilities and experience of the officer being assigned. The detailer told LeSchack he had two choices: go to sea, or be assigned to Max Britton's Arctic Program Office at ONR, the Office of Naval Research. The detailer said, "Ensign LeSchack, if you want a career in the Navy, you'd best go to sea now. On the other hand, I know ONR wants to have you serve with them—something about the Arctic experience you now have, and your working with the Air Force. But as an unrestricted line officer in the Navy, you must soon gain experience at sea if you are to advance in the Navy. Let me know shortly what your choice is."

LeSchack knew this would be a crucial decision for him. As far as "adventures" went, he sensed that either way, he would have them. Now 25 years old, he recognized that adventures seemed to seek him, rather than the other way round. If he chose sea duty, adventures would likely revolve about "sailing the bounding main;" duty at ONR would likely allow him to apply immediately his new-found knowledge of Arctic operations to what he perceived as a growing national priority as the Cold War "heated up." He also recognized as a young scientist, experience in Washington, D.C. and at ONR in particular, could come in handy at some point. He chose ONR.

Having made that decision, LeSchack reported to the Arctic Program Office of ONR in July.

LeSchack's first assignment upon commissioning is to Air Force Arctic Drift Station T-3 in 1959. Here he assists the Navy in surveying in, and orienting an acoustical array for tracking the submarine SSN Sargo, which made several test runs beneath this station. From this exercise, he now recognized the strategic importance of being able to track SSNs and SSBNs, both ours and the Soviet's, beneath the ice pack! Soon thereafter, he conceived the idea of "Project Coldfeet!" T-3's mess hall is at left, the radio shack at right. He served on T-3 from November 1959—March 1960.

The U. S. Navy and the Cold, Cold War Years—Office of Naval Research

In the long history of the world, only a few generations have been granted the role of defending freedom in its hour of maximum danger. I do not shrink from this responsibility—I welcome it. I do not believe that any of us would exchange places with any other people or any other generation. The energy, the faith, the devotion which we bring to this endeavor will light our country and all who serve it—and the glow from that fire can truly light the world.

And so, my fellow Americans: ask not what your country can do for you—ask what you can do for your country.

From President John F. Kennedy's Inaugural Address, 20 January 1961

Dr. Max Britton's Arctic Program was part of the ONR Geography Branch. During that time Evelyn Pruitt, a well-known geographer administered the Geography Branch. Ensign Leonard LeSchack was assigned directly to Max Britton's office. There LeSchack assisted Max in administering the ONR contract with the Arctic Research Laboratory, based at Barrow, Alaska, and helped to review unsolicited proposals to conduct Arctic research in the physical sciences. It was Max's office which funded the Laboratory through a contract with the University of Alaska. It also funded numerous principal investigators to conduct their research at the Lab or on the North Slope, or out on the ice. This office at ONR was then responsible for administering the contracts and grants it had let, and to help the Lab and researchers acquire needed equipment, and aircraft and ship support.

LeSchack spent months familiarizing himself with the Washington bureaucracy, and especially that at ONR. This was an entirely new experience for LeSchack—administering, rather than doing, as he had done at Shell Oil or in the Antarctic. That was the business of the Office of Naval Research. It had been established just after World War II in recognition of the fact that the Navy needed an advocate that could initiate, spearhead and administer basic and applied research, directly in the Navy's interest. Headed by a Rear Admiral, the office was military, but the majority of the workers were civil servants. While LeSchack now had some experience dealing with all-civilian organizations, and some experience dealing with all-Navy organizations, dealing with a hybrid organization would be interesting, he thought.

ONR was then physically located in World War II temporary buildings, then still standing, and still temporary, on Constitution Avenue Mall, right next door to the Washington Monument. Just across 17th Street and still on Constitution Avenue was the main Navy building; it was housed in a *World War I* complex of temporary buildings, also still standing. It was not until a decade later, when Richard Nixon took office, that the order came down to raze those temporary buildings and return the Mall to its pre-World War I state. Meanwhile these buildings, not much removed from the architectural élan of the OCS barracks he recently departed, were to be LeSchack's new professional home for the next two and a half years.

He found a ground floor garden apartment in Arlington, Virginia, just across Arlington Boulevard from Fort Meyer. This became LeSchack's first, real bachelor pad, one in which he was likely to stay for more than a year. He decorated it as only a single 25-year-old junior Navy officer on-the-make can. Was it tasteful? That was debatable. Did it work? Well, it did for LeSchack, most of the time. The apartment had a bedroom, a living room and a small study in which he placed his library and ham radio set. The kitchen was adequate. The apartment complex was close to ONR—a short bus ride. Another officer, Lt. James Willenbrink, and a beautiful young woman by the name of Carmen, had apartments in the same complex; both of them worked at ONR also.

ONR was an unusual military office. The organization had been

set up specifically to encourage, support and initiate both applied
and basic research in mathematics and the sciences that could
benefit the Navy at some future time. Although most offices had
at least one Navy officer, many with advanced degrees, most of
the scientists were civilians. Also, the military people rarely wore
their uniforms, just suits and ties, like the civilians. Perhaps once
a month it was decreed that officers would wear their uniforms,
just to remind both the officers, as well as the civilians that ONR
was indeed a military organization!

It took time for LeSchack to learn the Washington way of doing
things as well as specifically, his task, that of reviewing research
proposals in the physical sciences that involved work in the
Arctic. This required a lot of reading, going to technical meetings
of all sorts, and networking with both scientists and naval officers.
LeSchack also took advantage of a graduate school administered
by the U.S. Department of Agriculture to advance his technical
knowledge. The school, designed to promote advanced study in a
variety of subjects for federal employees, was starting a two-year
evening course in oceanography that would begin in September
1960. LeSchack enrolled. His reasoning was that if he remained
on active duty in the Navy, this would likely enhance chances for
promotion; if he chose to return to a civilian graduate school, this
would improve his chances of being accepted. It turned out that
this choice eventually enhanced both careers. What it would do in
the short term, however, was expand LeSchack's networking
ability within the federal government. And this is often what it
took to get the government's work done.

Now, several months into his career in Washington, LeSchack
recognized it was time to do some networking on his own
account. ONR had sent LeSchack to an underwater acoustics
conference held at the Navy Post-Graduate School in Monterey,
California, in the fall of that year. It was the first of many
conferences, seminars and technical meetings concerning matters
of interest to the Navy that he would be given orders to attend.
He had arranged to take a few days leave in California after that
meeting to visit Jim, one of his former Antarctic colleagues with

whom he traveled in New Zealand after they had returned from Antarctica. During the few days LeSchack stayed at Jim's home in the Bay Area, he was introduced to Maureen, who appeared to have been one of Jim's lovers. She was from New Zealand where they were likely to have met. During that short visit with Jim, the two men had occasion to drive Maureen to the airport to fly, she announced, to Washington, D.C.

Whatever the relationship had been between Jim and the most attractive Maureen, it seemed clear to LeSchack that that relationship was now at an end. Something in the way Jim let her off at the entrance to the terminal without getting out of the car to accompany her inside. Before Jim had a chance to pull away from the curb LeSchack inquired, "Jim, do you mind if I make an effort to see Maureen when I get back to Washington?" "Go ahead," he sighed, "Why don't you catch her before she boards her plane and talk to her? I don't think she's got anyone waiting for her there. I'll wait for you here." With a sudden jolt of adrenaline, LeSchack jumped from the idling vehicle and raced into the terminal where he found Maureen waiting in line.

"Maureen," he called to her, trying to disguise his out-of-breath state resulting from his mad sprint to catch up with this now suddenly interesting woman. "You said that you were flying to Washington. That's where I live. I will be returning there tomorrow. Would you mind if I called you?" "Oh please do," she smiled brightly. "Give me your phone number and I'll call you when I settle in. I'm not sure where I'll be staying yet, but I should be there for several weeks." With that quick exchange, they smiled warmly at one another, LeSchack thinking, "Perhaps I have found a new and interesting lover." LeSchack could not tell what Maureen was thinking, but at the very least, she appeared to have been pleased to meet someone else who, not only knew where New Zealand was, but had spent time there. Not many people even know where New Zealand is.

LeSchack returned to Jim's car, thanked him for providing the opportunity to meet Maureen, and the two drove off. The next day Jim took LeSchack to the airport and he too, flew to

Washington. But LeSchack would know where he would be staying—his bachelor lair in Arlington, a cozy spot that had yet to be graced by any lover of his. Although there seemed to be no connection to the strange scene that had just transpired at the airport, LeSchack's and Jim's paths never seemed to cross again. But LeSchack's and Maureen's did. And what a conjunction that was!

Upon his return to ONR, LeSchack became immersed in office work, administering existing research contracts and examining proposals for new projects. He began his course of oceanographic studies in the evenings. He also joined the Pentagon Officers Athletic Club, an indoor facility located on the Pentagon grounds. There he managed to keep fit, mostly by working out on the parallel bars and high bar, and swimming in the indoor pool. It was at that pool that he took his first course in scuba diving. And eventually one weekend, he got a call from Maureen.

She said she was staying at a hotel in downtown Washington, and wondered, "Len would you like to pay me a visit?" With that immediate surge of chemicals that he was learning to expect from his body whenever the potential for lovemaking suddenly appeared, LeSchack readily agreed to meet her. She gave him her room number.

Shortly thereafter, he was knocking at her door. It was a good-looking woman, at least ten years older than LeSchack, who came to the door to let him in. Although it was clear to him that Maureen was pleased to see him, she had a sad, weariness about her eyes. They sat down together in her rather small, rather shabby room and began talking of New Zealand, and generally getting to know a bit about each other. Not for long, however. It seemed to LeSchack that he had only been with her for a few minutes before they were in bed making passionate love to one another. And again and again. It was simply wonderful!

Eventually they disentangled damp arms and thighs from around each other, washed up, and went to the hotel's small restaurant for dinner. Over a completely uninspired meal, Maureen told LeSchack that there was a middle-aged man in town that she had gotten to know, who wanted to marry her. "He's a golf pro," she said, "and owns a putting range in town. All he seems to do is play golf. But he wants to marry me, and can support me, and I am ready to settle down. I don't know what to do, Len. He certainly does not like making love to me as much as I see you do." What Maureen left unsaid was, "I am ready for some security after being a party girl for so long."

Frankly, LeSchack did not know what to say. When they parted that day Maureen told him she wished to see him again, but she was seriously considering the offer of marriage from the golf pro. Several weeks thereafter, Maureen came to LeSchack's apartment in Arlington and remained over the weekend. As they had before, they made passionate love to one another and LeSchack doesn't even remember getting out of bed for those days. At the end of that weekend, Maureen said to him, "I am going to marry him Len. I need the security. I would like to invite you to my wedding. Would you come?" "Of course," said LeSchack sadly, but not really knowing why he should be so sad.

As that glorious weekend of love-making with Maureen came to a close, there was a knock on LeSchack's apartment door. It was Maureen's golf pro, ready to take her to wherever she now called home. As Maureen and her intended husband left, LeSchack thought to himself, "This was Maureen's Last Supper. She wanted to be, one more time, with someone, a U. S. Navy man, perhaps, who had a real connection with New Zealand, her home, and who really, really enjoyed making love to her."

LeSchack *did* attend Maureen's marriage, shortly thereafter. It was a private ceremony held at a nice home somewhere in Washington. An Episcopal minister officiated. Although there were a few dozen well-dressed people in attendance, Maureen was the only person there that LeSchack knew. "And I know her in the biblical sense," he mused, after listening to the minister's offerings. This wedding was truly an odd experience for LeSchack. Odder still, was the feeling he had during the reception. He only remembered speaking with one person after the ceremony, and that was with the minister who had presided. It turns out that somewhere during, what started out as trivial conversation, LeSchack gleaned that the minister was also a radio ham; together they launched into an animated conversation on a favorite subject.

As LeSchack left the reception, he thought to himself, "This has got to be the most bizarre experience I have ever had. I have *just* had a long conversation about ham radio with an ordained minister who I never before met, who *just* joined in holy matrimony a man I don't know, to a woman I *just* fucked, and most enjoyably so!"

The social highlight of that year, as far as Arctic explorers and scientists were concerned, was a large dinner party thrown by Colonel Lou DeGoes, head of the Air Force Cambridge Research Center's Arctic Program at Hanscom Field. In attendance were many of the world's old Arctic explorers, such as Vilhjalmur Stefansson, the Canadian anthropologist who was leader of the 1913-1918 Canadian Arctic Expedition, as well as many of the young Arctic drifting station researchers who worked on Air Force or Navy contracts. This event also signaled the peak of Air Force interest and influence in Arctic matters. At this point, with the Navy's increasing fleet of nuclear submarines capable of under-ice operations, Air Force interest in Arctic operations and research began to wane. Many of the invitees to the dinner were Navy people from the nearby Underwater Sound Laboratory in New London, Connecticut.

LeSchack and Max Britton were invited. LeSchack got his orders cut to include a few days working and networking with the colleagues he had gotten to know earlier that year at AFCRC. Max planned to stay at a Boston hotel. LeSchack planned to stay with Simone, which, of course was another reason he arrived a few days earlier.

By this time Max then aged 50, and LeSchack, half that age, had developed a relationship part way between that of a son Max never had, and a graduate student, of whom Max had plenty during his professoring days before ONR. Their relationship was developing well, and LeSchack looked to Max as a mentor both in science and in dealing with and manipulating the federal bureaucracy. Their relationship had a social side too—mostly martini lunches in Washington, just to avoid the drab government cafeterias. So it was no surprise to Max when he phoned LeSchack in Boston on some office business a day before he was scheduled to arrive there, and discover a woman with a French accent answering the phone at the number LeSchack had provided. Max, who had only recently married a beautiful Czech woman, well understood the charm that European women can have. "Ah, Len, I should have anticipated a young naval officer like you would find a woman with whom to stay on an official Navy trip!"

The party that Colonel DeGoes had hosted, was likely the last event at which many of North America's oldest explorers and scientists, like Stefansson, would all attend and share their wit and wisdom with their younger peers. Stefansson, one of LeSchack's polar explorer heroes, for example, was 81 when LeSchack finally met him in 1960. Stefansson brought his 40-year old wife, the vivacious Evie, to the dinner event. LeSchack brought the lovely, enigmatic and Gallic-looking Simone. He was simply amazed at how many men are attracted to women with French accents. Several of the men at the table at which LeSchack and Simone sat, tried out their college French on her. Smiling, she bantered gaily with them. It was then that LeSchack began to think seriously about learning to speak French. It was a fine event, after which LeSchack took Simone home to bed. When LeSchack finally left Boston and Simone's apartment, they agreed to meet again soon in Washington. But he left with that same odd feeling, that Simone was someone other than who she said she was. Nonetheless, he thoroughly enjoyed her company, no matter who she was.

While the Navy did not particularly encourage the wearing of the uniform in Washington every day, the wearing of the uniform elsewhere was *not* discouraged. And LeSchack was not unmindful of the affect that uniform had on some young women. He occasionally wore it on dates with women he knew in New York. Because he often was off-duty on weekends, he occasionally would return to New York City to visit his parents, and on Saturday night travel to Manhattan with a date. One of LeSchack's favorite restaurants there was an Italian place, Asti's, where the waiters and waitresses would sing arias from operas.

One night while there, trying to impress a young lady, a waitress with what LeSchack refers to as an operatic figure—big and buxom—came over and seeing him in uniform, told him her nephew had just become a naval officer, and she loved the Navy's uniform! She then asked, "Is there any aria you would like us to sing for you two?" Without hesitation, and remembering the power of that opera he had first heard at Byrd Station, he blurted out, "Oh yes, *Libiamo, Libiamo!*—the Drinking Song from *La Traviata!* Please." The waitress smiled happily, and then backed away from the table a bit, and began belting out that powerful, melodic aria to drink by! And moments later the rest of the serving staff joined in. They may not have been Metropolitan Opera caliber, but LeSchack thought they surely came close. He was most appreciative. On a few other occasions, LeSchack would show up at that restaurant, in uniform, and with a new date. If that buxom waitress was there, when she saw him in uniform, she would come up to their table and begin to sing "The Drinking Song," for him—and, of course, the Navy!

On the nineteenth day of January, 1961 it began to snow heavily in Washington, D.C. LeSchack watched through the gritty windows of his office on Constitution Avenue the big flakes falling. This was the first significant snowfall of the winter. After fourteen months in the Antarctic and four winter months in the Arctic, he was not much concerned about what a winter in Washington could produce. Earlier that day he and a new friend, Doran "Top" Topolosky, who occupied the office across the hall from him at ONR, had decided to go to dinner together. They had formed a routine of going out to dinner together, at least once a week, usually at a favorite steak house in Alexandria, Virginia.

At the end of the workday when LeSchack and Top set foot out on Constitution Avenue, they recognized a change in plans might be in order. The snow had accumulated to the point that traffic was at a standstill. The busses and autos that normally move briskly to carry government workers back to their homes in the Virginia suburbs were in gridlock. So LeSchack and Top made the decision to remain in town and go to a nearby restaurant that they knew well, one that was within walking distance. This they did, and they had "Blackie's House of Beef" nearly to themselves while others were fighting traffic. Many hours and martinis later, and after a good meal, they left the wonderfully cheery ambiance of Blackie's and walked back to Constitution Avenue with the hope that traffic would now have cleared up and they could find a late hour commuter bus. They found one going to Arlington where LeSchack lived, but none bound for Alexandria where Top lived. LeSchack suggested they both go to Arlington and Top could sleep overnight at his apartment on the couch. With that decision made, they banged on the closed door of the Arlington bus stopped at the usual pickup point at the corner of Constitution Avenue and Seventeenth Street.

The driver opened the door for them; they stepped on, dropped their quarters into the pay-here bucket, and waited, along with others in the crowded bus, for the traffic light to change to green. It did. Then back to red, and then green again. Traffic did not move. Gradually it dawned on LeSchack that this bus may have been there for a long time. He looked around and saw a sullen, unhappy group of people, some of whom he recognized from his office that got off work when he and Top had. "How long have you folks been waiting here?" LeSchack asked, fearful of their answer. It soon became clear that this busload had been at this one spot, without moving, for the entire time LeSchack and Top were being well fed and well lubricated at Blackie's. LeSchack said, "Top, let's get out and walk home, before these people stone us for being so boisterously well-fed."

And they did walk home. To the end of Constitution Avenue, then across the Memorial Bridge, which was thoroughly drifted with snow so that vehicular traffic could not possibly move, and then to Arlington Boulevard and LeSchack's apartment, and then to a few more drinks to chase away the chill of the night.

The next day hardly any traffic moved into town. All the city's snow-moving equipment had been commandeered for removing all snow and spotlessly cleaning the length of Pennsylvania Avenue from the White House to the Capitol Building. This was in preparation for the procession along that route for the inauguration of the 35th President of the United States of America, John F. Kennedy. LeSchack and Top knew it would be pointless to go into town, so they stayed at his apartment to watch the inauguration on television. One can hardly say that JFK won by a landslide: the popular vote stood at 49.6% for Nixon and 49.7% for Kennedy. And while LeSchack did not agree with all of Kennedy's policies, he did agree with Kennedy's style and élan. Well, hell, Kennedy was a naval officer also, and a Navy hero, and he was just eighteen years older than LeSchack!

Kennedy's inaugural address was the best one LeSchack had ever heard. That was the, "ask not what your country can do for you — ask what you can do for your country" speech. It was a stirring speech to LeSchack — and he *did* begin to wonder then what *he could do*. It was not long before he had such and opportunity to do something. And the very president who made that historic speech would be the one to authorize, shortly before his death, a presidential decoration for LeSchack that acknowledged that *he had, in fact, done something for his country.*

A bit less than a year at ONR, LeSchack asked Max whether he would authorize orders for him to travel to ARL at Barrow, Alaska, and then to the ice, to continue the ocean wave research he had begun on T-3. Max, formerly a professor of botany at a mid-western university, and a researcher himself, thought such a trip would be a good opportunity for LeSchack to experience Lab operations first hand, as well as to continue his earlier research. Max approved, provided, (1) LeSchack could scrounge any, and all geophysical equipment he needed for his research, and (2) he would return to Washington within two weeks of leaving.

LeSchack agreed to Max's conditions, and he obtained the equipment needed to conduct his research project on the ice, a recording gravimeter from the U.S. Navy Hydrographic Office (now the Oceanographic Office), and the microbarograph from AFCRC. The microbarograph was simple to obtain. LeSchack had met the officer that used such instruments at the Air Force lab at Bedford, Massachusetts before he left, and he knew that such an instrument was available and not otherwise in use. A simple Navy to Air Force request covered that arrangement. The recording gravimeter was a different story; such was not in the government inventory and would have to be rented from a private firm. Money would have to be spent, but as Max made clear, would not be available from ONR. This is where networking and LeSchack's enrollment in graduate studies paid off.

One of the courses in the oceanographic curriculum was "Ocean Waves." The instructor, Jack Schule, was a senior administrator at the U.S. Navy Hydrographic Office where the course was given. Jack had been an early researcher on ocean waves, knew the Arctic and had been there, and was a friend of the Navy—*the real Navy that wore uniforms.* Not all civil servants, even if they were employed by the Navy Department, were comfortable with its uniformed members! Many found them intimidating. But not Jack. So LeSchack approached Jack one evening after class to see whether he could convince him to get the Hydrographic Office to rent a recording gravimeter for his research. LeSchack knew his research would be valuable for both offices, especially since the Hydrographic Office had a "Gravity Branch" that could likely justify the rental costs. Jack's response: "We can't talk about this here in the classroom. Let's go across the street to Clancy's Bar after class, and discuss it over beer!"

In the dark, beery atmosphere of Clancy's, LeSchack learned an important lesson about doing business among governmental agencies. First you get officers from each of the agencies involved, all of whom want to see the discussed piece of business succeed, then *together* draft a letter of request. This is necessary since interagency letters, LeSchack learned, begin with the originator, and must travel up the chain of command for approval to be sent out by the chief of the originator's agency to the chief of the receiving agency for action. The proper words must be used that satisfy the needs and the politics of the originating agency, as well as the needs and politics of the receiving agency, which well may be different. This is best accomplished when officers of both agencies jointly draft the letter of request. Well, after the first few beers, Jack agreed that LeSchack's "ocean waves beneath the Arctic pack ice" measurement with a recording gravimeter was a good idea. So together, they began writing in LeSchack's notebook atop the bar. That hastily scribbled letter of request was duly transcribed by LeSchack's secretary the next day at ONR. She did this by typing from his now beer-stained notebook, and that letter went up the chain, and was ultimately dispatched. "Wherever did you write this, Len?" she asked him as she returned his stained notebook, shaking out the pretzel and peanut bits still in the binding as she did so. Nonetheless, the request was approved shortly thereafter. LeSchack now had the equipment he needed to go to the ice!

What was now needed for his research, however, was a new Navy drift station. During this equipment-gathering period, ARLIS I, the Navy's only drift station and LeSchack's intended base of operations, had broken up and was completely abandoned by 25 March 1961. It, like most drift stations, had been constructed on sea ice, and had been destroyed in a winter storm.

Fortunately, LeSchack did not have long to wait. Reconnaissance flights from ARL began in early May to find a suitable piece of ice for a new drift station. In anticipation of a station being established momentarily, LeSchack made arrangements to leave from Washington, D.C., to Barrow, Alaska, with all his equipment, on 18 May.

By this time in young LeSchack's polar career, he had learned that chances of needed equipment becoming lost, stolen or misrouted on their way to the Arctic or Antarctic were proportional to the importance of the equipment to the project. He had observed the manner in which the Army Corps of Engineers shipped their equipment to the Antarctic, where there were many transshipment points from original loading to final off-loading and therefore, multiple opportunities for loss of equipment. All their equipment boxes were painted international orange. All members of the crew *who would ultimately need the equipment* were assigned to watch the unloading and reloading operation at each transshipment point, counting the number of orange boxes at each location.

In this fashion, everything was accounted for all along the way. It is absolutely necessary to do this, because in no way can the shipper, whoever it is, apologize enough or financially make up for equipment loss that occurs during that small window of opportunity available for conducting long-planned polar operations. If a key piece of equipment is lost, the operation will be aborted and often, for a variety of irrelevant reasons, will never again be attempted.

Accordingly, LeSchack too, painted all eight of his equipment boxes international orange. He had the ONR Travel Office pre-arrange, with all the airlines being used to get him and his equipment to Barrow, to agree beforehand, *in writing,* that all equipment would go as *accompanying baggage.* LeSchack provided the carriers the dimensions of all boxes and specified that the largest box, the gravimeter, *must be shipped in an upright position.* All carriers agreed.

Imagine then, LeSchack's consternation on 18 May, aboard the Northwest Airlines 707 at Washington National Airport, watching his orange boxes being loaded aboard, when the Northwest loadmaster announced to him that the only way the large box can go is if they turn it on its side so that it will fit in the hold. LeSchack pulled out the baggage waybill and told the loadmaster Northwest agreed to ship it standing up, and suggested it will fit in the clothes closet in the forward cabin.

A stewardess recognizing that this disagreement might hinder boarding procedures, now joined in the discussion, announcing it is against company regulations to place baggage of this size in the forward cabin. LeSchack reminded the stewardess that the airline had already agreed, in writing, to carry the equipment in question as accompanying baggage and in an upright position.

The stewardess then threatened she would have to get the pilot if he didn't behave. LeSchack told her to go get him. The pilot then entered the passenger cabin and joined in the fray, and by fiat, declared that despite the prearrangement with the airline, they will either put the package in the hold, on its side, or leave it for another, unspecified flight. And if LeSchack did not immediately agree, the pilot would call the police.

At this point LeSchack, in the uniform of an ensign in the Navy, brought himself to his full six-foot height and told the pilot "my orders are to get the equipment to the ARL at Barrow **now**, and the plane **will not** leave without the equipment being carried as Northwest had promised. "As a military man who knows all about orders, though," he observed to the pilot, rather kindly he thought, "that you probably have your own orders too; and you must do what you must do." But then LeSchack alluded darkly that he was "a military courier and this was an urgent top security shipment and the Navy and the Department of Defense *would not be pleased* with the airline's abrogation of its contractual agreement."

The pilot stormed back to his cabin and ten minutes later, instead of the police, the Northwest Airport Manager boarded the plane, took one look at the situation and, most sensibly, ordered the box placed, *upright*, in the forward cabin. Alas, LeSchack had more than his allotted 15 minutes of fame, right then and there. Forty-five minutes late, the Northwest 707 took off with an entire cabin load of unhappy passengers looking angrily at him for being the obvious cause of the delay. The tension was palpable. As sternly and as dispassionately as a young Navy ensign can possibly look under the circumstances that prevailed, LeSchack straightened his uniform, made quick eye-contact with all the other passengers, and then proceeded to take his seat. When drink orders were taken, he ordered a double martini and downed it quickly. Just like James Bond would have done.

As it happened, LeSchack would shortly *anticipate exactly what James Bond would do, and before Bond would do so,* in LeSchack's "Project Coldfeet." But we get ahead of our story. Nonetheless, that incident with Northwest was yet another example for LeSchack of the logistics of science moving more smoothly when he was in uniform.

Because he was on official Navy business, he continued to wear his uniform on the last leg of his voyage, Fairbanks to Barrow. Once past the confrontation with Northwest—a confrontation whereby his uniform and his newly vested authority were tested in one of LeSchack's first battles of intimidation—he anticipated this last flight from Fairbanks would be one without further challenges. But one did arise, an enjoyable one for him. Halfway to Barrow, the Wien Alaska airline stewardess came up to LeSchack's seat and, with a brief mechanical smile, handed him a simple, mass-produced certificate that announced the bearer had crossed the famous Arctic Circle. LeSchack looked at the certificate, then at the stewardess, a magnificent-looking woman, at least ten years older than his now 26 years. He looked up at her and said simply, "Oh, thank you, but I've already crossed the Arctic Circle several times before."

With that, the stewardess performed the female equivalent of LeSchack's newly acquired manner of projecting "command presence"— that of standing ram-rod straight and puffing out his shoulders like a peacock. She too, straightened up, but then thrust, in LeSchack's direction, her ample chest, well outlined in her form-fitting uniform, and challenged him with, "I expect I have been farther north than you ever have!" The woman, with her mature good looks, exuded confidence and experience, and looked LeSchack directly in the eye as she said this. LeSchack looked into her eyes, and then quietly recognized that this woman was simply toying with him, a still quite boyish-looking Navy ensign. Sensing the game that was now being played out, and that

this adventurous woman had likely joined some polar bear
hunters out on the ice north of Barrow, he deliberately looked
directly at the stewardess' still outthrust chest and said simply, "I
doubt that."

The stewardess, now taken aback just a bit, naturally asked, "well
where *have* you been?" At this point, he raised his eyes and
generously looked into hers, "well, I spent four months stationed
on the Air Force Ice Island T-3." "Oh," she responded, now in
what appeared to LeSchack to be a downright motherly way, "I
guess you have been farther north."

LeSchack arrived at Barrow, with all equipment, on 20 May 1961.
On 22 May, the ARL pilots found an *ice island* at 73 01 N, 156 05W.
Max Brewer, director of the Lab, and the Lab's R4D and two
Cessna 180s, flown by Bobby Fischer, Bobby Main (who LeSchack
had met on T-3), and Lloyd Zimmerman, made the discovery.
The following day the nucleus of ARLIS II—for Arctic Research
Laboratory Ice Station number two—was established, and a camp
was set up. Flying to and from ARLIS II was unquestionably for
LeSchack an unique experience. Flights were made 23 times
during the initial phase of establishing the camp (from 24 to 28
May). He accompanied several of these flights to ARLIS II during
its establishment and prior to remaining there to set up his own
oceanographic research.

LeSchack flew with Lloyd "Zim" Zimmerman a number of times
and they got on well together. From LeSchack's notes at the time
he observed that Zim, an aviator of the "Terry and the Pirates"
school, was as colorful as he was good. He had previously flown
in Indochina and had a Vietnamese wife. He was now an Arctic
roustabout and had flown all manner of winged contrivances
throughout the North Country and was a student of...well, just
people. He knew, it seemed, all the folks from Nome on up
around the North Slope to Canada. Wherever he landed the ARL
plane, he seemed to find a home.

It was not infrequent, while roaring over the tundra, 500 feet off the deck, that he passed over a party of hunters looking for caribou or whatever was in season (or out of season too, for that matter), and they always recognized the colorful lab planes. They always seemed to know when Zim was in the cockpit driving, for they waved wildly to him.

Heading out to ARLIS II on the logistic support flights from Barrow, Zim would take the R4D up to 300 feet or so, to clear the ground fog that always hangs around the coast during the summer. Once clear of the coastal fog, he would dive down to get under the undercast. Then he would follow the radio beacon straight for ARLIS II at 200 feet off the ice. This is a strange sensation, roaring along at 120 knots with the vast, unending, ever-changing panorama of pressure ridges and pack ice racing toward you. He would startle a seal, sunning itself on the pack; with one graceful leap, it dove into an open lead and would be gone.

In May, 1961, ARLIS II—an ice island, glacial ice that broke off of the Ellesmere Ice Shelf—was only a little over a hundred miles from Barrow, and within an hour or so Zim would be nearing the camp. On a clear day, ARLIS II would loom up ahead quite strikingly; the large piles of rock—glacial moraines that had been deposited on the Ellesmere Ice Shelf and had drifted away when a piece of that shelf, now the ice island, had broken off—would contrast greatly with the brilliant white ice that supported those piles.

An ice landing is something to be experienced; second-hand description will not do it justice. After flying over the pack, which is remarkably smooth flying due to the uniformity of the air over the ice, Zim would prepare for a landing on the unprepared ARLIS II ice strip. It looked about the same as any other part of the ice island, except that it had flags along it to delineate it from the rest of the ice. And the camp was at the far end of the flags.

Zim would approach the far end of the strip and throttle down. He would just sail, slowly, gently settling over the runway. The R4D seemed to hang over one spot when coming in for a landing.

The only premonition that the landing may be something other than smooth comes from Zim himself. His easy "go-to-Hell" attitude slips away, and his jaw tightens a bit and the muscles in his face tense up.

The co-pilot has started reading the airspeed indicator. Hundred...hundred..... ninety...eighty-five.... Full flaps are down. The flags that line the strip are racing past the plane...the ice doesn't look quite as smooth and homogeneous when one is 30 feet above it. Then, after an eternity of gently settling, an almost anticlimactic teeth-rattling, jarring landing. Very much like landing an R4D in the Antarctic.

LeSchack liked flying in the Lab's R4Ds, and he had sense of accomplishment in doing so, since months earlier at ONR he had assisted Max Britton in prying loose those two very same R4Ds from the Navy's aviation bone-yard at Litchfield Park, Arizona. He had helped invent a reason why "United States Navy," emblazoned on these aircraft, should remain and not be painted over simply because they were destined for a contractor.

On 30 May Bobby Fischer and Bobby Main flew LeSchack and his equipment to ARLIS II in the two Cessna 180s. He remained there until 5 June. In those early days, the station was set up by ARLIS II foreman Kenny Toovak and manned by John Beck, the station leader, Frank Akpik, the mechanic, Charles Edwardson, Jr., the maintenance man, and Carl Johnston, the cook and baker. One, or some combination of these gentlemen, shot and prepared for dinner a marauding polar bear. Let me tell you, fresh polar bear stew, *au naturel*, i.e., without seasoning, and *al fresco*, i.e., without shelter, among the arctic breezes because no dining area had yet been built, was an experience.

During this time, LeSchack was busy. In a letter to his parents dated 4 June 1961 from "Ice Island ARLIS II, 73 13N, 157 19W", he wrote, in a most artsy green-colored ink:

"Here I am again in my element—the polar corners of this

globe; but not for long. I should be on my way home shortly. But in the short period of time that I have been North I have accomplished quite a lot. I have set up the first scientific measurements on the Navy's new ice island that was discovered in the Arctic Ocean a few weeks ago. I also was its first surveyor and navigator—oh well, all in a day's work!

Incidentally, I usually don't indulge in such exotic colors of ink, however, I forgot my Parker 51 blue-black and had to dip into the inkwell of one of my scientific recording machines for this delicious hue (digital recorders were not yet available then, only analog recorders with cantankerous, leaky pens)."

Well, LeSchack may have forgotten his fountain pen, but he remembered to bring everything else that he needed, a lesson he learned from both Antarctic and T-3 duty. He recognized that, "if you bring it with you, you have it; if you expect the Navy or the Air Force or the ARL or some other organization to provide it to you immediately, when you need it, in all likelihood you won't have it—in a timely fashion, that is."

This philosophy was to serve him well when Project Coldfeet, a substantial Arctic intelligence operation, yet to be conceived by LeSchack, would get underway.

Aboard ARLIS II, LeSchack had his own tiny shortwave radio. He might have expected that there would be a shortwave radio aboard the station. But there was none capable of receiving accurate time signals essential for calculating positions of the drifting station by celestial navigation. LeSchack's shortwave radio saved the day.

LeSchack and Bill McComas, who arrived at ARLIS II within days of LeSchack's arrival, set up the equipment to run LeSchack's oceanographic research program. McComas, a junior scientist, had been sent from the Hydrographic Office to continue taking the readings that LeSchack started, because several months of continuous recordings were required. He also was there to look after that office's considerable investment in equipment that LeSchack and ONR had borrowed.

LeSchack returned to Barrow on 5 June after recording the first geographic location of ARLIS II by shooting the sun. There, he made the first map of the circumnavigation of the periphery of ARLIS II, and he left the following day to return to Washington within the two-week period that Britton had authorized him to be away from the office.

Before LeSchack left Barrow though, Brewer, the ARL director, came over to him and, chomping hard on his pipe, asked him, with a twinkle in his eye, more about that circumnavigation of ARLIS II on foot that McComas and he had done to map the island. LeSchack went through the story again, recounting how that trip, following the sea-ice-ice-island boundary, pacing off distance and recording compass headings, was a long, arduous, walk. It was a bit scary, too, because they became lost in an ice fog and were fearful of visually loosing the boundary they were following. That boundary was crucial to their returning safely to their starting point at the camp. The ARL pilots had told LeSchack the shape and general dimensions of the ice island. He determined that a trip on foot was safely achievable by the two healthy young men. Had they wandered on to the sea ice and lost sight of the boundary, however, they could have walked and mapped forever without returning safely!

Brewer listened carefully and nodded sagely. He then told LeSchack that Kenny Toovak, his ARLIS II foreman, had observed that the M-1 rifle that he and McComas took turns carrying on the ice, and was always carried to protect against polar bears, had been returned to camp, after the circumnavigation, with a barrel packed full of ice and snow. "It's a good thing you had no need to fire it," he said, sarcastically. LeSchack, now a military man who presumably should have known better, was mightily chagrined.

Upon LeSchack's return to ONR he found on his desk official

orders promoting him to Lieutenant (jg). He was pleased, but of course, not surprised. It happens automatically after eighteen months of life as an ensign, provided you don't screw up. When LeSchack told Max about the promotion, Max looked up from his desk and said, "Good! In your own mind, I know that you always thought of yourself as a lieutenant, never an ensign! Now Len, with this promotion, it's time for you to think of bigger things!" Max was partly right. While LeSchack had not specifically thought about being a *Navy captain* just yet, in his own mind he was at least a lieutenant commander. *And he was* thinking of bigger things. He smiled a "thank you" to Max.

As the Cold War grew ever more frightening, and it was becoming clearer to LeSchack that the Arctic was going to become a major theater of confrontation between U.S. and Soviet nuclear submarines, he began to think more about the role Arctic drifting stations would play in a possible confrontation up North. With his return from ARLIS II, and his recollections of the USS SARGO acoustic experiments beneath T-3 the previous year, he began quietly to assemble information and stray thoughts about the strategic role drift stations play, or could play, for both the US and the USSR. This was one of the "bigger things" LeSchack was now thinking about. However, there was another big thing he was thinking about. Making love to Simone; she was coming to Washington to stay over that weekend with LeSchack at his apartment. But just before she showed up, LeSchack had another visitor.

By happenstance, there was another man in Washington who also was thinking about Arctic drifting stations and the role they play—and could play. Howard Simons was a young reporter for the Washington Post. A few days after LeSchack's return to Washington, Simons showed up at ONR's Arctic Program office to talk with him and Max about the establishment of ARLIS II by the Navy, and the scientific and strategic significance of these stations. Max outlined a brief history of the drift station program, both from the U.S. point of view, and from that of the Soviets. LeSchack went into some of the details of his adventures at this new station, and observed that he was one of the first men aboard her, and the first to map it and chart its position by celestial navigation. LeSchack, who had also taken photographs of the new ice island from Zim's cockpit, provided copies for use by the Washington Post. A few days later, under Simons' byline, there was a good piece in that paper about ARLIS II, and the Navy's drifting station program—with illustrations provided by LeSchack.

As a matter of historical note, a decade later Simons had become the Managing Editor for the Washington Post. However, it is not clear whether he was still thinking about Arctic matters any longer; as the Managing Editor, he was then directing a team of young reporters having their own adventures in a frigid world, the messy world of politics; their names were Carl Bernstein and Bob Woodward. They were the two reporters who investigated the break-in to the Democratic National Committee headquarters located in the "Watergate Apartment Complex," a robbery that was eventually traced to the White House and ultimately brought down President Richard Nixon.

That weekend with Simone was an absolute pleasure for LeSchack. This was the second time since he had moved from Boston to Washington that Simone had come to visit and make love to him. As before, they talked European and American politics, literature and music, and they dined well. And went to bed together. As before, LeSchack could not shake the feeling that there was something about Simone that was an enigma, and that somehow, she was not who she said she was; there was something that "was not quite right." But he could not define what that something was. Perhaps, he thought, "it's just my lack of experience with women. I don't yet know all their special signals and how to read them."

Nonetheless, whatever "that something was," he thoroughly enjoyed frequent lovemaking with Simone. And he assumed that feeling was reciprocated. Simone had an interesting manner in which to show this. She would awaken him from a sound slumber during which they were invariably entwined together and say something like, "Oooooh, Len, *Mon Chèr*, you ahhhrrr rrreaddddy! You ahhhrrr rrreaddddy!" observing, even before LeSchack had fully awakened, that if he *really* wanted to, he could easily enter her now, without further ado. To a less libidinous person, the manner in which she said this to LeSchack suggested she was merely bringing a trivial matter to his attention, as a point of interest, for whatever action *he* might choose. "However," he thought delightedly, "while I love the way Simone rolls her 'r's,' even more than that, I love the way she rolls her *arse*! And that, I believe, signifies she is 'rrreaddddy' too." Simone never seemed to be disappointed at his lusty choice. Enigmatic, perhaps. Disappointed, No.

It was clearly LeSchack's loving association with Simone that had awakened his interest in the French language and French and European history with its political intrigues throughout the ages, and of course, introduced him to popular songs in French. From Simone he learned, "*Plaisir d'amour*," and, "*Non, Je ne regrette rien*," two quintessentially French love songs—each displaying diametrically opposed points of view. *Plaisir d'amour*, speaks of the brief ecstasy of love followed by an eternity of sorrow, while *Non, Je ne regrette rien*, especially as sung by Édith Piaf, expresses a "love 'em and leave 'em, I don't give a damn," philosophy of love. LeSchack thought that the enigmatic Simone alternately embraced both points of view! Sometimes, even simultaneously!

When Simone indicated she would be going to Paris in August of that year, LeSchack told her he could arrange to meet her there. He would be able to take a month's leave at that time, and would love to join her. She happily agreed, and when she left at the end of that superb weekend, she gave him her address in Paris. What she left behind was one of her sweaters, the delicious fragrance of her wonderful perfume, "*crêpe de Chine*," and glorious memories for him. Also, some of the earlier nagging memories and doubts. LeSchack had, for example, an uneasy feeling that on this particular weekend Simone, a clearly sexually experienced woman, was now trying to become pregnant. Was it some sort of sixth-sense, this uneasiness, or was it LeSchack's paranoia? It was nothing Simone said or did differently as they embarked on their delicious lovemaking, just a feeling he had. But it was not something, at the height of passion, that he was going to comment on.

The scent of Simone's *crêpes de Chine* lingered on in LeSchack's mind well after she was gone. This was not surprising to him. He already knew that the memories of certain music and certain smells often are retained in one's mind, especially if they were linked to pleasurable events. What was surprising is that Simone's delicious scent lingered on in his bedroom, not just for a few days, but for weeks after she had departed. This was unexpected, but LeSchack paid little attention, because his mind was on other things those days—Arctic matters of national concern. Eventually, however, one weekend when he had a bit of free time, LeSchack determined to see if he could identify the source of this seemingly perpetual reminder of pleasures long-since gone.

He began crawling around the bedroom on his hands and knees, sniffing everywhere! Eventually he came across a small, rarely used wastebasket in an obscure corner of the room. It was more of a bachelor's bedroom decoration than a utilitarian object. Since LeSchack, then a quintessential bachelor, was not the most fastidious of housekeepers, he found, not surprisingly, the basket full of old tissues, likely the debris of a bad cold he had suffered months ago. Whether this basket was the source of the perfume smell, as his nose now suggested, it certainly was the time to dump the used tissues, and in fact, clean up the rest of the apartment!

To his surprise, as he dumped the wastebasket into a garbage bag, a tiny *crêpe de Chine* vial tumbled out. It had been smashed, and its contents had escaped and soaked the surrounding tissues. Tiny bottles of that size are not easily broken by, say, dropping them on a wood floor, or even throwing them hard against such a floor. They could, however, be smashed by hitting them repeatedly with the spiked heel of a high-heeled shoe, likely the only tool in the apartment that could have accomplished this while Simone was there. LeSchack never found out, but if that's what happened and it was Simone's way of keeping her memory uppermost in his mind, she had been most successful! Despite the enigma that surrounded her, LeSchack was determined to meet Simone in Paris as they had planned. He had even contemplated the possibility of proposing to her at that time. But until that time, Lieutenant (jg) LeSchack, spurred on by John Kennedy's ringing words a few months earlier, knew he had his plate full of non-romantic things to do.

*LeSchack's next assignment directly from the Office of Naval
Research (ONR) in Washington, was to assist in the establishment
of the Navy's new Arctic Ice drift station, ARLIS II, and to set up an
array for measuring ocean waves beneath the ice, as well as to map
the circumference of this station, and determine by celestial
navigation its exact position.*

The U.S. Navy and the Cold, Cold War Years-The Sky-Spies Hit Soviet Arctic Drifting Station NP-8

"Unknown, even today, is the spy war that raged at the top of world—the true Cold War. Here, the two superpowers came closest together—and were even joined, during the bitter winter, when America's Little Diomede Island and Russia's Big Diomede Island were linked by an ice bridge. It was also each nation's Achilles heel, where the distances were too great and the living conditions too intolerable to maintain an effective manned defense.......

"According to Gerson, one of NSA's (National Security Agency) pioneers in signals intelligence from space, at one point Russian and Canadian eavesdroppers nearly came eye-to-eye when a Soviet ice station drifted almost into Canadian territorial waters near Alert. Communications to and from these stations were a target of the (Alert) listening post. In fact intelligence interest was so great in the Russian espionage platforms that a highly secret and extremely dangerous operation was conducted in an attempt to find out just how sophisticated the icy spy bases were."

James Bamford, <u>Body of Secrets</u>, 2001

*"Len, is that rat-fuck operation of yours back on **again**?"*

May, 1962—Captain Daniel Walter, MD, USA, 82ⁿᵈ Airborne Division, the medical member of a strange Army-Navy-Air Force-CIA team, first conjured up over a martini-lunch in Washington, D.C.

"Len, I knew from my sources our Project Coldfeet was briefed to President John F. Kennedy shortly after its successful conclusion. Kennedy knew about it."

Connie "Seig" Seigrist, Senior CIA pilot on Project Coldfeet, in conversation with author, October 2005.

From time to time, a man named Nate Gerson used to drop in to the ONR Arctic Program Office to speak with Max Britton. LeSchack cannot remember whether he had ever met Nate. All he can remember is that Max simply remarked that Nate, a government employee, had "Arctic interests" which the two mutually discussed. Whether Max ever *knew* what Nate's interests were was never clear. It would not become clear to LeSchack what Gerson's interests *were* until author James Bamford published, "Body of Secrets: Anatomy of the ultra-secret National Security Agency" in 2001. In fact, Nate Gerson's interests were signals intelligence: spying by intercepting and decoding Soviet radio transmissions that could be received in the high Arctic.

The "extremely dangerous operation" Bamford referred to in his book published in 2001 was what LeSchack dubbed in 1961 "Project Coldfeet." That was the "bigger thing" LeSchack began working on, forty years before Bamford's book was published. Shortly after he returned from ARLIS II, he began to recognize the strategic, as well as scientific value of Arctic drifting stations. His experience on both Arctic drifting stations T-3 and ARLIS II, and his increasing knowledge of underwater acoustics gained from a course by that name in his after-work oceanography curriculum, led LeSchack to believe such stations could make ideal platforms for tracking the increasing number of nuclear submarines operating beneath the Arctic Ocean. For LeSchack, the ham radio operator, the use of such stations for collecting radio intercepts for NSA was a foregone conclusion. Now, with the advent of U.S. and Soviet nuclear submarines patrolling beneath the ice, the value of these stations for tracking submarines by underwater acoustics was also becoming clear. Such stations were valuable for both programs for many of the same reasons: lack of acoustic and electronic noise — interference — from manmade sources. And of course, the proximity of these stations to both Soviet and Free-World adversaries, as well as the limited likelihood of their being discovered by either side, made them ideal platforms for gathering data clandestinely in the Arctic.

From a global perspective, the strategic picture was simple. The heartlands of the two nuclear superpowers, the USA and the USSR, mortal enemies at this point in the Cold War, were geographically closest to one another across the North Pole. You can easily see this by looking at the globe. Both nations now had bombers that could easily and quickly reach the other's country, bomb, and still have enough fuel to return home safely. Soon both countries would have intercontinental ballistic missiles that could carry war to the other, even more quickly and effectively. There would be little need, as in wars past, to mount seaborne invasion forces to cross the Atlantic or Pacific Oceans. From the time of Sputnik until nearly the end of the Cold War, the Arctic was a major strategic theater. First for the Air Force, which had the bombers of the Strategic Air Command, and then for the Navy, whose intercontinental ballistic missiles could be carried swiftly and clandestinely under the Arctic ice cap for launch by nuclear-powered ballistic missile submarines. Both Soviet and U.S. air forces and navies now had this capability!

Knowing this, LeSchack wondered what the Soviets had been thinking about all of this. Their thoughts on these strategic matters would be carefully guarded secrets, of course, and not available to U.S. policy makers. However, thought LeSchack, "If the Soviet Arctic drifting stations were being used for anything other than unclassified scientific observations as they claimed, some evidence of secret activities might be gleaned from an investigation of such a station if it were hastily abandoned." LeSchack knew from historical experience that such stations, built on the pack ice, do require abandonment from time to time. Such abandonment is always precipitous because once the runway starts to breakup, everyone on the station knows it is just a matter of hours, rather than days, before the runway can no longer support aircraft. Within the 1959-1961 period, for example, the U.S., had abandoned precipitously Stations Alpha and Charlie when they commenced to break up. And guarded reports from the Soviets indicated that their drifting stations too, periodically had to be abandoned.

Abandonment, by force of circumstance, can be nothing other than chaotic. Once a drifting station that has been supported by fixed-wing aircraft breaks up, the ice runway is usually the first part of the infrastructure to disappear. The station occupants know that typically the remaining portions of the camp on the sea ice will then be short-lived. The camp buildings become ground up in the churning ice ridges and simply disappear, usually within a matter of weeks. As a result, there is little chance of ever again visiting or re-occupying such stations by landing fixed-wing aircraft on them. And in those days, helicopters simply did not have the range to fly from bases ashore to reach the beleaguered station. Accordingly, neither the U.S., nor the USSR gave serious concern about possible visitation by the other side, once a drifting station was abandoned. As a result, LeSchack knew that human nature being what it is, little effort would be made at the time of a hasty abandonment to cover up clues to clandestine activities, if any, if no one expected the station to ever again be visited. So, LeSchack reasoned, what a wonderful intelligence opportunity it could be should a Soviet Arctic drifting station be abandoned and a team of U.S. military investigators be prepared to occupy that station immediately thereafter.

The plan LeSchack developed was a simple, uncomplicated James Bond scheme: investigators who knew what to look for, would be parachuted on to the abandoned and crumbling drifting station, conduct their investigation, and then be retrieved by the Fulton Skyhook Aero-retriever system. Everyone knows about parachuting, but let me tell you a bit about the Skyhook. It is a system whereby a fixed-wing airplane, with a "V" shaped yoke on its nose, can fly into a 500-foot long nylon line that is suspended vertically upwards by a helium-filled balloon, and pick up a man on the ground, or in the water, at the other end of that line. The man is then winched safely into the aircraft. That new Skyhook system was being evaluated for the Navy by the ONR Air Branch in 1961. LeSchack thought it would work admirably for his plan.

The Air Branch had an ongoing program to provide the Navy with just such a retrieval capability for recovering downed pilots from denied or otherwise inaccessible areas. That Branch had even successfully conducted tests of the Skyhook in the Arctic. The pickup system worked, and a few live pickups had already been made under carefully controlled, ideal conditions at Fort Bragg and Quantico, Virginia. Simple and uncomplicated, right?

In concept LeSchack's proposed operation was, indeed, simple. Unfortunately, the schemes of Ian Fleming's James Bond, and the wondrous tools that "Q" had provided him to facilitate those schemes, were just now becoming well known. This was thanks to the publication of the James Bond novels contemporaneously with LeSchack's proposal. Why, even President Kennedy had remarked that he "enjoyed reading Fleming's James Bond stories." So it was not surprising that the plan of this ebullient and very junior naval officer should be looked upon with derision as he began discussing it at ONR. LeSchack first broached the subject with Max Britton at one of their martini lunches in downtown Washington. "So you want to become the American James Bond?" Max suggested, as he ordered yet another martini. This was essentially the same response LeSchack had to endure all the way up the Navy chain of command up to, and including, the Deputy Chief of Naval Operations for Air. However, LeSchack's plan did slowly and tortuously wend its way up that far in the command structure.

Upon sober reflection, followed by discussions with the ONR Air Branch, Max began to think LeSchack's plan *just might* have some merit. While he understood LeSchack's enthusiasm for personal involvement in the project—he clearly had the requisite scientific knowledge and polar experience to conduct the proposed investigation—Max wanted James F. Smith, now promoted to Air Force major, to be part of the investigation team. While LeSchack knew Smith only from his one contact returning from T-3, Max knew Smith well since the two had worked closely in funding and operating Drifting Station Charlie. Although both LeSchack and Max knew Smith was parachute-qualified—LeSchack would have to become jump-qualified—neither had known, however, that Smith also was an Air Force intelligence officer and a Russian linguist, attributes that combined with LeSchack's technical knowledge, could make a perfect team to investigate a Soviet drifting station.

Well, not quite perfect, thought the Chief of the Air Branch, Captain Robert Trauger; for political purposes to get LeSchack's scheme to fly, as it were, through Washington's DoD bureaucracy, it would be good, he suggested, to "include an *Army* member to the now Navy-Air Force team." The Army Liaison Officer with ONR, when presented with Trauger's suggestion, had just the solution: have assigned a parachute-qualified medical doctor from the Army's 82nd Airborne Division, just in case LeSchack's scheme creates injuries in some otherwise inaccessible location—as well it might!

LeSchack had made arrangements with ONR to take a month's leave during August 1961 to meet Simone in Paris. He left Washington with the "Project Coldfeet" plan wending its way up the Navy chain-of-command. By the time he had left Washington his plan had been approved by ONR's Chief of Naval Research, Rear Admiral Leonidas Coates. This was thanks to the plan being championed by a senior officer in LeSchack's office, Captain John Cadwalader. Cadwalader, a veteran of the Battle of the Coral Sea, as well as other World War II campaigns, also had considerable polar experience in the Antarctic. He knew LeSchack's plan was workable.

LeSchack flew to Paris from McGuire Air Force Base in New Jersey, taking advantage of DoD's ruling that military personnel on leave could fly, free, anywhere overseas that there was space available on a military aircraft. Upon arriving in Paris, he took a room at a small Left Bank hotel on *Boulevarde Montparnasse* that was often used by U.S. military personnel on leave there. After getting settled in, he procured a map of Paris and found that the address Simone had given him was within walking distance of his hotel. With rising excitement, LeSchack, with a small package containing the sweater Simone had left at his apartment a few months earlier, began a pleasant walk along the summery streets of Paris to his destination on the Right Bank, his hormones bubbling through his bloodstream.

Imagine then, LeSchack's disappointment when he arrived at the appointed address only to find it was the home of an American Express mail-forwarding office. He did inquire at that office whether anyone there knew Simone; a middle-aged woman behind both an intimidating desk and pair of thick spectacles did acknowledge, with a sickly smile, that she did know Simone, but was not at liberty to tell him her whereabouts. There had been no misunderstanding on LeSchack's part. He had letters from Simone acknowledging his planned arrival time in Paris, and that she had looked forward to their meeting. Notwithstanding his disappointment on this, his first visit to Paris, LeSchack decided he would remain there for the month and get to know the city.

Each day he would map out a walking trip to a different part of the city carrying with him his little Berlitz phrase book. As the month of August progressed, he would notice increased numbers of fresh bouquets left on the sidewalk, by a wall, on a window sill, frequently by engraved brass plaques, all observing both with sorrow as well as gratitude, that this was the seventeenth anniversary of the liberation of Paris from the Nazis. On the plaques were names of both French soldiers, as well as partisans, who had lost their lives on that spot in that August 1944 liberation battle.

On one of LeSchack's daily walks, he passed the U.S. Embassy. In those days, it was suggested that U.S. military personnel in a foreign country check in with the U. S. Embassy. Here, in Paris, he took this opportunity to do just that. While there, and on a whim, he stepped into the Consular Section, introduced himself, and asked whether that office kept records of French students who were enrolled in U.S. schools; "Was there a record of Simone from Grasse, France attending MIT?" A young woman in the Consular Section told LeSchack that was one her duties— to keep records of French students in the U.S. She agreed to examine her files. "No, no one by that name is in this file, Lieutenant, she smiled sweetly," and she also observed that LeSchack had come to the right office. "I maintain files of all students from France enrolled in U.S. schools and universities." Frankly, he was now not surprised. "Who is that enigmatic woman who had been my most powerful and voracious lover for over a year now?" LeSchack wondered.

He never was to find out. Simone never got in touch with him again. It was only after many years that LeSchack came across some research on "stalking behavior." What he had thought was simply "enigmatic" — strange, unidentified phone calls, messages, and incomprehensible letters that, in retrospect, could only have been produced by Simone— came into focus; today it is considered "stalking." "What was this all about?" mused LeSchack. "I was falling in love with her, if that was the goal of her "stalking." Well whatever else she might have been—illegal alien, runaway wife, spy even—LeSchack had to acknowledge that Simone had been a most satisfying lover, one who, for many years thereafter, inevitably became a yardstick against which he measured other lovers by—often to their serious detriment!

One day LeSchack and a U.S. Air Force officer on leave from his station in Turkey, chanced to meet, and decided that this was a day for café sitting. Over beers, they discussed Paris, its women, their respective military assignments, and the fact that there was a machine-gun-toting gendarme at each major intersection. In 1961, President de Gaulle was determined to pull out of Algeria. The French OAS, the "Secret Army Organization," a far-right group determined to keep Algeria French, was resorting to political terrorist acts in France, and especially, Paris, to voice its displeasure. Thus, they surmised, the armed gendarmerie. The two also groused about their lack of knowledge of the French language, and both recognized they would have more fun here if they knew it. At that point, a 40-year old American man at the next table, who couldn't help but overhear their conversation, asked them, "Well how long do you guys intend to remain in Paris?"

The man at the next table was a high school English teacher from California who was on a year's sabbatical in Paris. He observed to the two military officers that if they intended to remain in Paris for another three or more weeks, they might consider enrolling in the *Alliance Française*, a school that teaches the French language to foreigners. Gerry Goff, the teacher, allowed that he had been attending that school for the past year, and he knew that one could easily enroll, any time, at the Beginners Level. LeSchack invited Gerry to their table to tell them more. By the end of the conversation, LeSchack recognized that he would like to do this and now, with no Simone, had the time to do so. The Air Force officer with LeSchack said it sounded like fun, but he only had another day in Paris; however, he encouraged LeSchack to take advantage of the opportunity, observing as a more senior officer, that, "these days a military officer needs as many foreign languages as he can learn!

With Gerry's help, LeSchack enrolled at the "Alliance" the next day and began the first level of the French language. He found it fun. His courses were in the morning, as were Gerry's. It wasn't long before Gerry and LeSchack were taking afternoon trips to outlying suburbs of Paris and nearby cities, visiting churches, museums and eating and drinking well. And LeSchack, through Gerry's interest and support, was quickly learning to enjoy Paris and the French language and culture that Simone had introduced him to before she so abruptly disappeared from his life.

And then LeSchack's vacation was over! He took a commercial flight back to New York and then returned to Washington to continue reviewing a variety of Arctic research proposals for potential Navy funding, and to continue preparing for, and pushing Project Coldfeet. The autumn of 1961 was to be anything but uneventful for him: Shortly after he returned to the office, the Navy officially gave its approval to his James Bondian scheme! Then LeSchack was asked by the ONR Personnel Branch to please escort to the Navy Ball the gorgeous young lady chosen by ONR as its "queen." He had his first Fulton Skyhook pickup. He met another beautiful young lady with whom he would eventually fall in love. He went through Navy jump training and qualified. In the midst of all this—the further training and preparations for Coldfeet and his night-time course work in oceanography—one more thing occurred. On a dark November Arctic night, one of the ARL R4Ds—flown by Zim who he had flown with earlier in the year—was forced down on the ice on a return trip from ARLIS II, and LeSchack was the only one manning the Arctic Program office to answer frantic phone calls from all levels of Government and the media. LeSchack had his hands full during that last quarter of 1961.

*****

The U. S. Navy Ball, a traditional Navy social event commemorating the birthday of the United States Navy in 1775 is celebrated at many Navy facilities in early October. ONR, with many uniformed personnel, was no exception. As was traditional in that era, a "Navy Ball Queen" was chosen by votes cast by all personnel at ONR, both civilian and military, who had any interest in such things. LeSchack, during this fall season had too many things on his mind to even consider such frivolousness. He did give it lots more attention, however, when the ONR Civilian Personnel Branch called him and asked him to escort Carmen, one of ONR's secretaries, to the Ball. There was no mystery why Carmen was chosen Queen: Carmen, who had an apartment in LeSchack's Arlington apartment complex, was absolutely gorgeous. He knew her, and occasionally had casual dates with her. What was a mystery was why she had no date for the Ball. That being said, it was no mystery why

LeSchack was asked; there were no other eligible bachelors *in uniform* at ONR at that time. Not surprisingly, he reveled in this assignment. During the evening, several middle-aged Navy officers and senior civilian male employees, all with longing in their eyes, came up to LeSchack on the dance floor and reminded him how lucky he was. He didn't have to be reminded: he was dancing cheek-to-cheek, and holding Carmen as intimately as was acceptable in that 1960's era, and he was feeling wonderfully light-headed! His intuition was that at least one if not more of these men, all of whom were married, had been having, or at least desiring, an affair with Carmen. No matter. LeSchack was thoroughly enjoying this!

Commander Ben Levitt, Captain Trauger's deputy in the ONR Air Branch, was a naval aviator, a high-altitude balloonist, and an alumni of LeSchack's alma mater, Rensselaer. He was highly supportive of Coldfeet. He had made arrangements for LeSchack to be picked up by a Fulton Skyhook-configured P2V aircraft that was being evaluated at the Naval Air Station at Patuxent River, Maryland for future Navy operations. This evaluation was being funded by the ONR Air Branch. In mid-October 1961, LeSchack drove to Pax River, as the Naval Air Station was dubbed, first to watch the P2V pickup dummy loads, then the following day to be picked up himself.

Live pickups under *operational* conditions had never been attempted until Coldfeet. Some live pickups had been accomplished before that, but only under *carefully controlled conditions*, as would be the case for LeSchack—this time. All pickups had been restricted to military personnel. For reasons of liability, the FAA would not allow pickups of civilians. This would be LeSchack's first and only opportunity to familiarize himself with the Skyhook system prior to its first operational use. Moviegoers in the mid-1960s who saw "Thunderball," a James Bond movie, or "Green Berets" saw the pickup being used. Those scenes hardly do it justice. LeSchack, in an article he wrote for the United States Naval Institute Proceedings, and published a few years after that first ride, described his experience:

> "It was a warm, clear day at the Naval Air Station,
> Patuxent River, Maryland, when I was picked up by the

Skyhook. The preparations for pickup by the P-2 pick-up plane, that was already airborne and circling nearby, were unnervingly simple.

"Following the simple directions enclosed in the specially prepared pick-up kit, I withdrew a canvas bag that contained a neatly folded polyethylene balloon. The balloon was quickly laid out on the ground and, from another bag, I obtained a pick-up suit that was easily slipped on. The pick-up suit was essentially a one-piece flying suit with a fur-lined parka hood. A self-tightening parachute-type harness was built into the suit. After zipping up the suit, I inflated the balloon from two spherical helium bottles included in the kit. The balloon, fully inflated, looked much like a miniature blimp. It was pre-attached to one end of a coiled nylon line 500 feet in length. The other end of the line was terminated by a self-locking hook that was then attached to a D-ring fixed to the pick-up suit harness. The balloon, when released, extended the nylon line vertically upward to its full length. The release of the balloon was the signal to the circling pick-up plane that then began preparation for the pick-up run. I sat down on the ground with my hands clasped gently around my knees, my back to the wind. This whole preparation took perhaps ten minutes.

"The P-2 made a test pass at the balloon, flying level into the wind, at an altitude of 450 feet. I could barely feel the gentle tug of the balloon high above me. The P-2, quite distinctive with its protruding V-shaped pick-up yoke, turned and began its final run. It bore down on the line, aiming for an international orange marker attached to the line 50 feet below the balloon. Contact was made and the line was caught. At the same instant at the other end of the line, I felt a sudden thump, approximating a kick-in-the-pants, and I was airborne. As if lifted skyward by a giant swing, I saw first the patch of grass on which I had just been sitting, then the circle of observers now craning their necks to follow my trajectory, and then the entire promontory that was the pick-up zone, jutting out into the Chesapeake Bay.

"The rapidly receding ground spun quickly beneath me and I felt my jaw sag in response to a momentary increase in force. All this occurred within five seconds after pick-up.

"In less than ten seconds I found myself in a completely stable position, being towed through the air at 125 knots, facing aft. With my legs extended and my arms at my side, my body formed a reasonably good aerodynamic section. I had a remarkably good view of the entire area around the air station and the bay. My head, disturbing the airflow around my body, caused a bubble of air to form that made breathing no problem at all.

"During this time, the portion of the line caught by the yoke had been transferred to a winch in the after section of the plane. The line itself was now trailing out through the P-2's after hatch and I was being winched in at a rate of 250 feet per minute.

"While airborne I tried several body positions to see what affect these made on flight attitude. By bringing my legs up near my chest, the whole system became unstable and oscillation began, the period being a function of the length of the line. The oscillation was a particularly unpleasant sensation, but it was damped quickly by re-extending my legs; it was damped more quickly by extending my arms outward in addition to my legs. By extending my arms alone and using them as ailerons I could bank or even roll over 180 degrees.

"Within five minutes from pick-up I could see the after section of the plane directly above me. Once within the

P-2's slipstream some buffeting was encountered, but it was not unpleasant. Thirty seconds later I was drinking coffee in the after section of the plane."

*****

Although LeSchack's description accurately describes the mechanics of the Skyhook operation and what he did and saw once he was airborne, what it doesn't say is that from the time he saw the dummy pickups the day before, to the time he was safely pulled into the P-2's cabin, he was scared shitless! It was stark terror. In fact, LeSchack had been in a constant state of *subdued terror* from the instant, a month earlier, that the Navy had given approval for his espionage scheme--the one that James Bamford in his 2001 book, Body of Secrets, called a highly secret and extremely dangerous operation-- that he had now set in train—until its denouement seven months hence.

After he saw the dummy pick-ups and met the P-2's command pilot the day before that first live pickup LeSchack just described, he deliberately returned to Washington, rather than remain overnight at the Pax River BOQ, just to see a beautiful young woman and take her out to dinner.

William Manchester, in his memoir of the Pacific war, "Goodbye Darkness," observed, after a close call with death in combat:

> So close a call with death is often followed by eroticism. It is characteristic of some creatures that they are often very productive before their death and, in some cases, appear to die in a frenzy of reproductive activity. Desire is the sequel to danger. That is the reason for the recruitment, in most of history's great armies, of camp followers.

"Desire is the sequel to danger," Manchester had said. There was no doubt in LeSchack's mind that this was true, and combat *is* dangerous— and terrifying. But usually it is sporadic, shared with buddies, and is interspersed with long periods of inactivity—standing by to stand by. Espionage against an enemy, and on the enemy's territory, LeSchack also knew, is dangerous and terrifying. However, as opposed to combat, the terror of espionage—and its consequences, if caught—are *constantly* with the spy, are constantly gnawing on every particle of his being, and although sometimes less acute than at other times, he rarely has buddies with whom to share this terror. The spy is usually alone in his fears. In fact, he usually is physically all alone, especially when surrounded by a suspicious, alien people. In LeSchack's mind and psyche, formed by his knowledge of World War II history, Project Coldfeet was in many ways, a classic OSS spy operation, especially the part about dropping two agents into enemy territory by parachute. And as he became increasingly involved in this, his own espionage operation, his sense of danger expanded commensurately. So did his desire!

On two other subsequent occasions during the Cold War, LeSchack could be found spying on the USSR. Both times alone, and alone with his excruciating fears. And on both of those other occasions, too, his desire for a woman was, even for him, simply overwhelming. But at this present moment, faced with the imminent danger of his first Skyhook pick-up, Virginia was the clear target of that desire.

He had just recently met Virginia in Washington and felt that he could easily fall in love with her. It was not clear what Virginia was thinking that evening as LeSchack was gazing longingly at her across the dinner table, just bubbling with desire. It was highly unlikely, however, that she could possibly have divined what he, the incurable romantic, was thinking—"if I am to die at the end of that nylon cord tomorrow, let me have just one more time with a good-looking woman!" His desire, alas, was not assuaged that evening, but it soon would be. However, his terror mounted steadily.

Getting parachute-qualified was a bit more difficult for LeSchack—not physically, but bureaucratically. The only jump-qualified Navy personnel in 1961 were parachute riggers and their instructors. Navy SEALs, who of course, are parachute-qualified, had not yet come into existence. After trying the normal route of getting LeSchack orders for parachute training through the Bureau of Personnel—and failing— Commander Levitt did the Navy thing: look to see if he could find a Navy classmate assigned to the nearest Parachute Riggers training facility, which was located at Lakehurst, New Jersey, and ask a favor. And, yes he did. The CO of the Naval Air Technical Training Unit at

NAS Lakehurst was his buddy, Commander J. E. Little. Levitt explained the Coldfeet mission to Little who promptly agreed to provide a special accelerated jump course for LeSchack.

In the Navy, parachute riggers are usually assigned to carriers and naval air stations where the Navy's fighter pilots are based. The pilots use parachutes as part of their "working clothes," and such parachutes need to be regularly unpacked, checked and re-packed. To qualify as a Navy parachute-rigger, one must not only pass classroom work and a standard written test, but also pass a practical test; he must jump a parachute he has packed himself. There can only be two possible grades on the practical test—pass or fail. As a result of that practical test requirement, there were frequently aircraft at Lakehurst circling the drop zone and disgorging students performing the final test. Commander Little intended that LeSchack soon be among those brand new riggers dropping from the sky.

To qualify as a Naval Parachutist, one must have performed six free-fall jumps that are duly recorded. By free-fall, we mean jumping out of the open door of a flying aircraft, with no attachment whatever to the plane, like a "static line." You waited a few seconds while falling through the sky counting 1.....2...3... and then pulling a ripcord. Usually then, a parachute opens and you float gently to earth. To begin his training, LeSchack was taken under the wing of Chief Parachute Rigger Marvin Kubler, a rotund fatherly looking man, who recognized LeSchack's need for a quick, but thorough understanding of principles and procedures of parachuting, and an understanding of the need to master what is called "the parachute landing fall."

Chief Kubler, knowing the young officer assigned to him for accelerated jump training was a scientist from ONR, took pains to explain to LeSchack the physics of how a parachute worked. He also showed him the care with which parachutes were packed. There was no need, the Chief knew, to hype LeSchack with all that macho hoopla that Army Airborne trainees must endure as part of their jump training, or even for that matter, that given to the Navy's parachute riggers for their final test jump. The Chief knew that LeSchack's mission was hype enough to motivate his special trainee. What the Chief wanted to be sure of though was his ability to perform the "parachute-landing-fall," a maneuver that reduces the impact of landing on the parachutist, so as to minimize chances for injury.

A parachute landing, especially with a military parachute, at the best of times results in an impact on the parachutist similar to a free jump off a ten-foot wall. That can break bones if one does not land properly. To minimize the affect of the impact the parachutist must attempt to distribute the physical shock as quickly as possible after impact to all the least vulnerable parts of the body. In practice, this means landing, feet together, on your toes, and immediately rolling your body so that thighs, back and shoulders each take up a portion of that impact energy. It is not an elegant gymnastic maneuver, but it is effective. For LeSchack, who had been a gymnast and tumbler in high school and college, this was not a difficult procedure for him to perform. And after an afternoon of practicing jumping from a ten-foot platform at the Riggers' School, LeSchack was able to demonstrate to Chief Kubler that he had mastered the fall and would not injure himself once he started jumping. And that moment wasn't far off!

In fact, it was the following day. On 19 October 1961, LeSchack joined an R4D-load of rigger-students ready for their "graduation" jump. The R4D had its side doors removed and a canvas bench was placed along the length of each side of the fuselage for the students to sit on while waiting to reach the drop zone. In addition to some 20 rigger students, there were perhaps seven to ten rigger-instructors, all of whom were experienced jumpers, and all of whom were enlisted men. Other than the pilots, LeSchack was the only officer aboard, and certainly the only officer that would be jumping. As the aircraft began circling the drop zone, the instructors ordered all the riggers to stand in line, single file. After every two or three students, an instructor would insert himself into the line. As the line was being formed, the senior instructor came up to LeSchack and said, "I suggest you go to the head of the line, Lieutenant; I mean, *you are the officer, and your job is to lead, now isn't it?*" LeSchack noticed all the other instructors were grinning and nodding, "That's right, Lieutenant, you first!" LeSchack swallowed hard, but he recognized, though upsetting, their logic was impeccable.

When everyone was in line and ready, the aircraft was piloted one final time across the drop zone at an altitude of 1300 feet. The pilot throttled down and as the green light began flashing, all the instructors began screaming and pushing the riggers in front of them out of the open doorway, with LeSchack first to leap. It was clear why the instructors had devised this procedure of interspersing themselves in the line of students: to assure that no one would have a change of heart at this late moment, and that everyone would be jettisoned from the bowels of the aircraft during the three seconds it was over the drop zone!

When LeSchack became conscious of where he was, he was falling rapidly through the sky. "Shit! I have forgotten to start counting!" he exclaimed to himself. "With all that noise and smell and turmoil and excitement, I just forgot. I must have been falling for at least ten seconds or more!" With no further ado, he pulled his ripcord! Well, we've all had experiences where intense excitement does strange things to one's perceptions of the passage of time. In fact, LeSchack was still within the slipstream of the aircraft when his canopy opened explosively! It shook him like a rag doll. He was lucky to have cleared the aircraft's tail without striking it. And then he began descending slowly to earth. He landed and rolled properly, and within instants, he was surrounded by jump instructors all wanting to assure that their only officer student was safe. As soon as they knew he was, they bundled him off to the airstrip and the next flight. The instructors had learned that you must make the student who is intending to jump-qualify himself perform his second jump right after his first, so that he doesn't have time to analyze that first adrenaline-provoking experience!

LeSchack made that second jump, landed safely, but then was physically and emotionally exhausted, and went directly back to his BOQ room and promptly fell asleep. He made two more jumps on 24 October, and his final two jumps for qualification, the following day. Within a one-week period, he had qualified as a "naval parachutist." Just before leaving the Parachute Riggers' School at NAS Lakehurst, Chief Parachute Rigger Kubler, who like a few other senior people at the school knew why LeSchack was being trained, came up to him, unpinned his own jump wings from his uniform — the Army jump wings that the Navy then used — and pinned them on to LeSchack's uniform. "Congratulations,

Son. Be Careful!"

A week later, on 1 November 1961, LeSchack received a letter from the Chief of Naval Personnel officially designating him a "Naval Parachutist." The letter bore the Chief's—a vice-admiral—*rubber-stamped* signature. The First Endorsement, however, to that routinely stamped letter was from the Commanding Officer, NATTU, NAS Lakehurst, and bore the real signature of J. E. Little, *with a hand-written note:* "Forwarded, *and good luck!*"

More than forty years later, at lunch with one of his scientific colleagues, a brilliant petrophysicist, the question of parachute jumping inexplicably came up. The colleague, a beautiful and adventurous woman, many years younger than LeSchack, allowed that she had wanted to be a parachutist as a young girl, but that her mother had discouraged her because she thought it was too dangerous. So her lovely young daughter took up motorcycle racing instead. "What's parachute jumping like, Len," she inquired, looking directly into his eyes. LeSchack leaned back in his restaurant chair, tilted his head skyward, closed his eyes and began stroking his carefully trimmed white beard. He thought back to that tumultuous week at Lakehurst so many years ago where he became jump-qualified, and the weeks thereafter when he continued practice jumps until he made his jump that began Project Coldfeet.

LeSchack opened his eyes and looked at his young colleague. "In many ways it's like a man and woman making love—first there is the anticipation and buildup that occurs in the airplane; the noise: is it the plane's engines you hear or the blood pounding in your head? The smells: is it the pungent, but not-unpleasant airplane smells of AVGAS and engine exhaust you sniff, or the evocative odors of excitement that emanate from both men and women about to consummate their tryst? The moment of inevitability: is it the standing in the open door of the aircraft as you are about to hurl yourself into space, or the point at which you hurl your whole being into the whirlpool that is your lover? The orgasm is much the same in both cases," LeSchack said, looking deeply into the young woman's eyes. "When the parachute canopy abruptly tugs on your freely falling body careening through the sky and you look up to see that it is open and billowing voluptuously and fully above you,

you know you have come home—you know you will now be safe. And de-tumescence is the period during which all sound and noise stops. The loud roar of the aircraft's engines has gone. Your blood stops pounding in your head. Normal hearing and sensations return—you hear people talking on the ground below you. You are floating. There is just a gentle breeze wafting upward past your face. All is extraordinarily calm. And you are at peace. It is a marvelous, but of course, short-lived feeling, for you will soon come down to earth." As LeSchack's soliloquy trailed off, the beautiful woman across from him looked at LeSchack intently, and with a sly smile about her eyes said, "So that's what parachuting is like. I think for you, Len, having an orgasm in a woman might be more dangerous."

As October 1961 was coming to an end, another problem had become apparent as a result of the approval and planning process taking much longer than originally anticipated: it would soon be totally dark in the latitudes where there original target, Soviet drifting station NP-9 was expected to be. Although it was neither LeSchack's nor Major Jim Smith's choice, they could, if they had to, parachute to NP-9 during a full moon. It is often crystal-clear on an Arctic Ocean winter night. Both of them were loathe to delay the Coldfeet momentum at this point, since it had taken so much effort by so many people to get it to the point it now was. But parachuting in on a full moon was one thing, being picked up by the Skyhook was another. There would be no possible way a P2 pilot could see a half-inch nylon line in the dark, even with a full moon. The solution to that problem, proposed by Bob Fulton, the inventor of the Skyhook, was to string a series of strobe lights along the length of the line and make the lights an integral part of it. A pilot could surely see such a flashing line. And so, a night-time test of such a strobe-line pick-up was arranged at Pax River for the end of October. LeSchack was invited to watch the demonstration. He asked Virginia, his new girlfriend, whether she would like to join him that evening to watch the night-time pick-up demonstration; he suggested, with a gentle smile, that it would likely be too late after the demonstration to return to Washington that night. Virginia agreed to join him.

When LeSchack and Virginia arrived at the promontory at Pax River where he had been picked up a few weeks earlier, it was already dark. A pick-up balloon was aloft, and its line was attached to a dummy load. The strobe lights attached to the line were flashing in an eerily disembodied way beneath the balloon. There was a group of spectators, mostly the families of the P2's crew, standing around, waiting for the airborne spectacle to begin. Three night-time pick-up runs were made by the P2, the first two successful, the last not. The P2 hit the line incorrectly that last time, tearing off the balloon without grabbing the line. While the spectators appeared to enjoy the show, LeSchack was seriously disheartened: the statistics, two successful pick-ups out of three successive tries was not good enough for a successful operation in the field. Three successful pick-ups out of three tries would be required, two for LeSchack and Smith, and one for the intelligence materials to be retrieved during the real operation.

At the time of this night-time spectacular, LeSchack had only known Virginia for about a month. They had dated a few times. He certainly enjoyed her company but was not about to tell this lovely woman, who was not cleared for classified information, anything concerning the secret operation, Project Coldfeet. Imagine therefore, the innocent Virginia's surprise when the young wife of the P2's copilot came up to her, thinking she *was* LeSchack's wife, and nonchalantly observing that the dummy just picked up *was soon to be replaced by Virginia's husband, Len!* Virginia was aghast.... but also intrigued. None of her previous boyfriends—lawyers, doctors, dentists—had ever been involved in such things! Golf or tennis maybe, but this......?

When the P2 landed, the pilots, their wives and Fulton's engineer, who had designed the strobe-light array, all met LeSchack and Virginia in the Pax River Officers' Club for a drink. One of the members of this interesting group actually asked Virginia whether *she was* LeSchack's wife. Virginia responded gaily, "no, but I soon expect to be!" While LeSchack was surprised with her bold response, he certainly was not displeased. In fact, LeSchack was seriously interested in what could easily be described as Virginia's blatant proposal.

When the party at the Club broke up, LeSchack recommended to Virginia that they stop at a nearby motel off-base, and that if she was seriously interested in becoming Mrs. LeSchack, perhaps they should begin practicing that very evening! Virginia happily agreed, smiling her glorious smile at him.

There was no question that night that, *"desire was the sequel to danger."* And more than ever now, LeSchack sensed serious danger in the spy mission he had conceived. And that desire, within moments of their locking the motel door, exploded furiously within the clearly willing Virginia. And fueled by desire, that sequel to danger, as well as the unquestionable beauty, intelligence and wit of this eminently desirable woman, he took the chance and proposed marriage during that adrenaline-filled trip to Pax River.

That night-time exercise at Pax River raised major concerns in LeSchack's mind. Both he and Smith knew what winter/nighttime conditions in the high Arctic were. In addition to LeSchack's first-hand experience watching the exercise that night at Pax River, both he and Smith had concerns about whether the polyethylene balloons would stand up under the frigid, windy conditions that occurred in the Arctic during the winter. Smith, who was then stationed at Eglin AFB in Florida, had access to the environmental hangars on that base. The "weather conditions" in the interiors of these hangars could be varied from tropical heat to Arctic cold. Arrangements were made to test the "Project Coldfeet" pick-up gear under windy, -40 below conditions. The balloons were tested during the first week of November. They failed. New, specially designed mylar balloons were ordered. They would be ready for testing in December.

In mid November, another event occurred that really concerned LeSchack with respect to wintertime operations in the Arctic, an event that strongly impinged on the viability of Project Coldfeet being conducted during the Arctic night. Zim's ARL R4D went down in the Soviet sector of the high Arctic.

ARLIS II had drifted west from where it had been five months earlier when LeSchack was aboard. It was now north of Siberia in the Soviet Arctic sector. Zim had flown a logistic flight from Barrow to the ice island. He refueled the R4D at ARLIS II from barrels filled with diesel fuel, rather than AVGAS. There should have been safeguards to have prevented this, but those who have worked during winter time in the polar regions know how such a catastrophe could have inadvertently happened: The diesel drums and AVGAS drums obviously had not been adequately segregated. The big "D" painted on the diesel drums must not have been visible, covered with grease or snow, or had simply been rubbed off. It was too cold to smell the clearly different smells emanating from either the diesel or from the AVGAS barrels. And so it happened. Zim's plane with 11 aboard, including Max Brewer, had managed to take off from ARLIS II and fly toward Barrow for about 30 miles of the 550 mile-trip, before the engines began to sputter. Zim, recognizing he was in trouble, turned the plane back toward ARLIS II, hoping it would remain aloft until he could return. It didn't.

With the aircraft loosing altitude in the gathering darkness, Zim began searching the ice below him for a suitable floe on which to land. When he thought he spied a piece of adequate extent, he headed for it. As he approached, he turned on his landing lights and began waggling the plane's nose up and down to illuminate as much of the floe as he could during his remaining few seconds aloft. Seeing no pressure ridges in his path that could destroy his R4D, he set it down on the ice. He used what power remained in the engines to drag the aircraft's carcass to the end of the floe to allow space for a possible rescue aircraft to land.

Zim had obviously sent by radio "mayday" messages that had been received, and it wasn't long before LeSchack, in Washington, became aware of the disaster. Max Britton was away on office business in Canada, and when he heard the news, flew directly to Barrow. And a U.S. Air Force plane flying into the Soviet sector had seen the downed ARL aircraft, with the Navy Bureau Number still visible on the R4D's tail section, and reported that information, along with the fact that the downed aircraft had appeared to have suffered only slight damage.

Fortunately, no one was injured, there were adequate emergency supplies aboard the R4D for all to manage satisfactorily, and within a day or two of the aircraft crashing, a U.S. Air Force plane was able to land on the floe and everyone was brought home to Barrow safely. LeSchack, the young lieutenant, junior grade, spent those few days in the office all alone, fielding questions about the crash, the Lab at Barrow, who was aboard the flight and finally, what were ARLIS II, and an aircraft bearing U.S. Navy markings doing in the Soviet sector anyhow. All these questions came from action officers—bureaucrats, senior military officers and the media who had little understanding of the overall Arctic Program and its significance, but all of whom wanted some kind of reasonable answer to report to their bosses. LeSchack managed to provide such answers. Depending on the question and the tone in which it was asked, he responded with the truth, or a half-truth, or an outright prevarication, depending on who the interrogator was. It was a trying time for him. Fortunately, at this point he knew the Arctic environment, the aircraft and pilots involved, and the entire cast of characters in this whole event, and was able to sound plausible and in control.

The incident with Zim had one other ramification that was not lost on LeSchack. Night-time operations in the Arctic are to be avoided, if possible. LeSchack hoped that, one way or another, Coldfeet could be delayed until springtime without derailing the momentum the project now had achieved with so much difficulty. As it turned out, unforeseen circumstances, bureaucratic inertia, and an enormous number of logistics problems provided credible reasons for delay. However, wholly unexpected serendipity provided the pathway toward eventual success. All of this provided the time LeSchack wished for, ultimately allowing a spring operation during which time there would be perpetual daylight.

The litany of problems need not be recounted here. These problems were documented, and published in the official history of the operation, and then declassified years later. Suffice it to say, anyone who is familiar with complicated and secret operations, operations that depend on weather, new equipment, a recalcitrant bureaucracy, a need to maintain "cover-your-ass" safety, and which require diplomatic clearances to base from another country, have some sense of what LeSchack and his supporters at ONR went through. These problems simply multiplied when eventually, several other agencies of Government became involved.

During the winter of 1961-1962, the pressures of all these things began to weigh on him. LeSchack noted that during this period he developed an annoying tic in his left eye; because the tic disappeared after an extended martini lunch with Max, he recognized that his affliction was indeed, caused by nerves, and could be alleviated with alcohol. Accordingly, he encouraged more frequent martini lunches with Max. This tic also disappeared after he made love to Virginia, to whom he was now engaged. Unfortunately, Virginia lived at home with her parents at this point; the convenience and pleasures of frequent lovemaking—as had been possible with Simone—not only for its own pure enjoyment, but to reduce LeSchack's building tension, were not easily available now. Martini lunches were.

LeSchack found another way of reducing the extreme pressures building on him: parachute jumping. Before he left Lakehurst in October, those of his instructors who knew what LeSchack's mission was, strongly recommended that he and Smith use special parachutes that were steerable. The Navy didn't have such things, but his instructors told LeSchack they could modify the Army's standard T-10 parachute to create an excellent steerable parachute for the Coldfeet mission. LeSchack promptly called Captain Dan Walter at the 82nd Airborne, the medical doctor the Army assigned to join Project Coldfeet, and through him, the Army at Fort Bragg provided three T-10s to the Navy for modification. Once the riggers at Lakehurst made their recommended modifications, LeSchack and Dan went there together to be instructed in their use. LeSchack figured that Smith, a "master jumper," could try out his chute at a later date.

LeSchack and Dan found that the modified chutes were quite different from standard military parachutes, which are not steerable. The modified chutes had a static line that pulled out a pilot chute that *gently* opened the large canopy. There was no chance of being shaken "like a rag doll" as LeSchack had been during his first jump. And toggles connected to each of the risers permitted turning the chute either to the left or to the right, depending on which toggle you pulled. The result of these modifications was that for Project Coldfeet, where the drop zone would likely be strewn with the usual ice-station debris, random buildings and fields of antennae, such obstacles could be avoided just prior to landing so as to incur no injuries to the jumpers. Once taught how to use these chutes, LeSchack and Dan enjoyed jumping them, and they did so several times over the next few months. They also enjoyed each other's company.

Dr. Dan, as he began to be called by the ever-increasing Coldfeet team, was a about LeSchack's age, and had also served in Alaska. His medical specialty was gynecology, which seemed to LeSchack an interesting anomaly, considering his current patients—not a pussy amongst them; he was assigned to, and normally jumped with, one of the most macho groups in the military, the 82nd Airborne Division. And he was devilishly handsome. At least Virginia said so when they met, shortly thereafter. When LeSchack told Virginia that Dan was a gynecologist, her reaction was interesting, and perhaps foreshadowed events to come: "I wouldn't have a doctor that handsome touch me!" As the winter progressed and turned into spring, Dan and LeSchack kept in touch frequently. With all the twists and turns and setbacks the operation was now enduring, Dan dubbed LeSchack's operation —"Project Rat-Fuck"—a name apparently used frequently for "dicey" missions by the Fort Bragg people with whom Dan served, the Airborne, and the Special Forces.

The now increasing intensity of "Rat-Fuck," and the fact that LeSchack and Dan were the only junior officers involved in an operation which was now coming under increasing scrutiny and interest by many branches of government, brought these two ever closer together. While LeSchack would inform Dan of the latest twists and turns of his operation, Dan would report on gossip and scuttlebutt from the O-Club at Fort Bragg. More and more, its officers were returning from "advisor duty" in Southeast Asia: even in early 1962, their comments uttered in the well-lubricated atmosphere of the bar seemed to foreshadow the coming disaster in that theater.

As for contact with Smith, there was little during this period. Major Smith, the Russian linguist and intelligence officer, was going through arduous training to become the Assistant Air Attaché in Moscow, now a critical post at the height of the Cold War. Only as a result of a high-level request from the Navy, was Smith even allowed by the Air Force to become part of LeSchack's operation. Smith offered assistance where he could, as in the Cold Hangar tests at Eglin, or in joining critical training operations, but otherwise, LeSchack rarely saw him during this period.

In March 1962, two important and exciting things happened in LeSchack's life. A Soviet drifting station, NP-8, that had been established in 1959 on an ice floe, broke up and was hastily abandoned, and LeSchack and Virginia got married. LeSchack, Max and Captain Cadwalader all thought that NP-8 would make a more lucrative target than the originally chosen target NP-9. This was largely because NP-8 had been in operation longer—both before and after NP-9 had been occupied—and therefore would likely provide more clues, and *more recent clues* of the activities conducted on board, for example, acoustic tracking, than would NP-9. So Coldfeet focused on a new target. And LeSchack and Virginia decided—perhaps a bit too quickly—to focus on new targets also: each other. LeSchack was entranced by Virginia's beauty, wit, and intelligence, and Virginia liked his worldliness, sense of adventure and masculine good looks. They disappeared from Washington, the Arctic Program and Coldfeet for two weeks early in March and took a honeymoon in Mexico.

Upon LeSchack's return he and the entire Coldfeet gang suddenly switched into high gear. Up until this point, it had been assumed that the Navy P2V from Pax River, the only aircraft that the Navy had that had been configured for Skyhook pick-up, would be used for the planned operation. But the Navy would not let the P2 fly into the Arctic alone. The Navy required that the P2 be accompanied by a long-range support aircraft. Up to this point, there was not such an aircraft in Navy inventory that was available for such assignment; and the Navy had categorically refused to request the Air Force for assistance. However, by the time LeSchack had returned from his honeymoon, CINCLANTFLT had agreed to provide, for a limited time only, a C-130 Hercules aircraft from VX-6, the Navy's Antarctic support squadron with whom LeSchack had flown two years earlier. Now, in theory, Coldfeet could officially be launched, against the new target, NP-8, located then at 83° N, 132° W, 420 miles from the North Pole. Coldfeet, or "Project Rat-Fuck," as Dr. Dan now always referred to it, was officially on!

A full dress rehearsal took place at Lakehurst at the beginning of April 1962. All the key players were there, including two civilian aviators

LeSchack had not met before. They had been invited by Bob Fulton. LeSchack always wanted Bob as a participant to any operation that used his Skyhook invention. Bob had frequently alluded to the fact that he had an association with another organization that also had a Skyhook capability, the Central Intelligence Agency. He had invited Doug Price and Connie Seigrist to join the dress rehearsal as observers. This dress rehearsal would be the first opportunity for Smith to jump the new steerable chute, and for he and Dr. Dan to have an opportunity to be picked up with the Skyhook.

Dress rehearsals of any sort are conducted so that everyone "can practice their lines," and problems can be identified and presumably be solved, and the players can become comfortable with one another. Well, all of that happened, and problems *were* identified.

Two sets of pickup kits were para-dropped by a Lakehurst R4D for Smith and Dan to use for their first Skyhook pickups. Then both LeSchack and Smith jumped from that aircraft without incident, using their steerable chutes, and landed safely in the drop-zone. Dr. Dan was the last one out of the R4D; unfortunately, moments before he bailed out, there was some confusion in that aircraft owing to a minor mishap that distracted Dan as well as the jumpmaster. As a result, Dan jumped, unaware that his static line would deploy in such a manner as to entangle one arm as he leapt from the aircraft. That unorthodox exit caused Dan severe pain not only to his arm muscle, but also to his pride. Upon landing, he gingerly gathered up his chute and then inflated his balloon in preparation for his first pickup. Smith had already inflated his and was ready.

The P2 made two pickup attempts: the first one to pick up Smith was successful, the second one to pick up Dr. Dan, was not. In Dan's case, the P2 flew into the line but, once again, not correctly. The balloon was torn from the line, Dr. Dan was briefly lifted from the ground by a foot or two, and then fell back to earth unhurt, never to have become airborne. Smith was elated, like LeSchack had been the previous October, with his Skyhook pickup. Dan, however, not only missed the ride of his life, but now had a painfully throbbing arm, along with his damaged 82nd Airborne pride. As soon as he could disengage from the crowd on the drop-zone, he went directly to the Navy pharmacy on base, still in his Skyhook pickup suit and ordered the pharmacist mate to get a syringe and a vial of morphine for him. The Navy corpsman was simply astounded at that request: "Sir," he observed in disbelief, "you need a doctor's prescription for that!"

Dan, his left arm now in excruciating pain, grimaced as his right hand fumbled under the pick-up suit and into his fatigues where he retrieved a pad of paper. With his good hand he quickly, but with difficulty, wrote a prescription on the pre-printed pad—inscribed—Captain Daniel L. Walter, MD, U.S. Army, and signed his name. The shocked corpsman was now truly astounded. "Yes **Sir**. Right away, **Sir**." According to Dr. Dan, the corpsman was now beyond "astounded" when Dan filled the syringe with morphine and, in front of that corpsman, he injected himself to relieve the pain in his aching muscle. So shocked was the corpsman, according to Dan who related the incident at one of the many private "Jim-Dan-Len" Coldfeet drinking parties, that the corpsman fainted dead away as he watched the 82nd Airborne trooper before him, with great concentration and deliberateness, stab himself, and watch the needle penetrate deep into his bicep muscle.

The previous October, the P2 and its aircraft commander achieved two out of three pickups successfully; this time, one out of two. For LeSchack, these were worrying statistics! As it would eventually turn out, it was a good thing Fulton had invited the two CIA pilots to be observers. They would soon play a major role in Coldfeet, but not just yet; for now, they would only comment, "Hey, Len, that partner of yours looks like one hell of a tough cookie. We wouldn't want to meet him in a dark alley. He looks like he could slit your throat without blinking."

LeSchack really hadn't thought much about it. However, there was no doubt that the CIA pilots—Seig, who had flown with Claire Chennault of "Flying Tigers" fame, and Doug, who had flown 39 para-drop missions to support the French at Dien Bien Phu—were certainly likely to have seen "cut-throats and pirates." In their time in Southeast Asia alone, Seig and Doug would likely have seen more "throat-slitters" than LeSchack would ever have done during his short life. What LeSchack did know about Major James F. Smith was that he was part Cherokee Indian, had dropped out of high school, enlisted in the Army just before the Second World War and, due to sheer brilliance and merit, had come up through the ranks, and was eventually commissioned and at that time now a major, but eventually would make full colonel. In addition to Arctic and jumping experience, Smith had also been an Air Force survival instructor—you know, teaching young aircrews how to catch and eat raw bugs, snakes, rodents, and the like, to stay alive out in the wilderness. Virginia's comment upon meeting Smith simply was, "Oh my! What a hunk of a man he is, Len!"

NP-8 was nearly due north of Resolute Bay in the Canadian Northwest Territories. As a result, the original plan to base out of Thule, Greenland to investigate NP-9, the original target, was changed to the RCAF base at Resolute, on Cornwallis Island. This required diplomatic clearance, which took time to obtain.

Two weeks were spent at Resolute—the P2, the C-130, and the entire Coldfeet crew that LeSchack had assembled. At LeSchack's urging, Captain Cadwalader was placed in charge, not only owing to his polar experience, which was considerable, but because of his rank, which was important, especially in situations where men from different commands were lumped together. Although LeSchack had been the mastermind for the operation, he knew that an officer who outranked *all* other participants was absolutely necessary to orchestrate successfully the diverse elements that constituted Project Coldfeet.

The operation at Resolute was completely unsuccessful. The team received wonderful cooperation from the RCAF; the problem was the C-130—the search plane, and the plane from which LeSchack and Smith would be dropped—simply *couldn't find NP-8!* Two key things were learned from that fiasco: that Dr. Dan was superb, and that the P2 and its aircraft commander could not be counted on to perform the necessary mission.

Many tedious days were spent by the crew flying over vast stretches of sea ice searching for NP-8. They would return without success each evening and, dejectedly, join the RCAF crew in its mess hall. One evening RCMP constable Ron Gordon, who represented the Queen and the Government of Canada on Cornwallis Island, came into the mess and specifically sought out Dr. Dan; at that moment, he was the only doctor on the entire island. "Sir, there is a woman in the village who is having a miscarriage. She is the wife of my best friend in the village. Her condition is beyond my ability to help with first aid. Can you come with me to the village and help her?" Without hesitation, Dan grabbed his medical kit and parka, and jumped on to the back of the skidoo that Gordon was driving, and together, they drove to the stricken woman's home. In short order, Dan determined that an operation, in a real hospital, would be essential to save this woman's life.

The Mountie and Dan provided and administered plasma to replace her lost blood, and bundled the woman up on the skidoo and returned to the RCAF base. Dan radioed ahead and spoke with the RCAF commander, indicating immediate hospitalization would be necessary to save the woman's life. The RCAF commander, "Black Jack" Hall, knew that Coldfeet had a C-130, the only means of flying the stricken woman to the nearest hospital, 500 miles away at the USAF base at Thule, Greenland. Black Jack immediately asked Captain Cadwalader to fly that mercy mission, which, of course he did, rousing the exhausted C-130 crew from their bunks. That crew refueled the C-130, and with Dr. Dan aboard to minister to the woman, they took off for Thule. Dan radioed ahead to the Thule AFB hospital and requested that Air Force doctors meet him on the runway when the C-130 landed. They did.

Dan explained the medical situation as they were wheeling his patient into the operating room, and wearily requested that the Air Force doctors call him with a report when the emergency operation was completed. He would retire to the O-Club bar to unwind. Dan had had enough for that day. The C-130 remained at Thule until the hospital assured Dan that his patient was safe and would recover. The Air Force doctors made it clear to all, however, that without Dan's quick diagnosis and the action of the Coldfeet C-130's crew, the woman would have died. Upon hearing this happy news, Dr. Dan picked up a bottle of Jim Beam from the O-Club, and the crew returned to Resolute.

LeSchack, Smith and Dr. Dan shared a bedroom at the RCAF base. LeSchack and Smith had remained there awaiting the C-130s return.

They were unneeded for the emergency flight and had already spent too many long, tedious hours in the air searching for NP-8. When Dan returned to the room, he broke open the bourbon, offered drinks to LeSchack and Smith, and proceeded, with the able assistance of his roommates, to become seriously drunk. Finally, Dan observed to his roommates, slurring his words as he did so, "You know, delivering a healthy baby for a healthy mother is not difficult. About all you need to do is stand by with a catcher's mitt under her, and wait for the baby to drop out. In this case, sadly, parts of the stillborn baby came out in my hands." And Dr. Dan Walter, the gynecologist who jumped with that quintessentially masculine group, the 82nd Airborne Division, broke into tears of sadness.

The Coldfeet crew tried three more sorties to attempt to find the elusive NP-8 without success. The allotted hours on CINCLANTFLT's C-130 were now nearly used up, and the weather was deteriorating. Finally, Captain Cadwalader called off the operation. Before the crew left resolute, however, they staged a performance for the benefit of their RCAF hosts: a couple of parachutists dropped out of the sky from the C-130, and a couple of Skyhook pick-ups with dummies were attempted. Alas, the usual statistics that LeSchack had already noted pertained: one successful pickup; one failure where the P2's pilot again hit the line improperly and broke the balloon off the line without catching the line, itself. LeSchack shook his head sadly; he recognized the chances of a completely successful mission with this P2, and this pilot, would be highly unlikely. As the crew packed up and left to return to Pax River, LeSchack had mixed emotions. He was enormously disappointed that they had been unable to locate their target—likely they had been looking in the wrong place—but relieved that he and Smith would not have to rely on that P2 to save their lives.

By the end of April 1962 LeSchack and Captain Cadwalader were back at the Arctic Program Office at ONR and in a rather despondent mood, recognizing that nearly a year's effort to bring Project Coldfeet this far had likely been wasted. Shortly after they returned though, LeSchack received a phone call at home one evening from Walter Whitmann, the chief sea ice forecaster on Jack Schule's staff at the Navy Hydrographic Office. "Len, our Navy ice reconnaissance plane on patrol over the

Arctic Ocean just located your target!" and he gave LeSchack the coordinates. LeSchack was elated, but he knew that that he no longer could expect support from the two Navy aircraft he had just used, and ONR was out of money for funding his project, in any event.

Then, as LeSchack was continually to find out, serendipity plays a large role in life—certainly it always seemed to in *his* life. The trials and tribulations of the Project Coldfeet exercise, secret though it was, had become known to other agencies, and they did not, at this point, want to see it fail. Those agencies also knew by now of the Navy's lack of funding and assets for continuing the operation. The Office of Naval Intelligence (ONI) had learned about it through LeSchack; the CIA, as a result of Bob Fulton's *sub rosa* contacts; and it also had become known to a brand new organization, the Defense Intelligence Agency (DIA), that had just come into existence in 1961. Headed by General Joe Carroll, the DIA gave priority to specific requirements for intelligence concerning the USSR's ability to attack across the Arctic. From DIA's point of view, LeSchack's project appeared directly focused on that goal. DIA's Deputy Director for Collection, Admiral T.K McCormick, who had served several tours in Navy Intelligence, recognized that his agency could help establish itself as a player in gathering clandestine intelligence, one of its goals, by supporting Project Coldfeet. The Admiral also recognized he could strengthen ties with ONI in particular, by assisting the Navy with Coldfeet, as well as gain some other political points—so necessary in the Washington milieu, by supporting Project Coldfeet. He persuaded General Carroll to approve $30,000 to fund DIA's *first participation in a clandestine mission!* LeSchack's mission.

Bob Fulton, the Skyhook inventor, was the prime contractor for the ONR Air Branch on all matters pertaining to the development and ultimate deployment of his invention for the Navy. LeSchack and Bob frequently met and planned and schemed together as Coldfeet was unfolding. As a Navy contractor paid to develop the Skyhook capability for the Navy, Bob felt obligated to get Coldfeet operational with Navy aircraft. He was always with LeSchack as an observer on tests and dress rehearsals. As he had begun to see inklings of the Navy's inability to conduct satisfactorily the Coldfeet mission, he began to speak guardedly with LeSchack about another Skyhook-equipped aircraft. It was a World

War II B-17 bomber. Bob had secretly configured it as a Skyhook-equipped aircraft for the CIA. It was the only other aircraft in the world that then had been configured with the Skyhook capability. On several occasions he suggested that the organization that owned it, Intermountain Aviation Incorporated, a company wholly owned by CIA, might be convinced to assist Coldfeet accomplish its mission, should the Navy fail to perform.

LeSchack already knew a bit about CIA wholly owned companies, known as "proprietaries." Such companies had to conduct their business like real companies, and they had to be paid in "real" money for doing what they did despite the fact that such companies were heavily (and secretly) subsidized by CIA. Now that LeSchack knew he had $30,000 from DIA to work with, he was ready to ask Bob Fulton for assistance from "his friends." Bob facilitated this, and now he provided LeSchack a bit of background about Intermountain Aviation. Bob, who was on the board of directors of Intermountain, observed that to the outside world, it was simply an organization that provided flying services to a variety of legitimate private and governmental organizations. It flew smoke jumpers for the U.S. Forest Service and provided overnight logistics for automakers in Detroit. It also provided clandestine air support for CIA; for example, it flew air cover for the ill-fated Bay of Pigs invasion. Intermountain had also just planned to spring a CIA airman by the name of Allen Pope out of one of Sukarno's Indonesian jails. It had intended on smuggling a Skyhook kit into the jail, and had begun practicing the use of the Skyhook on a mock-up of that jail.

The key pilots to be used for performing this daring feat were to be none other than Doug Price and Connie Seigrist, the two pilots that LeSchack had already met. In early 1962, the entire Intermountain crew was psyched-up to a fever pitch to commence the secret operation in Indonesia; unfortunately for them, shortly before their operation was to take place, President Kennedy and Sukarno came to a diplomatic agreement that provided Pope's release through diplomacy. The Intermountain crew was sorely disappointed by that turn of events. It was at that point that Bob Fulton arranged for Intermountain and LeSchack to open contract discussions, since he knew that there was $30,000 available for the job. What transpired next, if it could have been set to music, would have made a wonderful Eighteenth Century farce for the Opéra Comique or a Gilbert and Sullivan operetta.

LeSchack by now had learned how to negotiate research contracts with the scientists that the Arctic Program funded for work in the Arctic. It was a straight forward give and take, based on the amount of money the researcher needed and the amount ONR was prepared to spend for that particular piece of research, and how valuable the research would be to the Navy's overall program. Project Coldfeet was quite another story, but LeSchack was told by ONR to conduct the negotiations as if it were a standard, arms-length transaction.

Intermountain pretended it was a real business, not a secret government office. It pretended Coldfeet was just another aviation job. LeSchack of course knew what the company was, and knew that it had been sorely disappointed at not being able to spring Pope out of Indonesia with the Skyhook. LeSchack also knew the guys at Intermountain were just itching for another Skyhook operation to justify all their training in perfecting that technique. LeSchack, himself, wasn't exactly a disinterested contract officer in this matter. And he knew that DIA had given ONR less money than Intermountain wanted for providing the only other Skyhook-equipped aircraft then available, as well as the logistic support aircraft that was also needed.

LeSchack and Intermountain went round and round, the desire by each to do the deal, palpable! And both sides pretending it was a neutral, arms-length transaction between the Government—Lieutenant (jg) Leonard A. LeSchack—and a private company (Intermountain Aviation). Finally, a price was agreed upon. It was less than Intermountain needed and more than LeSchack legally could commit. But commit he did! He reasoned, "If Coldfeet is successful, the money will be found afterwards to pay for it all; if it is not successful the most likely reason for failure this time will be unsuccessful pickups. And in that case," he said to himself with that wonderful bravado of callow youth, "I won't be around to face the music!"

The deal was made in mid-May 1962. That is the time of year when the visibility in the Arctic begins to deteriorate, and seriously so. There is an increasing amount of open water interspersed with the pack ice to assure a steady low-level ice fog, thus reducing likelihood of spotting NP-8 from the air. At that point, LeSchack and Captain Cadwalader recognizing there was not enough time to, once again, obtain diplomatic clearance to base out of Resolute, opted to base out of the ARL at Barrow, Alaska, over which ONR had control; this, despite Barrow's greater distance from the target. The B-17, designed as a long-range bomber, would have the range. LeSchack phoned Smith and Dr. Dan at their respective bases. "Guess what guys? Rat-Fuck is on again!"

On 23 May, the Intermountain C-46, the aircraft that would be used for logistic support, flew into Washington, D.C.'s National Airport and picked up LeSchack, Smith , Dan and Captain Cadwalader, and whisked them to Intermountain's secret air base at Marana, Arizona, just north of Tucson. That base, an old World War II Army Air Force training base in the desert, was well off the beaten track. The C-46 landed at Marana in the middle of the night. Nonetheless, the entire Intermountain crew, who had been denied the opportunity to whisk Allen Pope from Sukarno's jail, was out to joyously meet the arriving Coldfeet gang, a group that promised them a new adventure, easily as exciting as the one from which they were just deprived. They all retired to the base's bar, likely the original Army base's officers club. To LeSchack who had been a childhood fan of cartoonist Milton Caniff's "Terry and the Pirates" comic book stories of the 1940s, the Intermountain guys were right out of that mold. Adventurers they all were, with many of their adventures having taken place in Southeast Asia and Indo-China. Why "Seig," Connie Seigrist, Intermountain's chief pilot, even came with a beautiful Chinese wife; she looked to LeSchack like Caniff's caricature of the beautiful "Dragon Lady." She partied along with the entire gang! For LeSchack, it was most exotic.

The next day the B-17, piloted by Doug Price, took off and flew to San Francisco to pick up Bob Fulton and Bill Jordan, a polar navigator on leave from Pan American Airways, and then flew directly to Alaska. LeSchack, Smith, Dan and Captain Cadwalader, remained at Marana for two days while the C-46 was undergoing maintenance. These two days were a blessed respite for LeSchack. The sun was shining brightly and there were clear skies over this hidden desert oasis. On base, they found an outdoor swimming pool that, for just a few delicious moments, was just a wonderful place to relax at, in the hot, dry desert air. LeSchack, Dr. Dan and Smith checked and rechecked all their gear. And then, they were off!

The C-46 took an inland route and headed north, through Great Falls, Montana and Edmonton, Alberta. In those days the airport in Edmonton was the small, municipal airport, and the C-46 was able to taxi directly to the front door of the one-storey terminal building. There was a large crowd of Canadians out front, watching the intrepid Coldfeet gang disembark to stretch their legs. The young Lieutenant LeSchack, who by now knew the crusty Captain Cadwalader fairly well, ventured to inquire, tongue-in-cheek, whether the Captain thought "all these people were there just to *greet us?*" The acerbic Captain grimaced at LeSchack, intoning, "Yes (referring to the super-secret operation), they must be saying 'this has got to be the famous Project Coldfeet team we've *heard so much about!*'"

With Project Coldfeet now seriously underway again, Captain Cadwalader wanted to put into place a serious polar navigation backup team. He had obviously been mulling over for some time now the need for such a plan, and at one airport enroute to Fairbanks, Alaska, he told LeSchack that he had decided to call the Commander Alaska Sea Frontier in Kodiak and see whether he could count on support from Patrol Squadron VP-1 to assist in finding NP-8. Whether this was one of those captain-to-captain networking phone calls with which LeSchack became familiar much later in his career, or whether the project itself motivated the CO at Kodiak, LeSchack was never to know. However, Captain Cadwalader was to obtain unqualified Navy air support from this quarter for LeSchack's project! A P2V from that squadron was dispatched to Barrow the next day! It would turn out that VP-1's participation would be crucial to the operation.

Upon arriving at Barrow, LeSchack and Captain Cadwalader briefed Max Brewer, indicating what services they needed the Arctic Research Laboratory to provide. These included obviously the use of the runway and aircraft services, as well as the dormitory space at the Lab. LeSchack especially stressed the need for secrecy to the extent possible in that closely-knit environment—LeSchack, for example, already knew—and either had worked with, or was funding from ONR—several of the researchers there—all of whom wanted to know "what possible kind of research are you conducting, Len, with a B-17, a C-46, and a P2V?" He wanted to avoid them, and the usual bull sessions that abounded, lest the details of the mission become known. He also wanted to have a briefing room that was off-limits to everyone but the Coldfeet group, and for that group to have living quarters separate from the Lab's researchers. Because it was ONR's Arctic Program that funded the Laboratory, LeSchack felt it perfectly reasonable to insist on this. Max Brewer provided him what was requested, and LeSchack and Smith were provided a room all to themselves.

On Saturday morning 26 May 1962, a P2V from VP-1 at Kodiak, piloted by Lieutenant Larry Lowe, took off with Captain Cadwalader and ARL pilot, Bobby Fischer, aboard. Their mission was to find, definitively, NP-8. This mission differed in several respects from the fruitless searches that were conducted from Resolute using the C-130. Lowe had a recent position for NP-8, provided by Walt Whitmann. Then, this was Lowe's second tour of duty at Kodiak flying anti-submarine patrol duty over the sea ice; he and his crew were trained to see things amongst all that ice; he had skilled polar navigators, LT(jg)s Frederick J. Maier and Richard L. Olsonowski; and, lastly, he had the benefit of Bobby Fischer's Arctic flight experience, acknowledged by all as unsurpassed. After four and a half hours flying the search area, they found it!

The navigators confirmed their position, and the P2 returned to Barrow with a bare minimum of fuel remaining. Upon the P2's return, Captain Cadwalader called a meeting for both the P2 and the B-17 crew and, because NP-8 had definitively been sighted, planned the next day's mission for the B-17 alone. LeSchack and Smith joined that flight on 27 May, feeling fairly confident that this day they would be jumping on to NP-8. They were wrong. After five hours of searching, NP-8 was nowhere to be seen. Dejectedly, all aboard the B-17 returned to Barrow, no ones more so than LeSchack and Smith, whose bloodstreams were overloaded with the adrenaline of anticipation.

In utter frustration, Captain Cadwalader devised a plan whereby both the B-17 and the P2 would search independently for NP-8 the next day. On 27 May, Lowe's P2 with Bobby Fischer and polar navigators Maier and Olsonowski took off from Barrow two hours before the B-17. Lowe left at 0900 and the B-17 left at 1050. The plan was that if the P2 found the target first, it would radio the B-17 and guide it to the target. The B-17 reached its target area at 1600 and began its independent search. At 1700, after three hours of searching, the P2 found the target and transmitted the innocuous message, "the magnetic survey has been completed." LeSchack had suggested this message since he had previously commissioned airborne Arctic Ocean magnetic surveys under contract with the University of Wisconsin, and such surveys were already known about by the Soviets.

Lowe's P2 vectored the B-17 to the target, 42 miles distant, and remained circling NP-8 until the B-17 arrived. Upon arrival Seigrist, who was then at the controls, dropped to an altitude of 300 feet and began circling the abandoned station. Everyone peered intensely at the station to ascertain both that it was, indeed, the target, and that neither man nor polar bear was there to greet the two para-spies. When everyone was satisfied that those conditions were met, the level of excitement and adrenaline peaked! However, it was clear to all why the station had been abandoned. A long pressure ridge of ice cut the runway in half making it impossible to support air operations any longer.

Seig took the B-17 to 1200 feet, and the crew opened the "joe hole," the location where the World War II belly turret used to be. It was now the hole through which Smith, and then LeSchack, would jump! Smith pointed out to Seig the exact drop zone to be used for both he and LeSchack, and for all their supplies to be para-dropped as soon as the two officers landed. Seigrist, who had made hundreds of airdrops in Southeast Asia for CAT and Air America, both CIA proprietary aviation companies, knew just how to set up such a drop. And to add, just a bit more to this intrigue, Seigrist, who was an ex-Army Air Corps pilot decided it would be appropriate for him to drop, and subsequently pick up Smith , who had started his career too, in the Army, and for Doug, who had been an ex-Navy pilot, to be in charge of dropping and picking up LeSchack.

Smith positioned himself at the joe-hole, feet dangling beneath the aircraft while all his gear was double-checked by the jumpmaster who made certain that Smith's static line was secured to the plane's interior. As he was doing so, LeSchack leaned over to Smith, the master parachutist, to remind him to ignite a smoke flare immediately upon landing so that he, far less experienced in jumping, would have a guide to wind direction. Smith nodded agreement as the jumpmaster eased him out of the aircraft! His chute opened quickly in the ice-cold air but Smith observed with some alarm that he was drifting toward a field of vertical radio antennae! Fearing impalement, he tugged hard on both steering toggles to dump air out of the back of the chute to increase his forward momentum in such a manner as to pass over and avoid hitting the antennae farm. This he did successfully, and he immediately ignited a green smoke upon landing safely. He also urged the jumpmaster— using his hand-held UHF radio—to make the next pass 50 yards to the right for LeSchack.

Five minutes later, with the blood pounding in his ears, LeSchack sat over the joe-hole while the jumpmaster attached his static line to a D-ring attached to the bulkhead behind him. He checked his reserve chute and his jump kit attached beneath the reserve. As he was putting on his jump helmet, the very senior Captain Cadwalader leaned over to the very junior Lieutenant (jg) LeSchack, and shouted in his ear the encouragement that commanding officers give to their men going into harm's way: "Good luck, Leonard! I envy you!" Next, the Chief of the CIA Air Branch, who was also aboard the B-17 on what was destined to become an historic espionage mission, leaned over to shout in LeSchack's ear: "I told you before to be careful of what you wish and plan for. Sometimes it actually comes to pass! Good luck, Len!"

Moments later, the jumpmaster shouted, "jump!" and eased LeSchack through the joe-hole. It had been a long time since LeSchack had prayed. But he sure did at that moment! And the culmination of a year's worth of planning, aggravation, badgering senior officers, fruitless searches, and personal commitment all combined with the sudden, blessed opening of his canopy in the Arctic air to create for him a near-orgasmic state, slowly followed by the euphoria of now floating, in a noise-free, icy-cold environment. Looking down, LeSchack saw the green smoke that Smith had lit for him. Slipping downwards through the sky, it is easy to see which way the wind is blowing when a smoke flare is ignited on the ground. Using the toggles, LeSchack guided his chute toward the smoke. Soon he could hear Smith shouting instructions and encouragement to him. LeSchack waited until he was just above the ice surface to wheel his chute around so that his back was to the wind. This maneuver arrested his forward motion so that he made an almost vertical landing, and it was in a snowdrift. The best, softest landing he ever made!

Smith, with his hand-held UHF radio, radioed back to the B-17 that both he and LeSchack had landed safely and that there was no need for "Dr. Dan's drop-in surgical service, and thank him very much for standing by!" Also, that they were ready to receive an airdrop of their supplies. Eight cargo drops were made in twenty minutes, all loads neatly placed close together in the drop zone.

Moments thereafter, and after assurances that LeSchack and Smith were well and healthy, the B-17 wheeled, returned and flying low across the deck, directly over the two lone spies, in a thrilling performance, its four powerful reciprocating engines roaring and throbbing in unison, buzzed them and waggled its wings, goodbye. It then climbed and made a bee-line for Barrow before it ran out of fuel.

LeSchack and Smith stood standing, stupefied with physical and emotional exhaustion, in the middle of the camp for who knows how long. And then the isolation got to them! Eventually they mustered up the energy to search the various camp buildings to chose the best one for setting up house-keeping. After about an hour, they chose what appeared to have been the chief scientist's quarters. It had two double-decker beds—much the same as at OCS—a work table at one end, and a coal-and wood-burning stove at the other end. But before they settled in for the night, they arranged their drop bundles just outside their hut so they could be ready to start work early the next day.

As Smith lit up a sterno stove and began cooking some C-rations, LeSchack began emptying his jump kit onto the table. The jump kit had been designed by one of Bob Fulton's riggers to hold all the "must have with you immediately when you land" supplies. This included an emergency medical kit prepared by Dan. It contained morphine syringes, should their be a bad injury upon jumping. The jump kit also contained a .44 magnum Ruger, should they encounter polar bears; two Leica M-3 cameras and notebooks for intelligence-gathering; and, "ahhh yes," breathed LeSchack, in relief, as a mickey of Canadian Club whiskey slid out of the kit on to the table, "something to chase away the ice gremlins, Major." Smith looked up and declared most approvingly, "now there's a junior officer with initiative." They quickly prepared a drink known to many polar researchers and explorers: C.C. and snow!

Not knowing what kind of accommodations would await them on NP-8, LeSchack and Smith brought their own double sleeping bags, designed specifically for cold weather operations, and air mattresses. Even though the building they chose to camp in was, by far, the most commodious, it still was filthy and disgusting. The mattresses left by their unknowing hosts were repulsively grimy. LeSchack and Smith blew up their air mattresses, placed them on the existing mattresses, and then laid out their respective sleeping bags. Then they tried out their sleeping accommodations. For at least ten hours! The two men had not realized how exhausted they actually were.

Upon awakening the next morning the two "spies from the skies" made coffee, and planned how they would spend the next three days—the time allotted for their mission—to conduct their investigation. Despite the exotic way they arrived at NP-8, still in theory Soviet territory under international law, and despite the even more exotic way planned for their departure, there was no further similarity to a James Bond story. No luscious, dangerous women lurking about, no evil villains, no chases or wanton destruction, just meticulous, accountant-like investigation of all clues left on the station. They began with a preliminary survey of the entire station to prepare an order of priorities. LeSchack had with him a map of the station that he had the Hydrographic Office prepare for him, based on photogrammetric measurements made of the aerial photo that the Navy ice patrol plane had taken. LeSchack and Smith divided the map into four sectors, and then each would work independently. They would compare notes each evening, but if something startling turned up—some new unexplained piece of equipment, or some need for translation from the Russian—they would find one another to ask advice.

LeSchack had brought with him a then state-of-the-art ham radio transceiver for clandestine communications with Barrow—he hoped. He had modified the transceiver to operate (illegally) just outside the 20-m amateur radio band. He felt by so doing, he could maximize the chances of communication—without raising undue attention—and minimizing potential interference from more powerful ham transmitters. As a ham, he knew the 20-m band would likely be best for the distances to be covered between NP-8 and Barrow. And he could couch any transmissions in "ham jargon" which he knew well! LeSchack's first task then, was to setup the transceiver so that clandestine communications, as necessary, would be possible with Barrow.

One of the para-dropped loads contained four heavy-duty, fully charged truck batteries, and a children's toboggan that Bob Fulton had insisted they bring—just in case. It sure did come in handy! LeSchack towed the batteries and the transceiver to what clearly appeared to be the radio shack. There were numerous antennae systems attached to it, and all oriented differently, which lends credence to Nate Gerson's thought that in addition to science, these stations may also have been used as electronic listening posts on the West. Seeing all those antennae systems, LeSchack decided to try the one best oriented toward Barrow, rather than waste time stringing up an antenna of his own. It, and the transceiver worked, first try!

All day long, the two investigators trudged through the snow investigating their areas of priority. At one point, they met at the mess hall. It had a seating capacity of about fifteen. It was a mess hall, alright! What a shocking, disgusting mess! Food was still on the stove, frozen in greasy skillets—the Soviets clearly left in a hurry! There was dried blood all over, as if the actual trimming of meats was conducted in the mess hall. In an adjacent shed was the frozen food storage locker, not difficult to maintain at these Arctic temperatures. It was filled with carcasses destined to have eventually been served up. There were many sides of beef, as well as what looked very much like sides of dog in that shed. So perhaps, in fact, a side was brought into the mess hall to thaw, and then station members were allowed to cut off the piece they wanted!

In one corner of the mess hall, a dozen 16mm motion picture reels were found, indicating that the mess hall was also the social gathering place. Still on the walls were political posters exhorting the workers to increase their output. One large color poster, showing a determined Soviet male carrying forward the Red Flag with hammer and sickle, clutching a large book, with Lenin's picture on the cover, had a last minute message scribbled on it, on 19 March 1962, the date NP-8 was abandoned. Also on the wall was a map of NP-8 showing the progressive breaking up of this station. Both documents were liberated by the two investigators.

Then, they spent the rest of the day continuing their investigations at the various buildings and shelters they found. It was not a bad day for conducting such work in the Arctic. The temperature was 15° F with ten knots of wind. It was overcast and snowing. At the end of their first long day, they returned to their hut, cooked up another delightful C-rations meal, and compared notes. They crawled into their sleeping bags this night without benefit of the cocktail they so enjoyed the previous night, for they had consumed, and gratefully so, the flask of CC at that time.

The next morning they split up again; each of them began taking detailed notes and photographs of each hut and structure in the camp. They had to sift through mountains of debris at each location, and make quick decisions as to what was valuable and what was not. And what to try and take back. When in doubt, LeSchack and Smith would confer with one another. On this day among other investigations, LeSchack came across a building that had been used as a photographic darkroom. Like all the other venues, this one too was a disastrous mess. When he saw that there was an enlarger in one corner of the darkroom—and he had operated darkrooms before—the first place he looked for intelligence was in the negative carrier of the enlarger. Everyone in a rush leaves negatives in the negative carrier! He opened the negative carrier and, sure enough, this was no exception. A strip of negatives taken by NP-8 station personnel was there! The negatives, when printed back in Washington, showed several views of the station while it was operational. There was a photo of a re-supply aircraft on the ice runway, being fueled (and its license number—CCCP-04279); a group picture of several station personnel and the special clothing they wore; and a wonderful photo of a burly station member with the *clothing he didn't wear!* In that latter photo, there was a man in a bikini, sitting on the ice, smiling, as if he had just taken a dip in the icy open-water lead just behind him in the photo, and was now "drying off" on the ice. This type of information, recorded by the Soviets themselves, could prove to be valuable intelligence.

Smith discovered and translated a pad of personal radio messages from family members to NP-8 staff personnel. One such message was particularly amusing in its universality: a concerned Russian mother admonishing her son—undoubtedly an experienced Arctic hand—to wear plenty of warm clothes when he stepped outside. In many of the huts LeSchack and Smith found pinup girls: but not "Playboy" centerfolds; they were all pictures of ballerinas!

At the end of their second full day at NP-8, LeSchack and Smith were pleased with their progress, and both recognized that what they had already discovered was worth the effort expended. They felt that they could finish all they had set out to do the following day, at the end of which, the B-17 was scheduled to return and pick them up. As before, they had a meal of C-rations, warmed up on a Sterno stove, and crawled, exhausted into their sleeping bags and slept soundly.

On the morning of the third day, as agreed upon in the Coldfeet operations plan, LeSchack went to the Soviet radio shack and turned on his radio transceiver. On the previous two days, the plan was simply for ARL at Barrow, and LeSchack at NP-8, to monitor a chosen frequency at specific times, twice a day. Neither station would transmit—to maintain radio silence as long as possible—unless there was something urgent. On the third day however, twelve hours prior to the scheduled pickup time, LeSchack was to transmit a weather report, disguised as a ham radio conversation. This he did.

According to the plan, his transmission was to be acknowledged from Barrow. Hearing nothing, however, LeSchack assumed radio propagation conditions were poor. Radio propagation conditions vary according to a geophysical phenomenon known as the eleven-year sunspot cycle. In 1962, that sunspot cycle was at a *minimum,* and radio propagation in the Polar Regions could be expected to be sporadic. This contrasts with 1957-58, the time of the last sunspot *maximum;* that was the reason why the IGY was established at that time. Radio propagation was at the peak of its 11-year cycle, and at its best, particularly in the Polar Regions. LeSchack sighed, and closed down the transceiver. In fact, however, enough of his transmission had been received at Barrow for Captain Cadwalader to recognize weather conditions were acceptable at NP-8 to launch the B-17!

The B-17, with the V-shaped pickup yoke now attached to its nose, took off at 0935 on 31 May 1962. It flew alone to the position, 700 miles from Barrow and only 420 miles south of the North Pole, where four days earlier it dropped LeSchack and Smith. On NP-8, LeSchack and Smith knew they had at least six hours from the time of his radio transmission until the arrival of the B-17. During that time, they made last-minute decisions on which of their collected artifacts and intelligence materials they wished to bring back with them. They agreed that the smallest items, notebooks, rolls of film, and the most important documents they discovered, should be brought back in their pockets. It was intended that the remaining items and the ones of larger size would be hoisted up into the aircraft with a separate pickup kit that they would request the B-17 crew to drop for them. And so they packed these larger items in a duffle bag in such a way that it could be attached to the nylon pickup line, and such that the bag could fit through a man-sized hole in the B-17's tail, where the tail-gunner's turret used to be. Then they chose a pickup zone, nearby a forlorn-looking, likely pre-World War II D-4 sized tractor.

During the period between when LeSchack made his morning radio transmission and mid-afternoon, the weather deteriorated and the wind picked up. The two investigators now recognized they would have to change the original pickup plan from "pick up both men first, and then the booty" to pick up the booty first! The original plan was established with the thought that should anything go wrong with one of the first two pickup kits they tried, they could have the third kit be switched from a "booty pickup" to a live LeSchack or Smith pickup. However, with the wind-speed they observed that day, they recognized it would take both men to hold on to the booty bag after its pickup balloon was released, otherwise the wind would simply drag the bag rapidly across the ice. Hitting a stationary target line for a pickup crew is difficult; a moving line and fluttering balloon would be nigh on impossible! Accordingly, they arranged the plan such that both of them would inflate the balloon for the booty bag and release it first, then both of them would hold on to the bag until the pickup was made. And then first LeSchack, then Smith, would be picked up immediately thereafter.

At 1500, the time estimated for the arrival of the B-17, Smith turned on a U.S. Forest Service radio beacon that was provided by Intermountain. It had a range of five miles and the aircraft, if it came within range, could guide itself directly to the station. Also, they had earlier decided to create a visual signal. Each day they were at NP-8, as a change of pace, they collected burnable debris around the station and hauled it with Bob Fulton's toboggan, to the pickup zone. In addition to wood, diesel oil, and other garbage, they found many rubber tires lying about. They intended to light off a huge signal fire! Then, when they turned on the radio beacon, they set their pyre ablaze. They suspected the day wasn't going right when their signal fire that was supposed to create a black pillar of smoke to the sky, a pillar of biblical proportions, was quickly dissipated against the gray overcast by the ever-increasing wind! They *knew* it wasn't going right when the B-17 hadn't shown up, and the time had past by which it needed to have begun its return trip to Barrow to avoid running out of fuel!

Yes, LeSchack and Smith were disappointed, but they knew there was no need to panic at this point. LeSchack had brought along a month's supply of those delicious C-rations. He did bring three-day's worth of drinking water from Barrow, water which was brackish and frankly, revolting. But just in case that ran out, he also brought along a jerry-can full of gas, a large pot, and a plumber's stove, so they could melt ice for their own water. There was plenty of raw material for sparkling, good-tasting water just outside their hut. Well, actually, not exactly just outside the door, but within easy walking distance. So, no panic. And now, of course, they knew that if the C-rations ran out, there was at least a year's supply of frozen meat in the frozen storage locker. All they would have to do was go in, and saw off just the piece they wanted to cook. Smith, the ex-survival instructor, would certainly know how to do that! Well, that's what Len was thinking.

What Smith was thinking became immediately apparent once they arrived back at their home. "Shit! This place is revolting! Len, let's clean out this pig sty!" With that, Smith began deliberately tossing out the door all the useless and unnecessary furniture. Then he examined the tapestries hanging on the walls. Tapestries—wall hangings—can be found in many Russian homes and offices. But Smith, the survival instructor, master parachutist, and a man whom the CIA pilots did not wish to meet in a dark alley, *also enjoyed Russian art*. He had taken a year's total immersion course in Russian language and culture as part of his attaché training. LeSchack had seen him reading a magnificent book on Russian art during their many long, tedious search flights; it was the then recently published book, "Treasures of the Kremlin," by David Douglas Duncan. Major Smith, USAF, destined to be the next U.S. Assistant Air Attaché in Moscow, as soon as Coldfeet was over, knew what he liked in Russian art, *and what he didn't*. And what he didn't at NP-8 was tossed out in the snow! He then began vigorously sweeping the filthy floor. LeSchack cleaned out the heretofore, unused wood- and coal-burning stove, and finding numerous bags of coal lying about, started up a homey fire. While they didn't enjoy a noisy, seven hour, icy-cold B-17 ride home to safety that night, they did have, for the first time in a while, a warm place in which to take a sponge bath and to sleep!

LeSchack and Smith knew at this point that what they had already collected was an extraordinary intelligence haul. They also knew that despite the haste with which the last occupants departed there was much that likely would have been of intelligence value, but was no longer there. It was clear that all sorts of things had either been somehow stowed on board the last departing flight, or had been dropped through a hole in the ice. There were all sorts of indicators of equipment, once in place, but now gone. While they didn't know how much longer they would now remain at NP-8, it never occurred to them that all the secrets they had discovered might not ever get reported owing to them remaining there forever! They knew that a more aggressive search program for them would soon be initiated. LeSchack and Smith also agreed that after a night's sleep, they would develop a more leisurely plan for data gathering on the morrow. As they crawled, once again, into their sleeping bags they knew that they would sleep well, while Cadwalader, fretting and devising a new search plan, likely would not. They were correct on both counts.

Captain Cadwalader, remembering their inability to find the target from Resolute, as well as the first fruitless days of searching from Barrow, at this point already had a plan in place for "Rat-Fuck" should the B-17 miss finding, yet again, NP-8. As LeSchack and Smith were preparing their NP-8 home for a much longer stay, Cadwalader, some time during *his* seven hour, noisy, icy-cold return flight, sent a coded radio message to Max Brewer at Barrow. Upon receipt of that message, Max contacted VP-1 at Kodiak to activate "Plan B," send a P2V back to Barrow!

The next morning, prior to going to the radio shack, LeSchack discussed with Smith the advisability of breaking radio silence again to give a weather report. The experienced intelligence officer's advice was, "break radio silence only if you hear Barrow transmitting, and only if they ask you a question that requires an answer. We can't risk alerting the Soviets that you and I are here, especially since I am destined for Moscow as soon as I leave here! What an embarrassment that could be for the U.S. if the Sovs declare me *persona non grata*, the instant I land there owing to this espionage operation. And just two years after Gary Powers' unexpected visit!" LeSchack monitored the frequency, but heard nothing.

This day, 1 June 1962, Captain Cadwalader requested VP-1 polar navigator, Lieutenant Maier, to join the B-17 for another sortie to find NP-8 to pickup LeSchack and Smith. The B-17 took off at 1340. At 1500, Smith turned on the radio beacon. At about 1900, they *thought* they had heard the distant drone of aircraft engines, just as they *thought* they had heard the day before, but again they saw nothing and the aircraft was not in range of the beacon—either that, or it was not the sound of *their* airplane searching for them—a scary thought! So they continued their data gathering until the evening radio monitoring schedule, but hearing nothing, did not again transmit. They evaluated this day's haul over another wonderful C-rations dinner, and crawled into their sleeping bags.

The next morning, 2 June, they monitored the radio and heard nothing, and continued their intelligence gathering. They rearranged the artifacts in the duffle bag, added new and recently discovered ones and discarded ones of lesser importance, since there were clear restrictions on the size and weight that the booty bag could have — and still expect a safe and successful pickup.

At Barrow this day, Part 1 of Plan B was now in effect; Set up the search mission exactly the way it was successfully done to find NP-8 six days earlier, with Lieutenant Lowe and his P2 leaving two hours prior to the B-17. Part 2 of Plan B required all of Kodiak's P2s and all the polar navigators VP-1 had. In a captain-to-captain phone call with Kodiak's CO, Captain Cadwalader explained his concern that another day or two's delay in finding LeSchack and Smith would surely come to the attention of the Washington admirals who had strongly warned against pursuing LeSchack's scheme in the first place. You see, it would require the Navy then to request officially the Air Force Air Rescue Service to go hunt for the two James "Bondlets" now lost on the ice! Cadwalader, the CO of Kodiak and LeSchack all knew Navy brass was loathe to make such a request. So Plan B, part 2 was tentatively put into place, but part 1 was already roaring down the Barrow runway! Lieutenant Lowe's P2 was airborne at 1000 on Saturday 2 June. And the B-17 was soon to follow, but just barely.

Lowe found the weather conditions far less favorable than on his previous searches. He had to fly at ten thousand feet altitude to stay above the clouds so that navigators Maier and Olsonowski could make sunshots for navigation. When, hours later the P2 arrived at the predicted location for NP-8, it descended through the clouds to 500 feet above the ice. Visibility was no more than half a mile. But no matter. Within moments of beginning its search, the P2 picked up the radio beacon on NP-8 and guided itself toward the Soviet station.

LeSchack was first to see the P2 as it flew toward the station. He was trudging across the ice between buildings, pulling the toboggan. Smith was deep inside one of the buildings, continuing his investigations at the time. Now fully energized, LeSchack began jumping up and down and waving his arms at the P2. "Jim!" he screamed, "turn on your UHF radio. The P2 is overhead!"

Smith came out of the hut and turned on his tiny UHF radio that he had stashed in his parka. Contact was made. Lowe told Smith that they had at least two hours to wait before the B-17 arrived overhead. For a variety of reasons, including exhausted crew and mechanical problems, the B-17 did not take off for an hour and a half *after it was scheduled to do so.* It was the plan for the P2, should it again be the first to sight the station, to guide, by radio, the B-17 to NP-8, while orbiting the station. But as LeSchack and Smith made their final preparations for leaving, Lowe announced over the radio to Smith that he might not have enough fuel to continue loitering overhead awaiting the tardy B-17s arrival. "I burned more fuel than I planned by being forced to fly above the high clouds so as to get our sunshots. I am not sure we will have enough fuel to keep circling until that late B-17 arrives here, and still be able to make it back to Barrow, but we'll try." With that, Lowe throttled down to the point where, from the ice, it looked to LeSchack and Smith that the bird might simply "fall out of the sky."

On the ice they had time for, and one last opportunity to enjoy, another C-rations meal. After that, LeSchack and Smith spread out all their pickup gear and their booty bag at their chosen pickup zone, away from the congested campsite and by the dilapidated tractor. And then they watched the P2 circling painfully slowly overhead, and waited. At the last possible moment that Lowe calculated he could loiter overhead and possibly have enough fuel to make it home, he announced that he had the B-17 on the radio and it would be overhead momentarily. On the ice, they both strained to see, through the increasing whiteout conditions, the B-17 looming over the horizon.

At last, to the enormous relief of everybody, both on the ice and in the sky, a tired old World War II B-17, Number N809Z, one of only two or three still flying, resplendent with its distinctive yoke, majestically appeared through the white-out. On this occasion, likely the last military mission that a World War II Flying Fortress ever would fly, it roared low across NP-8, its four reciprocating engines throbbing with their special heart-quickening roar, and shattered the icy pristine silence. LeSchack and Smith stood together looking skyward as if transfixed.

Within seconds, Smith heard on his UHF radio Lieutenant Lowe's departing words, reflecting uncertainty now for both their fates: "I'm outa here guys. *I do hope we see each other at Barrow tonight!"* And without buzzing them or even waggling its wings, the P2 just broke out of its circle and headed directly southwest.

Once overhead and in contact, Smith radioed Seigrist to drop another pickup kit. "We've got goodies we need to bring back!" That done, LeSchack and Smith recognizing in that wind it would require two men to inflate and handle the unwieldy pickup balloons, inflated all three, and tethered them to the tractor, a safe distance apart. They announced to Seigrist that they wanted the booty bag to be picked up first. The weather was deteriorating rapidly, and visibility was becoming worse. LeSchack, who had found an anemometer in the Soviet weather shelter, measured the wind-speed on the ground at 15 knots. This was not good. Skyhook pickups had never been performed under such conditions.

When Seigrist announced that he was ready, LeSchack and Smith released the balloon that they had attached to the booty bag. Once aloft the balloon, although stable owing to its blimp-like shape, did not go aloft vertically. The strong wind blew the balloon down-wind and the nylon line appeared to be laying at 45 degrees to the vertical. Then they recognized that the additional tension on the line induced by the increased wind activated a safety release that Fulton had built into the line. Fulton had devised a system to provide quickly an additional 140 feet of line should a pilot strike the line improperly and *not* get it caught in the nose-locking mechanism at the apex of the yoke. That safety system suddenly added another 140 feet to the line that allowed the lengthened line to roll around the aircraft without tearing loose the balloon. Therefore, it gave the pilot a *second chance* at making the pickup with the same line. The release of the additional line was activated by a pull of greater than 80 pounds, which under normal wind conditions occurs only if the line is incorrectly hit. But these were not normal conditions! What LeSchack and Smith did note was that when the wind tore loose the extra 140 feet of line, there was a ten-second delay, during which time there was no pull on it until the balloon reached its additional height. At that time, however, the wind stress pull was even greater.

LeSchack and Smith both held on to the booty bag to keep it from being pulled downwind across the ice. Seig lined up the B-17 on the balloon, not an easy task in the near-whiteout conditions, with both the balloon and line slanted at an angle to the ice surface owing to the wind. Even though both men on the ground knew that Seig and Doug had far more experience picking up dummy loads with the Skyhook than had the Pax River P2V crew, they also knew that for all three pickups from NP-8, the B-17 would have *no second chance!* All three pickup kits available were now in use, and the Fulton safety feature on each line would disappear once the balloons were launched, and they pulled their lines taut. LeSchack and Smith knew that *this was living on the edge!*

Seig made perfect contact. The booty bag sailed into the sky. LeSchack would be next to go. According to plan, Doug, the ex-Navy aviator, switched with Seig to pickup Navy Len. Zipped into his pickup suit, LeSchack waited until the B-17 acknowledged that it had completely retrieved the booty bag and was now ready for him. Then, holding his balloon as close as he could to the ice, LeSchack walked to the pickup zone from the tractor. They had chosen this pickup zone because it was reasonably clear and downwind of most obstacles that could entangle them during their pickup. All clear except for the 10-foot-high pressure ridge, three hundred yards downwind, that had destroyed NP-8's runway!

LeSchack looked all around him before launching his balloon. Then, facing Major James F. Smith, USAF, Lieutenant (jg) Leonard A. LeSchack, USNR, threw the Major a sharp salute, wheeled around, and plopped down on the ice into the standard pickup position. He released his balloon. As he watched it deploy successfully, he pulled down a "ski-mask" over his face with only eyeholes cut in it so that his face would not be frozen flying through the frigid Arctic air at 125 knots. In a matter of seconds, the tethered balloon fully ascended.

Then, to his horror, LeSchack found that the ever-increasing wind had created enough upward pull on the balloon and nylon line to counteract his 185-pound weight and render him nearly weightless. He was pulled, slip-sliding along on the ice surface, at an ever increasing speed toward the pressure ridge's high jagged blocks of ice. In only seconds it seemed, his ski mask had twisted on his head making him unable to see his rapid approach to that pressure ridge and likely doom, should his line become tangled in the ice blocks, during pickup! He tried desperately to arrest his unwanted high-speed travel across the ice, praying for the 140-foot safety line to suddenly payout. And suddenly, it did! LeSchack now knew that while the "second chance pickup" safety feature was lost to him and Doug, he had gained his full weight back for ten seconds, during which time he had to scrape hand holds in the ice. And scrape he did, securing in those ten seconds of grace, two fragile hand holds in the ice that permitted him to stay put, *as long as he lay face down on the ice,* a pickup position that he knew no one had ever tried before!

LeSchack could feel the nylon line and pickup harness tugging on his body, trying to get it to move again toward the pressure ridge and certain disaster. He tightened his grip through his thick mittens on his frantically clawed hand-holds in the ice. He heard, what seemed to him like the tenth trial lineup pass of the B-17 overhead. And he waited in desperation wondering when the yoke would make contact with his line, and when it did, what unorthodox flight position would his body then assume. After what seemed like an eternity of waiting, he found out.

He felt the impact when the B-17 intersected his line. Within seconds, he was airborne. Being towed in the wrong direction! The harness, instead of pulling him from behind his head so that he would be pulled backwards through the frigid air, gathered instead in front of his sightless face, and towed him face into the wind. As LeSchack was quick to discover, a human being cannot breathe facing into a wind-stream of 125 knots, even with a facemask to block the full impact of that wind.

A typical Skyhook pickup requires between five and seven minutes to retrieve the dummy, or person in this case, and bring it, or him, into the pickup aircraft. LeSchack knew he couldn't survive that long without breathing. Under that constraint, it didn't take him long to remember the aerobatic maneuvers that he tried on that pleasant fall day at Pax river, eight months earlier. Sticking his arms out and using them as ailerons, he was able to rotate his body along its long axis so that he was now flying on his back, his face no longer facing the wind. He could breathe again! But only so long as he held his arms straight out from his side. Have you ever stuck your arm straight out the window of an automobile driving at 60 mph? Well, LeSchack was going at more than twice that speed, and it was hard work to hold his arms that way! If he relaxed his arms, his body would instantly flip over into its more stable position—face into the wind!

And so, for six and a half minutes, LeSchack kept himself flipped over, with his tired arms outstretched to do so, before he was dragged through the tail section of the B-17, simply exhausted. Dr. Dan was there to examine him as soon as LeSchack caught his breath, and declared no obvious ill effects from all that adventure.

One more pickup to make! Seig, ex-Army Air Force, now returned to the pilot's seat to pick up Army Jim, who started his military life also in the Army Air Force. Smith had observed LeSchack's pre-pickup trials and tribulations on the ice. He was determined not to repeat them. He decided to hold on to the tractor after he let go of his balloon. He tried, but the wind was too strong and he lost his grip. He too, was dragged across the ice some seventy-five yards towards the pressure ridge before he was able to hook his heels into an irregularity in the ice surface and halt his movement towards the ridge. Seig guided the B-17 into Smith's line and soon, he too, was airborne, but in the normal way. Three out of three consecutive pickups (with no safety margin) for CIA. To LeSchack's way of thinking, the Pax River P2V would have been highly unlikely to have achieved that statistic, and one or both of them might still be on the ice if that P2 had been used!

Now absolutely exhausted, both physically and emotionally, LeSchack and Smith crawled out of the tail compartment into the slightly more commodious, but equally frigid mid-section of the B-17. With operations at Soviet drifting station NP-8 now complete, that aircraft now wheeled in the sky and headed back towards Barrow. LeSchack, Smith, Dr. Dan with his medical bag open and still performing diagnostic checks on his charges, and Captain Cadwalader were now all spread out amidships, engaged in a quiet orgy of self-congratulation. Eventually a man who had been on the B-17's flight deck with Seig and Doug during most of the operation, came back to join the revelry. It was the Chief of the CIA Air Branch. A year earlier he had been in charge of air operations in Guatemala and Nicaragua to support the Bay of Pigs invasion in Cuba. Now, he was also the Intermountain Chief of Operations. When he joined the Coldfeet gang amidships, he had with him his ubiquitous attaché case.

"Well done," the CIA man allowed. Smiling, he opened his attaché case; its only contents—a bottle of Vat 69 scotch whiskey. Instantly, paper cups materialized, and it seemed that the Coldfeet crew literally inhaled the liquor. It was gone in a twinkling. In fact, so were LeSchack and Smith. Moments later, they fell into an exhausted slumber in that cold, noisy old aircraft. The last thing LeSchack heard as he slipped off was the gruff voice of an obviously relieved Cadwalader, famed for his acerbic sense of humor, admonishing the three "Rat-Fuck" officers, all junior to him, for "drunk and disorderly conduct aboard a military aircraft—clearly a court-martial offence."

Upon arriving back at ARL in Barrow, the weary crews of both aircraft and the Coldfeet crew all lined up in front of the B-17 for photographs, and then they retreated to the ARL library where Max Brewer then locked the library doors and threw a "classified" party. LeSchack remembers little of this, other than that Smith handed out Soviet cigarettes that he collected at NP-8 for curious smokers to evaluate. The evaluation had been unanimous: the "White Sea Canal" brand of cigarettes Smith passed around tasted ghastly!

The following day LeSchack and Smith returned to the ARL library that remained locked and began making a rough catalog of the intelligence materials they had collected. Captain Cadwalader sent a message to Washington announcing a brilliantly successful conclusion to Coldfeet, and LeSchack sent out two messages himself. The first to his office in Washington to call Virginia and let her know the operation (which, because she was not cleared for such secret information, she knew little about) had been successfully concluded, and that he would shortly be home. And the second one to LeSchack's Byrd Station friend, Sven, now living in Fairbanks.

Sven, was the former-Marine whose brother had been killed in a plane crash in Hawaii, when both Sven and LeSchack were prisoners at Byrd Station, Antarctica, four years earlier. Sven continued to work for the U.S. Coast and Geodetic Survey, and was now stationed in Fairbanks, Alaska, which would be an overnight stopping off place for the returning Coldfeet aircraft and crew. LeSchack's message to Sven: *Coming into Fairbanks, tomorrow afternoon on B-17 N809Z. Please meet me. Len LeSchack.*

LeSchack and Smith spent the rest of that day packing in cartons their hard-won haul. Although there would be little concern for the transport of these boxes aboard Intermountain's aircraft, LeSchack and Captain Cadwalader would be transferring to commercial flights destined for Washington, D.C., once they reached the Seattle-Tacoma Airport. At that point, all their booty would be carried as accompanying baggage to the ONR office, with all the risks of separation and loss that a commercial carrier would entail. LeSchack wanted to assure the maximum safety during such transportation of his treasures. Upon completion of this final packaging, another party broke out in the library. This night, everyone slept well, with the wistful understanding that members of this operation, which would turn out to be a wildly successful adventure as far as ONR, ONI, DIA and CIA were concerned, would be disbanding and returning to their home stations on the morrow.

The following day Lieutenant Lowe and his P2V and crew of extraordinary navigators left for Kodiak. And the Intermountain C-46 and B-17 with all of the happy "Rat-Fuck" members aboard, headed for Fairbanks, Alaska, a refueling, and an overnight stay. In those days, the Fairbanks Airport was not large. Intermountain's C-46 drew no attention, for such aircraft were common as cargo aircraft in Alaska then; but the B-17 sure did! And LeSchack's friend Sven from Byrd Station was there, amongst the gawkers. LeSchack saw him as he descended from the B-17, and yelled to him.

Because LeSchack's message from Barrow had been garbled in the governmental message system that delivered it to Sven's USC&GS office, he only knew to meet a B-17 at the Fairbanks airport that day. He didn't know what or whom to expect would arrive on it. "Oh so it was you who sent that message," he said as they warmly shook hands. "Well if you are staying overnight in Fairbanks, please stay with me and my new wife!" And LeSchack did, telling Captain Cadwalader that he would meet them back at the airport the following morning at the agreed upon time.

LeSchack's Byrd Station friend had no idea what brought him and his strange coterie to Fairbanks that day. And LeSchack couldn't tell him, since it was a highly classified mission. But Sven did find out about the mission, nearly 40 years later, when LeSchack and CIA historian Bill Leary jointly authored a book that described the now declassified story; Sven, now no longer a geophysical technician, but a retired professor of geophysics, had discovered the book, read it with glee, and wrote to LeSchack. LeSchack's response to Sven's letter pretty well described the emotions he felt that one night he stayed with Sven and his wife in Fairbanks:

> Dear Sven,
>
> What a wonderful and unexpected surprise your letter was. I am glad that you took the time to find me and to write. And I am certainly glad that you enjoyed the book. What you apparently either forgot, or did not recognize the significance of at the time, was that you played an important role, for me anyway, in Project Coldfeet.
>
> In June 1962, just days after the successful completion of Coldfeet, I returned, via Fairbanks, from our base at Barrow aboard CIA's B-17. I was physically and emotionally exhausted. I knew you were at USC&GS in Fairbanks at the time, and sent an official government message from Barrow to your office requesting that you meet my B-17 when I arrived. And you did meet me

(although you told me that the message was sufficiently garbled so that you did not know who or what it was you were meeting, only that it was coming in a B-17). After my arduous and hazardous experience, I was in need of the warmth and comfort that only an old friend could provide. So I was absolutely delighted for you to meet me at the plane in Fairbanks and to be invited to your home to stay overnight, while the rest of my Coldfeet colleagues had to endure the Travelers Inn.

And I had the opportunity to talk and laugh with you only of our Byrd Station adventures, something completely different from what I had been talking about for the previous several months; and because our project was then highly classified, I couldn't have told you about it anyway. I just felt wonderful basking in that old Byrd Station camaraderie that we once shared. It was good to be in your home, that night, with the warmth you and your wife, Anne, provided............

With warmest regards,

Len

The next morning Sven took LeSchack to the airport where, once again, he boarded the B-17, now destined for the Seattle-Tacoma Airport. LeSchack sat in the bombardier's plexiglass nose for much of the flight viewing the magnificent Alaskan countryside. Dusk was settling in when the aircraft began its approach into Sea-Tac. LeSchack had earphones on and listened to Seig make contact with the control tower. "This is B-17 N809Z requesting permission to land." The response from the control tower was an incredulous, "Sir, did I understand you to say, B-17?" Seig responded with a casual, "Yes....B-17 N809Z, can you give me a runway and heading?" The response from the tower was an "Oh, my! Oh, my! I and another flight controller here in the tower flew those big birds during the War. Will you be staying long enough for us to come visit?" Seig replied, "Just long enough to refuel."

At this point the tower officers, who likely had many B-17 adventures of their own, gave the first B-17 that they had laid their eyes on in 18 years, landing permission, with instructions to taxi to a quiet corner of the field. Getting other flight controllers to cover for them, they hastened to the spot on the tarmac where the B-17 was refueling. LeSchack could see as he met these now middle-aged men, out of breath from running to the parked aircraft, that for just a few moments, each alone with their own thoughts and memories as they looked at and fondled the aircraft, joined our Coldfeet heroes in an unspoken brotherhood. And these men *did* wait on that tarmac until the refueled aircraft was given authority from the tower to again take to the sky. They would wait to hear, once again, that heart-quickening sound of four B-17 reciprocating engines warming up and synchronizing the pitch of their propellers to produce the most exciting and romantic sound aviators of that era would ever hear!

Only moments thereafter, the tightest knit, most professional and dedicated team of adventurers that LeSchack had ever met, went their separate ways. The Intermountain aircraft and their CIA flight crews flew back to Marana, Arizona, and the four military officers took commercial flights back to their respective bases. LeSchack and Captain Cadwalader took the red-eye to Washington, D.C., Major Smith , USAF, flew back to Florida and Eglin Air Force Base, and Captain Dan Walter, MD, USA, the gynecologist who jumped with the 82nd Airborne Division, flew back to Fort Bragg in North Carolina.

Rat-Fuck was over.

****

Project Coldfeet would have a lifelong effect on LeSchack in many different and diverse ways. Even as he was flying back to Washington, he knew this in a general way, but he couldn't possibly have recognized all the ramifications that would accrue over his lifetime. For one thing, the operation was secret, and would remain so for many years. But in Washington, it became known to an ever-widening circle of admiring people in high places who had appropriate security clearances, and LeSchack was to enjoy, relatively quickly, the fallout of such recognition. ONR was, of course, the first organization to learn of Project Coldfeet's success, and LeSchack was welcomed back as a hero. But CIA, DIA, and some members of Congress were soon to learn about Coldfeet and want briefings. Seig told LeSchack that CIA briefed President Kennedy directly.

LeSchack only had another five months left during which time he physically would remain at ONR. He had applied for and been accepted as the "U.S. Official Representative with the French Antarctic Expedition, 1962-63." This was a program established under a bilateral arrangement between the two countries. LeSchack had lobbied for this assignment, first during his vacation in Paris in 1961, by meeting with Paul-Émile Victor, Director of the *Expéditions Polaires Françaises,* and then with the U.S Antarctic Projects Officer, in Washington. He had begun studying the French language seriously with a private tutor who lived in Washington. He would have to leave to join that expedition in December. Until that time, however, he now became consumed with examining his NP-8 data and describing the mission to many interested parties in government. He quickly learned that it was important to have Captain Cadwalader along on briefing assignments to other military organizations to assure that LeSchack's operation would not be co-opted by more senior officers from other services who would attempt to bask in LeSchack's or the Navy's glory.

Bob Fulton, who LeSchack had invited to join all phases of the operation, both from Resolute and Barrow, had recorded the highlights of this operation on 16mm motion picture film. Shortly after the successful completion of Coldfeet, Bob, the erstwhile cinematographer, had put together a fine movie presentation, a copy of which LeSchack used to illustrate the mission. One of the earliest requests for a full presentation was from General Edward Lansdale at CIA. Lansdale was the personable and resourceful operative whose activities were loosely chronicled in Graham Greene's, 1956 book "The Quiet American," and William Lederer and Eugene Burdick's 1958 book, "The Ugly American." Landsdale's crew was impressed with the data haul LeSchack and Smith brought back, but were clearly viscerally impressed, if that's the word, to see movies of the actual pickup! LeSchack and Smith smiled wanly at the collective, "uuugggghhhh!" and the way many male officers clutched their stomachs or their groins as they saw a Skyhook liftoff!

Of course there was a meeting with the new Defense Intelligence Agency that had saved Project Coldfeet's life with the $30,000 *down payment* on the operation. And of course, that organization had never anticipated their investment would be "spying on the layaway plan," and therefore were somewhat taken aback at the $100,000 overrun that LeSchack had accumulated. So, when he went to *that* meeting, with his movie and show- and-tell of all the intelligence gathered, he brought along Captain Cadwalader, Max Britton, Evelyn Pruitt, then head of the Geography Branch, and the ONR comptroller, for LeSchack knew the *DIA comptroller*, concerned with the unexpected overrun, would be at this meeting also! And as LeSchack had anticipated, with Coldfeet the resounding success that it was, DIA, to its credit, accepted the overrun gracefully, recognizing that its very first investment in clandestine intelligence gathering had certainly paid off, both politically and in substance; and LeSchack was not thrown into Portsmouth Naval Prison for financial chicanery with public funds.

These show-and-tells went on all through the summer of 1962 and into the fall. In September, an officer from the U.S. Naval and Marine Corps Reserve Composite Company 5-48 requested that LeSchack provide a briefing on Coldfeet to its members. This, however, was not your usual group of "weekend warriors." The 5-48 met on Capitol Hill, and its members were Congressmen and their staffers. It is uncertain if such a unit still exists today, for all of its members had to be ex-Navy men or ex-Marines, who maintained their reserve status. LeSchack's presentation elicited sufficient interest that he spoke before that unit twice; that month, and in October. There were amongst the unit thirteen members who were Congressmen, and on important committees: Armed Services, Atomic Energy, Foreign Affairs, Government Operations, Science and Astronautics and Ways and Means. On both times during which LeSchack was a briefer, there were other briefers there also: They were briefing the Congressmen on the sighting and buildup of offensive Soviet ballistic missiles in Cuba, just 90 miles offshore. And because LeSchack had the appropriate clearances, he was allowed to remain and to listen to the other briefers.

The other briefers in September showed CIA reports that medium range ballistic missiles might be part of that buildup. In October, briefers showed U-2 spy plane photos, taken on 14 October of that missile buildup: there were 36 medium range (1000 miles) and 24 intermediate range (2200 miles) missiles that could be counted in the photos. And from these spy-plane photos, it appeared that the Soviets were busily constructing launch pads. From Cuba, such missiles could do inordinate damage to the continental United States. Along with congressmen privy to this presentation, LeSchack recognized that what had been shown in these two briefings was serious in immediate and apocalyptic terms. He knew that President Kennedy and Premier Khrushchev would have a confrontation over this! And soon. He could see by the reaction of the congressmen that Kennedy would be forced to take potentially drastic action. And everyone in that briefing room knew then that when you are talking threats by medium range and intermediate range ballistic missiles 90 miles off shore, you are talking about a potential nuclear war. So it was with enormous foreknowledge and trepidation that a few weeks later, on 22 October 1962, LeSchack took his new bride by the hand and together they sat before the television set. "This is serious, Babe," he said, before the President even started. "I'm scared."

That night Kennedy said:

> I call upon Chairman Khrushchev to halt and eliminate this clandestine, reckless and provocative threat to world peace and to stable relations between our two nations. I call upon him further to abandon this course of world domination, and to join in an historic effort to end the perilous arms race and to transform the history of man.

> He has the opportunity now to move the world back from the abyss of destruction—by returning to his government's own words that it had no need to station missiles outside its own territory, and withdrawing these weapons from Cuba—by refraining from any action which will widen or deepen the present crisis— and then by participating in a search for peaceful and permanent solutions.

Kennedy had overruled the Joint Chiefs of Staff who had wanted to take out the missile sites in Cuba. Instead, two days later, on the 24th, he imposed a "quarantine," more diplomatic words for essentially a naval blockade of that island that prevented Soviet ships from entering Cuban waters. The naval blockade and behind the scenes diplomacy had worked, allowing both sides to save face Four days later, on 28 October 1962, the crisis was over and the Soviets began dismantling the missiles in Cuba and taking them home. A nuclear holocaust had been averted. But LeSchack knew that U.S. fingers had been on the nuclear trigger. Soviet fingers also, it turns out. Forty years later, LeSchack spoke of "the Crisis" with his friend, Natalya, a Russian-English interpreter, born in the USSR, but now living in North America. She was only an infant when all this had occurred. In her later professional career as an interpreter, she told LeSchack, however, that while still in Russia, she had worked with Vladimir, a Soviet interpreter—a military man about LeSchack's age she said—who had worked in the Kremlin war room when the White House-Kremlin "hot-line" had been installed. He told her that he *knew* in October 1962, Soviet fingers were on their triggers too. Vladimir told Natalya that he, too, was truly scared. Like LeSchack had been.

Referring to the Cuban Missile Crisis, Richard Rhodes, author of "Dark Sun: the making of the hydrogen bomb," wrote:

> What no one in the U.S. Government knew until it was revealed at a conference between Soviet and U.S. missile crisis participants in Moscow in 1989—was that contrary to CIA estimates, the Soviet forces in Cuba during the missile crisis possessed twenty nuclear warheads for medium range R-12 ballistic missiles that could be targeted on U.S. cities as far north as Washington, D.C., as well as nine tactical nuclear missiles which the Soviet field commanders in Cuba were delegated authority to use—the only time such authority was ever delegated by the Soviet leadership.

But in October 1962, Vladimir *knew*, while LeSchack only *suspected*. Such was the tenor of the times when LeSchack had instigated and conducted that intelligence mission against the Soviet Union, Project Coldfeet. Few people remember these times or their significance. LeSchack certainly does, and will till the day he dies.

For the remainder of the Cold War, another 29 years, the United States and the USSR never again came this close to nuclear war as they had in 1962. The Cuban Missile Crisis and the unequivocal threat of imminent nuclear holocaust were over on 28 October 1962! Three days later, on 1 November 1962, LeSchack and Smith were summoned to the Secretary of the Navy's office in the Pentagon. President Kennedy had authorized the Secretary to decorate Lieutenant Junior Grade Leonard A. LeSchack and Major James F. Smith with Legions of Merit on his behalf for Project Coldfeet.

LeSchack's and Smith's citations—which eliminated classified details that attested to the operation's success in gathering intelligence of a high order—were essentially the same. LeSchack's stated:

> The President of the United States takes pleasure in presenting the Legion of Merit to Lieutenant, Junior Grade, Leonard A. LeSchack, United States Naval Reserve for service as set forth in the following

> CITATION:

> "For exceptionally meritorious conduct in the performance of outstanding service during the months of April, May and June 1962, as a member of the Surface Evaluation Team of Project COLDFEET in the Arctic Ocean. Volunteering for this hazardous operation, Lieutenant, Junior Grade, LeSchack made many prolonged flights, averaging sixteen hundred miles, over the Arctic Ocean. At the culmination of these flights, he was dropped by parachute, with one companion and survival equipment, in a remote area of the Polar Ice Pack and remained there for five days in complete isolation, separated from the nearest other human

beings by several hundred miles of impassible ice. During this period, he conducted the required investigation with extraordinary skill and initiative, resulting in the acquisition of technical information of high order. At the end of five days, he was picked up by an aircraft employing the aerotriever ground-to-air recovery system, the first operational use of this system, and returned to his base. Lieutenant, Junior Grade, LeSchack's outstanding professional competence, fortitude, and devotion to duty throughout were in keeping with the highest traditions of the United States Naval Service."

For the President,

Fred Korth

Secretary of the Navy

Project Coldfeet and LeSchack's Legion of Merit would influence and alter the direction of the remainder of his life in both powerful as well as subtle ways. LeSchack sensed, in a vague way at that time, that it might. But he could not then figure how this might occur. It certainly showed him that persistence in promoting a good idea could overcome daunting odds, despite the inertia and the nay-sayers that surrounded him, and that he could ultimately become successful with his schemes. At least some of them. Coldfeet, then would become the model against which LeSchack examined all new ideas and projects for the remainder of his life. And, indeed, some would succeed, others would fail.

The Coldfeet story remained classified for a decade thereafter, so except for those with appropriate clearances, LeSchack could not share that story for whatever personal glory that might bring him. Nor frankly, did he want that story told just yet. For one thing, within a few months of their visit to the Secretary of the Navy's office, Smith was in Moscow as the Assistant Air Attaché. Knowledge of Coldfeet by the Soviets could compromise Smith and the United States in the eyes of the Kremlin.

Also LeSchack, himself, had plans to visit the USSR, and knowledge of that escapade could compromise him, also. Nonetheless, snippets of an action story like this do get around, rarely correctly, and often distorted. Military men—the Airborne and Special Forces—and intelligence officers in CIA, DIA and in the respective Armed Forces, all have security clearances and soon hear about things like LeSchack's operation. How could they not? And these kind of people enjoy telling such stories. For the remainder of the Cold War, and especially during periods he was in a milieu where military or intelligence people congregated, LeSchack's connections with Intermountain and the CIA, as tenuous as they were, always seemed for better or for worse, to color their perceptions of him, and his projects, whatever they were.

But for good or ill, the Legion of Merit now became part of LeSchack's persona, and that *was not secret information.* LeSchack was likely one of the most junior officers to be decorated with the Legion of Merit. It is a decoration, if awarded at all, usually given only to senior or flag officers. For LeSchack, it likely greased the skids for his regular promotion up the ladder to captain in the Naval Reserve, whenever he was under consideration for promotion before the Navy's Selection Board. But the Selection Board functions like a meritocracy—possibly the most perfect example of any that exists—not so the behavior of some of the mid-grade and senior officers that LeSchack was to run in to over the years. Jealousy and envy crept in from time to time. And the Legion of Merit and his parachute wings, then uncommon on naval uniforms, appeared to LeSchack to be intimidating to some.

It was LeSchack's experience then, as well as in later years, that military people rarely talk about their personal decorations. Possibly, they will with another person who has the same decoration. Or with a person known to have shared the same campaign or experience. The Legion of Merit ribbon—lavender with tiny white stripes on either end—that now became part of LeSchack's uniform, was rarely recognized, it seemed to him, by his peers in their 20s and early 30s. But it certainly was by senior officers who coveted one for themselves! And while they never knew, or were loathe to ask what the decoration was for, they knew the first and last lines of the citation for the Legion of Merit were always the same, no matter what it said in between: "For exceptionally meritorious conduct in the performance of outstanding service........ and;...... outstanding professional competence, fortitude, and devotion to duty throughout were in keeping with the highest traditions of the United States Naval Service." Or other service, as the case my be, for the Army, Navy, Air Force and Marines all have the same decoration.

This decoration, and the experience associated with conceiving, designing and executing Project Coldfeet then, like the beat he hears from that different drummer, would become a legacy that would shape the rest of LeSchack's life, whether in the military, or in any of his scientific or business endeavors to follow, or to the further espionage he was eventually to conduct against the Soviet Union.

■■■

Epilogue

Just as Coldfeet would become the benchmark upon which all other of LeSchack's future military as well as scientific projects would be judged by him, Giselle, his first serious and intense lover in Montreal, and especially Simone of Boston would be the benchmarks upon which all future lovers would inevitably be compared.

"Who is that enigmatic woman who had been my most powerful and voracious lover for over a year now," LeSchack had wondered that summer day in 1961 after he learned from the U.S. consular official in Paris that contrary to what Simone had told him when they were lovers, there was no record of her as a student from Grasse, France who was enrolled at M.I.T., and furthermore that consular office was required to have records for all French students enrolled in U.S. colleges or universities. At that time he wondered whether she was "an illegal alien, runaway wife or spy even. "Fifty years later, the likely answer to this question is "runaway wife !"

Surfing the web, a half century later LeSchack had discovered that Simone had both been born and died in Boston, and was married likely at the time she and LeSchack had become powerful lovers. He knew she had family in New York, for that

was where she was going when they first met on that New York
bound flight. LeSchack had no thought then, that that family
might include a husband, however!

LeSchack remembers vividly the night of their first date that
they deliriously become lovers. She took several stiff drinks prior
to pulling him into her bed, really just a cot, in her Boston
apartment. He had sensed at the time that these serious belts of
raw whiskey were designed to give her courage to move ahead
and consummate their affair! And that she was well prepared.
She came to bed with a diaphragm already inserted! Simone was
LeSchack's age and, at that time in 1960, he knew no other girls
that age who were already prepared with diaphragms on their
first date, and who knew how to make love so well and so
vigorously as Simone did that first night, and every night
thereafter when they chanced to be together.

As a result of her intellect and worldliness as well as her
lovemaking abilities she, just as would Giselle, inevitably
became women against whom all other subsequent women were
inevitably to be judged by LeSchack, often to their detriment!

*On 1 November 1962, just three days after President Kennedy
resolved the "Cuban Missile Crisis," that same president
authorized the Legion of Merit, a presidential decoration, for Air
Force Major James F. Smith and Navy Lt(jg) LeSchack. The
Secretary of the Navy is pinning it on me at left, and the
Secretary of the Air Force is pinning it on Jim, at right.*

Once the Office of Naval Research swallowed the concept of Lieutenant (jg) LeSchack's James bond-like scheme to mount a clandestine investigation of the just abandoned Soviet Spy station on the Arctic ice near the North Pole, by parachuting in, and after the mission, by being retrieved by the Fulton Skyhook aeroretriever system, the ONR Air Branch went into action! To provide LeSchack some experience with this system, ONR arranged for LeSchack to be picked up one sunny day in Autumn 1961, by a P2V at Patuxent River Navel Air Station. Here we see LeSchack already picked up, and about to be reeled into the aircraft. Shortly thereafter, the Air Branch was to arrange forLeSchack to become jump qualified.

The mission, dubbed "Project Coldfeet" by LeSchack is now underway in CIA's B-17. Both photos are taken from the Bombardier's nose. The upper view shows NP-8 dead ahead. The lower view shows a smoke flare dropped by the jumpmaster that gives us an estimate of the wind-speed and direction, valuable information for both the pilots and for us who are about to jump in!

Major Smith has already jumped, and LeSchack has now taken his position over "the Joe Hole," waiting for the jumpmaster's signal. Getting it a few seconds later, he drops into the freezing cold air and into history!

Once both safely on the ice, Smith and LeSchack begin searching the deserted station to familiarize themselves with the Soviet station, and to choose a hut in which to bivouac. This hut immediately caught LeSchack's eye. The numerous cables with hydrophones at the end strongly suggested that this hut was used for searching for nuclear submarines with an array of hydrophones. The weather station is seen in the background.

LeSchack in the "font yard" of the acoustic Array hut measures continuity of the hydrophone array system with an ohmmeter.

Smith examines the hydrographic hole, lifting up the tent in which a high quality hydrographic winch can be seen.

In another hut LeSchack discovered what had clearly been a darkroom. Seeing a photographic enlarger, he went to it fully expecting to find negatives still in the negative holder, owing to precipitous departure from NP-8! Sure enough, the Soviets had left negatives! This photo by the Soviets,

Chapter 7
shows one brave soul sunning himself on the ice after a
refreshing swim in the adjacent icy open water lead

A Soviet Bi-plane, the AN-2, is seen being serviced on the station's ice runway, prior to the station breaking up, forcing its abandonment.

The CIA B-17, already two days late, returning to pickup LeSchack and Smith, has finally arrived overhead, and begins its pick-ups! First to be hauled up, is a duffle bag full of LeSchack's and Smith's intelligence artifacts. Next to go up is LeSchack, and finally Smith.

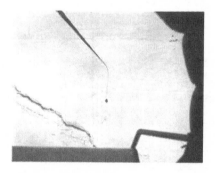

View from the aft end of the B-17 (which once was the tail gunner's station, and now is the entrance for everyone and everything being winched into the aircraft). In this picture we see Smith at the end of the nylon line, and in the upper right corner, a last view of NP-8. This is the final pickup. The intelligence artifacts have already been safely hauled into the B-17, followed by LeSchack.

Joy in the B-17 cabin! As Dr. Dan Walter, upper left, certifies that LeSchack and Smith have survived the rigors of their adventure, the CIA air boss presented the 'Sky Spies" with a bottle of Scotch! Smith, upper right, is already busily drinking, while LeSchack, lower right is recovering from shock! At lower left, Captain Cadwalader is enormously relieved that this dangerous, harrowing caper has ended successfully! The bald head between LeSchack and Cadwalader belongs to Jack Wall, the jumpmaster.

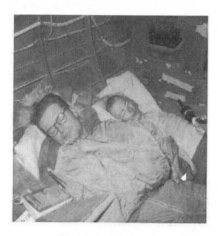

Smith and LeSchack, having finished the bottle of Scotch, and now exhausted, have retired to a forward cabin and collapsed!

After a cold lengthy flight back to Barrow, Alaska, the B-17 lands at the military airstrip at the Navy's Arctic Research Laboratory, and the entire Coldfeet crew form up for a group photo in front of the tired B-17, likely the last military mission

for any B-17, and have their photograph taken! LeSchack, with the red parka, already has a celebratory beer in his hand! Smith too, not surprisingly, also has beer!

To complete this historic occasion, we include a photograph of the Soviet crew that were forced to abandon NP-8 just a few weeks prior to the unexpected arrival of Smith and LeSchack.

The U.S. Navy and the Cold, Cold War Years-Argentine Antarctic Expedition

> *Teniente LeSchack, mi trabajador Americano, as you must have noticed when stationed aboard our ships, and working at the Instituto Antártico Argentino here in Buenos Aires, the Spanish language is far better used for writing poetry and for making love than it is for giving ship-handling orders or conducting oceanography.*
>
> *Admiral Rodolfo Panzarini, multilingual naval officer and scientist; Chief of the Argentine Antarctic Institute, March 1963.*

Lieutenant (jg) Leonard LeSchack had been looking forward to joining the 1962-63 French Antarctic Expedition. He had extended his three-year obligatory service commitment with the Navy for another several months to remain on active duty to perform that Antarctic assignment as a naval officer. He had been uncertain up to this point whether to remain on active duty after this Antarctic assignment and make the Navy his career; he had thought seriously about putting in for submarine school.

However, after he married Virginia, he felt that perhaps he should continue pursuing science as a civilian, instead of pursuing a career in the naval service. Virginia, despite the fact that her uncle was a Navy man, or maybe because of it, and because of what *she did know of his life*, clearly preferred a civilian life style for her family. For his part, LeSchack recognized that having the marvelous experiences and heady recognition he had up until now as a junior officer were unlikely to continue as he climbed the usual Navy career steps. He did, however, plan on remaining in the Naval Reserve.

He had arranged to obtain a study grant from the Arctic Institute of North America to write his report as the "Official U.S. Representative with the French Antarctic Expedition" at the offices of the *Expéditions Polaires Françaises* in Paris. His plan would be to muster out of the Navy and go to Paris as a civilian to complete his report and conduct further research. The French approved LeSchack's assignment to their expedition and the U.S. Navy, on 20 November 1962, cut his orders to go. The French language which he had begun learning with Simone and which he continued at the *Alliance Française* in 1961, and really immersed himself in with his tutor in Washington, was now becoming almost serviceable! And then one of those unexpected reverses occurred.

Just a few days after his Navy orders were cut, LeSchack received a phone call from the U.S. Antarctic Projects Officer. "Lieutenant LeSchack, the French have cancelled all cultural exchange programs with the U.S. for the moment. Whether this is due to some argument JFK and De Gaulle had, or their crisis in Algeria, or their Referendum crisis, or the increasing differences between the U.S. and French positions on the NATO Alliance, we just don't know. But all exchanges with the French are temporarily off! And that means your joining the French expedition is now off also. *However*, there is a U.S. Representative billet we have available for you to observe either the Argentine expedition, or with the South African expedition. Lieutenant LeSchack: we would very much like you to choose the Argentine expedition. For two reasons; your record shows that you studied two years of Spanish in high school, and we know you have recently been studying French — same linguistic roots, you know — and the other reason is that the Argentine expedition, unlike the South African expedition, is a *Naval expedition*....and you are a naval officer, right? *Say you'll choose the Argentine expedition!* We don't wish to send the only other available representative candidate we have to the Argentines — he is a retired Forest Service employee with no naval experience, and only speaks English. You will go with the Argentines, am I right, Lieutenant LeSchack?"

"*Sí,*" said LeSchack, wistfully thinking about the fun he might have had in Cape Town, the South African's port of embarkation.

And so, on 29 November 1962, the Navy cut LeSchack a new set of orders, this time to the 1962-63 Argentine Navy's Antarctic Expedition. On 2 December, Virginia's parents took LeSchack to the airport and he soon was enroute to Buenos Aires. He and Virginia made tentative arrangements for her to fly there to meet him after he returned from the expedition.

It was a long flight, stopping at Caracas and Asuncion for refueling and arriving at Buenos Aires' Ezieza Airport late that same evening. LeSchack was met by Lieutenant Bob Leopold, USN, the Assistant Naval Attaché at the U.S. Embassy, and by Teniente (lieutenant) Jorge Maggi of the Argentine Navy. Maggi was the operations officer for the icebreaker, "ARA GENERAL SAN MARTIN," the ship to which LeSchack was assigned. Maggi assisted LeSchack pass quickly through customs and then took him to the Hotel Shelton, an Argentine Navy-owned hotel, at which he would stay while in Buenos Aires. After registering, LeSchack, Bob, Jorge, and Jorge's lady friend, Señorita Carrillo, met in the Shelton bar for drinks. Bob was fluent in Spanish and spoke comfortably with Jorge and his lady. LeSchack's Spanish at this point was halting, but interestingly enough, he communicated well with Jorge's lady in French, for she had lived in Paris. This, and the fact that she was a sultry Latin beauty, entranced LeSchack. They talked in the bar until well past midnight. It was a long, but exciting day for him, as he began his new adventure—U.S. Official Representative with the Argentine Antarctic Expedition.

This adventure, however, would be less physical than the last several he had; this one would be more cerebral, more oriented toward politics, diplomacy and intelligence-gathering—"HUMINT," as it now is called— and would point LeSchack toward his eventual career in intelligence. This assignment would certainly be an excellent training ground for him. In 1962, when LeSchack arrived in Argentina, the fascist dictator, Juan Domingo Perón, had been ousted from power by the military only seven years earlier. He was one of the most remarkable Latin American figures of the 20th Century, who effected long-lasting changes in Argentina's politics. The change most obvious to LeSchack was political and economic instability after Perón's ouster. Just months before LeSchack arrived, the then incumbent President, Arturo Frondizi, and his government were overthrown by the Argentine military, and that caused vast political, social and economic confusion that was still ongoing at the time LeSchack arrived.

As LeSchack began to think about it, it seemed surprising that he was even in Argentina at all, for U.S.-Argentine relations had been strained nearly as badly during this period as U.S.-French relations had been

strained. The Kennedy administration had relied heavily upon
Frondizi's government to be one of the pillars of the "Alliance for
Progress," an economic initiative for Latin America the U.S. strongly
supported. It was therefore aggravating to the U.S. when Frondizi was
ousted. In the crisis days just prior to Frondizi's ouster, U.S.
Ambassador Robert McClintock, who LeSchack was soon to meet, was
active in exerting U.S. influence, unsuccessfully, against the military
coup. Perhaps, thought LeSchack, the Kennedy administration's
antipathy toward Argentina and its military were sufficiently assuaged
for LeSchack's official visit to go ahead as a result of Argentina's support
for Kennedy's stance towards Cuba during the missile crisis just two
months earlier, and the Argentine Navy's offer of some warships to
participate in the quarantine around Cuba.

Political uncertainty and instability reigned during LeSchack's entire
tour with the Argentines. Although reinstatement of constitutional
government was the most important event in 1963 with the inauguration
of the new president, Arturo Illia, the pre-election months during the
time LeSchack was there was a period of virtually unbroken crisis. For
example, there was a military insurrection just weeks after LeSchack
departed from his assignment there!

Knowing he would be required to prepare a thorough report of his tour
with the Argentines, LeSchack began a diary. It started with his arrival
and his early meetings with both the U.S. Naval Attaché and his
assistant, Bob Leopold, and continued with LeSchack's day-to-life
aboard ship with the Argentine expedition. His observations and
adventures during this austral summer cruise to the Antarctic are drawn
directly from his diary.

3 December 1962 Monday
I was awakened at 1015 by Bob Leopold who said he had set up a
meeting for me to meet Admiral Panzarini at the Argentine Navy's
"Instituto Antártico Argentino," (IAA) an organization with a large facility
in downtown Buenos Aires. A jeep from the *Instituto* picked us up. I
arrived there at 1100 with Bob. I had an opportunity to spend two hours
with Admiral Panzarini and to see the institute's facilities. I was highly
impressed by both. I inquired as to whether I could spend a few weeks

at the institute to write my report after I returned from their expedition's Antarctic cruise and re-supply mission, sometime in mid-January 1963. He said he would be delighted to have me there at that time, and the Admiral would make arrangements for me to do so.

The Admiral was fluent in English, and had taken a masters degree in oceanography at Texas A&M. He gave me an outline of the 1962-63 plan for Argentine operations in the Antarctic. It was an ambitious expedition. Next to the U.S. and the USSR, the Argentines usually mount the next most extensive annual expedition. It is largely driven by the Argentine Navy, the governmental organization most concerned with Argentina's large claim to territory in the Antarctic and its political interest there. Their task force, the *"Grupo Naval Antártico,"* was composed of three ships, the icebreaker, ARA GENERAL SAN MARTIN, the transport, ARA BAHIA AGUIRRE, and the tanker, ARA PUNTA MEDANOS (ARA stands for *Armada Republica Argentina*). The icebreaker was the flagship, and it carried two S-55 helicopters for ice reconnaissance and two Beaver aircraft for aerial mapping. The Task Force supported with personnel, supplies, construction, as well as other necessary logistic functions six Argentine bases; (1) the Navy's Deception and Orcadas Bases in the South Atlantic; (2) the Army's General Belgrano and Esperanza Bases; (3) the Joint base, Teniente Matienzo; and (4) the IAA Ellsworth Station. All but the Deception and Orcades bases are on the Antarctic continent. As well, the Task Force was charged with taking oceanographic and meteorological measurements and services all aids to navigation in the sector Argentina claimed (and the U.S. did not recognize), the Antarctic Peninsula .

I ate lunch alone at Officers Club in the *"Centro Naval,"* also in downtown Buenos Aires, and then spent the rest of the day wandering around downtown, getting familiar with the city.

4 December 1962 Tuesday

I was awakened this morning by Teniente Maggi who eventually made it clear that he wished to take me to his ship this morning (It is so difficult to speak Spanish over the phone). He picked me up and took me to his ship, the San Martin, along with some of my sea bags. He introduced me to the icebreaker's captain, *Capitán de Fragata* (Commander) Attilio

Barbadori.

Shortly thereafter, I returned to the hotel and met Bob Leopold for lunch. He introduced me to a "baby beef," a most delicious filet of pampas-fed beef. During lunch, he also began to introduce me to Argentine politics, U.S. Embassy politics, and his perception of the Argentine Navy—also politics. Bob is politically astute.

I joined Teniente Maggi, his señorita, his mother and another friend for drinks and dinner. Drinks were at 2100, and dinner at midnight—a typical social timetable in Buenos Aires. I had a most pleasant time and my hosts were most cordial.

5 December 1962 Wednesday
I was awakened by the phone at 1100, and with a splitting headache. The CO of the SAN MARTIN wanted a copy of the U.S. Navy's "Operation Plan" for this season's Antarctic operations. Fortunately, I had brought one copy with me. In fact, it was already aboard ship, packed in a sea bag I left there yesterday. I went to the ship and got it for him.

I then went to the U.S. Embassy where I met Bob, and the U.S. Naval Attaché, a captain. We talked at length then about U.S. positions with respect to Argentina, and what they, the attachés, themselves, wanted me to look for while on board Argentine ships. At one point during our meeting, the Attachés looked at me and pointedly asked, "were you, by any chance, ever picked up by that Fulton Skyhook?" I looked at them carefully and then said cautiously, "Whatever would make you ask that?" They explained that they had recently read in that secret publication, "ONI (Office of Naval Intelligence) Reviews" about a Lt (jg) who jumped onto a Soviet drifting station, and was then pulled off, "and you LeSchack, are a "jg" and have jump wings—we're just wondering."

I nodded in the affirmative.

While I was at the embassy, I cashed some travelers checks and went to their PX.

That night I had dinner with Bob and his wife, Peg at their home in the suburbs. During dinner there was a phone call from the Pentagon for Bob; "We hear there is a political insurrection under way in Buenos Aires and there are tanks in the streets." "I don't believe so," said Bob with a slight grin to me. "We just drove home from downtown, and everything was normal. But I'll call around and see if there is something I missed, and I'll call you back." "This is the kind of thing Assistant Attachés are called on to do," Bob observed to me. "I don't expect there is an insurrection here at the moment, but one can materialize in a twinkling. Excuse me while I make a few phone calls downtown to check this out. Oh, and by the way, do you think you would ever like an assignment as a naval attaché? He smirked wryly at me.

It was just a rumor. There was no insurrection. This time. I slept at Bob's and Peg's over night.

6 December 1962 Thursday
Bob took me to the Shelton Hotel where I packed up and checked out. I reported aboard the SAN MARTIN at 0930. We cast off at 1120, as a band on the pier was playing martial music. It looks like good weather.

Ate lunch in the wardroom (1230-1400); most leisurely. I was assigned my own stateroom (camorote) aboard, and took an after-lunch siesta until 1800.

There was a cocktail party in the wardroom for Teniente Maggi this evening (liquor is served aboard Argentine Navy vessels as opposed to the prohibition enforced on our ships). It was Maggi's engagement party to Señorita Carrillo (the sly dog had never even told me the lady with him was his fiancée; he made a splendid choice!).

Got a big bottle of water for various in-stateroom needs; we have strict water hours aboard, and the water is turned on only a few hours a day.

About midnight tonight, we will sail out the mouth of the Rio de la Plata, past Montivideo, and into the South Atlantic Ocean.

<u>7 December 1962 Friday –21st *anniversary of the bombing of Pearl Harbor*</u>
I awoke at 0930, and washed and shaved with cold, bottled water. Went topside and began talking with some of the civilian personnel who would be taken to Belgrano and winter-over there. I went into the chart room and began to copy navigation and weather data. We are now passing abeam of the beach resort city of Mar del Plata. Maggi told me I would be assigned a regular watch (or *guardia*) on the bridge to become familiar with ship-handling commands in Spanish. I welcomed the opportunity and started by standing the 1600-2000 watch with him.

Dinner at 2000 and a movie afterwards. It was "the Caine Mutiny" with Spanish sub-titles. This is the first time I've seen a movie in English with foreign-language subtitles. As I expected, there is something BIG lost in translation!

As I was preparing for bed I began thinking about today's ship' positions I saw on the chart up on the bridge, while on watch this evening. Early this morning, we were cruising just south of Montivideo and out the mouth of the Rio de la Plata. Twenty-three years ago *this week* the first major sea battle of WWII took place right there! Right where we had sailed this morning! The German pocket battleship, GRAF SPEE was cornered there by the British heavy cruiser, EXETER, the light cruiser, AJAX, and the New Zealand warship, ACHILLES. And it was a bruising battle. Graf Spee limped into the Port of Montivedeo to avoid further punishment.

I bet EXETER, AJAX and ACHILLES were right where we were earlier today, just laying in wait for a chance to finish her off as soon as she set to sea again. Of course, they never got that chance. Just north of where I was early this morning, the GRAF SPEE scuttled itself, when neutral Uruguay would not allow her stay in port more than 72 hours, insufficient time to effect repairs.

Just as I was about to go to bed I recognized, just 21 years ago today, *my Navy* took a rather bad drubbing also, on the other side of the world.

<u>8 December 1962 Saturday</u>
I awoke about 1030 this morning after a surprisingly restful night. So far

this cruise has turned out to be a vacation. We have had excellent weather, I have not had the slightest bit of *mal de mer* up till now, and wonder of all wonders, my eye has stopped twitching; this is the first time I haven't twitched since the onset of Project Coldfeet! I have developed a relaxed routine of walking about the deck from about 1030 till noon, talking with various officers and civilian technicians. My Spanish seems to be improving. My hosts, at least, seem to indicate this. In general, people must talk slowly and directly to me for me to understand them. In any event, a free passage of information is developing, although many gyrations, drawings and gesticulations are still necessary. We are now abeam of Golfo San Matías and cruising southwest along the coast.

After lunch, I copy the positions and weather and sea conditions from the ship's logs and make my own plot. Generally, I also manage a siesta after lunch, as I did today. I spent about an hour or so after siesta looking up words in my dictionary and translating an article on this year's Argentine Antarctic campaign that was left at my place at the dinner table in the wardroom.

During this time, there was an abandon-ship drill. Later on in the afternoon, the ship stopped to repair the hydraulic pump that operates the rudder. While this was going on, some sailors maneuvered a 20-ton boom over the side with a plankton net to catch fish for dinner. No fish were caught.

I am standing regular watches with Teniente Maggi now. We have the midnight to 0400 watch tonight.

9 December 1962 Sunday
Awoke at 0915. There was an inspection this morning. I was told to stand inspection with the Army personnel (*Ejercitos*) who were aboard. These people looked far superior to the Navy people, who really looked ragged. Shoes un-shined, tattered hats, loose threads and strings hanging (called Irish pennants in the USN) all over the place. However, this may, in the long run, be unimportant.

After inspection, I had just sufficient time to walk topside prior to lunch.

After lunch, and a siesta I went to the chart room to collect my daily notes. I stood the 1600-2000 watch with Teniente Maggi, during which time we had a long discussion on education, and the differences between the services in the U.S. and other countries. My Spanish is clearly improving. We are now passing abeam of Puerto Deseado.

Read a bit after dinner and hit the sack.

10 December 1962 Monday
When I began shaving with cold water again this morning, I had had it! I spoke with the boys in the oceanographic lab next door and convinced them to string a 110-volt cable from a transformer in to my cabin. I now have 110 volts for shaving with my electric shaver. The towel that I have been asking for, today finally arrived. It was so filthy, I can't believe it!

This has been another beautiful, calm day, although last night was quite rough. The weather all along has been generally clear and sunny, but today was perceptibly colder.

Up until today, the only land we could see from the deck was to starboard, and that was the east coast of Argentina. Today we saw a group of islands off the port side. As I was staring at these islands, my ever-present navigation chart under my arm, a group of my Argentine naval officer colleagues gathered around me. One officer pointed excitedly at the islands, *"Los islas allá son las Malvinas!* Those islands are the Malvinas!" The others nodded, forcefully, in agreement. A bit puzzled at their vehemence, I opened my chart, and having kept a daily plot of ship's position from my daily excursions to the chart room (I had just plotted our current position), knew exactly where we were. On my chart (which was dated October 1961) it said, "Falkland Islands-United Kingdom (claimed by Argentina)."

My Argentine colleagues, looking at the chart I had opened up, all pointed to the islands in question and made the point strongly to me that those islands were not, as noted, the Falklands, but the Malvinas, and with clear emotion, stated unanimously, **"and they belong to Argentina."**

Despite their vehemence, which surprised me, there was no rancor toward me, likely because, as a U.S. naval officer, not British, I was not involved, in any way, in that dispute.

Also this morning, I helped Teniente Tommy O'Connell, the oceanography officer, who speaks English more fluently than most officers I have met on board, to translate a letter from the U.S. National Science Foundation in Washington to the Argentine Navy to "please return some U.S. scientific equipment to them before they closed up the Ellsworth Station." During the IGY, Ellsworth was a U.S. station, but afterwards was turned over to the Argentines; so the requested equipment did, indeed, belong to NSF, and the NSF knew it was the Argentine plan to abandon Ellsworth because it was imminently about to calve off into the Weddell Sea. That letter (from a guy I know at NSF) was an object lesson to me: It was a letter in governmentese prose, that we know so well in Washington. Tommy was stumbling over English clichés and idiomatic phrases. I must remember to write (and speak) only literal and simple English when communicating with people whose maternal language is not English!

After lunch, a siesta, and then some reading about the legal aspects of the Antarctic Treaty.

Stood the midnight to 0400 watch with Teniente Maggi, thinking all the while about the scene this morning as we passed abeam of the Falklands. Back in the cabin, and before I went to bed, I found in the ship's library a book that discussed the history of those islands. This is what I found:

Three Hundred miles east of the Patagonian coast are two main islands, East Falkland and West Falkland, and 200 islets that surround them. The islands had been settled by the British continuously, peacefully and effectively since 1833, for 129 years at this point. Perhaps 2000 people, and 658,000 sheep, and several million penguins. The islands are cold and wet: on average, it rains 200 days a year. In 1690, an Englishman, John Strong, went ashore from the ship, *Welfare*, to inspect the penguins. He kept a record. He sailed through the strait between the East and West Island and named this body of water "Falkland Sound," after the third Viscount Falkland who was a commissioner of the Admiralty.

Then the French were there; Breton sailors from St. Malo who fished and hunted seals there in the early 18th Century. A map published in Paris in 1722 called the islands, "Isles Malouines," after the St Malo fishermen and sealers. In Spanish this becomes, *Islas Malvinas*, the name my Argentine colleagues insist upon using.

This historical and political saga of who did what there, and when, seemed to go on and on. From my reading so far, international law did not appear to be on the side of the Argentines. But I stopped there; that's all the history for tonight (really this morning, for it was 0400 when I got off watch). However, the political and nationalist vehemence my naval colleagues aboard the San Martin displayed today is a bit unsettling, worrisome even. Well, it's certainly nothing I could see the Argentines and the British ever wanting to go to war over. Time for bed. Better get plenty of rest. Tomorrow we'll be sailing the infamously rough Drake Passage!

11 December 1962 Tuesday
Today was pretty much a bust. I awoke about 1100, had a dreadful lunch, and because we were now in the Drake Passage, the ship was rolling badly. Too much for me. I put to the sack to keep things under control. Not appearing for dinner, *el mozo*, the steward, came down to my cabin with a steak sandwich and grapefruit juice, which really hit the spot.

Tommy came in later to see how I was feeling and he brought me some candies and a towel. I read in bed awhile; the Antarctic Treaty of 1959. I think this Treaty can be an international law model that will be valuable when we seriously begin to explore outer space.

12 December 1962 Wednesday
Today was a better day. I had no problems, and the ship settled down to its 5-10 degree roll. While I was on the bridge copying data, Tommy told me that any letters I wrote today and given to the BAHIA AGUIRRE would shortly be mailed at Ushuaia. Accordingly, I wrote to Virginia and Bob Leopold and gave the letters to Tommy, who would see that they got to the BAHIA AGUIRRE

After dinner, Tommy came to my cabin for a nip of Canadian Club. And then we were invited down the passageway for what Tommy called a *"pachanga,"* a special dinner party held by a group of the ensigns. The fact that we, more senior officers (but not by much) were invited was secret. We were special guests. Turkey, beer, and wine were served. This lasted well into the evening. After this, I had the midnight to 0400 watch.

This was an "ice watch." Because the San Martin was now well into the Scotia Sea, floating ice and bergs could be encountered at any time now. According to custom, the first watch that sights ice stands the wardroom to cocktails. Our watch didn't see any.

13 December 1962 Thursday
At exactly 0410, just ten minutes after Maggi and I left the bridge, Teniente Bellocq who had the 0400 to 0800 watch, saw the first ice. He suggested all sorts of skullduggery on our part….. such as keeping our eyes closed on watch!

We have now reached the South Orkney Islands where the Argentine base, "Orcadas," is located. I spent the morning preparing to go ashore here, loading my cameras, getting my cold weather clothing ready, etc.

We entered the harbor (Scotia Bay) at Orcadas at 1500. The BAHIA AGUIRRE was already there and anchored. There was much stooging around, captain's visits, inoperative launches and such, which kept us from going ashore until 1900. I received permission from the Exec (the executive officer or *el Segundo*) to go ashore on the first launch (a mike boat), and return on the second launch.

The people on shore were most helpful to me, particularly when I could speak some Spanish. A lot more helpful than we were at Byrd when visitors came!

The station was at first exquisitely beautiful and then, appalling and terrifying. This was my transition of reaction during the perhaps 90 minutes I was there. I am referring particularly to the setting. The camp was more or less like any other remote camp I have seen. Here, the setting is on a gray, gravel isthmus 300 yards wide, which has a beach on either side. The other two sides are bounded by jagged mountains from which glaciers literally pour off. These are about 400 yards apart.

When I first arrived, the sun shone for several minutes and the place was resplendent with a crude, elemental beauty. Then, as we walked to the other beach, past their cemetery festooned with crosses that added a macabre touch, the ice fog began pouring off the glaciers into the camp. The steady pounding of the breakers on the beaches, and the intoning, in both Spanish and English, of *el Viejo*, our guide, who had been an inhabitant of these regions for the past four years, began to put an unreal, unhealthy atmosphere on this entire scene.

I visited the main community building. It had separate messing facilities for officers and scientists, and for enlisted men. Power was provided by 17 KW diesel generator which powered and charged a room full of batteries. I saw the reasonably large radio shack. The only scientific programs I observed were a weather station and a geomagnetics building.

14 December 1962 Friday
The ship got underway with way on at 0230 this morning and began the trip to Ellsworth Station. I immediately fell back into the daily ship's routine, and indeed, my special routine. I did some reading, writing and translating.

The midnight to 0400 watch was crowded with people on the bridge, including two or three of the staff officers who joined us from the BAHIA AGUIRRE (to make the GENERAL SAN MARTIN the flagship). There were several stretches of heavy pack ice, which kept everyone highly alert. The radar picked up most of the surrounding ice and simplified what would have been a difficult job of steering in the dull haze of early morning.

15 December 1962 Saturday
I awoke late, had lunch, a siesta, and then had a watch on the bridge. Again, many people on the bridge. The staff, commander, exec, all there. Today was the first day that the ship launched the two helicopters for

observation of the pack. We remained stationary for approximately two hours while the choppers searched. After they returned we got way on again, with a significant alteration of course. Because of the damping effect of the pack, there is hardly any wave motion, and the trip now is smooth, except for the occasional collisions with pack ice.

As was mentioned several days ago, a bet was in progress—the first person on watch to spot the first ice would stand the wardroom to drinks. Well, it appears that a corollary bet was also in progress. El Segundo and Teniente Cassals bet that Tenniente Bellocq would, or would not be the first: El Segundo betting Bellocq would be first. Naturally, Cassals lost. As a result, Cassals threw a cocktail party for the wardroom; it was magnificent! Later on, Alférez (ensign) Revilla brought his guitar up to the wardroom and there was a gala songfest, with a large number of officers joining in. Maggi told me that these were typically songs of Salta, the northern province that butts up against Paraguay, Bolivia and Chile.

16 December 1962 Sunday
The usual routine in the morning, followed by lunch.

The ice occurs more frequently now, is getting thicker, and we have to make more stops for ice reconnaissance. Penguins are seen occasionally now, swimming in the water nearby the ship and lolling about on adjacent ice floes.

In the evening, the ship was stopped more or less permanently until morning when it would be light enough for the launching of the helicopters. Even though we are within a few days of Summer Solstice, we are still not far enough south to have 24-hour daylight (61°24′ S this evening).

Condition "B" was put into effect at 2310. This means that the ship is stopped, but may be put underway, with way on, in fifteen minutes. Only half the normal watchstanders are on duty.

That means I went to bed, rather than stand a watch today!

<u>17 December 1962 Monday</u>
We got underway early this morning. After lunch, I spent about an hour
with Señor Carlos Martin, who was running the cosmic ray program
aboard ship. Using my improving Spanish (and the French I had studied
so hard to learn for the French expedition, for Carlos was born in
France), and electronics diagrams and other scientific notation, we
communicated effectively.

Then I had the 1600-2000 watch, which was most interesting: Lots of ice
and many people on the bridge. I am beginning to understand the
engine orders and steering commands somewhat better now, and in
general, seem to be comprehending more of the language. However, as
my Spanish improves, more and more officers *are trying to speak English
to me*, and frequently ask me, in Spanish, "how do you say such and
such, in English?"

<u>18 December 1962 Tuesday</u>
Nothing of great interest today—the routine is deepening rapidly into a
rut. I am sleeping now much more than I need to, or should, and I miss
Virginia very much and I think of her constantly.

<u>19 December 1962 Wednesday</u>
I have been translating the Argentine Operations Plan; it has much
information of interest, and I can see that it will make up part of my
report.

I had a watch with Teniente Maggi this afternoon. It turned out to be his
last watch. This is because, as operations officer, he spends most of the
day on the bridge anyhow, and he has been relieved of a specific watch.
To celebrate...... guess what? He threw a cocktail party in the
wardroom!

<u>20 December 1962 Thursday</u>
Today, after very slow progress through the ice, we have approached,
more or less, the Antarctic Circle. It is difficult to say exactly, because
the cloud cover has been almost complete for many days now, and we
haven't been able to shoot the stars, sun or moon with such cloud cover.
Owing to the ice, our course has been anything but straight. Our

navigation is entirely "dead reckoning," meaning estimating the direction you are traveling, with magnetic and gyroscopic compasses, both of which are notoriously inaccurate in the polar regions, and estimating your speed in that direction. In any event, crossing the Antarctic Circle, no matter how imprecisely determined, calls for a ceremony, similar to the U.S. Navy's "crossing the line" ceremonies.

The ceremony began this evening, with several persons, mostly chiefs, I would guess, dressed up as various denizens of the deep. One or two were dressed up as girls. There was much drinking and merriment in general, and the telling of jokes, all of which were impossible for me to understand.

I went to the wardroom and listened to the Voice of America on the short-wave radio for about an hour until 0130.

21 December 1962 Friday
We remained in the pack most of the day today. Visibility was low. When there was an increase in visibility, helicopters were launched. Shortly after, one chopper developed engine trouble (clogged fuel line, I heard) and was forced down on the ice. The other chopper returned to the ship, picked up tools and a mechanic and returned to the downed helicopter, some seven miles away. Before the disabled helicopter, partially repaired, and able to fly (sort of) made it back safely, it went down on the ice again, this time 500 yards from the ship!

Today we completed the "crossing the line ceremony." There was no reason why it couldn't be a two-day ceremony, since my navigation notes from the chart room say that statistically we are neither on the Antarctic Circle, nor closer, nor farther away than we were yesterday. The difference today was that all ship's company was able to be present.

Everyone who has not previously crossed the line—and had proof of that crossing—gets called before the tribunal for "the ceremony." I was called before the tribunal of masked, painted pirates, simply by the name, *"Teniente Americano."* I sat down, and was sprinkled with "unholy water," and then told to sing a song. I chose to sing the first few bars of *"La Cucaracha,"* which drew much applause. Whether this light punishment was due to my status as a foreign observer, or the fact that I had crossed the line before (and presented my Deep Freeze II card), I can't be certain. In any event, even the "full treatment" was not bad compared to some of our line-crossing ceremonies. Under the worst conditions aboard the SAN MARTIN, a man got smeared with grease, glop and had an egg broken over his head. No beatings or brutality or crawling through a garbage chute.

23 December 1962 Saturday

I had a most interesting experience today. I spent several hours on the bridge while we were maneuvering through the ice. The Exec was talking through the tube to Bellocq who was in the crow's nest. Later Bellocq came down to the bridge and I asked him if there was sufficient room for two people in the crow's nest. He said there was. At this point, I decided to go up.

Well, let me tell you, that's a long climb without gloves, in your service dress khakis. I noticed this about half-way up. Around the ladder are numerous rings through which you climb to keep you from falling off in a high wind. And these rings were necessary. The wind is fierce once you are exposed, and no longer shielded by the ship. Once in the *"nido de cuervo,"* it was a fascinating and exciting view. I watched the hull of the icebreaker, far below, caroming off ice floes.

23 December 1962 Sunday

I had an amusing experience today. Señor José Basbous an assistant to Capitán Müeller from the IAA asked me for some information on this year's U.S. Antarctic Program that I gladly gave him. In return, he lent me a copy of the IAA program directive for this year's Argentine campaign. That was a rather straight-forward job of translation for me, but he began to translate it for me, out loud, page after page — more, it seemed, to show me that he could translate, than to be of help. I indicated to him several times that I understood most of the words, and that I would ask him specific questions later, after I had a chance to read it. To no avail, he plunged on and on, louder and louder.

I gave Tommy his Christmas present today — a bottle of scotch whiskey — hoping to cheer him up. He too, was missing his wife. He told me after dinner that he would go to his cabin to write a letter to his wife (who, judging from photographs is beautiful). Now, when a man writes a letter to his wife that can't be mailed for a month, he is filled with sadness. He liked the gift; it was in a stocking.

24 December 1962 Monday
I gave Teniente Maggi his gift today, and this pleased him greatly. In the afternoon, I attended Mass that was held in the crew's mess hall. There was a chaplain aboard who officiated. Christmas dinner was served in the wardroom beginning 2230. It was a formal affair, all officers in their blues. Chicken was served. The senior staff officers ate in the wardroom with us. After dinner, champagne was poured. At midnight, Buenos Aires time, the CO stood, as did everyone else, and toasted the Nativity. After that, much champagne flowed.

Many individual toasts were proposed, ranging from humorous to sentimental. As the officers at my table became sufficiently oiled, they began to try English phrases on me. This was most interesting, demonstrating to me the fact that most people are afraid to speak a foreign language for fear of making mistakes; when they have imbibed sufficient alcohol, they no longer give a shit, and go ahead and speak! But it also showed me that these people were friendly, genuinely so, when the strict Argentine naval formality was dropped.

Santa Claus came in with gifts for everyone. I received a framed photograph of our ship, and other souvenirs from Teniente Maggi.

25 December 1962 Tuesday
I awoke this morning just a little bit queasy. But it was a grand party! My lunch too, was a trifle shaky, but it got down satisfactorily.

There was much activity today because the ice was thick, there were many icebergs, and it was difficult to navigate. The helicopters were launched for reconnaissance. In the evening, the ship stopped so crew members could try detonating several 25 kgm charges in the ice to determine whether such blasts could loosen the ice so we could move forward. I watched, knowing it would be fruitless. I had detonated larger charges in the ice for refraction shooting on the Byrd traverse and knew that ice was simply too elastic—it would just absorb the energy without much happening. But as a U.S. Representative cum diplomat, I was loathe to say anything. But I did enjoy watching! It was a tremendous spectacle—full of sound and fury, signifying....*nada*! The last test (and these were only tests) was a genuine failure....it was a dud.

And then we continued plowing through the ice. Today was truly magnificent weather to view God's world. The water was mirror-calm and the giant tabular bergs made an awesome spectacle. There were several flocks of birds (skua gulls?) seeming to skim over the water in front of the bow.

26 December 1962 Wednesday
We arrived at the Argentine Army Base, General Belgrano, this morning at 1025. It was a beautiful, sunny day. Unloading of the ship began immediately, and continued around the clock. Men have eight-hour shifts; eight hours on, eight hours off. Things appeared to be well organized. There was some trouble, however, with the cargo boom. There was much difficulty in lowering a Sno-Cat over the side and a large metal winch frame slipped from the sling and dropped onto the deck, a distance of about 15 feet. There were no injuries or apparent damage.

An apparent slowdown of the ship's crew caused several hours of idleness of the crews on the ice. However, the stewards kept a steady supply of sandwiches, beer, wine, brandy and coffee flowing to the working crews on the ice.

27 December 1962 Thursday
After lunch today, I hitched a ride with Teniente Tramontana to the Belgrano Base. It is now completely under the ice. The only things above the ice were a few weather shelters and five antenna masts. Four masts appeared to support a rhombic antenna. I descended into the under-ice complex (eight feet of ice overhead), into the buildings. It was a rather appalling sight that I viewed. This was truly cave dwelling! It was considerably worse than Byrd had been.

The living, recreation, cooking, eating facilities, and generators were all in one long Quonset-type hut, I would guess to be 150 feet long by 25 feet wide. Ice movements and pressures had twisted the floor so that nothing was level. The individual *camorotes* or apartments held either one or two men, and the walls were simply made of blankets suspended from the ceiling.

There were two 5kw generators in this building, however, only one was running. There were not many light bulbs and they flickered considerably when the radio transmitter was keyed. Capitán Müller, the IAA representative, showed me about. We went to the kitchen for coffee and sandwiches. The kitchen was tiny, but adequate I think. Then I began talking to Teniente Cao (Army) who had spent the winter here. I had met and talked with him yesterday on the ice by the ship. We spent about an hour and a half together and he explained his work and took me through the camp. He told me of their glaciological work. During the spring they made several trips to record celestial observations at cairns on the Filchner Ice Shelf area between Halley Bay and Ellsworth Station. These were for the determination of ice movement, which was more than half a mile per year!

On one side of the Quonset there was a tunnel in the ice, being dug solely for ice for the snowmelter—just as had been done at Byrd to procure drinking and bathing water, but here I saw urine stains on the floor of the tunnel...hmmmm. Carved into the tunnel wall was a shrine. On the other side of the Quonset, there were long, labyrinthine tunnels that were tediously narrow and low-ceilinged. On the sides of many of these tunnels were shelves for provisions. These tunnels led to many isolated vaults or rooms, shops, storage areas, heads, and emergency quarters. It was obvious that the buildings had been constructed first, in a helter-skelter fashion, and then when the ice and snow began to accumulate and cover them, the tunnels were constructed.

The CO and Exec of the SAN MARTIN and the senior staff of the *Grupo Naval* conducted an inspection of the base today. They were truly appalled at the conditions. Capitán Dietrich, the chief of staff, was particularly verbose. He summed it up as "horrible." However, from my experience at Byrd, T-3, ARLIS II, and most recently, NP-8, I can easily understand how people stationed at Belgrano could fall into such slovenly habits.

28 December 1962 Friday
This morning we cast off from the Barrier adjacent to Belgrano and enjoyed an easy five-hour cruise to Ellsworth Station, also at the edge of the Barrier. I spent the better part of the day in the oceanographic lab aboard ship discussing an echo-sounder problem with Señor Furuya (an Argentine of Japanese descent). It seems that the mounting for the depth-sounder's transducer had been inadvertently placed in the noisiest part of the ship. As a result, the signal-to-noise ratio is so low that it has been impossible to obtain echoes of any depth while the ship is underway.

This evening I met the Argentine Air Force crew that was stranded at Ellsworth earlier this month when their modified DC-3 caught fire on the runway and burned before takeoff. They had planned to fly across the South Pole. There were only minor physical injuries, but it was a major embarrassment to the Air Force to have to be rescued by the Argentine Navy. I was astonished by the Air Force navigator of that ill-fated aircraft. After an introduction and general conversation with Tommy and me at the wardroom table for some ten minutes—he spoke English fluently—he launched into a discussion of his sexual adventures in intimate and excruciating detail. Interesting, I thought. On U.S. ships, discussions of sex, politics, and religion are not permitted in the wardroom. Neither is drinking spirits, of course, which has been done in abundance in this wardroom during my tour aboard—but never, never to the point of intoxication, I noted. "What subject will he regale us with next?" I wondered. Politics, I suppose. Sure enough!

As if on cue, the Air Force navigator *did* launch into politics.... Argentine military style. And that was more interesting to me, since none of the navigator's sexual adventures differed significantly from my own. Just that I wouldn't discuss them in any wardroom, or anywhere else, for that matter.

He spoke of the political confusion that intensified after President Frondizi's fall owing to bitter rivalries amongst the armed forces. He spoke of the clash, just three months ago, between the military "Blue

Group" which controlled the armored cavalry and a garrison outside of Buenos Aires—and had the backing of the Air Force—that *supported some accommodation with the Peronistas,* and the military "Gorilla" group that wanted *no Peronistas in government.* The Blue Group revolted against the dominant Gorilla faction and there were several *armed* clashes. The navigator sadly told us that his aircraft was ordered to load up with bombs and takeoff and bombard the rival faction's base. He said that the pilot and crew of his plane did, in fact, takeoff, as ordered, but refused to carryout the ordered mission against "their own countrymen." Instead, they flew out to sea and dropped their bombs over the ocean, believing that by the time they returned, cooler heads would have prevailed, and the revolt would be over.

Just as the loquacious navigator did not elaborate on the bra size or color of panties of his conquests, he did not elaborate on which military faction ordered his potentially devastating and murderous mission. In both cases however, he provided enough information so that I could guess. And there appeared to be no adverse repercussions to either his sexual adventures nor the decision made by him and the crew aboard his bomber to disobey their ill-conceived, and likely unlawful orders. There was no discussion of religion.

29 December 1962 Saturday

I got a new roommate today. Jim Barnes, the meteorologist-in-charge of the U.S. Weather Bureau's group assigned to Ellsworth Station. He, like all the rest of Ellsworth's crew would be returning to Argentina. He moved in early this morning, just after midnight. Delighted to be conversing with a fluent English-speaker, we began talking at great length about his year at the Station, and continued so for much of the night. He told me of the Argentine Air Force's ill-fated attempt to fly across the Pole. This is Jim's tale:

The Air Force had attempted to not only emulate, but to out-do the Argentine Navy's successful flight, a year ago, from Argentina to the South Pole and return. To out-do the Navy, the Air Force plan was not only to fly to the Pole, but continue on to McMurdo Sound, and then to New Zealand, before returning to Argentina.

They started out by taking a DC-3 and replacing the engines with larger DC-4 engines. They installed six additional fuel tanks in the fuselage capable of holding 1,000 gallons of AVGAS. Additional polar navigation gear had been installed as well as adapters for four JATO bottles. The aircraft had a ski-wheel landing gear.

This operation was ill-fated from the outset, according to Jim. After the plane landed at Teniente Matienzo Base on the Antarctic Peninsula, the crew discovered that they were unable to takeoff for Ellsworth without JATO bottles, none of which were available at Matienzo. The Navy's flight the previous year had not needed any here. After several unsuccessful attempts to takeoff, they requested that JATO bottles be flown to them by the Argentine Air Force. An Argentine plane picked up the requested bottles in the U.S. to fly to the crew at Matienzo Base. This plane, however, returning with the JATOs, crashed in Panamá, killing the entire crew of nine men.

The DC-3 at Matienzo made several more attempts to takeoff without JATOs, and finally on 1 December after nearly a month at this base, it succeeded. The plane landed safely at Ellsworth and preparations were begun for the trip to the Pole. Although Ellsworth had JATO bottles, there were no igniters available. Accordingly, they made their own. They were fabricated by an Army captain at Belgrano, using ground up match heads and black powder. An electric current through a resistance wire set the concoction off. Several tests were made. The first worked, but others didn't. Sometimes the bottles burned from both ends during the tests, instead of sending the rocket's thrust solely out the back as was designed. Well, with four of these lethal weapons attached to the DC-3, they prepared to takeoff on 10 December. The fuselage tanks were filled with all the AVGAS available at Ellsworth, 667 gallons. This brought the plane to 35,200 pounds gross weight. The plane carried a crew of nine (mostly senior Air Force officers) plus baggage. And they were ready to go!

According to Jim, this was the best photographed aerial catastrophe since the Hindenburg. Everybody from Ellsworth was out on the runway, with cameras, to wish *"buen viaje"* to the Air Force. According to eyewitness reports, the plane, after warming up, began its takeoff run on the shelf ice near the Station. Just after they began moving, the pilot fired two JATOs. Within a few seconds, the whole fuselage area, both in front and behind the JATO bottles was enveloped in flame. Seconds later, the entire fuselage was a mass of flames. The plane had been traveling so slowly at this point that the pilot shut down the engines and quickly stopped the plane. It had not traveled more than 700 yards. The entire crew jumped out of the plane through the emergency hatch in the cockpit, and only minor injuries were sustained, except of course, for their pride.

The plane was a complete loss, with the possible exception of the engines, which were later pried loose after the mess cooled down. Jim showed me photographs he had taken. About all that was left to identify that the photographed object had once been an aircraft were the fire-seared wings, with "Fuerza Aerea Argentina" burned off. What remained to be photographically recorded for history was the name of the previous aircraft owner; *Allegheny Airlines* could be seen clearly through the twisted, smoke-blackened debris.

Jim told me that eyewitnesses believe that a leak in the fuselage tank system was the underlying cause of the fire. It was suggested, although no one could say for sure, that one of the JATOs fired from both ends.

I felt that this accident was similar to the one that took five lives in a P2V at Wilkes Station last year. Both accidents were caused by fuel leakage ignited by JATO. The only significant difference was that the P2 at Wilkes was already airborne when the fire started. The fact that the Argentine aircraft had little speed, and was still on the ice at the time the fire started, unquestionably saved the lives of the crew.

This afternoon at 1530, I hitched a ride with a helicopter that was making shuttle flights back to Ellsworth Base. This was my first flight on a helicopter and it was interesting. The Base was completely buried under ice 15 to 20 feet thick. I went through the various buildings, storage areas and passageways. The construction was much like that at Byrd, the same orange 4 X 8 panels fastened by braces. The passageways were made with chicken-wire, barrels and wood. Everywhere there was evidence of the immense strain that had been caused by the weight of the ice above. Practically all of the wood uprights had been bent until they cracked, and the walls, floors and ceilings undulated. "I" beams were bent. And now that it was summer, everything leaked. There were splash pans everywhere and constant dripping. Many "Rube Goldberg" schemes for collecting water and draining it off were in evidence. The entire passageway system was festooned with stalactites and stalagmites of ice. It was slippery everywhere.

The ship's crew, upon going ashore, ransacked the place. Mostly hand tools and similar equipment. Most of the important scientific equipment was properly returned to the ship. More than NSF had, in fact asked for. The Ellsworth station chief was so incensed with the ship's crew's behavior that, after complaining to the CO of the SAN MARTIN, all this equipment was returned, and in addition, a work party from the ship was sent to help clean up the station. With the exception of that work party, the ship's company helped not at all with the last-minute work of the camp, although they did much stevedoring on the first few days. Needless to say, this irritated the already overworked camp crew.

While at the station, I went through the library and picked up some books for the SAN MARTIN, Bowditch's Navigation, an English-Spanish dictionary of naval terms, a technical dictionary, and some paperback novels in English, such as "Madame Bovary," and the autobiography of Ben Franklin.

In the process of driving a Caterpillar 955 Traxcavator to the ship for on-loading, it slid into a crevasse. It looked most forlorn, tilted at a 45-degree angle into the ice, with one track completely buried. I couldn't help but smile at the plight of this large piece of earth-moving machinery, a remnant of the U.S. Navy Seabees who in earlier years inhabited this station; painted on the rear of the Traxcavator was "FUBAR CONSTRUCTION COMPANY." I expect I was the only one there who recognized the humor of the fate of this equipment and its "company"name: FUBAR in U. S. Navy talk stands for, "fucked up beyond all recognition," the logical extension of "SNAFU".

30 December 1962 Sunday
At 0800 I took a chopper to the Ellsworth Station to be there in time for

the official closing ceremonies. These were held at 1000 by the flagpole. All the brass was there, the station contingent, and an honor guard of sailors with rifles. The bugle was blown, and the Argentine flag was lowered for the last time. Then there was a final captain's inspection throughout the entire station. Each building was inspected by the senior officers with the staff following after them. After the inspection, the buildings were all closed and a signed message, identifying the station, was taped over each door. Teniente Bellocq and I were the last ones out of the recreation hall. We played the last game of pool at Ellsworth. Despite the ceremony and the "sealing off" of each building, no one had much doubt that this station would never again be visited before the inexorably moving ice shelf, with the station upon it, would break off and sink into the Weddell Sea.

Furuya, the oceanographer, built a device to suspend the sonar transducer over the side of the ship and away from ship's machinery noise, and has since been able to record good data for mapping the bottom of the seafloor. The traverse party from Esperanza Base has not yet returned to Ellsworth, but should return shortly. On arriving, they will survey all caches and the camp itself, for future reference—in the unlikely event that the base inexplicably remains.

<u>31 December 1962 Monday</u>

We cast off all lines from the barrier at Ellsworth at 1030 and returned to the Belgrano Base, arriving at 1411. We tied up and nothing much in the line of off-loading was conducted. There was an accident with one of the helicopters this afternoon that had the potential for being a dreadful disaster. The helicopter was taking off when the Exec gave the boom operator an order to swing the boom around, unbeknownst to Teniente O'Connell, who was cargo officer, and therefore, in charge of boom operations. He had turned away to watch the chopper take off, not expecting the boom to be moved without his order. Meanwhile, the boom and chopper blades were headed for a collision, because Tommy O'Connel had not expected a senior officer to take charge of boom operations without properly relieving him. The chopper blade sliced one winch cable in two, just as the helicopter took off. While the cable snapped, the chopper, now airborne, but vibrating badly, put down safely on the solid ice several hundred yards from the ship. Several centimeters of propeller blade were hacked out of one of the rotors. This entire incident was a multiple bungle. Just as there can only be one conductor for a symphony orchestra, there can only be one officer directing cargo operations aboard ship. Fortunately, no one was hurt. And had this been the open sea and no ice on which to put down, we would have lost a helicopter, and possibly the crew.

There was a formal dinner tonight—blue uniforms—that began at 2230.

1 January 1963 Tuesday
At midnight the ship's whistle blew and there was much toasting and champagne. There were parties throughout the ship. I couldn't help thinking that for four out of the last six years, I celebrated New Years in the world's polar regions, and without a woman with whom I could sip champagne. Four of the ship's officers' promotions became effective today—more parties.

At 0200 I hit the sack and slept till noon. I had lunch, and then read Ben Franklin's autobiography until dinner. This afternoon, the ship's crews began to unload additional gear and AVGAS for Belgrano and completed this process.

2 January 1963 Wednesday
The SAN MARTIN chopped a better anchorage for itself today because there had been a tendency for the ship to swing loose in it's old position against the barrier.

I spent most of the afternoon writing notes and later on, went to Belgrano Base expressly for the purpose of taking flash photos inside the camp buildings; I arrived there without my flash bulbs. Fortunately, Capitán Peyrègne, the station's CO, had an electronic flash that he lent me. I hope the photos come out since I want to illustrate the poor shape of this camp owing to ice stresses. The common room was about 16 feet square, and the whole living space, including the common room and the crew's spaces was about 90 feet long and 7 feet high.

The Beaver aircraft flew to Ellsworth today to pick up the returning

Argentine Army traverse crew. Aerial photographs were taken of the base.

3 January 1963 Thursday

The SAN MARTIN cast off the barrier at Belgrano at 1140 and has had clear sailing parallel to the Barrier's edge in the Weddell Sea. I have settled back into the shipboard routine, and I finished reading two books already, "The autobiography of Ben Franklin," and "Nautilus 90° North." I have continued writing and expanding my account of the Air Force accident at Ellsworth for my official report, and have now started getting my thoughts in order for the writing of that report. I am now also beginning to determine the optimum schedule for conducting my work during the next month, and when I should try to return to Buenos Aires. The SAN MARTIN will soon reach Deception Island in the South Shetland Islands, just north of the Antarctic Peninsula, where it will rendezvous with the BAHIA AGUIRRE. Sometime between the 17th and 20th of January.

I had been invited to go to Teniente Matienzo Base near the northern tip of the Antarctic Peninsula. However, I am afraid that a round-trip to Matienzo at best would take two weeks more, plus an additional week to return to Buenos Aires. Considering the uncertainties of this part of the voyage—last year the ship was stuck in the ice near there for 20 days—I think it best to return to Buenos Aires to begin work at the Institute. This should give me enough time to finish my report and still meet the 15 March date specified in my orders to be back in Washington.

4 January 1963 Friday

I awoke around noontime. I spent the afternoon reading and writing. Very relaxing. One of the returning Ellsworth people threw a party this evening. It was his birthday.

5 January 1963 Saturday

I awoke about noon. I finished the report on the aircraft fire, did much copying from the ship's log because I decided to include in my log the ship's course and the type of clouds observed. I had not done this before. I had a chance to speak at some length with Dr. Lisignoli about his glaciological program. He conducted two glaciological traverses from Ellsworth during this past year; one short one, during last summer—March 1962—during which three glaciological pits were dug, and the second one this summer, during which five pits were dug. He followed the same program procedure we had used during the Byrd traverses in 1957-1959. He lost his ice augur early in the season, however, so that he did little ice coring. Each pit was four meters deep. I should like to see his work since his traverses covered an interesting area.

I read some more from "Madame Bovary," and continued plotting my own ship's course chart for inclusion in my official report.

6 January 1963 Sunday
I got up early this morning to watch a weather balloon launch. The balloon was a 600-gram U.S. Weather Bureau balloon filled with hydrogen from a cylinder. The radiosonde was a German-made instrument that transmits the observed weather-condition data back to the ship in Morse code as the balloon is ascending. A radio operator aboard ship copies this data. The launch was made from the helicopter deck. The balloon reached a height of 28 km before bursting.

I copied much logbook data this morning and spent time preparing a chart of our ship's course. I spent the afternoon reading. This evening I made radio contact through the official Navy phone patch with Bob Leopold in Buenos Aires. He agreed to send a message to Virginia and tell her to prepare to come to B.A. between 17 and 25 January. Bob could hear me, but it was difficult to hear him owing to interference from another shipboard transmitter being keyed at the same time.

7 January 1963 Monday
I did more ship's logbook copying. After lunch Jim Barnes, the meteorologist-in-charge of the USWB at Ellsworth, came to my cabin and we spent the afternoon discussing Ellsworth problems. I now have sufficient notes to begin work on the Ellsworth section of my report.

The late afternoon was spent in the navigation office copying data from earlier in the cruise. In the evening, I photographically copied some of Jim's photos of the Argentine Air Force disaster for my report.

<u>8 January 1963 Tuesday</u>
I finished reading "Madame Bovary" today and was much saddened by
the story. I find I have considerable empathy for women who desire to
have as broad a spectrum of loving experiences as men often have, but
are constrained from doing so, one way or another, by the mores of the
times.

After dinner, I spent time on the bridge. There was a fog over the ocean.
The sea was exceptionally calm and ghostly-looking, with billions of
bergy-bits scattered all over. It reminded me of the lines from
Coleridge's "The Ancient Mariner:" "The ice was here, the ice was there,
the ice was all around…."

Later in the evening, I spent some time in the weather shack with
Teniente Barrios, the meteorologist. He gave me the opportunity to
examine their radiosondes. It is a German-made "Grau H-50" and
weighs 500 grams. Teniente Barrios made three balloon releases from
the BAHIA AGUIRRE and six releases to date from the SAN MARTIN.

<u>9 January 1963 Wednesday</u>
The ship, now in open water, was rolling pretty heavily today, so I spent
a good deal of time in the sack, reading.

After dinner, an incident occurred that was most interesting. I was lying
in the sack in my skivvies and was reading. All the other lights in the
cabin were out except for a reading lamp. Around 2230 I was aware that
my cabin door was opening very slowly and stealthily. I looked intently
at the door, although it was difficult to see with the reading lamp shining
in my eyes. Suddenly, a sprinkle of water splashes my face, the cabin
door slams shut, and there is hilarious laughter outside, followed by the
clomping of bath shoes down the passageway.

Dressed only in my skivvies and shoes, I wandered down the
passageway, finally stopping at the cabin of Teniente Sosa and Teniente
Gemignani, inside of which I heard giggling. I opened the door and
there were about six young officers there having a party. Speaking in
Spanish, I said I was looking for a man wearing bath shoes. Teniente

Gemignani, looking very silly, asked me in his halting English:
"¿Did....he....have....water gun?"

Laughing uproariously, they all invited me to stay and have a piece of delicious rum cake.

10 January 1963 Thursday
Teniente O'Connell has begun making copies of the ice charts for me. When this is complete, I will have most of the technical data I will need for my report.

11 January 1963 Friday
Nothing much today. After lunch I took a complete tour of the engine-room spaces with Teniente Doldan. He showed me all the specialized machinery.

The ship has been rolling too much in the past few days to do much writing at my desk. Therefore, I have been doing a lot of reading.

12 January 1963 Saturday
Today, being the last complete day I would spend aboard SAN MARTIN, I threw a champagne and hors d'oeuvres cocktail party in the wardroom. It was a rather bad night for it because the ship was rolling heavily, and all those dainty little canapés began to look revolting after several large swells. Particularly the stuffed olives. On ships that roll a lot—destroyers and icebreakers, for example—dining tables have side strips that can be raised up around table edges so that dishes and tableware do not slide off the table and onto the deck as the ship rolls. Well, olives, owing to their shape, will roll off a plate of hors d'oeuvres and roll back and forth across the table, in response to the rolling of the ship. It doesn't take long for the sea-sick prone, watching the olives keeping time with the swells, to wish they were in bed! Or hanging over the railing!

For most of the officers in attendance, the party went well, and at my table there was much singing. Dr. Barcia, Teniente Barrios, Capitán Cassals, Capitán Fleuriquin were all at my table. It was sad for me that the party fell on a night that Tommy, Teniente Maggi and Teniente

Alberico had the watch.

Anyhow, I believe the going-away party I threw was good diplomacy and much appreciated.

13 January 1963 Sunday
There was much hurrying and scurrying this morning—packing up all my gear to move to the BAHIA AGUIRRE, with which we will rendezvous. The BAHIA AGUIRRE will return directly to Ushuaia, Argentina, while the SAN MARTIN will attempt to circumnavigate Antarctica. I have no idea when the San Martin might return, so I cannot take a chance of remaining aboard. My packing was completed by 1100. After lunch, about 1300, the BAHIA AGUIRRE drew alongside. A plan was devised whereby we would begin, at 1750, to transfer the gear of those who would be boarding.

After the gear was placed on the helicopter deck of the SAN MARTIN, the boom and cargo nets were used for transferring our gear to the deck of the BAHIA AGUIRRE. That is, until the boom broke, halfway through the transference task. About half the gear had been transferred when an electrical malfunction halted operations. A half hour went by with crew on both decks tearing their hair in frustration. Estimates of ten minutes to four hours were made for fixing the boom. Since the ships were side-by-side, separated only by fenders, I casually and diplomatically (since I was merely an observer) suggested to Palacio, a *guardia marina* (a midshipman), in charge of the winch repair crew, that it might be worthwhile trying to hand-carry the gear to the rail, and then hand it across the railings of both ships. The separation was only about five feet. Palacio agreed. Since there were many sailors hanging around, the job was completed in ten minutes!

When I left, the goodbyes were most sincere, and I was touched. I received several letters and packages to take back to Buenos Aires to wives and sweethearts. The CO of the SAN MARTIN called me into his cabin and made a personal goodbye. Tommy was particularly sad. We had become good friends on this cruise. He invited me for a drink with a friend of his aboard the BAHIA AQUIRRE.

There seemed now to be some indications that the BAHIA AGUIRRE might return directly to Buenos Aires.

14 January 1963 Monday

It was hot in the cabin to which I was assigned in the BAHIA AGUIRRE, and it was most difficult to fall asleep last night. Major Peyrègne, the chief of Belgrano Base during the past year, is my cabin mate.

Today, aboard the BAHIA AGUIRRE, we did a lot of stooging around. The weather reports suggested a storm in the Drake Passage, so we now plan to remain at BAHIA LUNA, where we rendezvoused with the SAN MARTIN, for the remainder of the day.

In the afternoon, all three ships—the PUNTA MEDANOS had now joined us—were side-by-side. I crossed over to the SAN MARTIN to copy the ice code symbols used on their ice charts. I also retrieved my dictionary that I inadvertently left in my cabin aboard the SAN MARTIN.

Teniente Giró, leader of the Army's traverse, lent me his report on that expedition. I have been reading it, translating and taking notes all evening. After dinner, Teniente Giró and I talked at great length about traverse problems—his and ours.

15 January 1963 Tuesday

This afternoon we left Bahia Luna at 1320 and sailed to Potter Refugio, arriving at 1813, where we will spend the day. It is farther north, but still out of the storm area.

A mike boat was sent ashore with some men to install a new acetylene tank in the navigation marker light.

There was much scurrying about at 1535 when the Argentine ship SAPIOLA, an oceanographic vessel, passed us a mile to starboard. No one appeared to know whose ship it was until we got within range to make visual contact and to see her distinctly. At about the same time we saw the British ship, PROTECTOR.

I spent much time continuing to read Teniente Giró's report on his traverse.

<u>16 January 1963 Wednesday</u>
Another day in the same spot. We are still waiting for good weather for sailing north from the Antarctic Peninsula across the Drake Passage to Patagonia. Although I have plenty to do, taking notes and preparing my reports, the others aboard ship are clearly getting bored. The unhappy Air Force crew is downright disgusted. The rumors of what route the BAHIA AGUIRRE will take—straight to Ushuaia in Patagonia, or non-stop to Buenos Aires, are running rampant.

I made it my business to get in touch with Teniente Gonzalez, the BAHIA AGUIRRE's navigation officer, to see and copy notes from his navigation log. The BAHIA AGUIRRE is a larger and more formal ship than was the SAN MARTIN—more Navy—it is more difficult to wander about the ship at will, as I did on board the icebreaker.

<u>17 January 1963 Thursday</u>
Another day at Caleta Potter and no real hope for a fast departure.

I spent several hours with Teniente Gonzalez, the navigation officer, and several hours in the chart room copying ship's course data. Teniente Gonzalez told me a little bit about the politics of "Antarctica Argentina," saying that the Argentine Navy is the primary driving force for claiming sovereignty here. He said the most important task the Navy has is that of maintaining the buoys and navigation aids—a step that international law recognizes as supporting any sovereignty claim.

<u>18 January 1963 Friday</u>
Another day at Caleta Potter (Potter Cove). Since today is Phil Gale's birthday (he is one of Jim Barnes' USWB associates from Ellsworth) a grand *"pachanga"* or party was held aft in the Chiefs' Mess. The senior chief (a man called Lucia) was master of ceremonies. He presided with a huge flat-blade sword, which he brandished frequently—he used it to pat recalcitrant singers on the tail.

A large variety of hors d'oeuvres and wines were served at this party.

The big attraction was the singing. Several guitars were brought out for accompanying the singers. One young sailor, in particular, had a fine voice, and was the center of the singing. Several sailors danced, both singly and in pairs. One sailor danced the *"Malambo."* The others sang and clapped in time.

Several tangos were danced admirably by two plumpish sailors. They did very well! Two other sailors performed a typical country dance using handkerchiefs, the ends of which they held while dancing. One fat sailor was pulled out of the sack to perform the "twist," then a popular dance. This he did, quite admirably, in his pajamas.

19 January 1963 Saturday

We got underway this morning, with way on at 0145. The storm in the Drake Passage has abated somewhat and we decided to make the crossing now. It is quite rough, and this morning, the combination of last night's *pachanga* party and the ship's rolling were too much for me. I spent the day in the sack.

I prepared and sent two messages today. Based on the information that an Argentine Navy plane will pick us up in Ushuaia on 23 January, I told Virginia to come to Buenos Aires on the 24th. Also, I asked Bob Leopold at the Embassy to make reservations for me at the Shelton Hotel.

20 January 1963 Sunday

Today was a real bad day. Maximum roll of the ship was 32-33 degrees. Most of the day was spent in the sack, although an hour or so was spent in the navigation shack to copy data from the ship's log. At present, there is still much doubt about planes, baggage arrangements and such, for the return to Buenos Aires from Ushuaia.

21 January 1963 Monday

We arrived at Bahia Ushuaia at 1015 and anchored after several hours of navigating up the Beagle Channel, named after Charles Darwin's ship of exploration, HMS BEAGLE. There was much wind coming down the mountains and it would be too difficult to dock, hence we anchored in the bay. This wind, however, is apparently predictable; they said it would stop around noon, and the ship would dock at that time. Docking was actually completed at 1407 when the wind subsided.

Later in the afternoon, Chicero, Gale and I went into Ushuaia. I changed some travelers checks to pay the bill for the personal messages I dispatched from the ship. Later I walked through the town and into the military section of the town, off to one side of Ushuaia. The town of Ushuaia was dreadful, dusty, a typical old-west setting. However, the military or naval housing appeared excellent. Accommodations for the officers appeared most comfortable, and the chief's quarters were far superior to anything in town.

<u>22 January 1963 Tuesday</u>
The day was spent organizing, packing and waiting. I brought the sea bag with my Antarctic gear up to Teniente Gonzalez' cabin. The ship had cast off from the dock and anchored again out in the bay to allow another ship to use the docking facilities at Ushuaia's only pier.

Departure from the ship is scheduled by launch at 0300. Several of us have determined to stay awake until then.

<u>23 January 1963 Wednesday</u>
I decided to take a nap at 0015 but couldn't sleep. At 0300 there was too much wind to use the launch. So, I went to sleep and remained in the sack till morning.

At 1000, we all climbed over the side and down a rope ladder to board a large launch. We reached the shore, and boarded a bus for the Naval Air Station. We then waited with much trepidation to see if all our gear would be placed aboard the aircraft to take us to Buenos Aires. Fifteen kilograms was the maximum weight of gear that was allowed, so we were told; I had three times this amount! We had been counting on Capitán Müller of the *Instituto Antártico* to help explain our weight requirements to the naval aviation officials, should we encounter difficulties getting all our gear on board. I was appalled, however, to find that he left on another aircraft sometime earlier, without informing us.

I found, however, that I was able to manage this concern on my own, without official assistance; my Spanish had improved to the point that I could argue effectively—and, of course, I observed to officialdom that I was an *official guest of Argentina* with what I alluded to as "diplomatic status." And I, and all my gear, got aboard. We took off from Ushuaia at 1338, arrived for refueling at Rio Gallegos two hours later and then flew on to Buenos Aires, arriving at 2243.

****

Serving as a military officer, a young man can often be given, or have thrust upon him, far more responsibility than is likely, or even possible, in any other profession. LeSchack had often heard that said, and with some justification, he thought. At 27 years of age, not only had he set in motion a major intelligence operation—Project Coldfeet—but now, in quite different circumstances, he represented the United States of America in a significant diplomatic mission to another sovereign country, Argentina. This 1962-63 season by arrangement between the U.S. Antarctic Projects Officer and the U.S. Department of State the United States exchanged official representatives, under separate bi-lateral agreements between Argentina, Australia, Chile, South Africa and the United Kingdom. LeSchack had been chosen for Argentina, a country that not only mounted a major naval expedition, but continued to have contentious sovereignty issues with Chile and the U.K. in their area of operations. In the case of Argentina, more than diplomatic finesse was required of the Official Representative. Status as a naval officer was also required for easy access to personnel aboard ship and to the ship's bridge. LeSchack felt he had this, and represented his country well. Not only that, he was having a marvelous time while doing so! This seems clear from LeSchack's diary.

His diary not only gives you some idea of a young officer's life at sea, the hours upon hours of uneventful watches, punctuated by the occasional and unexpected tense situations that inevitably arise at sea, but also, the camaraderie amongst shipmates that occurs while on such a cruise. All of these sensations are heightened by sailing, unescorted by other ships, through Antarctic ice, on the only type of ship that can reasonably do so, an icebreaker. LeSchack's diary also provides a glimpse of the diplomatic requirements for representing his country under these seagoing circumstances—gently spying, but being acknowledged as a gentle spy—that is, being an official observer, not just another naval officer, from a country that categorically *does not* recognize any of the historical territorial claims of the host country. Yes, LeSchack enjoyed himself, but it was a bit like walking on eggshells, or better yet, on thin ice. But now that he had returned to Buenos Aires, a city he thought was deliciously sensual, he *really expected to enjoy himself*, and without the implied restraints of his Official Representative status.

LeSchack took up residence at the Navy's Shelton Hotel where he planned to stay for at least six weeks working on his report at the *Instituto Antártico Argentino*. His beautiful wife, Virginia would be joining him shortly, although it was not clear yet on which day she would arrive. He was enjoying being debriefed by the Assistant Naval Attaché, Bob Leopold, and by the new senior U.S. Naval Attaché, a Navy captain, and the U.S. Ambassador to Argentina, Robert McClintock. LeSchack felt good about himself. His capability in the Spanish language had improved to where it was now serviceable, both for general conversation and for working at the Instituto, which he now was doing. And his previous Antarctic experience during the IGY had given him, despite his junior rank, a knowledge of the icy continent that few others had, and many of his superiors as well as peers, admired.

Before leaving the San Martin, Teniente Maggi had given him a parcel to take to his fiancée in Buenos Aires. LeSchack was looking forward to that. He had been bewitched by her Latin beauty and overt sexiness when he met her before his cruise. LeSchack called her, once he settled in at the Shelton, indicating he had Maggi's parcel for her. She invited him to bring it over that evening. Señorita Carrillo lived in an apartment within walking distance of the Shelton, so LeSchack jumped at the opportunity that evening to do so, and began walking.

Away from the grand boulevards of downtown Buenos Aires, many of the streets, although picturesque, are poorly lit and narrow, and seemed to LeSchack to exude an enormous sexuality, as if tangos were being danced in every darkened apartment, and political insurrections were being planned in each basement. While these streets appeared physically safe, they exuded sex and mystery around each corner. Or perhaps LeSchack, in his current state of mind, was just perceiving sex and mystery where it was not. Nonetheless, this was the way he felt as he walked to Señorita Carrillo's apartment.

He was not disappointed when he arrived at her apartment. She was alone and dressed in a most sophisticated outfit. LeSchack presented Maggi's package to her and they began talking, as they had before the cruise, in a combination of Spanish and French. "Your Spanish, after seven weeks of total immersion aboard ship, is noticeably improved," Señorita Carrillo—Lola—observed with an appraising smile. But LeSchack continued to intersperse his Spanish sentences with French sentences. For one thing, during his passionate affair with Simone two years earlier, he learned words and concepts in the French language that were not particularly useful aboard ship, but were now appropriate in Lola's apartment. Also, and not surprisingly, he had no occasion to learn those same words and sentiments, in Spanish, aboard ship.

LeSchack and Lola talked of the cruise, and when the ship would likely return, of her fiancé, and most particularly, of Argentine politics. Both past—her brother had been incarcerated by Perón seven years earlier for political reasons, and present—she was interested in the problem of Argentine sovereignty in the Antarctic. LeSchack learned that Lola had studied international law in Paris—where she perfected her French—so Argentine sovereignty in the Antarctic, as a matter of international law, was a question of particular interest to her. In fact, she lent LeSchack a copy of a tract in Spanish for him to read concerning Argentina's specific interests in the Antarctic, with a view, LeSchack thought, that was considerably to the political right.

The two talked well into the night, and with increasing animation and obvious enjoyment. To LeSchack, Lola became ever more sultry and exciting with each passing hour of conversation, until finally his head began to swim with lust for her. Whether his mind had become beclouded with his own hormones or whether he sensed that she too, was becoming increasingly excited, he would never be sure. But he had the feeling that if he made a move toward Lola then, they would have been together in bed in a twinkling.

He chose not to find out. With his beautiful bride of less than a year shortly about to arrive, and with the friendship Maggi, the Operations Officer, had shown for LeSchack aboard ship, he divined that making such a move might be less than appropriate. Not to mention the diplomatic unpleasantness that might arise from taking advantage of his official status in Argentina. Alas, the young LeSchack—just aching for this intellectually exciting and sexy woman—was not about to proceed to that next, incredibly inviting, and seemingly inevitable step, as enjoyable as he expected that would be!

LeSchack settled down to a comfortable, social and academic routine. After morning coffee at the Shelton, he would walk in the summer sunshine to the *Instituto Antártico Argentino* where Admiral Panzarrini had provided LeSchack an office in which to work. At lunchtime, he would either meet Bob Leopold, or walk to the Officers Mess at the Centro Naval for a lunch alone. Within a week of his settling in, Virginia flew in to Buenos Aires to spend the remainder of his tour in Argentina together with him.

Bob and Peggy Leopold took LeSchack out to Ezieza Airport to meet Virginia's Pan Am flight, arriving as his had months earlier, late in the evening. Virginia, never a good flyer, was a bit woozy and stressed out from the lengthy trip from Washington. Fortunately, the Assistant Naval Attaché helped Virginia quickly through customs and then drove the four of them back to the Shelton. After a quiet drink at the Shelton Bar, the two couples parted and LeSchack took his bride to bed.

The next five weeks were most pleasant for LeSchack. Typically, he and Virginia had breakfast—Argentine breakfast is juice, coffee and a roll or croissant—and then he left for the *Instituto*. They would meet together for a leisurely lunch either at the *Centro Naval*, or at one of the many wonderful restaurants or cafés in downtown Buenos Aires. Occasionally they lunched with Bob Leopold. After lunch, LeSchack would return to the *Instituto* and continue writing his report, translating useful or supporting documents from the Spanish, and then wander back to the Shelton to meet Virginia and go out for dinner together.

Calle Florida was a street within walking distance of the Shelton that was a fun place in the evenings, full of fancy and exotic boutiques, with many side-street restaurants. One of their favorite places for dinner was *"el Palacio de las Pappas Fritas,"* literally the "Palace of the French-Fried Potatoes," a not particularly fancy restaurant, whose ambiance and excellent steaks intrigued LeSchack and Virginia. For steak lovers, which they then were, there was nothing, they believed, that could compare with Argentine Pampas-fed beef. A typical meal included the *"bife de lomo,"* a superb-tasting filet. The *pappas fritas* were what the French call, *"pommes soufflés,* basically a double-fried potato that looks like a swollen potato chip. They were served hot and not greasy. You would order a bottle of cheap red wine with this meal and cut the wine with soda water from real old-time seltzer bottles, New York-style. LeSchack and Virginia found it all quite wonderful.

Shortly after Virginia arrived in Buenos Aires, LeSchack suggested she might enjoy her stay more fully if she could speak a little Spanish—some useful words and phrases helpful in everyday life. Virginia, who had studied French in both high school and university, had the general linguistic basis for learning Spanish. She agreed learning Spanish could be useful, and even fun. And it would give her something to do while he was working at the *Instituto.* He helped her enroll at Berlitz, the language school, located close to the Plaza de Mayo, nearby their hotel. On those days when she attended Spanish lessons—she had a tutor in the mornings—they would meet after her lessons on one of the grand boulevards nearby the Plaza de Mayo, and off they would go together for a leisurely, and usually splendid lunch.

The month of February 1963 was totally delightful for LeSchack. His work at the *Instituto* was fascinating: writing, translating, meeting new and interesting Argentine naval officers and Antarctic scientists, and it was being conducted at a pace of his own choosing. No deadlines, save the mid-March one by which he needed to return to Washington to muster out of active duty. Despite, what for LeSchack was a leisurely pace, Admiral Panzarini often referred to LeSchack as *"El Trabajador Americano,"* the hardworking American. And with Virginia, LeSchack enjoyed a pleasant social life. He and Virginia had a number of social events with the Leopold's, whose company they enjoyed: lunches, dinners, weekend outings to Tigre, along the Rio de la Plata, and a boisterous dinner party at Spadavechio's, in the "La Boca" district, where there was dancing and singing in the aisles between the tables!

Teniente Giró, the Argentine Army officer who led several traverse parties on the Antarctic Peninsula and whom LeSchack had gotten to know aboard the San Martin, invited LeSchack and Virginia to a family *asado*—a barbeque—one weekend at his family's estate. And it *was* an estate! Located on the outskirts of Buenos Aires, Giró's family—his father was a retired Argentine Army general—owned a magnificent home with swimming pool, on a large piece of land. LeSchack and Virginia spent a Saturday there, talking, swimming and eating delicious barbequed things from the pampas. There were a number of beautiful teen-aged girls there, presumably from the Giró family or their friends or relatives, and they wanted to try out their high-school English on Virginia; they did so, quite successfully. These girls wanted to talk about Hollywood movies, and even wanted to know whether Virginia came from Hollywood! It was an enjoyable weekend.

Many people's constitutions rebel against foods that are foreign to them, and of course, the water. While these stomach upsets rarely affected LeSchack in his travels, they did seem to bother Virginia. This had happened to her on their honeymoon in Mexico also. But LeSchack dismissed that from his mind because he knew many people became ill in Mexico. In Buenos Aires, she complained of severe constipation. He paid immediate attention to her health concerns here because firstly, he knew the water and the food in Buenos Aires to be as healthy as it is in Washington, and secondly he had learned that as soon as Virginia became concerned with any bodily malady it, not surprisingly, immediately inhibited her desire to make love. After all those weeks at sea away from her, this was what he wanted most to do. "How can I help you, Babe? Where does it hurt?" LeSchack asked in a spirit of helpfulness.

"Len, my plumbing is clogged. How about "Roto-Rooter?"...... or at least an enema bag?" Even in adversity, Virginia never lost her acerbic humor, LeSchack noted to himself. "Well," he offered, "there's a pharmacy right on this block I noticed. Shall we try there first?" "Oh yes, Len, and the quicker, the better!"

LeSchack armed himself with his little Berlitz "Spanish for Travelers," and a pocket dictionary– he left the only other language book he had with him, "Naval Phraseology," English, French, Spanish, Italian, German, and Portuguese ship-handling terms and scenarios, back in the hotel room; he divined that tome as likely to be unhelpful. "Let's go Darling, we'll try out our medical Spanish."

Without further ado, LeSchack and Virginia went up the street to the *"farmacia."* In his Spanish-English dictionary, the word for "enema" in Spanish, appeared, helpfully enough, the same as in English—enema— pronounced "en-ay-mah." LeSchack, spotting the pharmacist, went up to him. *"Mi esposa necesita una enema. ¿Tiene Usted una enema?"* A simple declarative sentence, and simple question such as he learned to make aboard ship. The simpler his statements or questions, he found, the simpler the likely responses would be. "My wife needs an enema. Do you have one? The pharmacist's bewildered response of *"¿Que? ¿Como?* stymied LeSchack. He had exhausted his medical Spanish, and was unable to formulate further questions. At that point, Virginia, now noticeably doubled over with pain, took over.

She knew her limited Berlitz would be useless, so she began drawing pictures on a piece of paper and pointing, surreptitiously, to various orifices. Within seconds, it seemed that a vast audience within the farmacia and from off the street surrounded her as she drew and pointed. The pharmacist, clearly trying to be helpful, began procuring from his storeroom, various devices and contraptions of rubber, which appeared to be similar to the shapes that she had drawn. One after another, he brought them out of the storeroom, as Virginia shook her head. LeSchack had never seen so many rubber devices like this before. As the crowd around her grew larger, Virginia, in desperation, clearly stuck her index finger up her ass. There was a cheer from the crowd as the pharmacist now procured the correct implement from the back.

"Pay the man, Len! If I wait here much longer, I won't need it anymore!..... But they'll never let us back in *this* drugstore again! " Virginia gasped, amidst a mixture of laughter and tears. LeSchack, the neophyte linguist, paid the pharmacist, but he couldn't refrain from asking, *"¿Qual es el nombre de esto en Español?* What's this thing called?"

"Lavativa," said the pharmacist *"Lavativa?"* repeated LeSchack, slowly, "Well what is this?" he asked, pointing to the word "enema" in his Spanish dictionary. "Ah Señor, en-ay-mah is en-ay-mah....... but in *Madrid!* In Buenos Aires is *lavativa!* Es same ting!" As Virginia was dragging him out of the drugstore, LeSchack yelled over his shoulder, "If you knew what en-ay-mah was in Madrid, why couldn't you have known right away that's what we wanted right here in Buenos Aires?" LeSchack couldn't tell whether there was a response or not. Virginia had frantically yanked him out of the drugstore and was half-way back to the hotel already.

LeSchack had to acknowledge that the event was clearly funny, but there was something a bit disquieting about it for him also. He had been living with this beautiful woman for nearly a year now, and these kind of maladies seemed to have a habit of arising when he most wanted to make love. Before they were married, on their honeymoon, and now here, one malady or another always seemed to come up like this. But he also recognized that perhaps he might be causing her great strain—all those previous months of "Coldfeet" secrecy and clandestine military trips—so he dismissed the thought. He was having too much fun here in Buenos Aires, doing his work and being with this funny, intelligent and attractive woman. Was he imagining things?

LeSchack began wrapping up his activities in Buenos Aires during the first week of March, 1963. He had finished his reports to the Naval Attaché, Ambassador McClintock, and to the Antarctic Projects Officer in Washington. Admiral Panzarini and the Instituto staff threw him a going-away luncheon. He had confirmed their return flights via PanAm and noted there would be only a marginal amount of connecting time from New York's Idlewild Airport to the last flight of the day to Washington, D.C. And, on the last night of their stay at the Shelton, LeSchack received a phone call from Tommy, Teniente O'Connell. The SAN MARTIN had returned to Buenos Aires, unable to complete its circumnavigation of Antarctica owing to ice and bad weather conditions. When Tommy learned that this was to be LeSchack's last night in Buenos Aires, he arranged to meet him and Virginia at the Shelton.

Tommy brought his wife with him. She was even lovelier than in the picture Tommy had shown LeSchack aboard ship. And she brought a glorious bouquet of flowers for Virginia. The two couples remained in the Shelton bar talking all evening long. LeSchack was glad not to have been aboard the SAN MARTIN when she attempted the circumnavigation. Tommy said the roll of the keel-less icebreaker, was extraordinarily uncomfortable! LeSchack was glad that he and Tommy could meet one last time, and they could meet each other's wives about whom they had talked so glowingly on their voyage together.

The flight home was long, tedious and uneventful. And the aircraft was full. As appropriate for a naval officer with an official red passport, and traveling under official orders, LeSchack was wearing his service dress blue uniform. Virginia, as usual, was stylishly dressed and brandishing the bouquet of flowers which Tommy's wife had given her the previous night. "You know the Department of Agriculture man who will be awaiting us at Idlewild will fuss over your flowers, don't you?" LeSchack opined. "I'll take my chances with him," Virginia smiled sweetly. What LeSchack was more concerned about was making the tight connection at New York with the last plane out to Washington. He really did not wish to sleep over at the airport hotel at Idlewild, and with the plane he was now on, disgorging its hordes into an undermanned customs hall, LeSchack felt they had a good chance of missing that last flight. He explained his concerns to the chief stewardess who recommended they sit at the rear of the aircraft, since she expected economy-class travelers would debark from the rear exit.

She was wrong. Upon landing in New York, the purser announced that all passengers would debark through the forward exit only, now leaving LeSchack and Virginia likely to be the last to leave. This turn of events disheartened LeSchack, particularly since nobody was allowed to leave the aircraft, now parked at the gate, until the public health officer came aboard with a spray can to disinfect the plane of unwanted, foreign microbes!

LeSchack's spirits rose, however, when the public health officer entered the aircraft. The officers of the United States Public Health Service did, at that time, wear uniforms undistinguishable to the average citizen from U. S. Navy uniforms. As the public health man walked slowly down the cabin aisle, spraying his aerosol, this way and that, LeSchack formulated a plan. When the USPHS officer finally reached the rear of the cabin, and saw LeSchack in uniform, he nodded recognition. LeSchack beckoned him to lean over and talk briefly. "Can you help us get out of this aircraft first?" Brandishing his official red passport, he continued, "the last plane for Washington will leave in less than an hour, and I must report for duty first thing tomorrow. We can't miss that plane!"

LeSchack, of course, was stretching a point about an early morning meeting in Washington, but the USPHS officer, as a professional courtesy, felt like obliging him and Virginia. "Okay," he said with a silly smile, "you two guys follow directly behind me up the aisle." And having done all the spraying he was going to do in this aircraft, he said, "Are you guys ready? Let's go!" and two men, both in nearly the same uniform, and one beautiful young lady, smiling prettily behind them and clutching a bouquet of now wilting flowers, marched up the aisle past a plane load of tired, irate passengers, out the cabin door to the ramp, and directly to the customs counter!

At this late hour of the night, and with LeSchack's official red passport, customs went like a breeze, especially since he and Virginia were first in line. But the customs officer was concerned about Virginia's flowers. "I'll have to call over the Department of Agriculture guy," he announced, and then yelled across the customs hall, "Hey Johnny, c'mere! Da lady's got flowers!" A man from the USDA sauntered over, looked at LeSchack and Virginia, looked at the wilted bouquet, shook his head and waved the two weary travelers off. "Scram youse guys, and **welcome home!**"

LeSchack and Virginia just managed to board, with all their baggage, the last plane to Washington, D.C., thus ending not only their Argentine adventure, but LeSchack's life as a junior officer on active duty in the U.S. Navy. He couldn't possibly have known then that he would return to active Navy duty again and again, both as a mid-grade officer and then as a senior officer—and all "at the convenience of the service."

Epilogue

Although the abrupt cancellation of LeSchack's orders to join the French
Antarctic Expedition were puzzling to him at the time, and his lifetime
adventures were in no way upset by that development, he wondered for
years what was the root cause for the order cancellation. He felt he had
the support of Paul-Émile Victor, the director of the Expéditions Polaires
Françaises in Paris. Nonetheless, pure Cold War politics was likely the
root cause, and LeSchack's order cancellation was an unintended
consequence thereof. His first inkling of this came five years later from a
piece published on page A3 of the April 15, 1968 edition of the
Washington Post, entitled "Paris set for a spy scandal." Quoting the Paris
newspaper, Le Canard Enchâiné, it said that "the details of a three
cornered spy case including charges that a French official close to
President de Gaulle, is an agent for the Soviet Union, are about to be
known."

A few days later, the New York Times of 20 April 1968, in a piece with
the headline, "Ex-aide asserts de Gaulle suppressed data on spies,"
began:

"Philippe Thyraud de Vosjoli, a French intelligence officer in the United
States, who resigned from the French service in 1963, has criticized the
Government of President de Gaulle of allegedly hushing up evidence of
Soviet penetration of the French Cabinet and intelligence services."

As a liaison officer with the CIA, de Vosjoli played a key role in
obtaining in the summer of 1962 the first reports that the Soviets were
introducing offensive missiles into Cuba. The article went on to say,
"The available evidence indicates that Mr. de Vosjoli's assistance to the
United States was not appreciated by President de Gaulle. The French
leader is said to have been embarrassed by the role of the French
intelligence service in helping bring the United States and the Soviet
Union to the confrontation over Cuba."

A more detailed explanation emerged after the conclusion of the Cold
War in Tom Mangold's book, "Cold Warrior—James Jesus Angleton: the

CIA's master spy hunter." In the spring of 1962, CIA director John McCone, at Angleton's instigation, convinced President Kennedy to send a letter to President de Gaulle advising of a "KGB mole infestation" in the SDECE, the French intelligence service. This letter simply exacerbated the increasing policy differences, then extant, between America and France.

In October 1962, six months after Kennedy's letter was sent to de Gaulle, and a month before LeSchack's orders for the French expedition were cut, the Franco-American intelligence relationship grew ever more bitter. Then, the CIA's Angleton, Chief of Counter-Intelligence, Anatoliy Golitsyn, a KGB defector, and Philippe de Vosjoli, SDECE's liaison officer with the CIA and FBI from 1951 to 1963, were the unusual team that insinuated that French Intelligence had massive leaks to the Soviet Union. During that month, senior CIA officers told General Paul Jacquier, the director of the SDECE, bluntly that the French service "is infiltrated!" This could hardly have made relations between the U.S. and French intelligence services—and therefore French policy toward the U.S., with Charles de Gaulle at the helm, more strained.

While at that time, LeSchack, despite his Coldfeet spy mission, had not really thought of himself as an intelligence officer—just as an unrestricted line officer—others clearly thought differently of him. The U.S. Navy, for example, briefed him—as if he was an intelligence officer—on what to look for and what to photograph. And likely the French *assumed he was* an intelligence officer, and LeSchack's order cancellation to join the French Expedition was nothing more than the old tit-for-tat spy game that countries played with some regularity during the Cold War.

According to Mangold, James Jesus Angleton was likely clinically paranoid and Golitsyn was an outright fabricator of most moles, although he had identified a few notable ones. As for de Vosjoli—the model used in his 1967 novel, "Topaz," for Leon Uris's French intelligence officer in Cuba prior to Castro's revolution—he was simply too closely involved with the Americans to be trusted by the SDECE any longer. But all together this threesome significantly soured the intelligence relationship between France and the U.S. as LeSchack—

whom the French no doubt thought was yet another intelligence
officer—was preparing to join the French Expedition.

Whether or not that *was* the reason his orders were precipitously
cancelled, the outcome for LeSchack couldn't have been better. He
joined the Argentine Expedition, had a lot of fun, and learned Spanish.
And, despite the sudden change in expeditions, his study grant to work
at the *Expéditions Polaires Françaises* in Paris thereafter, his key reason for
wishing to join the French expedition in the first place, was not revoked.
And, with great exuberance, he would soon be on his way back to spend
April in Paris!

*Back in Buenos Aires after his tour as United States Official
Representative to the 1962—63 Argentine Antarctic Expedition,
Lieutenant (jg) Len LeSchack begins to unwind and enjoy the life of a
Porteño at Spadavechio in la Boca. From left to right, Lieutenant Bob
Leopold, USN, Assistant Naval Attaché, Embassy of the United States of
America, his wife, Peggy, Len, and Virginia. February, 1963.*

LeSchack's Personal Cold War in Paris, Madison and Montréal

> *Plaisir d'amour ne dure qu'un instant, Chagrin d'amour dure toute la vie.*

> —*First line of popular French song written by Jean-Pierre Claris de Florian, born a Pisces, on LeSchack's birthday, only 180 years earlier.*

> *Non! Rien de rien ...Non ! Je ne regrette rien*
> *Ni le bien qu'on m'a fait, Ni le mal tout ça m'est bien égal !*

> *Non ! Rien de rien ...Non ! Je ne regrette rien...*
> *C'est payé, balayé, oublié; Je me fous du passé!*

> *Avec mes souvenirs, J'ai allumé le feu*
> *Mes chagrins, mes plaisirs, Je n'ai plus besoin d'eux !*

> *Balayés les amours, Et tous leurs trémolos*
> *Balayés pour toujours ; Je repars à zéro ...*

> *Non ! Rien de rien ...Non ! Je ne regrette rien ...*
> *Ni le bien, qu'on m'a fait, Ni le mal, tout ça m'est bien égal !*

> *Non ! Rien de rien ...Non ! Je ne regrette rien ...*
> *Car ma vie, car mes joies, Aujourd'hui, ça commence avec to !*

> – *Another French song, but with a different approach to love, presented in its entirety, and written by Charles Dumont for the Parisian singer, Édith Piaf.*

Simone, LeSchack's erstwhile lover who spoke French fluently, had introduced him to these two quintessentially French songs. The first states, *"The pleasure of love lasts only a moment, the heartbreak of love lasts all your life."* The second, simply, *"No! I regret nothing!"* Simone had been LeSchack's second long-term lover. His first lover, Giselle, also French-speaking, was from Montréal, a very French city, where that romance had ended sadly, seven years earlier. For the enigmatic Simone, and

308

increasingly for LeSchack, it seemed that these two songs captured both the ying and the yang of love....and life, itself. He would sense this most strongly when he returned to Paris to live in 1963—after being stood up there by Simone, just two years earlier. Also, when he returned to live in Montréal, in 1965, the home of his first lover, Giselle. He thought of neither of these songs, however, when he lived in Madison, Wisconsin to attend graduate school; he neither had the time, nor the inclination to do so in that troublesome milieu.

Lieutenant (jg) Leonard LeSchack, USNR, had been released from active duty in mid-March 1963. These next several years were wonderful/horrible. They were full of learning experiences, some of which were good, others that he could just as soon have done without. The beat of LeSchack's "different drummer" was now confused sometimes by the obtrusive and overly raucous sounds of that conventional marching band that always seemed to follow him around. And the kind of intimacy with women that he had learned to expect and to enjoy with, for example, Giselle, Maisie, Simone and Maureen, his lover, just prior to meeting Virginia was, alas, no where to be found in that most beautiful woman of them all, his new wife, Virginia! Frankly, with respect to all aspects of his life now, LeSchack had no idea where these next several years were leading. During his tour with the Argentine Navy, his application for a study grant to the *Expéditions Polaires Françaises* in Paris had been approved by the Arctic Institute of North America. Never mind that the application had been predicated on his original plan to join the *French* Antarctic Expedition. The Arctic Institute had funded his study in Paris anyway, despite the last minute change to the Argentine expedition. LeSchack was not going to argue! Also, his application to the geophysics program at the University of Wisconsin Graduate School in Madison, had been approved. So he knew where he and Virginia would be for the next year or more.

He had applied to graduate school because that's what the conventional wisdom had said he must do to pursue his science. But truth be told, LeSchack hated school, and had done so since nursery school, and through university. He enjoyed learning, but he hated being preached at. "And that's what they do at schools," LeSchack thought. He disliked being forced to listen to largely uninspired instructors that always seemed to be the ones assigned to teach him. The different drummer had him march to enlightenment by learning in his own special way, while the conventional drumbeat led him to uninspired grades at undergraduate school.

LeSchack knew he had been accepted to Grad School by the intervention of Professor George Woolard, a world-class geophysicist, who knew LeSchack through the numerous ex-IGY Antarctic scientists at Wisconsin. LeSchack had been declined by the Grad School in the first instance, owing to his undistinguished undergraduate grades. Woolard, however, had written to the admissions board requesting that LeSchack's application be reconsidered. He noted that LeSchack had achieved good grades at the USDA Grad School, along with the powerful argument that, "if President John F. Kennedy saw fit to award LeSchack a high decoration for 'scientific achievement'—Project Coldfeet was, after all, an investigation of Soviet science—then the University could at least give LeSchack a chance for Graduate School." That was a successful and more palatable argument than had he simply bludgeoned the admissions board—largely Democrats—at an ultra-liberal school, with the fact that LeSchack was directly responsible for having awarded several well-funded military research contracts to Woolard's department from ONR—that was also true.

With the knowledge that they had at least a year of stability, LeSchack and Virginia packed up and flew to Paris. Within a week, they found a tiny apartment in the 8th *Arrondisement,* a few blocks from the Place de la Concorde. He began to work at *the Expéditions Polaires Françaises* (EPF), across the street from the *Bois de Boulogne* during the afternoons; and both he and Virginia enrolled at the *Alliance Française,* in the student quarter, in the mornings, so that they could improve their French. By the next week, they had purchased an appropriate form of transportation for these two now slightly aging students: an Italian "Vespa" motor scooter. And it was now springtime in Paris, and they were in love!

For the first time since they had married, LeSchack and Virginia had begun to have long stretches of time—uninterrupted by his secret and far away Navy assignments—in which to get to know one another well. There were wonderful sidewalk cafés and bistros in their neighborhood where they often stopped. It was walking distance from their apartment to the Place de la Concorde, the Tuilleries Garden, and the Champs Elysées, and they often walked there together, hand-in-hand.

Depending on the weather, they either took the Paris Metro to the Alliance Française, or they drove there together—and most defensively—through Paris traffic on their Vespa. LeSchack loved the Vespa; Virginia barely tolerated it, which for him, was a pity, because he so enjoyed it. Something about motor scooters being unladylike, she said. Well, that might have been true in Washington, D.C., but certainly not in Paris! Frequent sightings of luscious young *Parisiennes* scooting about on *Les Grandes Boulevardes*, skirts a-flying, either alone, or as giddy, sexy, smiling, rear-seat passengers, continually delighted the eye. To LeSchack, it seemed "most continental," to see young ladies on scooters. And intensely romantic!

Their ability in the French language picked up quickly. Especially so for LeSchack since he took more course work at the Alliance, and then used what he learned in the mornings at the EPF in the afternoons. Just as he had aboard Argentine ships, LeSchack found that learning a new language as an adult was like being reborn: with each new word and grammatical construct he learned—and used—he could almost sense his horizons expand on a moment-by-moment basis. But Virginia was no slouch with French: she soon became comfortable in shopping alone for both food and clothing, and of course, for books.

LeSchack was absolutely smitten by Virginia's beauty—as were many of his colleagues who had met her. And he admired her quick wit—often sardonic or acerbic—and her intelligence. But, bit by bit, as they had increasing amounts of time to spend together, he began to observe her lack of enthusiasm for emotional involvement with him. She seemed to *enjoy talking about it*, just not actually getting involved. In the previous year since their marriage, LeSchack had been gone so much, and when he was with her, had so much on his mind that he was forbidden to speak about, that he hardly had space in his brain or time to think about comparing Virginia's lack of enthusiasm for emotional involvement with the enthusiasms that other women he had known had displayed. But now unburdened by official duties that had often involved life or death matters, and with plenty of free time between his self-assigned tasks in

Paris, he *did* have the time to ponder about the entire spectrum of love-making. And here in Paris, the two songs that Simone had earlier introduced him to helped powerfully to define that spectrum. Of course, that led to making comparisons—and then he began to wonder.

From the time LeSchack first began to think about females in a sexual way—which was early in his life—he always thought making love had to be a mutual sharing of pleasure. He recognized a need for "desire" on the part of both parties. He also recognized that for him, he had to sense a "mutual chemistry" between himself and a potential lover. By the time he was at university, he observed that it would be fruitless for him *even to pursue* a woman with whom such "chemistry" was not immediately apparent. And thereafter, absent that chemistry, he never even tried.

Having that attitude, LeSchack could never understand how men could physically become hard enough to enter forcibly an unwilling woman. He knew he wouldn't be able to do so. To be actually "in love" was wonderful—as it had been with Giselle, his first lover, whose desire for LeSchack increased steadily (as did his for her) over their three years as lovers. They were both in love and *in lust*. But "love" wasn't necessary. Mutual desire—just lust—plainly visible to LeSchack—with or without love—was, however, as it had been between him and Maisie in New Zealand, Elsa in Chile, Simone in Boston, and Maureen in Washington, all bombastically passionate women. Since these voracious women represented the majority of the women LeSchack now knew intimately, he deduced—erroneously—that this was a true example of the wonderful way women would behave with him.

Furthermore, as LeSchack the scientist would say, mutual desire was a necessary condition, but not necessarily a *sufficient* condition for him to proceed. He did, after all have to become hard! However, desire alone often satisfied that condition. Also as a scientist, he had to consider one permutation to that condition of mutual desire: a prostitute has desire—a financial one, to earn her fee. And that seemed also to have worked for him.

So LeSchack, now with free time in Paris—the city of love—also had time to be troubled about Virginia. He knew Virginia loved him. He knew he loved Virginia. He knew that several of his previous lovers had told him that he *was a good lover*, and told him so gratuitously and without prompting, both verbally and by their actions. Therefore, he believed he was. So what was wrong? That question powerfully arose one sunny, balmy Saturday in Paris. After a wonderful, leisurely day of walking along the Seine, watching *péniches*—barges—plying lazily along the river, having a delightful lunch, *al fresco*, followed by shopping, café-sitting and drinking wine, he and Virginia decided to return to their apartment for a "nap." He felt as romantic as he can ever remember.

If ever the ambiance for romance was perfect, this was it! Paris in the springtime. A leisurely walk along the Seine. No pressing worries. Lovers everywhere strolling arm in arm, along both banks, exuding l'*amour*. And then LeSchack and Virginia enter their cozy apartment, disrobe and jump into bed. LeSchack's blood is pounding in his head, his hormones bubbling through his system. He just couldn't wait to fondle his beautiful wife and then merge their bodies and souls. But he was made to—till perhaps a week or two later! All Virginia wanted was, literally, a nap.

Virginia did not appear ill. She was on birth-control pills. To LeSchack there was no excuse not to continue to the expected conclusion, and Virginia offered none. She had in no way signaled a lack of desire up till this moment as far as he could discern. What more romantic day could she be waiting for? He was so furious that without thinking he angrily pushed her out of bed. He couldn't believe he had so misread her. Never before, nor since, has he ever been this upset with a lover. LeSchack will always remember that incident with sadness. Had this been a singular incident, he likely would have let it pass. But it was not. In the year that they had been married, too many such rejections had now accrued. This was simply the most egregious and disheartening. It marked the beginning of the gradual withering away of what LeSchack thought—and fervently had hoped—was a true and enduring love. But as he did with most unpalatable incidents and thoughts, he stowed this rejection deep, deep in the recesses of his brain so that it was out of sight—most of the time.

LeSchack's work, however, was going well at the EPF. In addition to the director, Paul-Émile Victor, who he already knew from his 1961 visit, he began getting to know a number of the administrative and scientific personnel at the EPF. He had easy access to all the information he needed and received genuine encouragement in speaking French from his colleagues, not the well-known haughty looks of disdain that are given by Parisians to most visitors attempting to speak French. The beautiful receptionist, Joëlle, even helped LeSchack with his homework from the *Alliance.*

It did not take LeSchack and Virginia much time to become acclimatized to life in Paris. They enjoyed their funky little apartment on Rue de Surène. The apartment was completely furnished and consisted of a bedroom, a small, separate living room, a bathroom with a small, but high-walled bathtub and a place for cooking that Virginia called the "kitch." "Why a kitch, not kitchen?" he inquired. Virginia replied, "It's not large enough to get 'en.'" In fact, it was not much more than a closet, with a small stove, small fridge, and small sink. But it worked.

The apartment was on the fourth floor of a five storey building. You reached the fourth floor by a remarkably small, slow, very European elevator. The concierge strongly recommended using it only to go up! He alluded darkly that coming down was problematic—"it might descend faster than you might wish." Like many European apartments, this one was built surrounding a completely enclosed courtyard. The bedroom and living room windows of their apartment gave on this courtyard. That courtyard, perhaps 30-feet square and five-stories tall, acted as an efficient and unwanted echo chamber for the German family on the fifth floor who used to stick their heads out of their windows on the courtyard to yell at one another, rather than walk into the adjacent room in their apartment for quiet, private conversations. He and Virginia had, unwanted, the opportunity to learn German also.

LeSchack and Virginia enjoyed trying the many different restaurants, all within walking distance of their apartment. If you liked French cuisine, as he and Virginia then did, there was no such thing, they felt, as a bad French restaurant—just restaurants with different prices. Most of the time when they went out they would head for bistros or restaurants frequented by students. Occasionally, they went to the Chez Tante Louise, a nearby upscale restaurant. During one such dinner there, when Virginia wanted to discover the mystique of escargot, she ordered a plate of these snails baked in their shells, and steeped in garlic butter. And then she attempted to properly extricate them from their shells. Most of the time she did so easily, but not all the time. There was one particularly obstinate snail that clung to its shell, no matter how she pried and poked with her little snail fork. Until it abruptly flew out of its shell, scattering garlic butter everywhere along its trajectory, at the end of which it splashed down onto a table on the far side of the restaurant.

The blast-off, like those at Cape Canaveral, as well as the sub-orbital trajectory of that snail, were observed by all present! However, Gallic behavior toward beautiful young women, LeSchack noticed, is quite different from that reserved for the rest of us beset by similar embarrassing circumstances. In this particular case, instead of stares and gasps of dismay, there were merely good-natured smiles and winks directed at the clearly embarrassed and effusively blushing Virginia, her dripping escargot fork still daintily dangling innocently from her garlicky fingers.

As spring wore on and the weather continually improved, LeSchack looked forward to his afternoon Vespa rides along the Champs Elysées, around l'Etoile and the Arc de Triomphe, and to the EPF in the fashionable 16th Arrondisement. He was enjoying himself. This was the "student life" he never had at engineering school or OCS, and he enjoyed the leisurely pace with which he now learned things. He enjoyed, just for this little while, the lack of deadlines. He knew his current schedule would not last too much longer, although he frantically tried to think of ways to extend his stay. But he knew then, as he had learned earlier in life, to enjoy pleasures as they occur; nothing this good lasts as long as you would like, and certainly not forever.

He took that trip to the EPF several afternoons each week. On one such trip, as he was circling the Arc de Triomphe, he saw a ceremony, accompanied by a military band, about to take place under the arch. He guided his Vespa around to the inside lane so that he could "hot park" by that impressive structure. Hardly had he come to a stop at the curb around this famous monument and shut off his motor, when the band commenced playing *La Marseillaise*, the French National Anthem. Wherever you hear it, LeSchack thought, *La Marseillaise* is an impressive

315

and stirring piece of music. When you hear it played under the Arch of Triumph, it can bring tears to your eyes, even if you are not a Frenchmen. Not only was it the French National Anthem, Simone once tearfully told LeSchack, but during the Second World War it was also the anthem adopted by many non-French soldiers and partisans — the European Diaspora who had battled the Germans — *not only the music of La Marseillaise, but the words too.*

In fact, those very battles occurred less than twenty years earlier. Paris was coming upon its nineteenth anniversary of its liberation from Germany while LeSchack was studying there. In most of his classes at the *Alliance,* he not only was the sole American student, he was one of the few male students. Most of the other students in his classes were young *au pair* girls. They were studying to learn a second or third European language to become multi-lingual secretaries for businesses; they supported themselves as nannies — *au pair* girls — for wealthy Parisian families. And most of these girls were from Germany. Although they were likely to all have been born after the war, LeSchack could sense his French instructors' antipathy toward these young women. Madame van den Baumgarde, a middle-aged woman, for example, knew from class discussions that LeSchack was a U.S. naval officer. She went out of her way to tell him what life was like in Paris during the War, and how her home had been destroyed then by the Germans. She made no apologies for her anti-German bias toward her German students and her pro-U.S. bias toward LeSchack.

LeSchack had noticed a change in Paris since his stay there two years earlier. In 1961, the Algerians were fighting their war of independence from colonial France. Acts of political terrorism were frequent not only in Algeria, but in Metropolitan France, and particularly in Paris. President de Gaulle had been determined to extract France from Algeria by 1962, and he had done so, but not without anguish and bloodshed. Now, in 1963, with that mission accomplished, there were no longer machinegun-toting gendarmes at every street corner as there were when he first visited. And the Foreign Legion was invited back to town, after an absence of many years!

The fourteenth of July is Bastille Day in France. It is the French national holiday. Traditionally, there is a major parade — largely military — along the Champs Elysées. LeSchack and Virginia awoke early that morning and walked to the famous tree-lined boulevard to secure a spot for themselves to watch the parade. They chose a spot about halfway between l'Etoile and La Place de la Concorde. There were brass bands all around them. It was not long after that that the sidewalks and parks that bordered this thoroughfare were jammed with Parisians. And then the parade started. It was a standard military parade; tanks, armored vehicles, marching soldiers. *La Marseillaise,* was played frequently, and received polite applause by the citizenry. A flight of Mirage jets, trailing red, white and blue smoke, swept across l'Arc de Triomphe, and roaring at tree-top level along the Champs Elysées, flew over la Place de la Concorde and out of sight. LeSchack thought it was a dramatic, impressive spectacle. It too, just received polite applause from the Parisians.

Then *la Légion étrangère*, the fabled French Foreign Legion, immortalized by the 1939 movie, "Beau Geste," and by the then popular singer, Édith Piaf, marched past, dressed in their kepis and black aprons, performing their distinctive "slow step" march. Their band played, in slow-step time, the Piaf song that the Legionnaires had much earlier adopted as their own, *"Non, Je ne regrette rien"* —No, I regret nothing. The crowd, which clearly supported that sentiment, as far as Algeria was concerned, surged forward, and loudly and tearfully applauded the Legionnaires. This was the first time since the onset of the war of independence in Algeria, some eight years earlier, that they had been invited to return to France to march on Bastille Day. Algeria was where most of the Legionnaires had been stationed since their ignominious return from Indo China in the mid-1950s. The Legionnaires, who were supposed to be apolitical, had not been so when it came to Algerian independence, and disagreed vehemently with de Gaulle's position. But it was clear to LeSchack how the Parisian citizenry felt! And with the Algerian catastrophe behind him, de Gaulle now felt comfortable in letting them back in town! LeSchack, ever the romantic, enjoyed watching them, and thinking—clandestinely—of the lover who introduced him to "their song."

LeSchack was falling into a quiet, altogether generally pleasant rut. For the first time in years, his work schedule was easy and he enjoyed *la vie*

Parisienne. The nervous twitch in his eye seemed gone for some time now. No one was writing FITREPS—the Navy's evaluation of performance—on him, nor was anyone now *even concerned* with his performance. No one, including his wife. Imperceptibly he was coming to recognize that life with Virginia was not likely to be characterized by the sexual pyrotechnics with which he had earlier become joyously accustomed—and which he had come to believe were normal behaviors between men and women who found each other attractive. And while Virginia's lack of emotional enthusiasm bothered him a bit, he had no intention of, nor desire, for straying from his marriage vows—at least at this point in his life, for he hoped things would improve with time. Frankly, despite his lazy days playing the role of a student of independent means, he had plenty of other things to think about, and his mind was always active, creating strategies and planning new projects. However, he got into the habit of assuring there was a bottle of cognac, easily obtainable at the grocery store up the street, stashed away in the living room closet. In that way, he had something smooth and voluptuous to sip on, while reading or just thinking, all alone in their tiny living room, in those instances when no other social activities were on the agenda, either out in night-time Paris, or in their bedroom.

LeSchack became well enough known at the EPF, and his French sufficiently useable, to begin to enjoy social conversations with his polar colleagues, either at the EPF, or afterwards at nearby cafés. He became friendly with two glaciologists in particular; Jean, an ex-paratrooper—or "para" as the French referred to them—and Pierre, who had a taste for fine wine, and lived in the valley of the Loire, known for its wines. With Jean, they mostly drank and told each other "jump stories." But Pierre had invited LeSchack to join him one weekend at his family's home in the Loire Valley, so that he could take him on a wine-tasting tour of the Loire.

Frenchmen rarely invite casual associates to their homes. They entertain them in restaurants. LeSchack felt delighted, therefore, by this invitation from his colleague to the family home. Pierre pointed out however, that such a trip would most easily be accomplished on LeSchack's Vespa. Pierre did not have a vehicle in Paris. The Vespa could carry two people, but not three. That LeSchack recognized would, for him, be a diplomatic problem, not a logistics one. Virginia neither much liked traveling

318

astride the Vespa nor wine drinking. So he just suggested to her that he wished to have a "boys weekend" out alone, on the Vespa, visiting with Pierre and his family. By this point, LeSchack knew he would not be missing more enjoyable activities at home in Paris that weekend. And that Friday afternoon, Pierre and LeSchack took off on the Vespa.

LeSchack enjoyed himself. On the weekend, Pierre borrowed a family *deux-cheveaux*, a tiny automobile shaped like a fat sardine can on wheels, and they spent a day and a half whipping and bouncing around the Loire Valley, stopping at uncounted wineries for tastings, and visiting numerous old chateaux on the way. It was a wonderful, alcoholic, fun-filled weekend for the two young polar scientists. And once again, as he had aboard the SAN MARTIN, he found his ability at a foreign language improved noticeably with each drink he took! The two sobered up at the end of the weekend and took turns driving the Vespa back to Paris.

At some point during the summer, Virginia's middle-aged cousin and her husband whirl-winded through town. Four days was all their busy and well-planned schedule permitted in Paris. What they didn't have in terms of time, they made up for in money. Recognizing that LeSchack had achieved a reasonable fluency in French and would be desirable as an interpreter, they were prepared to take Virginia and LeSchack with them to as many fancy restaurants and sex shows as they could jam into four days, and pay all expenses. It was an extraordinary experience for LeSchack. Even if he had that kind of money to spend, LeSchack would not have spent it the way Virginia's cousins did. And he certainly would never again wish to eat that much! But he had gotten to go to Maxims and le Tour d'Argent, two well-known, extremely fancy restaurants.

Le Tour d'Argent is located on the Left Bank of the Seine, just across the river from the Nôtre Dame cathedral. The two couples had a table by the window with a clear view of the cathedral. While the food in the restaurant was extraordinary, the night-time *son et lumière*, a musical light show that surrounded the cathedral that night just as dessert was being served, was something LeSchack will never forget. This was the 800th anniversary of Nôtre Dame, and the *son et lumière* was the city's way of celebrating this historic event—with music, light displays and lastly, a major fireworks finale. It was also, by coincidence, the 19th anniversary of General Charles de Gaulle's dramatic visit to this very cathedral just after Paris was liberated from the Germans in 1944.

With De Gaulle leading the way, General Leclerc, and the Free-French Second Armored Division had marched down the Champs Elysées to cheering crowds—punctuated by sniper fire aimed at them from remnants of the *Wehrmacht,* as yet undestroyed—de Gaulle deliberately and unflinchingly, as the bullets flew, marched into Nôtre Dame to attend mass. De Gaulle, the tallest man in almost any group, was clearly a prominent target. Yet unperturbedly, he marched, not only down the Champs Elysées, but then down the aisle of the cathedral—and, inexplicably, there were snipers inside the cathedral also, and they too began shooting—and de Gaulle remained unharmed. This was unmistakably his imperial, albeit highly risky way of announcing to the world, *"Le Bon Dieu est avec nous*—You see, God is with us!" This is what LeSchack was thinking as he finished his dessert at Le Tour d'Argent that night. The fireworks extravaganza had just reached its dramatic conclusion, with brilliant fingers and flashes of colored light blossoming over top of the cathedral. Idly, he wondered what the others at his table were thinking, particularly Paul, the cousin's husband. He had served in the U.S. Army in France in 1945.

LeSchack didn't have to wonder what the others were thinking when they took in the shows at "le Crazy Horse Saloon," or "les Folies Bergères." These overtly sex-oriented shows mildly amused LeSchack because he knew when to laugh at the naughty French jokes; the others didn't. However, he never considered sex a spectator sport, even when he was first introduced to the concept of "strippers" at college. If he wasn't involved, he wasn't interested. About all he got out of these performances was the opportunity to say that *he had seen them,* should anyone ever ask. But nobody did. And it stirred some memories of past delights that he would have just as soon left unstirred. Just as quickly as they came, and spent a bundle of money, the cousins left. LeSchack and Virginia fell back into their earlier routine.

There have not been many times in LeSchack's life when he has had the luxury of time—time to sort out and catalog in his brain all that has gone before, and its meaning. The first such time was during the 1958 Antarctic winter at Byrd Station. To be sure there were projects to then

think about, but there was enough time for cataloging also. Although
this time in Paris five years later would be shorter than his Antarctic
winter, it was an appropriate time for him to re-arrange thoughts and
events of the past five years, and merge them with those of his earlier
life. And this he did, sitting alone in the Tuilleries Gardens by the Place
de la Concorde, or in the Luxembourg Gardens near the *Alliance,* or
occasionally in the Bois de Boulogne. And sometimes in his living room
late at night with a snifter of cognac. But try as he might, he had
difficulty in projecting where all his accruing knowledge and experience
were taking him, and what enrolling in graduate school within the
coming two months was going to accomplish. But push on he would!
And he felt confident that he would be pleased with an outcome that he
as yet could not visualize.

As LeSchack's "student days" in Paris were coming to an end, Paul-
Émile Victor, the director of the EPF, invited LeSchack and Virginia for
lunch at his home, a charming *péniche* tied to a quay along the Seine. His
other home was in Tahiti. Victor, while small in stature, was a heroic
figure nonetheless, and in France, he was well-known as a polar
explorer, scientist and author. He had been a French naval officer and
had several polar expeditions to his credit prior to the onset of World
War II. At the onset of the war and before France capitulated, he was
assigned as the French Assistant Naval Attaché for the Scandinavian
countries. When France surrendered, *he did not return* to his native
country but went directly to the U.S. where he enlisted in the U.S. Army.
He was quickly commissioned an officer in the Army Air Corps,
qualified as a parachutist, and was soon thereafter sent to Alaska where
he eventually commanded a search and rescue squadron. LeSchack's
kind of man! He was in his late 50s when LeSchack first met him and
was fluent in English.

And while very French, in the nicest way, and oozing Gallic charm, he
also likely knew Americans—especially American women—quite well
by the time the War was over. At the time he had invited LeSchack and
Virginia for lunch, he inquired delicately, for he had already met her,
whether Virginia would be upset to find his mistress, a beautiful woman,
perhaps half his age, joining and in fact, presiding over lunch. LeSchack
laughed, knowing just what would make Paul-Émile ask, but said,

"Don't worry. She'll be just fine." Paul-Émile's *péniche* was tastefully decorated in a Polynesian motif and the lunch was excellent, as LeSchack had expected. As it would turn out, LeSchack and Virginia would be able to reciprocate just two years later when they lived in Montréal.

Although his study grant provided airfares to return to the States, Virginia indicated that, if they could in any way arrange it, she would like to return home by ship. He agreed with her that this might be the only opportunity they might ever have of making a trans-Atlantic crossing together; and while LeSchack now had several ocean voyages to his credit, he knew a cruise on a civilian ship would undoubtedly be different from icebreakers and cargo transports. Unfortunately for LeSchack, the only passage available within their time frame was aboard a German ship, leaving La Havre.

"A German ship, Virgnia? Good God! It will be loaded with Germans! Some of whom were likely Nazis! And still may be! They were our mortal enemies less than 20 years ago! I'll be paranoid by the end of voyage!" Virginia pleaded: "Ohhhhhh Please, Len........It willl be our best chance for a Trans-Atlantic voyage together!"

"Alright, I'll do it for you dear," he acquiesced, "I just hope I can sufficiently let bygones be bygones to be comfortable aboard her. She allowed rather lamely that, "she hadn't really thought of *that* Nazi aspect." But they went anyway.

The passage home was a strange, haunting experience for LeSchack. The only previous experience he had on ships had been aboard ships of war. And for the past three years he had been a warrior, had served with older, decorated warriors who he admired, and he had learned to feel like one himself. He felt uncomfortable aboard this ship, not from *mal de mer*, because this ship, unlike the keel-less icebreaker, did not roll heavily, but because nearly everyone aboard was German, and his anachronistic childhood fears and upsets bubbled up from the recesses of his core being, demanding that this warrior "do something about it."

However, there *were* some similarities with his past cruises. He enjoyed the sea and the feeling of the sea breeze in his face while standing on the bow; and he had about as much lovemaking on this ship as he had on his previous cruises. There was another similarity between this ship and his cruises with the Argentine Navy: there were plenty of wines and spirits served aboard this ship also. But here, he was extremely cautious about what, and how much he drank—always his cautionary reaction whenever his body and soul sensed a potentially threatening environment.

A few days into the cruise, LeSchack was now anxious to get home. His brain was working overtime to place into perspective all that he had learned in the past two years, not only his two recent forays into learning to adapt to different cultures, but from the excitement and high drama of Coldfeet and the Cuban Missile Crisis. "This is a complicated world we're living in," he often mused while standing on the bow, with the sea breeze in his face. "What shall I do with my newfound knowledge?"

LeSchack was again standing on that bow several days later when the ship entered the Ambrose Channel. To Starboard in the distance was Coney Island. Dead ahead, also in the distance, was New Jersey. Then the massive liner slowly wheeled to starboard and entered Lower New York Bay. Now dead ahead he could see the Verrazano Narrows Bridge under which they would soon sail. And soon enough she did. LeSchack looked up at the understructure of this landmark as they cruised beneath. It was not long after that that this ship, flying under the flag of his erstwhile enemy, a country from which his aunt and uncle barely escaped with their lives in 1938, sailed past that quintessential symbol of LeSchack's *country*, the Lady with a Lamp. When the Statue of Liberty was off the port beam of the German ship, LeSchack's body involuntarily came to attention. While he did not salute—he would have, had he been in uniform—he cried instead. Then, after a bit, he smiled, remembering how, as a child growing up in New York City, he and some of his elementary school chums had climbed to the top of her head and marveled at the view of the harbor from her crown.

Moments later, the ship sailed past Ellis Island where 57 years earlier his father first made landfall in the New World. LeSchack, the first generation American, mused at the difference between father and son: LeSchack and his bride, both with American passports, would descend the gangplank at the 42nd Street Pier, and for the second time in six months, enter the United States of America without any questions and a minimum of hassle. LeSchack knew it had not been so easy for his father and his family. In addition to learning to speak passably in two different languages during the past year, LeSchack had a sudden flash: "maybe now, I know a bit more of what America is all about." But this understanding and feeling of patriotic fervor were about to be seriously challenged when he arrived at the University of Wisconsin in the next month. There he would be thrust back into the real Cold War, which had been invisible to LeSchack during his idyllic sojourn in Paris.

******

The Department of Geology and Geophysics at the University of Wisconsin was well-known and respected. In addition to Professor Woolard, there were other world-class geologists and geophysicists on staff. The school was also the home base for a number of the scientists with whom LeSchack had worked in the Antarctic during the IGY. That was the big attraction for LeSchack. The school, a public, coeducational Land-Grant College, had been established in Madison, the state capitol, in 1848. And he and Virginia packed up their belongings in Washington, stuffed them into a U-Haul trailer, and drove to Madison in September 1963, and into an entirely different life than that they had shared for the previous eighteen months.

They rented a small, barely affordable but nice two-bedroom garden apartment on the outskirts of Madison. LeSchack enrolled in Graduate School and signed up for a course load heavy in mathematics and in geophysics. Charlie Bentley—the same Charlie Bentley who was the Byrd Station traverse leader during the IGY—was his advisor, and suggested these courses. LeSchack agreed that this was what he wanted and needed. Virginia, who had been a high-powered legal secretary in Washington, took the only job she could find in Madison—a simple secretarial job. With the stipend that LeSchack had obtained from the University, and Virginia's salary, they could barely get by.

LeSchack's day was spread between formal course work on campus in downtown Madison, and research and administrative work at a large mansion on the outskirts of town that housed the "Geophysical and Polar Research Center" of the University. It was at the downtown campus that he saw a different world from that which he had previously experienced. There was, of course, the abundance of nubile co-eds, which delighted his eye. The last coeducational experience that LeSchack could remember had occurred ten years earlier, and that was his Red Cross Water Safety Instructors' Course—an experience that stands out since the majority of the students were healthy women, 20 to 30 years of age, who wore only bathing suits to class! What caught LeSchack's eye at Madison, however, was the overt political activism that abounded. He had never seen this kind of behavior before.

When one considers political activism at U. S. universities, the University of California at Berkeley comes to mind first. Madison, however, with its large liberal arts faculty and student body was not far behind. And the focus of this activism was concerned with the increasing United States involvement in Indo China. LeSchack generally knew about that U.S. involvement, and that it was less positive than portrayed by the White House. During preparations for Coldfeet, he regularly received scuttlebutt from Dr. Dan, via talk at the Fort Bragg O-Club from Special Forces advisors returning from Southeast Asia. That talk was usually pessimistic, and contrary to White House claims. But frankly, over the past three years, LeSchack had professionally been paying far more attention to the threat of Soviet submarines in the Arctic, Soviet missile buildup in Cuba, and plans for a U.S. invasion of that island as hinted at by his Coldfeet partner, Major Smith. That had been followed by concerns about Argentine politics and Argentina's claims in Antarctic waters, and most recently, France's final disengagement from Algeria, with which he first became aware through conversations with Simone, and then from living in France. That disengagement was the denouement of French colonization; Algeria was the last significant European colony to be let loose, preceded, of course, by France's hasty retreat from Indo China, after they were beaten at Dien Bien Phu ten years earlier. So, at the time he arrived in Madison, LeSchack had paid little attention to that part of the world that was the focus of student activist upset.

While LeSchack's primary focus had always been on his science, his mother, an Eleanor Roosevelt liberal and an historian, had insinuated some of her views on him, but most particularly the need to understand history. Fresh from several years of being immersed in the governmental orbit, he was dubious about some of the positions the activists took, particularly vis à vis Southeast Asia. However, remembering a key reason for his joining the military in the first place—to keep a watchful eye on his government in his own best interest—he observed attentively, and with an intellectual eye, the unfolding student unrest.

LeSchack quickly immersed himself into his class work, and began writing some technical papers covering his previous geophysical and oceanographic work on the Arctic drifting stations. As per his agreement with the Department, he earned his stipend by providing guidance to the administrators of the Geophysical and Polar Research Center on the preparation and handling of research proposals, many of which were submitted to ONR. Jack Long, LeSchack's old tractor mate from the Antarctic, worked at the Center also. With his Antarctic experience, he had become the senior civilian logistics officer for administering the National Science Foundation's contract to the University for the management of Antarctic programs. Jack had enrolled in the Department of Mechanical Engineering and was paying his way through school in this manner. As for Virginia, she settled unhappily into a secretarial job at the University that was far less challenging than her legal work in Washington. As people displaced into the hinterlands from Washington often do, she became amazed at the parochialism of views in her office. LeSchack had considerable sympathy for her, and cajoled her with "together we are working toward a more secure future for us." But he surely didn't have any idea of what that might look like.

When LeSchack enlisted in the Navy he signed a commitment for six years—three on active duty and a minimum of three more in the reserves. As a result, he needed to affiliate now with a drilling reserve unit. There was a "Navy Research Reserve Unit" associated with the University, and it drilled on campus. This was convenient and seemed an appropriate place for himself since the Research Reserve was affiliated with his old office, ONR. The unit was composed entirely of officers, all of whom were affiliated with the University, and all of whom had already served on active duty. The unit met one evening a week, and the meetings were a welcome change from the pure academic grind.

In fact, anything different from the academic grind was welcome. Even joining Virginia to watch the occasional television program was welcome, and LeSchack had never watched much television before, except for the news. Mostly, he spent all his free time studying in their apartment's second bedroom, which he converted into a study. His reserve unit filled LeSchack's need to spend time with older men who had shared the Navy experience — though none of his colleagues had anywhere near the romantic active duty assignments that he had just had. Surprising to him was the pleasure of again putting on the uniform — once a week, required for attending drills. It was only then that he began to realize how much responsibility and prestige had accrued to him during his, so far, limited service in uniform, responsibility and prestige he never before had in his life, and ruefully he thought was certainly missing now. But it was in this academic milieu — so different from Rensselaer — that LeSchack felt he had to be furtive when on campus and in uniform. The anti-military environment made him feel uneasy, but fortunately, drills were held in the evenings, and walking on campus in a black uniform (with the white uniform cap hidden from view) made it unlikely to be easily identified.

As he was soon to learn, a substantial number of Navy Reserve drills are a waste of time. It was cliché that reservists typically trained for the last war, not for any future conflict. It was certainly so in this unit. But a key purpose of reserve drills is to remind its members of their military service and to teach them to remain comfortable in uniform if ever they are called back to active duty. To this end, the CO of the unit, a research professor at the University, had arranged for a two-day trip to visit the McDonald-Douglas aircraft plant in Saint Louis, Missouri to examine the latest fighter planes coming off the assembly line. Truax Air Force Base in Madison provided a DC-3 and crew that would fly them there and back.

On the appointed day, in autumn of 1963, the members of the Navy Research Reserve Unit, in uniform, assembled at Truax and boarded the aircraft. Whether it was a new requirement or not LeSchack never knew, but the unit members were required to strap on parachutes. In all his Antarctic and active duty service where combat was not expected, no such requirement was ever levied in military aircraft. And the reason is simple: if no one is shooting at you, and the aircraft is forced down, it is safer for all aboard who are not trained as paratroopers to remain with the aircraft. But LeSchack had no reason to question the donning of parachutes, if that is what the Air Force required.

However, when the active duty Air Force sergeant instructing the frankly concerned unit members on the finer points of wearing parachutes began recounting all the parachute malfunctions possible, and all the parachuting horror stories that LeSchack had already heard before, he had had enough. LeSchack knew most of the horror stories about chutes that didn't open, or partially opened, or knocked the parachutist unconscious as they did open. These things did happen, of course, but only a tiny fraction of the time. He sensed this smug enlisted man was simply wanting to terrorize LeSchack's Navy colleagues—not an unheard of scenario perpetrated by enlisted men on officers, when they have the opportunity. Finally LeSchack, the most junior officer aboard, opened his bridge coat, displaying his jump wings on his uniform, and said for all to hear, "Cut the bullshit, Sergeant! You are unnecessarily frightening the men." LeSchack had noted that the sergeant who had been regaling all the assembled, and obviously concerned Navy men, *did not have jump wings on his uniform*. The sergeant, spotting LeSchack's wings, abruptly desisted!

By mid-autumn LeSchack was well into his coursework. His two classes in his major subject, geophysics, were small, and he knew the professors, Charlie Bentley, who had led the 1957-58 and 1958-59 Byrd Traverses and Ned Ostenso, who LeSchack had replaced as assistant seismologist on that traverse. Of the dozen students enrolled in this curriculum, two were young women, one of whom was the widow of Ed Thiele, a geophysicist LeSchack had known in the Antarctic, and who was killed in a P2V crash there two years earlier. Because he had known Ed, and Ed had also been an ONR contractor with the Arctic Program, Lieutenant LeSchack had been tasked with writing, for the Admiral's signature, ONR's official letter of condolence to Ed's young widow. "There but for the grace of God," thought LeSchack, sadly, remembering his own hairy adventures in P2s—for he knew two other colleagues, both naval officers, who also were killed in separate P2 crashes. It seemed as though Ed's wife was attempting to take over her late husband's work. It was not clear whether she could successfully do this. Every time he saw her in class, LeSchack remembered the last time he and Ed talked, returning to New Zealand together on the WYANDOTTE, and he thought of how, at ONR, he had agonized over writing that letter to her. But he never told her it was he who wrote the Admiral's most caring condolence letter.

The other young woman, Hilda Kessler, a charming, vivacious and worldly young lady, was a brilliant mathematician who was also helping LeSchack with the mathematics needed for some of his research. He enjoyed that collaboration! It was a congenial group that made up those two geophysics classes.

LeSchack was in this class on 22 November 1963 when news came of John Kennedy's assassination. The entire school seemed to shut down directly thereafter. LeSchack was devastated. He almost felt he knew this ex-Navy man who had his office on the Ellipse, just two blocks north of LeSchack's Constitution Avenue office at ONR, and who had authorized his decoration just a year earlier. It was worse for Virginia. She had worked for then Senator Kennedy back in Washington on his presidential campaign. Watching the funeral on television, Virginia sobbed that she was so sad that she was not back in Washington now.

And they pushed on. Virginia liked her job less and less, and she was beginning to get anxiety attacks; they were disabling. LeSchack, still uncertain where all his studying was leading, pushed harder and harder, and learned interestingly enough, if he had several stiff drinks just prior to his occasional exams, he would do observably better on them than without such drinks. Obviously, LeSchack too, had anxiety. He would take snorts of cognac surreptitiously in his parked car, and walk from there to wherever on campus the test was being given. He was thoroughly sober after the exam was over.....and then he drove home.

As more and more discouraging news trickled out of Viet Nam, an art exhibit—paintings of unhappy war scenes in Southeast Asia—appeared on campus. Along with it were memorials to some Wisconsin grads killed in action: some had been in the Special Forces, others civilian aid workers. Increasingly anti-war songs began to be sung at drinking parties, and on campus. The words and lilting melody of Pete Seeger's song, "Where have all the flowers gone?" was particularly sad for LeSchack. He heard that song often during his time at Graduate School. Although he still supported the Government's position, he was beginning to wonder if they knew what they were doing.

One day while at his office at the Geophysical and Polar Research Center, he met a Navy captain who represented ONR. He was there discussing research and contract matters on one of the ONR-sponsored programs being conducted at the University. LeSchack introduced himself to the Captain, indicating a bit of his Navy background and that he was now affiliated with the Naval Research Reserve Unit that drilled at the University. In passing, LeSchack observed unhappily that it was a non-pay unit, and that grad students benefited more from units that paid for the reservists time, for he knew that there were such units somewhere. "What's your designator, Lieutenant," the Captain asked. "I'm an unrestricted line officer, Sir," he replied. "Well, I know that there is a Naval Intelligence Reserve Unit drilling here at the University, and it's a pay unit," the Captain observed. "But you would eventually have to change your designator to intelligence, if you were to affiliate with that group. Would you wish to do that? And, more to the point, do you think you have the qualifications to be a naval intelligence officer?"

LeSchack thought for a moment and answered, "Well, Sir, to answer your questions, I *need* a pay billet, I haven't had enough sea duty to be promoted as an unrestricted line officer, but I expect I should have adequate qualifications to change to the intelligence designator and be successfully promoted in the reserves." After more reflection he continued, "how about speaking ability in two foreign languages, duty as Official U.S. Representative to the Argentine Naval Antarctic Expedition, study grant in France," and then as an afterthought LeSchack added, "I was also involved in an intelligence mission against the Soviets two years ago. I got the Legion of Merit for that one."

The Captain blinked at that. "And you're only a lieutenant (j.g.)?" LeSchack replied, "Well, I should make full lieutenant this month." "I see," replied the Captain, a bit startled. "I expect you *might indeed* have the qualifications. The CO of the Intelligence Unit is a Professor of Agricultural Economics at the University, a lieutenant commander in the Reserve. I'll get him to call you."

Shortly thereafter LeSchack was invited to join the Naval Reserve Intelligence Unit—for pay—that drilled on campus. This would turn out to be a significant turning point in both his naval career and his civilian activities also. It caused LeSchack to increasingly begin to *think* like an intelligence officer—and also, *think of himself as one*. And in December 1963, he *did* receive orders promoting him to the rank of Lieutenant in the Naval Reserves. One day after classes LeSchack and Virginia happily visited a haberdashery, about a block from campus on State Street which happened to carry Navy lieutenant's shoulder boards and devices, and could stitch gold braid on to his sleeves to update his uniform. After purchasing these accoutrements signifying promotion, they went out for a quiet dinner, alone, and at a nice restaurant. These days they rarely had much to celebrate, or money to effect such celebration, but they took the occasion of his promotion to do so now.

Although LeSchack could sense that he was learning much of what he wanted to learn, he still did not enjoy the process. He missed the exciting life of recent years. What he was doing now was, frankly, boring. It was worse for Virginia, who missed Washington, and the excitement of national politics. LeSchack began wondering whether he wanted to be a scientist after all. On a whim, he visited Professor Kirk Stone in the University's Geography Department. LeSchack knew Professor Stone as a Principal Investigator on research grants from Evelyn Pruitt's ONR Geography Branch. He also knew that Evelyn, knowing LeSchack had enrolled at Wisconsin's Grad School, likely made Kirk aware—just in passing—of some of LeSchack's previous secret Navy activities. When LeSchack observed to Professor Stone that he had just been accepted into the Intelligence Unit drilling on campus, and was enjoying it, the Professor observed, "And now you were wondering whether I would introduce you to the CIA recruiter in this neck of the woods?"

"Of course," responded LeSchack who by now knew just who would likely have such connections. Not too long thereafter, LeSchack received a call from a man who said he would like to talk to him about a career in intelligence.

331

Graduate students are required to write a thesis on independent research that they have conducted. LeSchack was amazed at what anguish that seemed to cause his fellow grad students in his curriculum. Few of them seemed to have research projects in mind, nor seemed to know where to begin. To the extent that he overheard conversations between his classmates and their instructors, it appeared that the students were depending on their thesis advisors to come up with ideas! LeSchack judged that the advisors encouraged such dependent behavior on the part of the students so that they would remain "scientific sycophants" and continually put off conducting their own research, and would spend yet another year helping their advisors conduct *their own research*. LeSchack sensed that the advisors took advantage of their students, attempting to keep them in some form of academic bondage, in an intellectual "boot camp." LeSchack was not one of those students. He had his own data, and he knew what to do with it. Also, he knew how to write. And he was determined not to go through *any* boot camp experience again in his lifetime! However, he kept these thoughts to himself and just watched the others agonize.

LeSchack and Virginia just kept their heads down and soldiered on, enjoying the experience less and less, but at least he was learning something. Virginia was just marking time. They began to increasingly "cocoon" in their apartment, particularly during the cold Wisconsin winter. Aside from occasional student and faculty parties, their social life included only Jack Long and his wife, and Jim Sparkman and his wife. Both Jack and LeSchack had met Jim on the tedious airplane trip to New Zealand that launched the IGY for all three of them. Jim, an ex-reporter from the Christian Science Monitor, had entered geophysics on a whim. He had been interviewing Professor Woolard for a Monitor piece, when Woolard asked Jim whether *he* would like to change professions and carry a gravity meter around the world during the IGY. Woolard suggested that Jim might like to record measurements for a worldwide gravity database that was being created under Woolard's direction. Jim promptly changed professions. Jack Long and Jim were LeSchack's closest friends at the University and remained so afterwards. Virginia was not impressed with either of their wives. LeSchack was just beginning to learn that Virginia did not enjoy the company of many women.

As spring arrived, so did the CIA recruiter, sent by Professor Stone. LeSchack filled out the enormous quantity of paper work and submitted the package through the recruiter. He had no idea of the outcome, but it gave him a diversion from the academic grind. Also arriving, much to LeSchack's and Virginia's delight, was a Navy check for a thousand dollars that represented his back parachute-jump pay. It had been applied for over a year earlier, and owing to the peculiar circumstances involved in the origins of Project Coldfeet for which parachute jumping was required, but not otherwise needed by a Navy officer in an ONR "research billet," the intervention of the Secretary of the Navy was ultimately required for approval. But it happened, and LeSchack and Virginia most desperately needed the funds at just the moment the check arrived.

Also that spring, LeSchack learned that the Hydrographic Office, now officially called the U.S. Navy Oceanographic Office, was sponsoring the "First Navy Oceanographic Symposium" in Washington, early in June, and after the Spring Semester was over. LeSchack requested the Navy to issue him "active duty for training" (ACDUTRA) orders—with pay—so that he could attend. To his surprise and delight, they were forthcoming, and the Navy would pay for the round-trip by automobile back to Washington. Both LeSchack and Virginia were delighted to have an excuse to get away for awhile. Just before they left, he received a telegram from CIA requesting he call, at his earliest convenience, an anonymous phone number in Langley, Virginia.

As soon as classes were over, they packed their car with LeSchack's uniforms, and just enough other things to support a two-week trip to Washington and return. Such a trip is a comfortable two-day drive each way. Somewhere in Ohio, they found a nice motel and stopped for the evening. It was a warm spring day and the motel pool was open. "Time for my first swim of the year," announced LeSchack, after they had unpacked for the evening. "Too cold for me, Len," Virginia replied, just shivering at the thought. "I'll stay in the room and read until you return." LeSchack wanted to read also, but out in the fading sunshine by the pool. He had begun reading a book, just published: "The Invisible Government," by David Wise and Thomas B. Ross. It was a book about

CIA activities. LeSchack thought it might be useful, under the circumstances, to find out more about that organization.

Sitting by the pool, he nearly fell out of his chair reading about the Agency's air operations in Guatemala and Nicaragua in 1961. A remote jungle base near Retalhuleu, and later, Puerto Cabezas, supported the Bay of Pigs invasion. Wise and Ross had interviewed a number of Cuban exile pilots who had been involved, and they provided details, such as they knew them. When asked about who was in charge, the exiles could provide only nicknames and general physical descriptions of the key players. Nonetheless, they had without any question in LeSchack's mind, identified the two senior men on the B-17 who flew his Coldfeet mission! This was the first indication that he had that Intermountain Aviation had been involved with the Bay of Pigs fiasco in 1961. It also provided LeSchack a dramatic object lesson for intelligence officers: even partial, incomplete, or half-true information to an audience who already has a framework in which that fragmentary bit of information can be placed, often results in extremely valuable intelligence. LeSchack now had information about his Intermountain colleagues that they had withheld from him and ONR, information that would not become public knowledge for many years to come. Once he digested this, he smiled to himself. "Time to go for a swim," he said, as he dove into the pool.

Since LeSchack and Virginia had given up their apartment in Arlington, they stayed at Virginia's parents' home in Chevy Chase, Maryland. Within a few days of their arrival, the Oceanography Symposium commenced. To get to the venue of the symposium, LeSchack took an old familiar route into downtown Washington, the Sligo Creek Parkway. He used this route throughout his brief courtship of Virginia, who was then living with her parents. In those days, the parkway was a bucolic return through time. It was a narrow, winding paved pathway running through mature growth forest with numerous bridle paths criss-crossing the forest. Where streams crossed the route, one had to ford them. There were no bridges. In late spring, the water was generally high enough so that the prudent driver slowed down to a crawl when crossing the streams to avoid wetting the brakes or splashing the engine block.

Because LeSchack was going to the symposium under Navy orders, he was wearing his dress khaki uniform with brand new lieutenant's shoulder boards—two broad gold stripes. He was feeling good at this moment as he slowed down to cross the first of the fords on Sligo Creek Parkway, on that first day of the symposium. As he slowed down nearly to a stop at the first crossing, he spied a beautiful young girl on horseback also about to cross the ford. As he looked at her to see what she and her horse planned to do, prior to his fording the stream, she saw him. She immediately sat up straight in her saddle, and giving LeSchack a magnificent smile, saluted smartly! He broke into a wonderful grin and returned the salute. The entire exchange took perhaps five seconds. Then he slowly drove the car across the stream. But that transaction made his day! After a year of academic drudgery as a lowly graduate student—they were not held in high esteem at Wisconsin—a salute from a pretty girl on a horse made all the difference in the world to him then. He felt like a man once again! As he drove away he thought, "This is a fine omen. Good things will happen at the symposium."

Symposia are designed both for transfer of knowledge and for networking among colleagues. Both happened for LeSchack. Jack Schule, who had made it possible for him to conduct his gravity meter experiments on ARLIS II in 1961, was there. "Len, when are you going to write up the results of your work on the ice?" Jack inquired. "I was planning on using it as my master's thesis at Wisconsin," LeSchack replied to his old mentor and instructor in ocean waves. "Why not write it at the Oceanographic Office? We'll pay you. We could probably get you a GS-11 salary. And you will have access to our computers as well as our specialists in gravity and ocean waves." LeSchack was astounded, and frankly fascinated with that idea. "I think I'd be interested, Jack. Let's talk further at your office right after the symposium is over."

When LeSchack told Virginia about the conversation with Jack Schule, she urged, "Oh Len! Do please make it work out. I've had enough of Wisconsin, and a GS-11 is a good salary!" LeSchack was beginning to feel that way also. And because he could see the developing conflict in Viet Nam equally well from the viewpoints of both the government, and the anti-war movement, he was becoming increasingly uncomfortable remaining in this conflicted university milieu. He had enough credits he thought for a master's degree, and all he needed to complete was a thesis. But he cautioned her that "if I took up Schule's offer for a government job, it would only be temporary; if I had wanted a career government job, he reminded her, "I would have remained in the active duty Navy." LeSchack knew that Virginia, a product of two career civil servants, wanted him to have the stability of a secure government job— even if it killed him. And LeSchack knew it likely would, not necessarily physically, but surely, he felt, creatively, and probably emotionally. But then again, maybe not, if it was an exciting job with CIA! "Exciting" was the operative word.

And that too, had now become a serious possibility.

After the Navy symposium was over, LeSchack met Jack Schule at his office in Suitland, Maryland. Jack took him to the "Civilian Personnel Officer" who provided him the forms to fill out for temporary employment at the Oceanographic Office. As LeSchack left that office, Jack assured him he would make every effort to push his application through the bureaucracy. LeSchack felt certain that he would.

LeSchack felt a little better on their return drive to Madison. He felt he now had a few more options. But none of them were a certainty; just good possibilities. By the time they got back to their apartment in Madison, it was now a full-blown Wisconsin summer. Thanks to the recent arrival of his back jump pay, they had a brief financial cushion that allowed LeSchack and Virginia to consider thoughtfully what to do next.

The decision was made within the next two weeks. A letter arrived from CIA saying he had tentatively been selected for employment pending "intensive background investigations and reviews which concern professional competence and personal qualifications such as general dependability, physical and emotional health, and loyalty." A phone call to Jack Schule revealed that his application had been favorably acted upon, the only question left was Civil Service adjudication of the GS-11 grade. And Charlie Bentley, LeSchack's major professor, had decreed that *contrary to his original agreement* with him, LeSchack would no longer receive his stipend for acting as an assistant administrator at the
336

Geophysical and Polar Research Center, but only if he would agree to do the donkey research work for his professors, like all the other grad students were doing. LeSchack nodded sagely to Bentley at this new understanding brought about by unmitigated fiat, then did an about-face, and walked briskly out. That was it! The decision was made.

By the end of the following week, LeSchack and Virginia had packed up their belongings into another U-Haul, had settled with the landlord of their apartment, said their goodbyes to Jack and Jim, and were on their way back to Washington. LeSchack was now prepared to write his thesis at the Oceanographic Office—a thesis that he already knew to be more appropriate as a doctoral dissertation—and take his chances at sometime later being granted a master's degree.

By the end of July 1964, LeSchack had a desk at the U. S. Navy's Oceanographic Office—and a steady paycheck—and he had begun analyzing all the ocean wave data he had collected with his gravity meters on Arctic Drifting Stations T-3 and ARLIS II. During the first week of August, he had three days of interviews and testing at the Agency pursuant to his application. That process passed by in an unmemorable blur. However, two things stood out in LeSchack's mind associated with the testing process:

The polygraph test—this was the first time he had ever taken one. LeSchack had no problems with it and answered all questions honestly. The only question he was uncomfortable with concerned Communists that he knew—this remember, was in the latter part of what was still called the "McCarthy Era." Well, LeSchack knew a few. They were his parents' peers, harmless, old idealistic folks who were completely open about their Communist sympathies: they were card-carrying Communists who openly subscribed to the "Daily Worker." LeSchack was certain that, because they were so open about their sympathies, those in government who *wanted to keep track of them,* already had. LeSchack didn't know any clandestine Communists at this point in his life. Nonetheless, when asked to "name the Communists that you know," he did so, but was a bit uncomfortable about the question.

There was a whole battery of tests that were designed to test one's "emotional health," with questions of the type, "on a scale of one to five, how much do you enjoy chocolate? One, very much; five, not at all." Most of these questions seemed innocuous to LeSchack. However, the question, *"Do you have a satisfactory sexual relationship with your wife? (one to five),* stopped him dead in his tracks. The very blatancy of the question shocked him. Even guys in the locker room don't ask a question like that so blatantly. For over two years now, LeSchack had deliberately avoided asking himself that very same question for fear of hearing his own answer. However, he now had enough intelligence experience and world travel to know the purpose of CIA's question, *and he knew it to be a valid question.* The conventional wisdom in the early 1960s was that a sexually unsatisfied married man searching for pleasure outside his family was a prime target for compromise—owing to blackmail and co-option—particularly in a foreign country where Agency employees with LeSchack's experience would likely be stationed.

LeSchack had to stop and think. He spent the longest time over that question. Half of that thinking time was spent reviewing his delicious affairs prior to his marriage. It was the best and most powerful and vigorous of those affairs--the one with Simone-- that he had been thinking about when he had answered a previous question—"Do you enjoy making love to compatible people of the opposite sex?" (one to five). And he had already marked, with an indelible pencil a "1," (very much enjoy). The other half of the thinking time spent on the present question concerned which box he needed to check to obtain a "correct" answer. A check mark in any box other than the one signifying, "no, I do not have a satisfactory sexual relationship," i.e., it's the shits, LeSchack recognized now would be an outright lie! He chose the box that he, in his wisdom, expected to be the "school solution," and went on to finish the battery of exams. But for the first time in his married life, he was forcibly brought face-to-face with the fact that sexually, he had a most unsatisfying marriage, a fact that like all unpleasant matters, he had filed in the least accessible portions of his brain. Now, unwanted, that fact bubbled to the surface, and he had to deal with it. Why it was so, he didn't know. He just remembered that women he knew before Virginia enjoyed making love with him. And Virginia, despite all her other attractive attributes, simply didn't.

338

LeSchack had done all he could do with respect to the Agency. The rest was up to them. And basically he forgot about his application.

He had settled into working on his Arctic data at the Oceanographic Office. As a scientist, he enjoyed unfettered behavior at the office. He could conduct his work as he saw fit. He knew, from his old ONR days, a number of the civilian scientists and a few of the naval officers assigned there. No one bothered him, with the occasional exception of Jack Schule. From time to time, there were oceanographic working groups that Jack wanted to assign a "naval officer-scientist" to as a representative. LeSchack was requested to go. He knew this was now the *quid pro quo* for Jack's earlier assistance to him. It was interesting to LeSchack that so few civilians at the Oceanographic Office actually understood the uniformed Navy's mission. That is why Jack had asked him to participate in those working groups. And so he did. LeSchack observed in his new "Civil Service milieu" how many junior and mid-grade civilian employees of this Navy facility actually found the naval officers assigned anathema. Largely because, having had no previous active duty military experience, they were afraid of them.

Recognizing they likely had some stability, either with the Oceanographic Office or the Agency, LeSchack and Virginia rented a nice two-bedroom apartment in Silver Spring, Maryland and began to live like, what they used to call, "real people" again. That meant restaurants and theater, and some of the good things that they had been missing in Madison.

To continue his Naval Reserve affiliation, LeSchack joined the Naval Reserve Intelligence Division that drilled one night a week at the Washington Navy Yard. As opposed to the units of about ten officers he had drilled with in Madison, the Washington unit he began drilling with had between 150-250 officers. Many of these officers were senior civilians in the many civilian and military intelligence organizations that had headquarters in the Washington, D.C. Metropolitan Area. With time, LeSchack began to get to know many of them and this formed one of the most astounding groups for networking that he ever encountered. And took advantage of.

With the summer of 1964 well underway, LeSchack was happily digging into his Arctic data, having the Oceanographic Office's computer personnel crunch the vast volumes of numbers that represented that data, and he was enjoying the occasional help from some of the serious scientists at that office. He enjoyed going to the swimming pool at his apartment complex with Virginia when he returned home. Virginia too, was working again at what she enjoyed doing: being a legal secretary for patent attorneys. For the time being, it was a comfortable life. LeSchack didn't know how long it would last, nor how long he wanted it to last.

When it came to work that LeSchack enjoyed doing, he spent considerably more time on it than the standard eight-hour workday. When an interesting result cropped up in his analysis during the office workday, he would continue to ponder it during the evening—on those evenings that he and Virginia did not have social commitments. So, it was with some irritation that LeSchack listened to reminders from the dull, gray mid-level civil servant, Ed, who nominally was head of the section in which LeSchack was working, concerning LeSchack's occasional morning tardiness. LeSchack would say nothing, but he would screw up his face unpleasantly, as if inadvertently stepping in some offal. Naval officers, even on shore duty, were on call 24-hours a day, if that were necessary, not just nine-to-five. And LeSchack worked on all his projects in this fashion, both while in uniform or out. And he soon recognized that Ed was one of those employees who was fearful of the Navy in uniforms.

Every Tuesday evening was Naval Reserve drill night for LeSchack at the Navy Yard. Since that large complex on the Potomac River was on his way home to Silver Spring, he went there first on Tuesday nights. He hung his uniform in the car Tuesday morning, and changed into it after work and went directly to the drill site. Sometimes he would change at the Navy Yard, but on those occasions when Ed had recently become a nuisance, LeSchack would change in the head around the corner from his office. Promptly after civilian working hours on those days, he would duck into the head and emerge in the uniform of a full lieutenant in the Navy, resplendent with decorations and intimidating jump wings; any one who had seen WWII or "Green Beret" movies, as were common then, would recognize jump wings, and the power and *machisimo* so implied. Then he would walk back to his desk to "pick up a few papers

340

he had forgotten to take with him." Ed, who also was usually still dawdling and fumbling over his papers, always seemed shocked when LeSchack showed up looking like this. "Good!" thought LeSchack, "that's the effect, I intended!" and then he left the office, smiling.

At the onset of autumn, LeSchack was well into his thesis, but he now recognized it would take several more months to complete it. Also, he finally received a letter from the Agency. Regretfully, it stated, "the position for which he had been considered had been filled by someone else." Whether this was true or not, LeSchack never could be sure—he had heard rumors that his job had been predicated upon receipt of requested supplemental Government funding, funding that never materialized. He absently wondered whether his fudging on the question of "getting enough sex?" had been cleverly discovered, and the Agency psychologists had divined that, should he be hired, he would promptly screw every foreign woman in sight, thus compromising the whole United States. However, it turns out LeSchack was only mildly disappointed at the rejection. He recognized that the Oceanographic Office would certainly keep him on the payroll until he finished his thesis, and likely permanently should he so desire. Or at least, until he conjured up some new adventure. And adventure, LeSchack had finally come to recognize, was what his entire life was about—with not only exploration and science, but world travel and women also.

Interestingly enough, nearly a decade later, in 1973, LeSchack was to find out from a trusted friend within the Agency that his entire file was still there, moreover, he was listed as a "retired CIA officer." That might have explained some unusual happenings that befell LeSchack in 1980, when he showed up in Panamá as a captain on active duty, on a sensitive intelligence assignment. But that's another story.

As the year came to a close, LeSchack was nearly finished with his thesis, and two new potential projects popped up. Bob Fulton, inventor of the Skyhook, was interested to see whether LeSchack could start a division of Fulton's company that could apply his Skyhook to civilian applications in remote areas. What they discussed together were ways to determine if the success that accrued from the military use of the Skyhook in Coldfeet, could be transferred to civilian applications in remote areas where commercial resource development was ongoing. After Coldfeet, the Department of Defense certainly became aware of Skyhook's value, and Fulton's company began receiving contracts for its further development. Bob, like LeSchack—always thinking and scheming—was now looking to investigate non-military applications for civilian clients.

Also, the Arctic Institute of North America, whose main office was in Montréal, wanted to know whether LeSchack had any interest in taking on the job of "Polar Regions Project Officer" for the then forming Canadian Corporation for the 1967 World's Fair—EXPO-67—to be convened in that city. The AINA had been retained to find an administrator who had polar experience, had contacts with the world's polar institutes, who spoke French, and, most importantly, was available. To LeSchack the job in Montréal sounded fascinating, and in one of his favorite cities. But it was only tentative and likely would not occur until the summer of 1965.

At the end of January 1965, LeSchack finished his thesis. The Navy, which liked it, said it would publish it as an official technical report. He sent a copy off to the University of Wisconsin, where it was accepted, and then he washed his hands of that matter. And he promptly joined Bob Fulton to pursue a plan for civilian Skyhook applications.

Fulton had his office, laboratory and Skyhook manufacturing facility in Newtown, Connecticut. LeSchack had visited Fulton often during the planning stages of Project Coldfeet. On such trips he would stay at his parents' home in Westport, Connecticut about a half-hour's drive from Newtown. Because LeSchack and Virginia now had a home in Silver Spring, and Virginia had a good job in downtown Washington, they decided that what would make sense for the time being was for LeSchack to work out a schedule of working alternate weeks at each location, one week in Connecticut, the next week in Washington. This made business sense also, since the Agency for International Development, and U. S. Forest Service were both located in Washington, and were major organizations that Fulton believed should be courted as potential clients. While in Connecticut, LeSchack would stay with his folks.

When LeSchack was in Newtown, he would spend time becoming more familiar with both Fulton's technology as well as his business operations. He also spent more time learning about the "civilian" capabilities of Intermountain Aviation in Marana. This was simple to arrange since Bob was one of Intermountain's "directors." In Washington, LeSchack began writing proposals and making contacts. As part of business development, he wrote a piece describing potential applications in the resource development business; it was published in the Engineering and Mining Journal. He wrote another piece covering Skyhook mechanics and applications in detail; that was published in the U.S. Naval Institute Proceedings.

LeSchack learned many things from this attempt to establish a business venture with Bob's company, and not all of them had to do with business. He learned more about Bob, the man, the inventor, the writer, and the adventurer. He learned that while Coldfeet's use of Skyhook was an extraordinarily difficult concept to get across to unusually conservative military minds, *it could be done*, if one could find a high-ranking champion to batter down opposition by dint of rank and forcefulness. This was especially so if your parent organization's stock in trade, like ONR, was the selling of new technological ideas. The same thing is far more difficult to accomplish in the civilian world unless the top dog declares *that it will happen*, and has the money to make it so. New ideas have enormous difficulty in moving ahead in a milieu in which new ideas are a foreign concept—which LeSchack was to learn, occurs at many organizations.

He learned that in many ways, Bob's brain worked much the way LeSchack's did—Bob like LeSchack, was left-handed, and therefore, right-brained. This was not always necessarily a good thing.

LeSchack also learned more about himself; he had more free time to ruminate over CIA's "emotional health" question that he found so disturbing—*are you getting enough?* The trip from Washington to Connecticut was some five hours each way. And he had time alone in his old family bedroom several evenings every other week. Plenty of time for rumination. He determined that he still loved Virginia, for the very reasons he was attracted to her in the first instance—her beauty, her intelligence, and her sense of humor. But his mind had the time now to make unfortunate computations which, for example, suggested he had made love to Simone more times in three months than he now had with Virginia in three years. To be fair, he tried to factor in the time he was away on various missions; nonetheless, that computation did not augur well, LeSchack thought, for a "marriage made in heaven." Over that three-year period, LeSchack had certainly, and most delicately, brought up the subject of more frequent love-making with Virginia, however, all he could determine was that from time to time, when she was ready, she would signal, "I'm in the mood." "What a dreadful waste of a gorgeous body," thought LeSchack, disconsolately, stuffing that unpleasant reality deep down in his mental archives, out of sight.

He began to keep a notebook in which he scribbled down his sexual fantasies. Intuitively, he knew this was *not* a good sign. Especially when he noticed that as time went on the fantasies were becoming more elaborate and increasingly lascivious. He also dredged up long ago thoughts about what he would do with his life if he *couldn't* make love to women— if, for example, his balls were shot off in battle, or some other catastrophe had occurred rendering him sexually impotent. Those erstwhile thoughts all suggested that as compensation—or sublimation—his daredevil adventures—parachuting or Skyhook pickups, for example—and exploration of ever-more dangerous faraway places would likely increase. That would be LeSchack's substitution— *sans* sex.

There was one other passion that inflamed LeSchack besides women— classical music. Alas, he was beginning to recognize also that Virginia simply did not seem to have appreciation for Beethoven and Mozart, LeSchack's favorites. Their music could bring him to tears, much as could consummation of an exquisite amour. That lack of appreciation became patently obvious not only to LeSchack but to Virginia's Uncle Charlie one Sunday afternoon. LeSchack, Virginia and her family were visiting Uncle Charlie at his Washington home. Uncle Charlie was a Navy man and a musician. In fact, he had then just recently retired as a commander with 49 years of active duty service, a record likely exceeded only by Admiral Hyman Rickover, the father of the nuclear Navy. Uncle Charlie and Admiral Rickover had achieved that longevity for the same reasons: both officers, whether they were loved or hated by their superiors, were clearly favored by Congress. Over and over again, when the Navy wanted to retire them, the Congress passed special bills keeping them on active duty because the *congressmen liked them.* For many years, Uncle Charlie had been the leader of the United States Navy Band. Not surprisingly, Uncle Charlie and LeSchack found common cause in music and the Navy.

On this particular Sunday, family members were roaming all over Uncle Charlie's house, drinks in hand. Not surprisingly, Uncle Charlie had a "music room" in his home and his stereo, playing non-stop classical music, like a magnet, drew LeSchack in. He sat down in an otherwise empty room as the final movement of Beethoven's Seventh was approaching its majestic crescendo. As it did so, tears started streaming down LeSchack's cheeks; it was just at the moment that Virginia walked in, obviously searching for him, with Uncle Charlie close behind her. "Oh Len, stop crying. That's embarrassing—seeing a grown man cry!" It is not clear whether Uncle Charlie, well known in the family as a "ladies man," was following the frequently astounding motion of Virginia's exquisite hips as she swished into the music room, or whether he was drawn in by hearing the final magnificent bars of the symphony. Whatever the reason, when he heard Virginia's unfeeling comment to LeSchack, Uncle Charlie gently took her hand and said simply, "There, there, my dear, *I certainly understand* why he's crying. Come, let's leave him for a moment by himself."

In May 1965 LeSchack served his second ACDUTRA, this time at the Navy's amphibious base at Little Creek, Virginia. It was the first of several prescribed two-week training courses that would qualify him for his new "intelligence" designator in the Naval Reserve. The Little Creek course specifically covered beach and amphibious warfare intelligence. Several of his instructors had recently returned from advisor duty in Viet Nam. LeSchack got the sense from them that the general malaise expressed by Dr. Dan's Special Forces colleagues, also returning from advisor duty there in 1961 and 1962, had not dissipated, but had gotten worse. In that two-week training period LeSchack obtained a much better appreciation and understanding for what the Navy called the "Alligator Navy."

By the beginning of summer, both LeSchack and Bob Fulton recognized that it appeared to be hopeless to convince non-military organizations of the potential for Skyhook applications in remote areas. With the ever-increasing action in and over the jungles of Southeast Asia, the DOD had increased the level of contract work for production of Skyhook gear for military purposes. Therefore, Bob Fulton was beginning to devote more time to military activities, in any event. And, for reasons that LeSchack could not actually fathom, he was not unhappy with their decision to call it quits. Also, there had been further conversations with AINA about the post in Montréal, although nothing was yet definite. LeSchack was comfortable in remaining at their apartment, reading during the mornings, swimming at the pool during the summer afternoons, and taking Virginia out for dinner when she returned from work. Now thirty years old, LeSchack had learned that, for him, providence did, in fact, provide—so he waited not impatiently.

In July LeSchack, the AINA, and the Canadian Corporation for the 1967 World's Fair negotiated an employment agreement that LeSchack liked. It was with great pleasure and a bit of wry amusement, however, that he accepted his position with the World's Fair Corporation. Pleasure because Montréal was the city where ten years earlier his first lover had lived—and where they passionately made love together. He had fond memories of that city.

The amusement for LeSchack, the quintessential American, was to be offered the position in the first place, owing to the political situation that then prevailed in Québec. In that era, Montréal and the whole Province of Québec were rife with French Canadian ferment, talk of separation from Canada, and terrorist activities by leftist fringe political groups. This overlaid a quiet, long prevailing anti-Americanism. The mere fact that he got the job was an indication that, as hard as the World's Fair Corporation had searched, it had not been able to identify a person, first in Québec and second in all of Canada who possessed the appropriate requirements. That position called for a person knowledgeable of the Polar Regions; had contacts with polar officers around the world; had the administrative experience necessary for the job; and was available at this time to take the position. *And* who could speak French. LeSchack qualified in all these areas through his extensive Navy Arctic and Antarctic experience *and* from living and working in Paris.

346

LeSchack had accepted the job in Montréal, savoring the idea of returning to this most European city in North America. He and Virginia moved to Montréal and found an attractive two-bedroom high-rise apartment on the western side of the mountain, Mount Royal. He already had the makings of a social network in the city because, Victor, his old classmate from RPI, had returned there and married his childhood sweetheart, who LeSchack also knew. They and LeSchack and Giselle had often double-dated a decade earlier.

During the course of several months of orientation, LeSchack became familiar with the structure and working of the World's Fair Corporation; he also took time to reacquaint himself with Montréal. He discovered that the World's Fair Corporation was what Canadians call a "Crown Corporation." This means, in effect that although it is controlled by the government, the corporation need not follow civil service rules for salary, tenure and such, so that it can be more free-wheeling. In the case of the World's Fair Corporation, the effect of this crown corporation status was to permit the developing of a corporate structure that would be a nightmare to any business consultant: At the top was a high-ranking diplomat. Directly under him was a retired Canadian Army colonel. The colonel brought in many of his retired Army buddies to staff his office. Below that were mid-level civil servants "on loan" from their parent agencies. What "on loan" means in this context is that memos were circulated earlier throughout each department in the over-staffed civil service bureaucracy requesting personnel. The request to ministers and department heads was to choose "highly imaginative officers who could function well in a non-standard, artistic-type environment to 'enhance chances for the World's Fair to become a commercial and artistic success.'" As any experienced government bureaucrat knows, however, such a memo means, "at last! We have a legitimate way of dumping dead wood," which is, otherwise, nearly impossible to do, with the hope that such drones never return.

Beneath these layers were the actual worker bees. But yet, more layering. The top level of the "worker bee" structure were artistic types from various museums, art galleries and design centers who brought to the work place extreme right-brained thinking, uncertain sexual preferences, and absolutely no capability of interacting in a positive manner either up or down the chain of command. Beneath them, another level of bureaucrats from various agencies; political hacks who obtained their jobs through patronage, because after all, this was a political environment that the Fair was operating in; and finally the technocrats who actually developed the theme pavilions as they were, in fact, seen at the 1967 World's Fair. LeSchack was amongst these lower rung employees.

For LeSchack's first five months in Montréal, the work was pleasantly interesting, if not inspiring. There were an extraordinary number of meetings; they appeared to serve more as forums for individual officers to hear themselves talk than to produce concrete results. To LeSchack, not much of value was being accomplished but, most assuredly, much paper was generated. His immediate superior was a retired Royal Canadian Navy officer, Captain Tony Pickard, a man LeSchack took to quickly. He agreed with LeSchack's assessment of the World's Fair's unwieldy structure. They frequented a nearby bar after work hours for martinis; this assisted them to arrive at their mutual conclusion. And to talk of their respective navies, and tell sea stories to one another.

LeSchack and Virginia's new social life was far more interesting than was his work, as well as far more vibrant than their previous social life elsewhere. This was not thanks to Victor and his wife, Hortensia, who like the wives of most of LeSchack's friends, Virginia did not like. It was due to their introduction to Hortensia's brother, Felix, who came with a "trophy" girlfriend, Annabelle, who *Virginia did like*. Felix and Annabelle were social butterflies and were well-connected in Montréal society. And that, Virginia liked! Frankly, so did LeSchack. They went to concerts, art exhibits and the ballet together and often dined together. This was far more sophisticated than the Montréal of cheap dates consisting of hot smoked meat sandwiches, French fries, known there as *"frites,"* and beer, that he and Giselle did for dates on a student's budget, ten years earlier. On the other hand, for LeSchack, there had been far more inspired loving during that earlier epoch. On reflection, it seemed that perhaps Annabelle and Virginia were more kindred spirits than any of the other wives had been; coincidentally, LeSchack divined that Felix did not get much action either.

Virginia certainly was a consummate and gracious hostess, however. During the autumn of 1965 Paul-Émile Victor, the director of the *Expéditions Polaires Françaises,* was in Montréal representing France with respect to the Polar Regions Pavilion. LeSchack invited him to their home where Virginia had prepared a splendid dinner. As LeSchack had expected, Paul-Émile gallantly and effusively kissed Virginia's hand upon entering their apartment, announcing that she "was even more beautiful than I remembered you to be when you dined with me on my *péniche* in Paris." Virginia was simply enchanted by his Gallic charm.

On the first week of November, LeSchack, along with a number of other Expo-67 officers, would be asked to fly to Europe for a round of meetings with representatives of other countries that would be exhibiting at the various Theme Pavilions. LeSchack's itinerary called for him to visit France, the USSR, Finland, Sweden, Norway, England, Belgium and Denmark, all countries with significant polar interests. It would be a long trip for LeSchack. He wouldn't return home to Montréal until a few days before Christmas. Although it was never clear whether any of the activities of LeSchack, the Polar Regions Project Officer, were used on Expo's behalf at the time the 1967 World's Fair opened—for he was no longer there then—it was to be an extraordinarily valuable trip for LeSchack, *the intelligence officer,* for it would increase his exposure to government-to-government diplomacy and clandestine espionage, both of which would strongly influence the rest of his life.

LeSchack and Virginia, summer 1963, returning from France aboard ship. He had just been released from active duty a few months earlier, and he was in Paris for the spring and summer working at the Expéditions Polaires Françaises on a study grant from Arctic Institute of North America. They were reluctantly returning, and on their way to the University of Wisconsin so that he could continue his studies in geophysics.

Montreal to Moscow, 1965: KGB: "You are from the Ukraine, are you not, Mr. LeSchack?"

The Setting from Russia with love

The gears automatically begin to turn in Moscow whenever someone applies for a visa to enter the Soviet Union. The visa application, possibly accompanied by a report from the KGB Residency in the country where it was submitted, is ordinarily referred to an evaluating officer in the 7th (tourist) Department of the Second Chief Directorate. He requests from the computerized records of the 8th Department, the central KGB archives, and the operational archives of the Foreign Directorate all information that the KGB possesses about the applicant. This may include intelligence gathered over the years by KGB agents as well as data from open sources. The evaluating officer then notifies other KGB departments likely to have a special interest in the foreigner because of his occupation or background.....

After consultations among various departments and evaluation of what is known about the foreigner, the KGB decides whether to grant the visa. If it is issued, the KGB tentatively decides whether it will try to neutralize, influence, recruit, or merely watch him. This decision is based upon estimates of whether the visitor is a spy, his potential value as a controlled Soviet agent or unwitting purveyor of disinformation, and his vulnerability to recruitment.

KGB: The Secret Work of Soviet Secret Agents, by John Barron, 1974, in his chapter entitled, "Surveillance and Seduction."

Chronology of Relevant Events

June, 1962: Spy mission, "Project Coldfeet" successful; Lieutenant LeSchack and Major Smith return with substantial intelligence haul from Soviet Station NP-8

Summer, 1962: *"I understand your people have recently been visiting our Arctic drifting stations." –KGB officer to CIA officer at Washington diplomatic cocktail party, as told to LeSchack by a CIA aviator who was a key participant in Coldfeet.*

October, 1962: *Cuban Missile Crisis; U.S. and USSR come as close to a nuclear war as ever occurred during nearly 50 years of the Cold War.*

1963: *Major Smith sent to Moscow as U.S. Assistant Air Attaché.*

June, 1964: *Major Smith kicked out of the USSR, persona non grata. Meets LeSchack at dinner party back in Washington. "Jim, did they kick you out because they knew about Coldfeet?" he asks. "No Len," Jim responds, shrugging his shoulders, suggesting he really didn't know, "I don't think so."*

December, 1965: *LeSchack shows up in Moscow working for the Canadian Government—"Welcome to the USSR, Lieutenant LeSchack. We have read about your Arctic work in the ONR 'Naval Research Review! Your are from the Ukraine, are you not?"—KGB officers and operatives upon meeting him.*

Leonard LeSchack, the Cold Warrior, and now confirmed as an intelligence officer in the Naval Reserve, was offered an unusual opportunity to visit the Soviet Union, then the avowed enemy of the United States. It was the height of the Cold War, just three years after the successful completion of the spy mission, Project Coldfeet. That mission that he had conceived had specifically targeted the USSR. Although released from active duty just two years earlier, LeSchack would officially remain a U. S. naval officer unless he resigned his commission.

The opportunity resulted from his employment with the Canadian Corporation for the 1967 World's Fair in Montréal—EXPO-67. Five months after joining EXPO-67, it became clear that for a variety of reasons, LeSchack needed to meet with officials in Moscow. The Soviets had by far the largest polar interests of any country in the world. While the U.S. has Alaska, and Canada has a long Arctic coastline, neither of these countries have the population, nor the industrial interests in the Arctic as had the Soviet Union. Accordingly, it was clear that no World's Fair Polar Regions Pavilion would be complete without Soviet participation. Further, the Soviets, like many other countries, were planning on having their own "Country Pavilion" and wanted to assure cooperation with the Canadians. Therefore, it was determined to send LeSchack, as Polar Regions Project Officer, to Moscow for coordination.

He was both elated at the prospects of the trip and, at the same time, in view of his background in espionage, extremely concerned about the potential political repercussions. In fact, he was concerned about his own safety, should he undertake such a trip. Firstly, LeSchack knew from a CIA contact that the Soviets had gotten wind of the clandestine incursion onto their "territory;" but did they know it was by him and his partner in Project Coldfeet, Air Force Major Jim Smith? Secondly, Major Smith, a consummate intelligence officer and Russian linguist, had been assigned to duty in Moscow as Assistant U.S. Air Attaché shortly after the conclusion of Coldfeet, and within a year of that assignment, had been kicked out of the USSR, *persona non grata*. Was there a connection? Had the Soviets discovered *it was their incursion* and used it as an excuse to get rid of Smith? Because military attachés have the same diplomatic immunity as do diplomats, the Soviets could not have done much else to him.

Only a year before LeSchack's contemplated trip to the USSR, he had bumped into the recently returned Major Smith at a Washington dinner party and had asked him, point blank, whether Smith was declared *persona non grata* because of Project Coldfeet. Smith thought not, but LeSchack would never be sure. Only two years earlier, Professor Barghoorn of Yale University, while visiting the Soviet Union was picked up for "spying" by the KGB and thrown in jail. In fact, he was merely a pawn, caught up in the Cold War "tit-for-tat" game, "you throw my spy in jail, we throw your spy in jail." In October 1963, the FBI had captured three KGB officers in New York, armed with legitimate evidence of their spying. Two of the KGB officers had diplomatic immunity and were released. The third, Igor Aleksandrovich Ivanov, did not, and was thrown in jail. In response, the Soviets randomly grabbed Barghoorn off the streets of Moscow to force release of Ivanov in New York. President Kennedy, assured by all U.S. intelligence agencies that Barghoorn was not spying for the country, personally intervened and demanded that the Kremlin release the professor. They did. But that's what it took: the President's intercession.

LeSchack knew that should he accept the assignment to Moscow he would have *no diplomatic immunity,* as did Major Smith, and further, he knew that, although representing the Canadian World's Fair Corporation, he would still be traveling under a *U.S. passport.* Would President Lyndon Johnson intervene on *LeSchack's behalf* should he be caught in a situation similar to Barghoorn's? Even if, in the unlikely event Johnson chose to do as Kennedy did before him, could this President honestly say that LeSchack *was not a spy,* considering his background? He felt that his only hope for safety centered on his assumption that the Soviets would not likely provoke an incident with a representative of the Canadian Government at a time when they strongly wished to exhibit at its World's Fair. This uncertainty, however, dogged LeSchack throughout the preparations for the Soviet trip, and certainly, throughout the entire period he spent in the Soviet Union.

LeSchack also did not wish to embarrass the Canadian Government *vis à vis* his own government should an incident, provoked or otherwise, arise as a result of his trip. As a result, he felt he needed to alert a senior officer of the World's Fair Corporation of the potential for an unpleasant incident should the Soviets choose to create one. He felt he was obliged at least to officially alert such senior officer (and that officer only) and give him an opportunity to decline sending him, should he feel it was prudent to do so. But how to do this, wondered LeSchack, without sending a sensitive memo up the chain that would be routed through a labyrinth of whom he knew to be geopolitically inexperienced bureaucrats?

Ultimately, he began discussing it with his immediate superior, retired RCN Captain Tony Pickard—a man LeSchack thought could be trusted with such information. He assumed the Captain would have an understanding of his unusual concerns as a result of years of military experience and of numerous deployments overseas resulting in associations with diplomatic personnel at foreign ports. The Captain did, indeed have such an understanding of the problem, and said he felt it best to discuss it with a fellow theme pavilion curator, M. Bertrand. Bertrand was on loan from the Department of External Affairs (the Canadian State Department). Should this career Foreign Service officer chose to do so, he could bureaucratically go directly for assistance to the senior World's Fair official, a diplomat of ambassadorial rank from his own Department of External Affairs. By so doing, he could circumvent the undoubtedly leaky chain of bureaucrats in between who, at best, lacked understanding of Cold War politics, and at worst, might leak sensitive information that could jeopardize LeSchack's assignment.

Canada is officially a bi-lingual country. Canadians know this. As a practical matter, however, it can generally be assumed that if you speak fluently in both English and French, you are a French Canadian. Canadians living outside Québec are rarely truly bilingual, largely because they have never taken the time to learn the other language. So it was not surprising then, or even now for that matter, that members of the Department of External Affairs are largely French Canadian, because upon entry into that service, they already know two of the world's diplomatic languages, and are more amenable to learning additional languages, as necessary. The point is that it appeared that LeSchack's competence in French, unexpected because he was American, made a substantial difference in the outcome of how he was perceived when he entered M. Bertrand's office to broach the subject of the proposed Moscow trip.

LeSchack's office was one of these completely soulless cubicle offices that had become the rage in office decor. In the adjacent cubicle sat Mlle. Ouellette, the beautiful and vivacious secretary for M. Bertrand, and a young woman who sent LeSchack's head spinning every time LeSchack encountered her. Because of the proximity of the desks and telephones in the adjacent cubicles, there was no such thing as a private conversation. And normally, in the course of daily business, LeSchack spoke in English over the phone, since everyone that he needed to talk to understood that language and frankly, he felt more comfortable using it. On one occasion, however, shortly before the meeting with Bertrand, LeSchack received a phone call from Jean Dumont, his old *Expéditions*

Polaires Françaises colleague with whom he had worked in Paris. That colleague, a glaciologist and ex-French military paratrooper, was in Montréal, and had heard LeSchack was working there now and wanted to renew their acquaintance.

This was a wonderful surprise for LeSchack, recalling the fun times they had in Paris together. Not surprisingly, upon hearing Jean's voice, he began an excited and animated phone conversation in French, as they often had in Paris, regaling each other with outlandish jump stories, as paratroopers are wont to do. Mlle. Ouellette overheard the conversation, as she could not have helped from so doing in those cubicle conditions, and apparently with some excitement, reported to her boss, M. Bertrand, that "M. Len LeSchack speaks French! Did you know that?" It was something she had never expected to hear from an American.

The ramifications of all this became clear to him when he entered M. Bertrand's office. LeSchack not only needed to broach the subject of his intelligence background, prior to the trip to Moscow, but also to request a letter of introduction for him from the senior World's Fair official. He wished that official apprized of the possible international complications owing to his background. The letter of introduction, he felt, would be as close to a "safe-conduct pass" as he could hope to obtain for his trip to the USSR.

LeSchack's meeting with the diplomat was quick and to the point, once he laid out the story and his concerns about his previous intelligence background, a background that he knew at least a seasoned diplomat would understand. M. Bertrand listened, nodded, and asked him only one question, "Are you currently under orders from your government?" LeSchack told him he was not. The diplomat's response was positive. Fine, he said. I will discuss this matter directly with Ambassador Dupuis, the senior officer of the World's Fair Corporation. "And, by the way, Len," Bertrand observed with an exaggerated Gallic wink, "Mlle. Ouellette ran in to my office the other day and quite excitedly told me she overheard you, *an American*, speaking French over the phone. She appeared quite delighted. You might consider paying some attention to Mlle. Ouellette. I believe she would like that. And thank you for your candor in that other matter. I will take care of it for you."

LeSchack thought that little bit of "French relatedness" with the seasoned and experienced foreign service officer made all the difference in how his concern was received, which might otherwise have been considered a bit theatrical. He also thought, a bit ruefully, that had he not been married to Virginia at that time, and had he not still subscribed to a certain Nineteenth Century morality, he certainly would have enjoyed paying *a lot of attention to Mlle. Ouellette.*

As plans for the Moscow trip developed, it became clear that LeSchack would also need to spend time visiting the polar activities of other countries in Europe as a part of what originally had been planned only as a trip to the Soviet Union. This was fine with him since he had developed friendships with colleagues in many of the polar organizations in Europe over the years. As it turned out, his first stop was Paris, and it was late in the autumn when he arrived. The *marronniers* were dropping their chestnuts on the Champs Élysées, and the smell of roasting nuts was everywhere. It was a gorgeous fall in Paris. His colleagues at the *Expéditions Polaires* invited him to a wine and escargot festival in the basement of the polar institute. The party in the basement among his old colleagues was fine and the wine and escargots, drenched in garlic butter, were good. But LeSchack, always the paranoid intelligence man, felt uneasy about the party being held in this particular basement. He knew from his earlier studies there that the *Expéditions Polaires* building had been taken over by the Nazis when they entered Paris in 1941. This basement, it seemed to LeSchack, would have been perfect for "interrogations." He overcame this fleeting concern by drinking more wine. As it was, the windowless basement with the solid, soundproof walls, were just the thing to contain the increasingly raucous joviality of LeSchack and his wine-drinking polar colleagues.

That autumn in Paris was good for LeSchack. He knew that his stay in the Soviet Union would be much different from these lovely days in Paris, and he would have to be extremely careful and continually on his guard. Accordingly, he took every opportunity he could to revisit his old haunts and restaurants, to go to the Paris Opera and listen to his favorite, *"La Bohème,"* and to take advantage of all the parties that he and the Canadian entourage with which he traveled were invited to attend. He felt comfortable here in Paris, where he once lived and studied, whereas he knew his life would be stifled at his next stop, Moscow, if he ever actually got there. At this point, after a week in Paris, his intelligence officer's mind began to wonder.

It had been six weeks since the World's Fair Corporation had submitted his visa application to the Soviet Embassy in Ottawa, and LeSchack had not yet received it; other members of the entourage, all going on to Moscow also, already had. And their plane to Moscow was scheduled to leave le Bourget in two days. What was the hold up? Had they gotten wind of Coldfeet? Or where they just concerned that his father had been born in Russia, and perhaps LeSchack would be planning to meet up with family still there (something that was frowned upon for westerners, particularly Americans, to do in 1965, still the height of the Cold War). In any event, LeSchack suspected the delay meant his application was receiving special scrutiny.

He continued enjoying Paris. On one evening after a particularly satisfying dinner on the Left Bank, he passed a bookshop that displayed a book in the window for which he had been searching for several years, ever since he saw Major Smith reading it on one of their missions together. The French translation of David Douglas Duncan's book "Treasures of the Kremlin" was in plain view. Knowing that he might have the opportunity to visit the Armory in the Kremlin (assuming he got his visa in time), he eagerly returned the next day and purchased it. Slowly he began plodding through it since, of course, the book was written in a style more suitable to artists, than were the French technical and naval books with which LeSchack was more familiar.

****

On the scheduled departure date from le Bourget to Moscow, LeSchack, along with the rest of the World's Fair people going to the USSR, waited in the airport. Although everyone else had already been issued their visas, LeSchack was still awaiting his. It was at the last possible moment that an official of the Canadian Embassy in Paris carrying LeSchack's visa, just issued from the Soviet Embassy, arrived in front of the Departure Lounge, waving his visa. Fifteen minutes later the Canadian World's Fair entourage was aboard a four-engine Aeroflot aircraft that appeared to LeSchack to be a marginal copy of the twin-tailed Constellation.

Although it had been a wonderful, pleasant autumn in Paris when he left, he and the Canadian entourage, after an uneventful flight, landed late that night at Sheremetyvo Airport, in mid-winter Moscow. While the entourage milled around the airport waiting help from the Canadian Embassy personnel to get them sorted out, LeSchack found an official foreign currency exchange kiosk where he was able to exchange U.S. Dollars for Russian rubles at the official exchange rate. In those days, rubles were only legally available within the USSR, so that it was not practicable to have obtained them at, for example, a Canadian bank. From earlier experiences traveling out of North America, LeSchack had learned how important it is to have some currency of the host country at the outset of the visit.

His Canadian colleagues derided him for not waiting to exchange his hard currency with free-lance money traders on the street in the morning at a much better exchange rate. Right! Thought LeSchack. The easiest entrapment scene there is. There were likely plenty more opportunities for him to become entrapped than with illegal currency exchanges. LeSchack, the intelligence officer, felt that if it was necessary to take risks that involved possible entrapment, he thought such a risk should be taken only for something worthwhile, like valuable intelligence data, not for cash or women. As it turned out, the kind of vision or ability to "second guess" that people trained as intelligence officers often develop, came to the fore here. The Soviets had just run one of their periodic sweeps to rid the city of illegal moneychangers, and those of LeSchack's World's Fair colleagues expecting to reap a bonanza trading hard currency on Red Square, in front of the Kremlin, found themselves out of luck. And so he became the "bank of last resort" for those early days in Moscow, since he was the only one with rubles.

The Canadian group spent the next several days preparing for discussions with, and presentations to, their Soviet counterparts. Ambassador Dupuis, the senior World's Fair official, attended most of these preparation sessions. He had a wonderful bit of pantomime, loaded with pure Cold-War symbolism that he frequently used during the preparation sessions: if one of the presenters had something laudatory to say about the Soviet hosts, Dupuis would make the signal "to speak louder," and then point his finger toward the inevitable crystal chandelier. His pantomime was clear: "Speak to the chandelier, folks. There's a hidden microphone up there. Let them hear something good about themselves for a change. It's good politics!"

Early on in their stay in Moscow, LeSchack and one of his other World's Fair colleagues, Dr. Fred Roots, met with Robert Ford, then the Canadian Ambassador to the USSR. Ambassador Ford was impressive. He was the epitome of what LeSchack thought an ambassador should be—tall, elegant, knowledgeable, a foreign service professional, and most importantly, spoke Russian. Not only did he speak Russian, he was reputed to be able to write poetry in the Russian language, an ability that endeared him to his hosts. Ambassador Ford walked with a limp, and used a cane to assist him. It was not clear to LeSchack whether the limp was an old war wound or whether the remnants of polio, which in the early part of the Twentieth Century still capriciously afflicted North Americans. Either way, the limp added to the ambassador's panache, and it was reputed that Premier Khrushchev went out of his way at official diplomatic functions to assure there was a ramp or easy steps specifically installed so as to ease the route for Ambassador Ford. It was at this reception with Ambassador Ford that LeSchack got his first taste of real Russian Vodka and true Caspian Sea caviar.

The first few days in Moscow were consumed with World's Fair meetings between members of the Canadian entourage and their Russian counterparts. There were also splendid social events, official cocktail parties and dinners, and trips to concerts and ballet, put on by the Soviet hosts for the Canadian visitors.

LeSchack loved it all, and although he was only 30, he was comfortable in this diplomatic milieu, since he had already experienced the rarefied atmosphere on Capitol Hill that surrounds senators and Congressmen in Washington, and ambassadors and attachés in Buenos Aires. Nonetheless, despite all this high-level conviviality, he also was cognizant that there were KGB officers all around, and LeSchack was determined not to make a slip. He never drank at official Soviet functions, although he pretended to.

At the conclusion of the formal discussions and presentations, the entourage that had accompanied LeSchack to Moscow departed. He remained another ten days to complete Polar Regions Pavilion business discussions with his Soviet counterparts. On his own during that period, LeSchack's paranoia increased, and with cause. He could sense that he was never alone, and that he was constantly being watched, and tailed. He learned to expect a phone call each day, at about two in the morning. When he roused himself out of bed to answer, there was a grunt of some sort at the other end of the line, and the caller would hang up. At which point, with some irritation, he would stagger back to bed. The phone call was simply a check to see if he was safely in his hotel room and not out creating anti-Soviet mischief.

Most of the Soviets that LeSchack met as part of his official meetings on behalf of the Polar Regions Pavilion were scientists and technologists experienced in the Polar Regions. But not all were. On one officially sanctioned meeting, at the Hydro-Meteorological Ministry in Moscow, LeSchack was met by an interpreter, supplied by this ministry, and they were ushered into the sumptuous office of the deputy director. It was a large office with oriental tapestries hanging from the walls. Soon this office began to fill up with a dozen or so men and women invited to the meeting. As each person filed into the office LeSchack inquired of the interpreter, "who is that person? What is their position?" The interpreter, a young man, responded to each request, and LeSchack jotted this information down in his notebook. There were oceanographers, meteorologists, geographers and sea-going officers, all with polar experience. All were dressed in business attire.

The deputy director was about to start the meeting when one last man arrived, a bit rumpled-looking, and in casual attire. To LeSchack, he looked out of place at this meeting. He asked his interpreter who this new man was. The young and not so politically experienced interpreter said simply, "Oh he's from the Foreign Department." Immediately there was a flurry of dissenting murmurs from the audience assembled, and the young interpreter "corrected" himself. "Ah no, he's an engineer!" "Aha" thought LeSchack, hoping that there was no change of expression on his face, "We have discovered the KGB man in our midst!" "Would the interpreter's verbal misstep have been recognized by a non-intelligence officer?" LeSchack wondered. He had suspected this man as soon as he entered the office. Bit by bit over LeSchack's career, he had learned that spooks from all over the world, of all political persuasions seem, almost instantly, to recognize each other by some sixth sense.

As the meeting progressed, LeSchack spoke about the Canadian World's Fair Polar Regions Pavilion, and what Soviet polar artifacts he would like to have exhibited there. It became clear during this meeting that most of the people he was speaking with had serious polar experience, either in the Arctic, along the Northern Sea Route, on Arctic Ocean drifting stations, or in the Antarctic during the International Geophysical Year and afterwards. It was clear that a number of people in the room had worked in both Polar Regions. To establish relatedness with these Soviet scientists, LeSchack spoke of his own Arctic and Antarctic scientific experience and research. He strongly felt that his Arctic and Antarctic military experiences, with the possible exception of Project Coldfeet, which was still highly classified, was already known to senior members of his audience, thanks to the resources of the Soviet intelligence services.

During the course of the meeting, LeSchack inquired whether he could visit the Soviet Maritime Museum while he was in Moscow. The Maritime Museum was administered by the Hydro-Meteorological Ministry. The response was, of course, we will take you there. LeSchack then cautiously asked whether he would be permitted to take photographs inside the museum that might be used in the Polar Regions Pavilion at the World's Fair. During this time, at the height of the Cold War, the Soviets were known to be adamantly opposed to foreigners taking photos of almost anything in the Soviet Union. Accordingly, LeSchack knew that official permission would be required, and this would be the best time to request such permission, while the deputy director was in attendance.

LeSchack phrased his question as diplomatically as he could and watched carefully while his interpreter translated the question into Russian. All eyes in the office, including those of the deputy director, involuntarily turned toward the "engineer." After a brief moment of thought, the KGB man discreetly nodded a Yes. Then the deputy director spoke to LeSchack. "Yes, of course you can." LeSchack's intelligence instincts had been confirmed.

As the meeting broke up, the KGB man, Nudlemann, came up to

LeSchack and, with a carefully appraising look said, "I'll be taking you to the Museum, tomorrow. You know, you spent the same year in Antarctica that I did." LeSchack then became aware of just how important was the relatedness he had created with his intelligence counterpart: Nudlemann had spent the International Geophysical Year at the Soviet station, "Mirny," during the same time that LeSchack was at the American Byrd Station, a remarkable coincidence, since not many persons of any nation wintered over in the Antarctic during the IGY. Nudelmann had acted as the historian documenting the Soviet activities in the Antarctic for that period. He then went to his office and returned moments later with a three-volume history that he had written documenting this period, and gave it to LeSchack. Interesting, LeSchack thought, how mutually shared but unusual experiences can often transcend political differences.

When LeSchack went to the Maritime Museum, he was struck by the setting; it seemed as though he had been there before, despite the fact that this was his first trip to Moscow. The way the streets, buildings and the overall setting appeared to him, all seemed familiar. There were overhead power cables to provide electricity to streetcars and these also appeared similar to someplace that he had previously experienced. LeSchack wondered about this as he and his retinue from the Hydro-Meteorological Ministry proceeded to the Museum. He also wondered whether the stress that he was under in this closely monitored environment had not begun to play tricks with his mind.

How much did his Soviet hosts really know about him?

In addition to visiting the Canadian Embassy, he had also visited the Science Attaché at his own Embassy. An appointment was made by phone from his hotel, the Sovietskaya, a phone LeSchack expected was monitored. Although the phone conversation was innocuous, his greeting by the ubiquitous Soviet guard in front of the U.S. Embassy was unnerving. The guard's job was not so much to protect the embassy— there are US Marines there for that purpose—but to assure that Soviet citizens don't go in. As LeSchack approached the embassy gate in civilian attire, the Soviet guard, while saying nothing to him, or in any way impeding his entrance, came to attention and smartly saluted him. In utter surprise, LeSchack stifled (he thought) the natural urge to return the salute. Was this a test, he wondered, a way of confirming a visitor's military status? Or did he already know LeSchacks military status? Was this performance for his benefit, or was this standard procedure for Soviet guards in front of the U.S. Embassy? In either event, it unnerved him.

He also had been startled, shortly before, when two of the many Soviet officers he met asked, or rather stated, in passable English, "Ah Mr. LeSchack, you are from the Ukraine, are you not?" LeSchack was not, of course, but his father was born in Lvov. And from comments made to him by an elderly uncle who also had been born there, he expected there may still be family in the USSR. From the ramblings of the high level Soviet defector, Oleg Penkovskiy, as published in his memoir, there was a story about a Red Army major by the name of LeSchack—transliterated from the Cyrillic as Loshak in the book—who was the son-in-law of a senior Red Army general. The major was arrested by *"Smersh,"* tried by a military tribunal and was shot as a traitor to the Soviet Union for selling Red Army supplies on the black market. His description sounded much like one of LeSchack's family members. He too, had been born in Lvov, and was Jewish. Red flags, literally, went up for LeSchack! So not surprisingly, he was under considerable stress—all these unexpected questions floating about in his brain concerning his KGB dossier—and paranoia was a constant companion during this trip.

Nonetheless, he did have opportunities to take advantage of some of the less threatening aspects of Cold War Moscow. Ambassador Ford's wife, Thereza, a charming Brazilian lady, had personally taken LeSchack to a number of Soviet tourist attractions around the city. Owing to the fact that Ambassador Ford and she had another engagement the same night they had tickets to the opera—Boris Gudonov—she gave their tickets to LeSchack. He was absolutely delighted to watch and hear this quintessential Russian opera, as it was meant to be performed, on the stage of the Bolshoi Theater. He also had the opportunity to visit the Armory in the Kremlin, and see the treasures that were so eloquently described in David Douglas Duncan's book LeSchack purchased in Paris, just a few weeks earlier. He also began to travel by himself on the Moscow subway. It was difficult for him to determine whether he was *really alone* or being followed through all those crowds.

The Moscow subway system is that artwork in marble that Stalin had built. For sheer beauty (and cleanliness), it put to shame the New York subway system or the Paris Metro. But each evening as he returned to his hotel, the Sovietskaya, he had to pass by the watchful eyes of men, who frankly, looked exactly like old fashioned, right-out-of-central-casting, seedy hotel dicks. In reality, they were KGB officers. Intelligence officers develop a sixth-sense about such things. And of course, he would go to sleep each night, after a dreadfully served, boring, tasteless meal at the hotel restaurant, to await being awakened at two in the morning, just so that Soviet officialdom could see that he was safely in his room. Although LeSchack's training had prepared him for this, the constant surveillance was increasingly beginning to bother him.

At the conclusion of LeSchack's work in Moscow, he flew to Leningrad to visit the Arctic and Antarctic Institute. This organization sponsors scientific research for both Soviet Arctic drifting stations, and stations in the Antarctic. LeSchack's flight on Aeroflot was met by a delegation from the Arctic and Antarctic Institute. Not just picked up at the airport, the delegation met him at the foot of the ladder descending from the aircraft. Although LeSchack *might have wondered* what they knew about him in Moscow, *there was little doubt* upon his arrival in Leningrad; "Good morning, Lieutenant LeSchack," said the senior member of the delegation in English, "We have read about your work in the U.S. Naval Research Review (published by ONR)." With that introduction, LeSchack knew that, despite his clear affiliation with the Canadian World's Fair, both his scientific work as well as his U.S. military background, were known.

The delegation of official greeters accompanied him to the Institute where he met many of the staff and several scientists whose work and activities he had followed and cited in his own scientific publications. He was assigned Anya, a good-looking young English-speaking woman on the institute staff as his interpreter. She accompanied LeSchack all day throughout the many meetings he had. These related to World's Fair business, as well as to discussions with individual scientists whose names he knew from reading their books and papers. Because Leningrad, whose name has now reverted to its pre-revolutionary "Saint Petersburg," is the most beautiful of Russian cities, even in mid-winter, LeSchack wanted to go sightseeing. Anya obliged and took him across this city, showing him the Winter Palace, where the Russian Revolution of 1905 occurred, and the wide boulevards and statues. He specifically requested that they visit the Hermitage, Leningrad's magnificent museum of art, now housed in the Winter Palace.

The Hermitage Museum overlooks the Neva River. This museum contains one of the world's greatest collections of art. Included are extensive holdings of Italian Renaissance and French Impressionist paintings. The winter Palace was the winter home of Russian emperors before the Revolution of 1917.

For LeSchack, entrance into this museum was an education in Soviet behavior. There was a block-long line of Soviet citizens waiting to gain entrance. The line was moving at a glacial pace. LeSchack and Anya clearly would have to wait in the winter cold for hours to gain entrance, if they took their place in line. Anya told him that, "we will try and gain immediate entrance by requesting diplomatic status since you are an official guest from Canada." She led LeSchack to the head of the line and began presenting her story to the uniformed guard at the museum's entrance. *"Nyet,"* he said. Anya was not fazed. She did not move and she repeated her request. *"Nyet."* Again she did not move, and using slightly different words, repeated her request again. This exchange was repeated over and over again for at least ten minutes, with neither Anya nor the guard raising their voices nor appearing to show irritation. Eventually, after what seemed to LeSchack, Anya's hundredth request, the guard threw up his hands and said, *"Da, da, horosho,"* and waved them in. To LeSchack, this appeared to be the Soviet way to do business, and what he witnessed he believed was not at all unusual.

LeSchack was entranced. There were works of art in the Hermitage that have not been seen by non-Soviet citizens since 1917 owing to the difficulty of traveling there and especially since the "Iron Curtain had descended across Europe." The collection included some works by Rembrandt. He and Anya, who appeared quite knowledgeable of the art, had a most pleasurable afternoon together at the museum.

On another occasion, shortly before LeSchack left Leningrad, and the Soviet Union altogether, he and Anya, a married woman, were alone together. This was a far more unsettling experience for LeSchack. Anya was wearing a tight sweater that revealed ample breasts beneath. Around her neck she wore a necklace with an obvious *Star of David* dangling from the end of the chain and nestling comfortably between her breasts. "Uh Oh," thought LeSchack. "What's happening here?" 1965 was the height of the Cold War, and the Soviet Union was then celebrating a period of maximum atheism. Both Judaism and Christianity were strongly frowned upon. Communism was the religion. During this very trip on a guided tour through St. Basil's, the world-famous church on Moscow's Red Square, an official Intourist guide made gratuitously snide remarks about the beautiful church as once, long ago, being a place of worship, and stated baldly, "We don't believe in that anymore." In view of Anya's blatant display of a Jewish symbol — worn on the only occasion they were completely alone together — during this period of Soviet history, LeSchack had to ask himself, "Is this a classic setup, such as we learned about in intelligence school? How is this supposed to play out?"

Although not a practicing Jew, LeSchack was born of a Jewish family, and according to his father, the family in the Ukraine was certainly Jewish. Did Soviet intelligence research the religious status of his family, either in the Ukraine or in America? And had this research become a part of LeSchack's dossier as held by the KGB? They certainly knew he was from the Ukraine, and that he was not a Canadian, but an American naval officer. That was made clear to him earlier on during this trip. While continuing to talk amiably with Anya in their comfortably secluded room, her star bounced deliciously on her breasts with every very deliberate movement of her body. And, naturally enough for LeSchack, that elicited a clear and powerful reaction: desire, that sequel to danger, so eloquently expressed by William Manchester, was certainly bubbling furiously now in LeSchack's loins. He had felt it building up — in parallel with his fear and paranoia — throughout his stay in the Soviet Union, particularly so after the remainder of the Canadian delegation had departed and he was there on his own. And especially so, now that he was all alone with just her.

LeSchack began thinking at breakneck speed: "What is the end-game supposed to be? To ask Anya whether she is Jewish? Then what? If she says yes, what's next? An invitation to her apartment, to a clandestine synagogue, to a Hadassah meeting?" Any one of these events could be compromising and result in his being arrested for anti-Soviet behavior. He knew this from his recent intelligence training. He would then become a Cold War hostage like countless other unfortunate tourists, visiting professors—like Barghoorn—or businessmen. Perhaps even like Gary Powers. Or, perhaps this was simply more of LeSchack's paranoia. Perhaps this was only a coincidence, and Anya just saw the six-pointed star as a non-religious piece of jewelry that had a lovely, but non-symbolic shape. But LeSchack saw that necklace, nestled as it was between her ample warm breasts, as the key to entrapment.

In the end, he said nothing about the star dangling on her lovely breasts. But for the rest of his life he wondered what would have happened had he asked Anya about the necklace, and whether Anya was a "swallow," a woman trained by the KGB in the art of entrapment and co-option. Instead, he continued talking about polar matters, the beauty of Leningrad, and the pleasure they shared at the Hermitage. And then Anya sighed and said it was time for her to go home. LeSchack's hotel was not far from where they now were, and Anya pointed the direction, and quietly left. He, most pensively, wandered back to his hotel through the winter night, passing by the statue of Peter the Great on his horse. When possible, he walked close to store windows on Nevsky Prospekt so that he could surreptitiously use them as mirrors to determine whether he was being followed. Although he could not be sure, this seemed to be the first time in his whole stay in the Soviet Union that he felt that he probably was not trailed.

LeSchack left the next evening on a Finnair flight for Helsinki. His Institute hosts escorted him directly to the Finnair aircraft boarding ladder. Whether to insure that he got aboard, or simply as a diplomatic gesture, he could not be certain. What he was certain of was the magnitude of the stress that never left him while he was inside the Soviet Union. As soon as the flight got off the ground, he allowed his brain to slip into neutral, and he began to tremble. In the icy, winter of 1965, he had been "out in the cold" in every way possible. As a spy, of course; he was in the USSR as EXPO-67's "Polar Regions Project Officer," photographing and taking notes whenever and wherever he could, but not *all* his notes and photos were destined for EXPO-67. It was just three years after he had masterminded that successful intelligence mission against the Soviets, and only a year after his partner in that mission, the

U.S. Assistant Air Attaché in Moscow, was tossed out, *persona non grata*. Those thoughts had been with him constantly.

Sexually, he also was in the cold; he desperately needed to make love to a complaisant woman, more so now than ever, for as William Manchester had observed, "desire is the sequel to danger." And LeSchack felt that he had been in constant danger, whether real or imagined. On top of this, he agonized, "I haven't been regularly satisfied for the three years since I have been married," for Virginia, alas, was not a passionate woman like Giselle, Maisie, Elsa, Simone and Maureen all had earlier been. He vividly remembered the strain of spending time alone talking with the lovely Anya, a few days earlier, when he really just wanted to get into her pants, not talk—and he knew perfectly well she was a likely setup, a "swallow," in KGB parlance.

And finally, with the prescience of an intelligence officer, he sensed from message traffic from Montréal, that all his work for EXPO-67 would be in vain, owing to recent changes in office direction and politics back in the office, even in the short time he had been gone.

Flight time from Leningrad to Helsinki is only an hour. LeSchack could not wait till the aircraft crossed the border into Finland. On this nighttime flight, it was plain to see from the aircraft window just when that occurred. Once over Finnish territory, it seemed that there was a festival of lights below. It seemed as though every farmhouse had been lit up just to welcome him back to the Western World. With the plane commander's announcement that his aircraft was now over Finland, a stewardess began pushing a "duty free" cart of gifts, cigarettes, and liquor for purchase by the passengers. LeSchack had not had much to drink since the reception at Ambassador Ford's residence. At this moment he felt that, in aid of relieving some of the stress of the past ten days, he would enjoy getting a bit drunk in his hotel room in Helsinki. Accordingly, he took advantage of the passing cart and bought a bottle of French cognac, just to know there would be alcohol immediately available to him upon arrival. He promptly stowed his new treasure in his carry-on bag, and shortly thereafter, the plane began its descent into Helsinki.

An official driver from the Canadian Embassy in Helsinki was at the airport to pick LeSchack up and take him to the Palace Hotel. In short order he had checked in, and once in his room, with a hand now trembling with relief, opened the cognac and poured himself his first drink. Then he walked into the gleaming bathroom and stepped into a steaming shower. At least fifteen minutes later, he reluctantly got out of the shower, toweled off, and lay naked on his bed with his second cognac. He was about to doze off when the phone rang. "Welcome to Finland, Mr. LeSchack." It was Laase Oka, the Finnish Trade Commissioner to Canada, who was back in Helsinki on official business. He normally worked at an office in the Finnish Consular Section in Montréal. LeSchack knew him since he was Finland's representative to the Canadian World's Fair. And the Trade Commissioner had learned that he was going to be in Helsinki during this same period.

"Come join me for a drink," said the Trade Commissioner. "I'm already drinking," said LeSchack, wearily, "and I am half asleep." "What are you drinking?" asked the Commissioner. "Cognac," answered LeSchack. "Well, you can certainly find that upstairs in the bar, where I currently am awaiting you. It's on the top floor of the hotel." LeSchack, recognizing that it would now not be diplomatic to refuse, allowed that he would come join the Trade Commissioner as soon as he put his clothes back on. And so he did, recognizing that it would likely do him good just to have a drink with someone from the "Free World" at this point.

LeSchack took the elevator to the top floor and entered the elegant bar. The Trade Commissioner, sitting comfortably on a plush stool at the bar, saw him enter and waved him over. Life was returning to LeSchack at this point and the two heartily shook hands and embraced. He was now very glad to see someone he knew, so shortly after his Soviet, "walking on thin ice" experience. He ordered another cognac and the two began a spirited conversation. Although the Trade Commissioner knew none of his espionage background, LeSchack knew enough about recent Soviet-Finnish frictions to know that the Commissioner would understand some of the stress that he had been under during his stay in Cold War Russia. And they talked a lot about that, and what it was like for Finns to live adjacent to the Soviet Union from prior to WWII until now, 1965.

What they did not talk about was the amount of stress that LeSchack had been under during the past two weeks, the wondering, always wondering, how much of his background, i.e., the Project Coldfeet espionage, did his Soviet hosts really know. And why was Major Smith, his partner in that espionage, thrown out, *persona non grata*, from his attaché billet in Moscow just a year earlier. If Coldfeet was the reason Smith had been thrown out, then they probably knew about LeSchack too. Had LeSchack's only protection been the fact that the USSR wanted very much to exhibit at the World's Fair and chose not to create an international incident that might upset this? And so they chose only to watch his every move? LeSchack and the Trade Commissioner must have talked and drank for nearly an hour, at which point he said he really was exhausted and ready to retire. "Oh, not now, our waiter has just signaled me that our dinner is ready in the dining room." A bit wearily, LeSchack agreed to join him after he had gone to this much trouble to greet him.

He was unprepared for what happened next. As the two men approached the elegantly set table located by a large picture window overlooking Helsinki Harbor, he saw on the table along with a lovely bouquet of fresh flowers, a standard with crossed Finnish and Canadian flags. "A nice diplomatic touch," smiled LeSchack to himself. Owing, of course, to his position with EXPO-67, his existing familiarity with Montréal, his French-speaking ability, and his knowledge of things Canadian, few people associated with the 1967 Canadian World's Fair — with the clear exception of his Soviet hosts — knew that Lieutenant LeSchack, USNR, was *not* a Canadian.

But a bit to his own surprise, LeSchack, the quintessential American, began trembling uncontrollably upon seeing the Canadian Flag — not his flag, but that of the country next-door. Giselle's country. He had come to know it well from his visits there over the years they had been lovers. While the overly romantic LeSchack may have conflated his love for his adored Giselle with the country of her birth, there was absolutely no confusion in the Cold Warrior's mind about his country's ally when crunch time came three years earlier in October 1962. Canada *immediately* placed the ships of the Royal Canadian Navy, flying the famous White Ensign, on battle stations in support of America's quarantine of Cuba during the harrowing "Missile Crisis" that had so petrified LeSchack.

Tears welled up in his eyes and then overflowed. The stress and paranoia of constantly being under surveillance by the KGB behind the Iron Curtain in 1965, so shortly after his secret Project Coldfeet espionage against the Soviet Union, followed by that Missile Crisis that had seriously threatened nuclear Apocalypse, just simply overwhelmed him. It all just came tumbling out at this moment. Just from seeing the Canadian Flag crossed with the Finnish Flag, he knew, at last he was safe. He had come in from the cold. He was extraordinarily happy to be in Finland and out of the Soviet Union.

****

In the icy Russian winter of 1965, LeSchack was "out in the cold" in every way possible: as a spy, of course; he was in the USSR photographing and taking notes whenever he could, under cover as the "Polar Regions Project Officer" for Canada's EXPO-67. The dagger and gold shield boys of the KGB had already accosted him with: You are from Ukraine, are you not, Mr. LeSchack?" What else did they have in his dossier? It was just three years after he had masterminded "Project Coldfeet," a successful intelligence mission against the Soviets, and only a year after his partner in that mission, then U.S. Assistant Air Attaché in Moscow, was tossed out, persona non grata. Was it because of Coldfeet?

Sexually, LeSchack also was out in the cold; he hadn't been properly loved for the three years that he had been married—the beautiful Virginia was not a passionate woman like so many of his previous lovers had been. In Leningrad he remembers vividly the strain of spending time alone just talking with the lovely Anya, his Arctic and Antarctic Institute interpreter, when he really just wanted to get into her pants, not talk—and he knew perfectly well he wouldn't try; she was likely setup, a "swallow," in KGB parlance. And finally, with the prescience of an intelligence officer, he sensed that all his curatorial work for EXPO-67 would all be in vain owing to changes in office politics—a palace coup—back in Montréal.

A Bloody War or a Sickly Season

> *Toast of the Day* — *Royal Navy, Canadian Navy, and in fact, all Commonwealth Navies*

> *Monday* — *Our ships at sea*
> *Tuesday* — *Our men*
> *Wednesday* — *Ourselves-since no one is likely to think of us*
> *Thursday* — *A bloody war or a sickly season*
> *Friday* — *A willing foe and sea room*
> *Saturday* — *Wives and sweethearts-may they never meet*
> *Sunday* — *Absent friends*

"A bloody war or a sickly season" was the Toast of the Day for Thursday in the Royal Navy, and by derivation, the Royal Canadian Navy also, in which Captain Tony Pickard, LeSchack's EXPO-67 boss, had served. He learned the seven toasts from the Captain in their favorite after-work bar, in *Place Ville Marie*, in Montréal. The toasts, in fact, were common to all the Commonwealth navies that, *served alcoholic drinks* in the wardroom (as opposed to the U.S. Navy where aboard its ships, it was absolutely forbidden). Some of the toasts were timeless, like Monday's — our ships at sea; Tuesday's — our men; Saturday's — wives and sweethearts; and Sunday's universal — absent friends. Thursday's and Friday's were anachronistic and harkened back to the days of warships under sail: "A bloody war or sickly season" was, in those days, the only way young officers had any chance for promotion; and a "willing foe and sea room" was the only way naval engagements under sail could ever occur.

Captain Pickard, knowing LeSchack to be a U. S. Navy lieutenant, thought it was high time he came to learn these toasts now that he was living in Canada. For the first martini of the evening the Captain started with the "Toast of the Day;" with the second martini, which he called, "the other half," he felt a simple, "cheers," would do.

It was Thursday 25 November 1965 in Rovaniemi, Finland, a charming city on the Arctic Circle in Finnish Lapland, when LeSchack thought of Thursday's toast. His visit to the city had been arranged by his hosts in Helsinki. They wished him to feature Rovaniemi, that Arctic urban marvel, at the Polar Regions Pavilion. And this LeSchack wanted to do. He had spent time in villages above the Arctic Circle in Alaska and Canada. None of those villages could be considered architecturally attractive. Most of them have not appreciably changed from the lumbering, mining or fur-trading centers they once were.

He had spent the last 24 hours with Rovaniemi's town planner and architect, a fetching woman, named Lempi, perhaps in her early forties, who had taken LeSchack on a detailed tour of the city. Whimsically, over cocktails, at what would be their last meal together before he flew back to Helsinki, he proposed Thursday's Navy Toast of the Day. In his mind this was a private, diffident *double entendre*, since frankly, he recognized that he, himself, was becoming *sickly*—likely owing to the extraordinary stress of recent weeks—and he knew he would be facing a *bloody* bureaucratic war upon his return to Montréal. Also because historically the beautiful new city of Rovaniemi had been reconstructed as a direct result of *a bloody war*. The one twenty years earlier, with the Nazis.

What LeSchack could not have known, except through clairvoyance, when he proposed that toast to the fascinating Lempi, was that the first major, all American, and *very bloody battle* in the Ia Drang Valley in Viet Nam was just, this day, coming to a close. And that he was also toasting the onset of, what for him, would be a decade-long, metaphysical "bloody war or sickly season." He acknowledged to himself that his whimsical toast was likely prescient. There were bloody wars, both ongoing real ones, as well as bureaucratic ones, which now were impinging on his life. And the sickly season was his own—even though mostly metaphysical—it had all sorts of undesirable repercussions in his life now that he expected would, unfortunately, last for a long time to come.

Lempi, a Finnish citizen, who had lived and studied in England for many years, seemed to recognize the Royal Navy toast. "Ah, you are a naval officer, yes?" she said; and to LeSchack, her dancing eyes also seemed to say, "Well then, sailor, why didn't you take me to bed last night? You knew I was available to you." He groaned inwardly at what he read from her eyes; it was true. She had been available. After a wonderful evening meal at the restaurant above Rovaniemi's best hotel, the Hotel Polar, during which time they talked at length about the city's history, Lempi took him to her apartment, where they continued to talk and talk......and then to fondle.

He was strongly attracted to Lempi—good-looking, well-traveled, well-educated, buxom, and available. And LeSchack was certainly needy! Desire, the sequel to danger, was bubbling up within him—he had left the USSR and his paranoia of the KGB just four days earlier. But the bloody war closest to him was the one going on within him. How long could he remain faithful to his wife—which, deep down, he wanted to do—when she was rarely interested in making love, a condition that now seemed unlikely to change?

Also, he knew he was coming down with some malady. He was rarely sick or had "ailments." But when these maladies occurred, it was often just after, and associated with, long periods of stress. Good examples were the twitching eye associated with Coldfeet, and coming down with bad colds just after completion of school exams. And when he was in Lempi's apartment, feeling the wonderful luxuriousness of her full breasts, he also felt the dreadful discomfort of his nose now, about to start running, as well as all the other associated aggravations of an oncoming cold. He knew, alas, for all these reasons, he would not be able to consummate this delicious opportunity! So, everything considered, he had, with some sadness, stopped those wonderful lovemaking preliminaries.

It was Lempi, the architect, who told LeSchack the history of this beautiful, new attractive city in the Arctic. Rovaniemi was a city of 8000 people in 1944. At that time, the fortunes of war changed and Finland, fighting the Russians with German assistance, sued for a separate piece with the Soviet Union in September, 1944. The Germans now became *persona non grata* in Finland and departed the country by going to the north around neutral Sweden, and down through German-occupied Norway. Not surprisingly, the Germans completely destroyed Rovaniemi, the administrative capital of Finnish Lapland, that lay in their path of retreat. The citizens of Rovaniemi, of necessity, left the ruins of their home and crossed over the border to nearby Sweden (many Finns speak both Finnish and Swedish), where they spent the duration of the war, planning however, the future reconstruction of their old home.

At World War II's end in 1945, their plans could be implemented. Obtaining a team of architects headed by internationally famous Finnish architect, Alvar Aalto, construction of the new Rovaniemi was begun, literally from the ground up. A new network of roads including peripheral and main streets was developed, allowing for easy expansion of the population as necessary. Schools, shops, churches, city administration and office buildings were all designed prior to the commencement of construction, thus avoiding the haphazard suburban sprawl now common. LeSchack was impressed. He called it the "jewel of the Arctic," a lovely, thriving metropolis. And he wanted Rovaniemi to be on exhibit at the Polar Regions Pavilion in 1967.

LeSchack's trip would last another month. Largely now because of inertia, because he had appointments set up in several more countries, and because the trip had already been prepaid. Also, because he would meet many more of the world's famous living polar explorers, a number of whom were elderly. He knew this might be the only opportunity he would ever have to meet them. But his malaise was lingering on mostly, he expected, because he sensed no one back in EXPO-67 now intended to make use of what he had been intent on presenting.

LeSchack returned from Rovaniemi to Helsinki where appointments were set up for him at the Wartsila Ship Yard. Finnish icebreakers were made there, and LeSchack, who now knew something about icebreakers, was interested in seeing how they were made and used in the Gulf of Bothnia. He was also invited to his host's sauna club. He took part in the Finnish sauna ritual, which included being scrubbed and rubbed by the "lady of the bath." Despite her teasing title, there was absolutely nothing prurient about this experience, even though he entered her domain buck naked. The "lady," really a large female animal, hefty enough to hoist him bodily up on to her wash table and then slam him down upon it, was not in any way sexy. She was simply a strong cleaning woman. And clean him, she did. First by dousing him with a pail of scalding water, followed immediately by a powerful pummeling, and finally, followed by a rough rubdown. Arousing, it was not. But it did alleviate somewhat, LeSchack's continuing feeling of unhealthiness.

375

After this ordeal, he and his host, sat for hours talking and drinking before a roaring fire in a huge fireplace. The following day he flew on to Stockholm.

LeSchack arrived in Stockholm over the weekend. He had a room reserved at the Continental Hotel and remained quietly there, nursing his cold, and not venturing outside. He spent the weekend examining the photographs he was allowed to take in the USSR—he had them processed as soon as he reached Helsinki—and writing up his notes and captions for those photos. They would eventually be sent by diplomatic pouch to the Office of Naval Intelligence in Washington. And eventually, he received a laudatory "Letter of Appreciation" from the Department of the Navy with the observation that a copy of that letter was being inserted in his official promotion jacket held by the Chief of Naval Personnel.

The next few days in Stockholm were spent on administrative matters concerning the Fair, and arranging possible support for a cinematographer on contract with EXPO-67 to film Laplanders rounding up reindeer with snowmobiles—which was the way they did it; most exciting and colorful too. Although LeSchack's as yet unidentified malaise was not getting better, he found that being invited to lunch by a Swedish magazine writer he already knew there, and trying three types of herring (plain with lemon, in mustard sauce, and with sour cream), washed down by copious quantities of schnapps, did not hurt! He also managed a pleasant few hours having cocktails with the Canadian Ambassador and his wife. Just before he left for a flight to Oslo, he picked up a message at the Embassy for him from EXPO-67 confirming his suspicions that a "palace coup" had occurred back in Montréal, and his office, and its priorities would not be as he left it a month earlier. His malaise, whatever it was, now got worse. He determined, at this point, that he should simply focus on meeting polar explorers he already knew, or had always wanted to meet, and enjoy northern Europe, as much as one could, in the middle of winter. And not waste time arranging for exhibits that were no longer wanted for the Polar Regions Pavilion.

LeSchack landed in Oslo on 1 December. He was met by a Canadian Embassy driver who took him to his hotel. Shortly thereafter, he checked in with the Embassy Vice Consul to go over his mission from EXPO-67 (as he now understood it, for it had appeared to have changed). In a more congenial setting at the bar of LeSchack's hotel, he and the Vice Consul continued their conversation. He told him he was particularly interested at what the Norsk Polarinstitutt had to offer, since it is responsible for all Arctic research, as well as the hydrographic and topographic charting of the Arctic islands that comprise Norway's Svalbard. Additionally, LeSchack told the Vice Consul, he wanted to visit the Fram.

The Norwegian ship "Fram," was preserved in a nearby museum. The Fram was a wooden ship, deliberately frozen into the Arctic Ocean ice in 1893 by Fridtjof Nansen, and allowed to drift across the Arctic Ocean for nearly three years with its crew, gathering meteorological and oceanographic data. It had served as the model for latter day drifting stations on the Arctic ice, like T-3, ARLIS II, and NP-8. And the data gathered aboard the Fram formed the starting point for much of the present-day understanding of both the geography and environment of the Arctic Ocean. Nansen, too, had been one of LeSchack's childhood heroes.

After cocktails, he retired to his room to sleep. His malaise for this evening manifested itself as a stomachache.

The following day was spent on administrative matters dealing directly with EXPO-67 via official messages through the Canadian Embassy, and with Norwegian Government personnel who officially dealt with EXPO-67 matters. The Norwegian Commissioner-General for the Canadian World's Fair personally drove LeSchack to the museum in which the Fram was housed—only to find it closed for the winter. He immediately placed some phone calls and arranged to have the museum opened especially for him. The day being Thursday, the earliest they could open it for LeSchack (and turn up the heat for comfort in the museum) was on Saturday.

On Friday, much of the day was spent at the Norsk Polarinstitutt discussing polar politics and science with Dr. Tore Gjelsvik, the director. He and Captain Lundquist, the Polarinstitutt's hydrographer, showed LeSchack some original charts drawn by Nansen. For him, this was most exciting—having the history of polar exploration, which up till now, had represented much of his professional career, spread before him in this dramatic fashion. He felt much the same way seeing Nansen's original charts as he had, ten days earlier, from crawling inside Papanin's original NP-1 hut, and preserved at the Arctic and Antarctic Institute in Leningrad. NP-1 was the historic first Soviet Arctic Drifting Station established in 1937, and Papanin, the station leader, had lived in it. The remainder of the afternoon was spent, as military attachés euphemistically say, "gathering intelligence," i.e., drinking and dining, first with the Norwegian Fair people, then by taking the Canadian Vice Consul to dinner.

LeSchack spent most of Saturday at the Fram museum. He was allowed to clamber all over the all-wood ship. "Good God," thought LeSchack, "what a tiny ship to remain aboard—without liberty—for three years drifting around the Arctic." Below decks, he could not stand up straight. The overhead was clearly not "over *his* head." He was not sure even if it would be over the head of a five-foot tall sailor. At six-feet tall, he had to creep around the Fram to view all the separate quarters, and that included the quarters of the Fram's captain, Otto Sverdrup. LeSchack knew well hòw rigorous *modern-day* polar exploration was—he had been involved—but "fifty years ago, it really was Hell," he mused.

On Sunday, he spent most of the day in his hotel room, writing up his notes and a private letter to Captain Pickard. That took most of the day. He wrote in his diary, "In the evening I felt so lonely I placed a trans-Atlantic phone call to Virginia. It was so exciting to hear her voice, I couldn't believe it! Although I felt much better after the call, I felt light-headed, and could no longer work." It was just ten days after his stay in Rovaniemi with the bright and voluptuous Lempi, who certainly had reminded him of the pleasures of the flesh. What he thought, after that phone call with Virginia was, "I love her so, and I believe she loves me. Why the Hell doesn't she want to make love to me?"

Why, indeed? He went out of the hotel into the icy cold Oslo winter night for a walk, and to think. After an hour, not having resolved anything in his mind, he returned to the hotel and went to sleep.

LeSchack flew to London the next day, where he had enough commitments to remain a week. It was a good thing too. He was feeling so run-down, he knew it would take a week to otherwise do what should have been accomplished in three days. Whatever the malaise was, *it had never happened before* with all his previous travels. Shortly after he arrived at his hotel, he collapsed into bed and did not arise till the next morning. The following day, Tuesday 7 December 1965, he went to Canada House, a building that housed the Embassy and consular offices and provided apartments for bachelor officers and official guests. There he met with a Canadian official who handled EXPO-67 matters vis à vis the U.K. As well, LeSchack met Ron Howard, a man his own age and a bachelor, who was, amongst other things, the travel officer for the Embassy and the Consulate. LeSchack was pleased to meet him, since Ron was the first person that he met in the last month with whom he could talk, in English, without having to be constantly on guard for political *faux pas*.

As opposed to in the Soviet Union where LeSchack was unfortunately known as the "Ukrainian who became a U.S. Navy officer—and now for reasons unknown, but likely dubious—was working for the Canadians and therefore a man to be carefully watched," in the U.K. LeSchack was known simply as a polar explorer and a geophysicist, now living in Canada. And he was clearly welcome. Upon his arrival at Canada House there were already two invitations awaiting him from well-known British geophysicists. Also, this day he had an appointment with Dr. Gordon Robin, director of Scott Polar Research Institute. LeSchack met Robin and was invited to spend more time at Scott Polar later in the week. And most gratefully, Ron was available to join LeSchack for dinner that night in Soho.

A well-known British Arctic photographer, Frank Illingworth, who was working for the U.K. office coordinating with EXPO-67, requested through the Montréal office, a meeting with LeSchack when he arrived in London. In one of the last messages LeSchack received from his office, he was specifically told *not* to speak with Illingworth, presumably because of office politics, and that the office no longer wanted him involved in making policy with respect to the Polar Regions Pavilion. LeSchack's response was predictable: "Fuck them, I'm meeting Frank anyway, whatever they say. I have known Illingworth long before I

began working for you peculiar people, and I intend to see him."
Without responding to his office, he did just that. And on several
occasions while in London. Frank and he had a most pleasant lunch that
day.

Although he would have arranged in any event to see Illingworth,
contrary to EXPO's explicit instructions, owing to his previous relations
with the photographer, he got a perverse pleasure now in hearing from
the First Secretary of the Office of the High Commissioner for Canada,
that the High Commissioner, himself, was in turn, displeased with
EXPO's way of doing things!

That afternoon LeSchack went to visit the British Antarctic Survey office.
He had a pleasant meeting with Sir Vivien Fuchs. Although this was the
first time they had met, he observed that he was a member of the U.S.
Antarctic traverse from Byrd Station in 1958-1959 when Sir Vivien and
Sir Edmund Hillary of Everest fame, made a trans-Antarctic traverse of
their own; they missed each other by 300 miles, but they both were on
traverse at the same time. That, as they say "broke the ice," and
LeSchack and Sir Vivien continued to talk as equals. Again, that
evening, LeSchack and Ron Howard meandered through Soho together.
The following day he would meet General Sir William Oliver.

General Sir William Oliver was the U.K.'s senior officer assigned for
liaison with Expo-67. He met LeSchack to talk about what Great Britain
would want to contribute as well as what LeSchack wanted the U.K. to
contribute for the Polar Regions Pavilion. He told Sir William he already
had considerable familiarity with the Scott Polar Research Institute
associated with Cambridge University, since he had already met its
director, Dr. Robin, and had quoted liberally a technical paper by Robin
in the thesis that he wrote at the Oceanographic Office. And he had a list
of what he thought Scott Polar should contribute. Sir William invited
LeSchack to lunch at his club, the "Travellers."

Over smoked trout, roast beef, cheese and red wine Sir William began
the conversation by discussing with LeSchack his previous and
distinguished military career. His most recent assignment, he said, had
been the U.K.'s High Commissioner for Australia, and earlier he had

been a senior military officer in Malaya, sometime during the "Emergency," the Communist insurrection in the Federation of Malaya from 1948 to 1960. LeSchack nodded in an understanding manner.

"I understand you are a *leftenant* in the U.S. Navy, LeSchack." The General pronounced "lieutenant" in the British manner. "Why, yes sir, I am," responded LeSchack in simple acknowledgement. Sir William then gratuitously and most pedantically added, "You know your people are going about this Viet Nam thing in the wrong way;" he continued, "We learned how to handle those Wogs long ago with our 'resettlement program' (basically, concentration camps). You should handle it the same way we did."

In fact, LeSchack was aware from Dr. Dan's Fort Bragg scuttlebutt in 1962, that a similar U.S. plan *had begun then*, called the "strategic hamlet" program—also basically concentration camps. It was designed to deny the Vietcong support from the peasants in South Viet Nam. It was less than successful. And in any event, the situations LeSchack knew were not comparable: The insurgents in Malaya had been largely ethnic Chinese hated by the Malays, while the Vietnamese peasants and Vietcong were indistinguishable from one another. Further, Malaya was always short of rice, so that the insurrectionists could be starved into submission, while South Viet Nam had ample supplies, so that food could not easily be denied to the Vietcong.

LeSchack was not happy about having to defend U.S. policies with which he had little connection, or involvement at this time. So instead of actually comparing the British and U.S. policies, he mildly observed to the senior British officer who was just finishing up his last bit of stilton, "Well John Sherlock, in his book about the Malayan Emergency, didn't seem to think your resettlement program was so successful." LeSchack was speaking of an historical novel, "The Ordeal of Major Grigsby," published the year before, and written by a British author who appeared to have served there during the time of the "Emergency." And he presented this information as if he were merely giving an oral book review in a high school English class. He had not expected the General to have read it. *LeSchack was dreadfully wrong!* Moreover, he simply was unprepared for General Sir William Oliver's bombastic response.

Sir William, his face suddenly livid, leaned across the table, thrusting his face so close to LeSchack's that he could clearly smell the smoked trout, roast beef, cheese and red wine on the General's breath. The General apparently would have liked to have grabbed him by his necktie and pulled his face even closer. But generally officers don't do that—and *general* officers certainly don't. Instead, he spit out, "That book was a bunch of balls! Sherlock just hated the Army!"—an exact quote, as recorded in LeSchack's diary at the time. He now guessed that Sir William, had, *in fact, read the book*. And he quickly went on to other topics more germane to EXPO-67. Young LeSchack had just experienced a perfect example of why one doesn't talk politics in the wardroom! And especially, during this epoch, the politics of Southeast Asia.

That evening, LeSchack took a cab to the offices of the BBC where he picked up Frank Illingworth and his charming wife, Jenny. From there they then took a train to the Illingworth's home in the London suburbs. Frank and Jenny were splendid hosts. And Frank and LeSchack picked up from where they had left off several years earlier when they first began communicating, during the time LeSchack had been stationed at ONR.

The next several days LeSchack spent shuttling back and forth between London and Cambridge University. The only connection that these days had to do with EXPO-67 was that Dr. Thomas F. Gaskell, a well-known oceanographic geophysicist, had earlier met him at the EXPO offices in Montréal; Gaskell was representing British Petroleum's (BP) interest in supporting the 1967 World's Fair. For example, LeSchack asked Gaskell to get BP to fund an exhibit to be produced by Dr. Robin of the Scott Polar Research Institute; he agreed to do so. Knowing he was also a geophysicist, and was the Polar Regions Project Officer, Dr. Gaskell arranged for LeSchack to receive several social invitations to meet people with an interest in those subjects. And they were good fun.

The first such event on Friday evening was a lecture presented at the Royal Society of Arts by Dr. Tonking, deputy director of the Mohole Project. That project was a major endeavor to drill a hole through the ocean floor and through the earth's mantle. LeSchack had been well aware of the origins of this project, since ONR was one of its early supporters during the time he had been stationed there. Cocktails were served in the library after a fascinating lecture. A private dinner had been arranged afterwards that included Dr. Gaskell and Sir Philip Southwell, the two gentlemen who had organized the lecture, LeSchack, and two others.

LeSchack found the dinner simply splendid. It was held in the Garrick Club in a private room with fireplace and wood paneled walls that supported some 40 portraits of distinguished men. Dinner: smoked salmon—vin blanc; roast grouse—vin rouge, cheese soufflé, coffee and brandy. Whatever his malaise was, it didn't appear to interfere with this sumptuous feast. Just yet.

The next morning however, was quite another story (not a hangover, mind you; poor stomach I believe—he wrote in his diary). It took him half a day to get up the energy to board a late train for Cambridge—he missed several earlier ones, phoning ahead to Gordon Robin each time that he "would make the next one." Eventually he arrived at Cambridge and Dr. Robin, with a wry smile, met him at the station and inquired about "Tom Gaskell's alcoholic party the previous evening." LeSchack smiled his silly smile, and observed that, "Well, whatever happened, I did get Tom and BP to agree to support the construction of *your model* of advancing and retreating ice-sheets for EXPO-67!"

Dr. Robin took LeSchack to the Scott Polar Research Institute where they had an opportunity to examine rough sketches of the ice-sheet model. Gordon suggested that the model might depict Montréal being inundated, should severe melting of the world's ice sheets occur. "That would be effective—and certainly dramatic," remarked LeSchack. Even in 1965, these two earth scientists knew that periodically the earth alternately warmed and cooled, enough to substantially diminish or enlarge the world's ice sheets and cause major changes in the sea level while doing so. The earth's geologic record already showed that. And these fossil records stretched back well before man started using fossil fuels.

While at Scott Polar, LeSchack was introduced to Dr. Terence Armstrong a geographer, who was then the West's expert on Siberia and the Soviet Northern Sea Route. He would have much more time to get to know

Armstrong eight years hence, when together they would travel through Siberia.

That evening in Cambridge, there was a black-tie dinner—the Arctic Dinner—held in a huge "King Arthur" type hall, constructed circa 1600. LeSchack had been invited along with many others who had some Arctic connection. He sat next to Terence Armstrong. Also seated beside him was Peter Mott, managing director of Hunting Aerial Surveys, a firm in nearby Cambridge. That was another connection that LeSchack would maintain over the years. According to Gordon, "the meal and the service in this hall were quintessentially British." According to LeSchack's diary, "the meal was brilliant!"

The following day, a Sunday, was a quiet one for LeSchack at Cambridge. He had been invited to a Sunday-morning-coffee event at Caius College, and then met, and went with Terence Armstrong once more to the Scott Polar Research Institute. The highlight of the day for LeSchack was seeing in the geography library a recent listing by the Board of Geographical Names. It confirmed that a mountain in Antarctica, along his 1958-59 traverse route, had been officially named for him. "Now that—Mount LeSchack," he thought with genuine pleasure, "is true immortality!"

That afternoon LeSchack took the train back to London and went to MacDonald House, where Ron Howard's apartment was, and where he had left his excess gear before going to Cambridge. Ron had recommended that before he left for Cambridge, he check out of his London hotel, leave his baggage with Ron, and spend what would be his last night in England in Ron's apartment upon his return. LeSchack was glad that Ron had made that suggestion; this opened the way for a quiet evening together on his last night in London.

Joined by one of Ron's bachelor colleagues who also lived at MacDonald House, the three young men from Canada began exploring an observation that Ron had made to LeSchack on earlier bar-hopping evenings. Ron had observed that the chief conversation of middle-aged British men at bars concerned not sexual adventures, but their World War II adventures and victories, events that had occurred 20-25 years earlier. Further, Ron recognized that despite the wartime deprivations, the London bombings by the Luftwaffe, the loss of their friends during the war, and everything that both preceded and succeeded these wartime events, their fondest memories, and what they wished most to talk about, was the war, and their experiences in it. Very little else. Ron had marveled that nothing before or since, was ever as exciting to them as the wartime adventures for these middle-aged men. Ron's friend had agreed with him, and while LeSchack understood it, he thought it sad.

It was sad for LeSchack because he had learned that, as Thoreau said, "The mass of men lead lives of quiet desperation." And for the men that Ron had been talking about, it seemed that only wartime had relieved them of their lives of tedium. This was not a new concept for him. But LeSchack, the reluctant warrior, had begun to subscribe to a different dictum: John Milton's, "Peace hath her victories—No less renowned than war..." and that was the path he intended to follow. LeSchack was not prepared to let his Coldfeet adventure, clearly a Cold War military victory, be the one and only adventure in his lifetime. He had thought about this "lifetime path of adventure" in a general way over the past three years, but Ron Howard's observations had given LeSchack strong impetus now to begin to codify his own path for living a life of ongoing adventures. Adventures that could take place serially. Even if, as in his old fantasy conundrum, "for whatever reason, his balls were physically—or as was more likely in his present life—psychically shot off." No "life of quiet desperation" for me, he vowed!

On Monday, LeSchack cleaned up loose ends: he returned the tuxedo he had rented at the Moss Brothers haberdashery for the black-tie Arctic dinner, and while in Soho, spotted a fancy lingerie shop where, on a whim, he purchased a filmy, lacy "teddy" for Virginia. It was a camisole with a difference—it was designed only for delicious intimacy; on this elegant piece of apparel, instead of gossamer fabric cups for womanly breasts, there was...well.....nothing. But on Virginia, with her stunning body, LeSchack knew it would look superb! He hoped it would please her.

He met Ron at Canada House, took him to lunch, then picked up his things at Ron's apartment. He then cabbed to Heathrow and flew on to

Brussels, for Belgium was one of the signatories to the Antarctic Treaty and also had interests in the Antarctic.

Although LeSchack had been weakened by whatever malaise had followed him out of the USSR, his stay in England had been enjoyable nonetheless; not because of his work—he now knew that would be irrelevant—but because of the social activities and interesting people he had met in London and Cambridge. Now he traveled on to Brussels to visit Baron Gaston de Gerlache de Gomery, chief of the *Expédition Antarctique Belge Néerlandais*, the organization that operated a research station on the Antarctic continent. He was back to speaking French again. There appeared to be only marginal interest in Belgium for promoting any exhibits at the Polar Regions Pavilion, but at this point, LeSchack didn't much care. Two days were enough to conduct his business there, and he did so, perfunctorily. And then he packed up and flew to the last stop on his itinerary—Copenhagen.

Denmark has an enormous Arctic interest—Greenland, the largest island in the world, is part of Denmark, and lies mostly north of the Arctic Circle. Since Greenland is adjacent to northern Canada, LeSchack thought it appropriate to assure some Greenland exhibits were on display at the Polar Regions Pavilion.

He arrived in Copenhagen on a Thursday, just a week before Christmas. He was enormously weary. He was disheartened because there was a delay in his being picked up by a driver from the Canadian Embassy, normally the procedure when one is on official business. Eventually he went to the information kiosk checking to see if there were any messages for him left by the Embassy. The lady behind the counter indicated not, but said she would be pleased to call the Embassy on his behalf. As she was doing so, a man came to the kiosk, and standing next to LeSchack, asked the same woman placing the Embassy call for him to page "a Leonard LeSchack" after she finished her call. It was the Embassy driver standing directly beside him—an hour late, but there he was! "An auspicious beginning," thought LeSchack, as the driver took him to the Imperial Hotel.

Another harbinger of irrelevancy struck LeSchack the following day at the Embassy. Although diplomatically pleasant, the cognizant officer assigned to EXPO affairs clearly displayed the attitude of, "Oh, what again? More of those EXPO people from Montréal?" This motivated the exhausted LeSchack to become quite specific, identifying exactly what people in what Danish offices he wanted to see. On official business. He was able to start that day, but because it was Friday, he knew he would need to remain over the weekend and continue on Monday, and perhaps Tuesday.

LeSchack spent a quiet, pleasant weekend at the Hotel. He slept late to attempt to recoup his energies, wrote up his notes, wandered around the Tivoli Gardens, which were relatively drab in mid-winter. While wandering, he took advantage of Copenhagen's permissive atmosphere regarding the sale of literature of all sorts. He purchased some lascivious magazines, not yet permissible for sale in North America, to see if he could rekindle his now failing libido. Also, he received an invitation for Sunday dinner from the Anderson's, a Copenhagen family that had befriended Captain Pickard at some earlier date when the Captain's ship had docked in Copenhagen's famous harbor—you know, the one with the mermaid on the rock. He accepted that invitation, picked up a bouquet of flowers, and took a cab there in the afternoon. As he went to bed that Sunday night, he knew it wasn't only his libido that needed rekindling, it was everything! He was just discouraged and bone weary. "Just two more days and I'll be flying home! But to what, I just don't know."

During the next day and a half, LeSchack visited the Embassy to handle further administrative matters, visited Dr. Helge Larsen at the National Museum, the Danish Government's Film Office, and a private film distributor that had exciting and artistic cinematography of Greenland. Finally, he visited a Greenland Government Office where a potential model of the capitol Nuuk (formerly Godthåb) could be constructed for display. Like Rovaniemi, Nuuk is a small, modern Arctic city. And then, most wearily, he boarded an SAS flight back to Montréal.

Once back at his office in Montreal, he found that in his two-month absence, office politics *had* drastically changed. Owing to these politics, LeSchack and several of his colleagues who had traveled to the USSR with him, as well as some other theme officers left behind, had essentially become non-persons in their offices. Considering the basic makeup of the Canadian World's Fair Corporation, this in itself, was not surprising. All along, there had been subtle undercurrents and backstabbing by the "artists," the political hacks, and the low-level career civil servants. But the result was that LeSchack found he had no further EXPO business to conduct now, had time on his hands, and an office in which to think and scheme on his own. He knew such a situation could not last long, at most, only another six months, before someone in authority would notice this small group of non-people occupying space, but no longer on the "team" — such as it was. He knew he had best use this remaining time to prepare for the next phase of his life.

LeSchack recognized that, at this juncture, his next step would have to be organizing his own business. He just had a massive dose of what the worst of civilian bureaucracies could inflict, and he wanted no more of it. Not that military bureaucracies were much better. But, at least, thought LeSchack, in the military you wear your rank on your sleeve, your history and successes on your chest and, as they say, you and every other military person know where you stand. Well he had decided now to stand, or fall, based on his own choices made in his *own* business. And the business he chose was one in which an increased level of physical and intellectual adventure would be generated. Thanks to two years of duty at the Office of Naval Research in Washington, LeSchack learned not only how to read and evaluate proposals, but also how to write them and, furthermore, make things happen.

Although LeSchack had an office in which to work, and he remained on salary in Montréal, he began to recognize that was only part of what was needed in his life for him to function properly. He had to have a mission that meant something, a mission that he knew could be successfully accomplished, and he had to have bright, stimulating people around him. Not political hacks and toads. But he also recognized all he could count on in Montréal — and only for a short, unknown period — was an office and a salary.

The business he chose to think about and develop involved using the tractor-train and traverse logistics that he became familiar with in the

Antarctic, modified for use in another type of remote area, the tropical jungle. LeSchack began conducting library research and doing a lot of reading, and writing to various government offices in Washington, and Ottawa, and to a variety of potential suppliers. He began collecting reports on jungle operations all over the world. Meanwhile, his after-USSR malaise continued to deepen and began diversifying into numerous unpleasant symptoms. He came down with acute abdominal pains, serious anxiety problems, and not surprisingly, eventually sexual impotence — to match the feeling of professional impotence he now felt and probably because of it. Not all symptoms manifested themselves at the same time, but over a period of depressing months. It was all quite horrible.

Their Montréal social life with Felix and Annabelle continued vibrantly, however. And quite enjoyably so. But LeSchack couldn't help but muse wistfully, as they went out amongst the Montréal glitterati, "two couples, two beautiful women, and now *two* sexually impotent men." Strangely, however, during this epoch LeSchack's impotence did not greatly disturb him. *All* his stress-related maladies now essentially numbed and incapacitated him mentally and physically; and Virginia's reaction to that sexy camisole he brought her from Soho was the final straw. When, in their bedroom, she put it on and found that it *was not intended to cover her breasts*, but instead to let them be displayed in all their magnificence, she said, "Ohhhhh no!....you'll never catch *me* wearing this!" Virginia, in fact, looked glorious. "Many women," thought LeSchack, despondently, "would kill to be able to look like this in their bedroom!"

LeSchack did not speak to Felix of their mutual affliction, but he did speak of his own acute abdominal pains and anxiety attacks. Felix recommended he see his doctor, which LeSchack did. The doctor diagnosed the pains as "acute pancreatitis" and prescribed antibiotics, and tranquilizers for the anxiety attacks. Both prescriptions appeared to work. But LeSchack expected the abdominal pains were just another way his body reacted to his current level of stress — an advanced form of "eye twitch" — and had little to do with pancreatic afflictions.

In fact, EXPO-67 didn't get around to firing him, and a number of his other colleagues in the same circumstances, for nine months. Within this time period LeSchack had come up with a serious plan. He had already begun promising discussions with the U.S. State Department's Agency for International Development (AID) in Washington. While it was clear that he and Virginia could not find some common ground to discuss sexual matters in any mutually agreeable way, they could comfortably talk about business plans. They agreed to return Washington, where she knew she could secure a legal secretary's job. Also, Virginia's parents agreed to let them live at their place in Chevy Chase until LeSchack's new business got "on its feet." And in October 1966 they relinquished their apartment in Montréal and drove back to Washington.

As for Thursday's toast—A bloody war or a sickly season—LeSchack, back in Washington, became increasingly aware of the former, the one now taking place in Viet Nam, and becoming increasingly bloodier with time. It was beginning to impinge more and more on his life. The sickly season, although remaining with him, had changed. It became less caused by work-place stresses, because he had much greater control over his professional life than ever previously, but increasingly so from lack of vibrant connubial fulfillment.

*****

Montréal's EXPO-67 sent this light plane around the world as a publicity stunt in 1966 to advertise the following year's Canadian World's Fair. LeSchack was Polar Region Projects Officer at EXPO-67 at the time. Here the aircraft is on Marcus Island in the Pacific Ocean, where it was forced down owing to engine trouble. Marcus Island was a US Coast Guard Loran station at the time. Perhaps it still is. The two folks on either side of the military officer are the EXPO people. The military officer standing between them is Lieutenant Larry Brooks, who was the CO of the Loran station at the time. He sent LeSchack this picture years later. By then they had already met at an Arctic sea ice conference. Brooks, eventually joined Chevron Oil Company and worked on sea ice problems related to Arctic off shore oil exploration. It was in that context that Brooks and LeSchack began working together from 1975 until 1985.

A Taste of Volume II: As LeSchack's life evolves, he becomes further involved in diplomacy, espionage and fieldwork in foreign lands and dangerous locales--in support of U.S. Realpolitc-- Latin America, Soviet Union, Viet Nam, OPEC's energy challenge to the U.S. of the 1970's, Political Terrorism, and Castro's export of revolution to the Caribbean and Central America; exploration in, and ballistic missile threat from the Arctic Ocean; An intelligence officer in Puerto Rico, Panama, and as a scientist, he creates a joint oil industry/Navy project to overfly a nuclear attack submarine for correlating airborne laser profiler data of the sea ice surface with the submarine's upward-looking sonar data of the same under ice surface; and at the U.S, Forces Caribbean Command in Key West, where he is tasked with establishing a dedicated Reserve Intelligence unit to Support this Command, and he becomes its first Commanding Officer. It is in the Florida Keys that he meets his soul-mate. 1967-1990.

391

393

399

400

traverse expedition and, 78–
79
Virginia and, 344–345
*Mutiny on Board H.M. Ship
Bounty and Minutes of the
Court Martia* (Bligh), 118

N

Nadi (Fiji Islands), 43
Nansen, Fridtjof, 377–378
Napoli, Lieutenant (jg), 135–136
Natalya, 252
NATO, 259
nature, 81
"Nautilus 90° North"
(Anderson and Blair), 286
naval aviators, 137
Naval Reserve Intelligence
Units, 330–331, 339, 340, 345
navigation, 141, 152, 226, 262,
274
Nazis, 373
networking
gravimeter and, 175–176
Montréal and, 347
Oceanography Symposium
and, 335
ONR and, 166, 170, 174
Project Coldfeet and, 225,
250
U.S. Navy and, 128, 132, 133,
141, 152
Washington, D.C. and, 339
Neuburg, Hugo, 117
Newtown, Connecticut, 342–
343
New Years' celebrations, 285
New York City, 21–22, 23–24,
27, 127, 323–324. *see also*
Waldorf Astoria Hotel
"New Yorker" (magazine), 93
New York state. *see* Freeport,
Long Island; Rensselaer
Polytechnic Institute (RPI)
New York Times (newspaper),
71, 73, 104, 305
New Zealand, 14, 43–49, 95,
111, 113, 114, 167
Nixon, Richard, 165, 186
"*Non, Je ne regrette rien*" (song),
187, 308, 317
Normandy beaches, 13
Norsk Polarinstitutt, 377–378
Northern Sea Route, 383–384
North Pole, 149

Norway, 376–378
Nôtre Dame cathedral, 319
nuclear holocaust/weapons,
13–16, 43, 122, 251–252
"Nuclear Strategy and
Diplomacy" (Encyclopedia
of American Foreign Policy)
(Hagan and Skinner), 4
Nudlemann (KGB man), 361–
362
Nuuk, 387

O

Oceanographic Office, 331, 333
oceanography, 166, 168, 191,
262, 279, 292, 326, 377
Oceanography Symposium
(Washington, D.C.), 334–335
oceans, 1. *see also* beaches
O'Connell, Tommy, 268, 269–
270, 275–276, 279, 284, 289,
290, 291, 302–303
OCS. *see* Officer Candidate
School (OCS)
OCs (officer candidates), 141
OCSA (Officer Candidate
Seaman Apprentice), 130–
131
Office of Naval Intelligence
(ONI)
LeSchack's research review
and, 263, 351, 364
Naval Intelligence Reserve
Unit and, 330–331
Project Coldfeet and, 221,
245
research contracts and, 310
technology and, 343
University of Wisconsin
and, 326
Office of Naval Research
(ONR). *see also* ARLIS II
(drift station); Britton, Max
E.
amorous adventures and,
167–170, 186–189
ARL and, 174–175, 180–186,
226
assignment to, 162–163
bureaucracy and, 164–166
DeGoes' party, 171–172
equipment and, 175–178
interagency letters and, 175–
176

404

T

408